The Epicure's Almanack

EATING AND DRINKING IN REGENCY LONDON

Rowland

RALPH RYLANCE

The Epicure's Almanack

EATING AND DRINKING IN REGENCY LONDON

THE ORIGINAL 1815 GUIDEBOOK

EDITED BY
JANET ING FREEMAN

THE BRITISH LIBRARY

© in this edition 2013 Janet Ing Freeman

First published 2012
This edition published 2013 by
The British Library
96 Euston Road
London NW1 2DB

ISBN 978 0 7123 5704 3

British Library Cataloguing in Publication Data
A CIP Record for this book is available from the British Library

Designed and typeset by the author
Printed in England

CONTENTS

ILLUSTRATIONS

The map details of central London are taken from Richard Horwood, *Plan of the Cities of London and Westminster, the Borough of Southwark, and Parts Adjoining*, published in thirty-two sheets over the years 1792-99 (British Library Maps 148.e.7). The maps on pp. 47 and 48, showing the West and East India docks, are from William Faden, *A Plan of London and Westminster, with the Borough of Southwark* , 1823 (British Library Maps Crace VI.219), and those of outer London from John Cary, *Cary's Actual Survey of the Country Fifteen Miles round London*, 1786 (British Library Maps C.29.d.19).

The frontispiece image is a detail from a print by Thomas Rowlandson, depicting the interior of a Fleet Street establishment variously identified as the Rainbow Tavern or the Wheatsheaf eating house. This and the remaining two illustrations are reproduced from originals in the collection of Arthur and Janet Freeman.

EDITOR'S PREFACE

IN THE SPRING of 1815 a publishing novelty tempted London bookshop browsers: the capital's first dedicated 'good food guide', surveying some 650 establishments in and around the city and promising to direct the reader to those in which he might 'dine well, and to the best advantage', be they Mayfair hotels or tripe shops in Shoreditch. Unlike equivalent modern directories that rely on public feedback or teams of inspectors, the 1815 *Epicure's Almanack; or, Calendar of Good Living* was the work of a single man, Ralph Rylance, who – perhaps with a little help from his friends – visited and described not only City chop houses and West End *pâtisseries,* but also ancient coaching inns, dockyard taverns, suburban tea gardens, and village pubs, throwing in for good measure an account of London's markets, a directory of local merchants stocking everything from anchovy sauce to kitchen ranges, and an 'alimentary calendar' to direct both cooks and diners to the best seasonal ingredients. Advertisements for the new guidebook stressed that it had been modelled on the celebrated *Almanach des gourmands* published at Paris between 1803 and 1812, and Rylance repeated this claim in his opening sentences. But his handbook in fact has little in common with Alexandre Grimod de la Reynière's series of French *Almanachs* beyond its title and general outline: where Grimod's *gourmand* is devoted to the exquisite and the sensual, Rylance's epicure is altogether a homelier sort, concerned not so much with gastronomy – 'precepts for eating', as the term was defined in 1814[1] – as with convenience of situation and access, speed of service, and above all value for money.

   Longman, the publisher of the *Almanack*, had high hopes for its success, issuing 750 copies and projecting an annual revision to sell alongside their principal guidebook to the capital, *The Picture of London*. But while the latter continued as a staple of Longman's lists through 1833, the *Epicure's Almanack* died in its first year, perhaps passed over by Londoners with somewhat weightier matters on their minds: on 20 March 1815, when the *Almanack* was still at the printers, Napoleon returned in triumph to Paris,

---

[1] *The School for Good Living; or, A Literary and Historical Essay on the European Kitchen* (1814), p. 19. For a discussion of the development of gastronomic literature, see Denise Gigante's introduction to *Gusto* (2005).

and months of settlement negotiations followed his final defeat at Waterloo in June. And although Rylance had urged readers and proprietors to supply him with corrections or suggestions before he 'resum[ed] his peregrinations, preparatory to a second Volume', by the beginning of 1816 he was laid up in the Marylebone Infirmary, where he remained some six months, completely unfit for work. The promised sequel to the first volume never appeared, and at the end of 1817 the remaining copies of the *Almanack*, some 450 in all, were 'wasted' or pulped by Longman.[2] For the next hundred and fifty years London was without a comprehensive guide to dining, until in 1968 Raymond Postgate published his *Good Food Guide to London*, which even with the inclusion of nightclubs and discothèques listed only 337 establishments.

Originally intended as a practical vade-mecum for the hungry man walking the streets of the capital, the *Epicure's Almanack* is today consulted in rare book rooms for its time-bound evidence. Historians of London and of gastronomy have repeatedly delved into it to read accounts of long-vanished taverns and coffee houses, extract one of the few contemporary descriptions of England's first Indian restaurant, or explore such topics as the growing interest in continental cuisine in the post-Napoleonic years. Social historians have studied the *Almanack's* comments on meal times and women diners, biographers and editors of letters have combed it to identify inns and eating houses mentioned by their subjects, and over the years a few readers, charmed by the occasional passage, have speculated on the identity of the anonymous author. In 1906 George Edward Weare, quoting several paragraphs from the guide in *Notes and Queries*,[3] remarked that the words 'By R. Rylance' were pencilled on the title-page of his own copy, an attribution that can be confirmed from Longman's archives and Rylance's own correspondence.

The present edition of the *Epicure's Almanack* is designed to make this engaging and informative text more readily available, and to provide an introductory commentary on the book and its author, and on the wider subject of eating and drinking in London at the beginning of the nineteenth century. The notes to the main text include brief histories of the principal establishments mentioned, with missing addresses and names of proprietors supplied when possible. For many taverns and eating houses I have been able to find nothing more than a string of directory entries, but the increasing availability

---

[2] Today the book is comparatively scarce: I have found fewer than twenty records of institutional holdings worldwide, but additional copies undoubtedly survive in private collections.

[3] 'The Epicure's Almanack', 6 January 1906 (10th ser., vol. 5), pp. 4-5.

of digitized periodicals and newspapers, through resources such as *The Times Digital Archive* and the British Library's *British Newspapers 1600-1900*, has enabled me sometimes to cite contemporary advertisements or record bankruptcies, auctions, and demolitions, and even – in one particularly satisfying instance – report the midnight collapse 'with a tremendous crash' of a famous chop house once frequented by Dickens.

Although I have corrected several obvious misstatements by Rylance, errors and omissions, both his and mine, certainly remain. In trying to keep my notes and bibliography to a manageable size I have sometimes omitted references when the facts in question are easily verifiable, but I have endeavoured throughout to confirm details, cite reputable sources, and tread carefully among romantic legends. As the authors of *Licensed to Sell*, English Heritage's 2004 survey of the history of the public house, have remarked, 'once erroneous tales are born, they seem destined for a long and robust life because local tradition and those who write about pubs are all too prone to recycle the same information'.[4] In the Internet age this is truer than ever, with website after website placing Samuel Johnson beside the fire in Ye Olde Cheshire Cheese and Dick Turpin's horse in the stables of the Spaniards Inn on Hampstead Heath. Tall tales also continue to proliferate in print, and while it is easy to dismiss some claims, others are more tenacious. Was the Town of Ramsgate at Wapping indeed the successor to the Red Cow, where the famous 'hanging judge' George Jeffreys was captured in late 1688 (page 60); did Pocahontas stay at the Belle Sauvage in 1616 (page 85); did Shakespeare drink at the Three Pigeons in Brentford (page 234); or – returning to Hampstead – was the Spaniards once the home of the Spanish Ambassador to James I (page 259)? In general I have taken a cautious approach to these and similar stories, but readers are free to form their own conclusions.

Perhaps the most frequent question I am asked about the *Almanack* concerns its survivors – those taverns and public houses mentioned by Rylance that are still in business today. A list of fifteen establishments that qualify is provided in Appendix II, divided between those in central London (six) and those in outlying districts (nine); all remain in essentially the same premises that were described in 1815 – remodelled or renovated qualifies; entirely rebuilt does not – and retain the same name or a near variant. Not surprisingly, suburban taverns have had a better survival rate than those in Westminster or the City, but the Seven Stars in Carey Street is just about the same age as the remaining south gallery of the George Inn at Southwark: both

---

[4] Brandwood et al. 2004, p. 165.

date from around 1680. The George at Twickenham is known as a coaching inn from 1737, and the building itself has late seventeenth-century origins, as do those that house the Old Bell in Fleet Street and its neighbour Ye Olde Cheshire Cheese.[5] There are, of course, also a number of other pre-1815 establishments still in business today that were bypassed or overlooked by the *Almanack*, such as Durrants Hotel in Marylebone and the Olde Mitre in Ely Court; others further afield include the Dove at Hammersmith, the Flask in Highgate West Hill, and the Grapes and the Prospect of Whitby at Wapping.

A NOTE ON THE TEXT

The original *Epicure's Almanack* is a small duodecimo, with pages measuring about 5½ by 3½ inches; the paper is thin and the printing, by Barnard and Farley of Skinner Street, London, is undistinguished, with many pages over- or under-inked and type occasionally misaligned. The text presented here was transcribed from a copy of the *Almanack* in my possession, and checked against that in the British Library (shelfmark 1037.f.23); the page numbers of the original are given within square brackets, and all references in my introductory matter that specify 'page' rather than 'p.' are to the original pagination. I have retained the peculiarities of spelling and punctuation of the 1815 *Almanack* (holibut, potatoe, sallad, confectionary, Sunday's, and so on), inserting *sic* in square brackets only when it seemed necessary. Errors in the spelling of a place name or personal name (e.g. Bryanstone for Bryanston and Tattersal for Tattersall) are corrected either in a note or in the index.

In 1815 the *Almanack* concluded with a nineteen-page index (pages 333-51), principally listing the names of districts or streets and occasionally particular establishments or foodstuffs, but in view of the four indexes that follow the present text this has not been reproduced. In the first index, itemizing establishments, proprietors, and purveyors of foodstuffs and other goods, I have included earlier and later names of the establishments discussed in the *Almanack*, and where possible have added to or corrected information given by Rylance. Thus, for instance, the index shows that 'Mr. Derrell' of the Angel

[5] Brandwood and Jephcote 2008 and the volumes of *BoE* and *SL* provide the most reliable dates. Stuart 2004 should be consulted with great caution: the 'earliest remaining sections' of the Cittie of Yorke in High Holborn, for instance, do not 'date from the mid-1600s' (p. 32), for the pub is a 'rebuild of 1923-4' (Brandwood and Jephcote, p. 9), and the Hand and Shears in Middle Street has not 'stood here for over 400 years' but dates from 1830 (Stuart, p. 46; Brandwood and Jephcote, p. 19).

Inn, Islington, was in fact Richard John Derrett, and it distinguishes between the Mr Pardy of the Spread Eagle Inn (William) and that of the Lamb Tavern (James). The second index concentrates on places: towns, villages, counties, markets, churches, and major streets and buildings. Food and drink are covered by the third index, and the fourth includes topics, terms, and persons that did not find a place elsewhere.

Ralph Rylance, a lover of Shakespeare and Milton and a frustrated poet himself, frequently enlivened his text with snippets of verse or Latin and French tags; where his sources are not obvious I have tried to identify these and provide translations in my notes. Rylance's own occasional notes are indicated (as in the original) by asterisks, and a terminal glossary defines words not otherwise discussed. The maps of central London, reproduced from one of the British Library's copies of Richard Horwood's 1799 *Plan of the Cities of London and Westminster* (Maps 148.e.7), will, I hope, not only provide a guide to areas of London that have changed substantially in the past two centuries, but also allow today's reader to follow in the footsteps of Ralph Rylance as he wandered the city in search of places where a man might 'readily regale himself, according to the relative state of his appetite and his purse'.

ACKNOWLEDGEMENTS

Some twenty years ago my husband, Arthur Freeman, bought a tattered copy of the anonymous *Epicure's Almanack*, intrigued by the idea of a nearly two-hundred-year-old 'good food guide' to London. With an eye both to the book's charm and to its research potential, he painstakingly photocopied the loose sheets before having it rebound, and a few years later he handed over the project to me. He cannot have known then how many of his own lunches and dinners would be delayed while I was time-travelling to 1815: for this, my apologies, and for his companionship and help, my gratitude and love.

In the twelve years that I have been working on this project, nearly all of my friends and colleagues have listened patiently while I talked about the *Almanack*, and many have added useful information or suggested sources that I might investigate. I cannot name them all here, but I would like to thank the following for answers to specific questions, or otherwise essential assistance: Nicolas Barker, Lizzie Collingham, John Coulter, Ian Jackson, Ricky Jay, Jill LeMin Lee, Janet Nassau, Jan Piggott, Omar Senussi, the late Michael Silverman, Susan Walker, Stuart Walker, Andrea Tanner, and Ron Woollacott.

For access to manuscripts and published materials, I am grateful to the following libraries and archives: the British Library, the Camden Local

History Library, the City of Westminster libraries (Westminster Archives Centre and Marylebone Library), the Corporation of London (Guildhall Library and London Metropolitan Archives), the Institute of Historical Research, the Liverpool Record Office, the London Library, the Special Collections Department of the University of Reading Library, the Shropshire Archives (Shrewsbury), the Society of Antiquaries of London, and the libraries of the University of London (Senate House) and University College London. The final stages of my research and writing were made immeasurably more pleasant and rewarding through an appointment as Honorary Visiting Professor in the Department of English, University College London, and I would like especially to thank Susan Irvine and Henry Woudhuysen for facilitating this.

In the later stages of writing I was fortunate to be advised by two readers who added much to what follows: Christopher Wright, who from his deep understanding of the period suggested many new directions and emphases, and Peter Ross, who offered advice on all matters gastronomic, and (among other things) introduced me to the 'tossing-up pieman'. The book as it now appears would not have been possible without the help of everyone associated with British Library Publishing, including Sally Nicholls, who arranged for the illustrations; Andrew Barron, who designed the jacket; and Andrew Shoolbred, who oversaw the final design and production of the book, and offered friendly and necessary advice to a novice typesetter. My thanks above all go to David Way, for his decision to take a chance on the *Almanack*, and his unfailing assistance at every step of the way.

My considerable debt to earlier scholars will be obvious from my notes and bibliography. I would like particularly to single out the extraordinary efforts of John Paul DeCastro, whose four massive volumes of notes on London taverns (a term he interpreted very broadly), now in the London Metropolitan Archives, were compiled at a time when searching through newspapers and journals was a slow and inky-fingered process; and of Bryant Lillywhite, whose *London Coffee Houses* of 1963 remains the standard source for the history of many of the establishments described in the *Epicure's Almanack*. Finally, I would like to pay tribute to all of the many, often unnamed, researchers and writers who have contributed to three ongoing series of books that I have found essential: the *Buildings of England*, the *Survey of London*, and the *Victoria County History of England*.

INTRODUCTION

In 1815 the *Epicure's Almanack* may have seemed a novel concept, but the work can in fact be placed in a tradition of guidebooks to London that reaches back to the early seventeenth century, when John Taylor (usually called the 'Water Poet', as he was not only a writer but a waterman on the Thames) published *Taylors Travels and Circular Perambulation through … the Famous Cities of London and Westminster* (1636), consisting principally of an 'Alphabeticall Description of all the Taverne Signes in the Cities, Suburbs, and Liberties aforesaid'.[1] Taylor's conceit was that in his tour he had passed through all the signs of the zodiac – though he admitted he had not searched for the sign of Cancer, and had been forced to accept a Green Dragon in lieu of Scorpio – as well as through several constellations and by way of animals from antelopes to swans, and personages from shepherds to kings. In all he listed 366 tavern signs, giving a street direction ('The White Lyon at the end of Tower street, neere to the Hill'; 'The Peacocke in Thames street neere the old Swan') and occasionally commenting in verse on an establishment. Thus, the Crown Tavern in West Smithfield receives the following notice:

> Within this Crowne hath many Crownes been spent,
> Good Wine, Attendance good, and good Content:
> Theres Liquor of the best, from *France* and *Spaine,*
> Which makes this Crowne full weight above a Graine,

and behind the Royal Exchange readers might

> At Antwerp Taverne meet shake hands, be merry,
> Ther's Clarret, White, Canary, and good Sherry.

In his preface Taylor warned that although at the time of writing all the signs listed were 'shining and adorning our Terrestriall Hemisphære with most hopefull, resplendent, refulgent, and translucent Luster', some establishments might have disappeared before his book was published: perhaps 'some of my Suns have been eclipsed, with a Cloud of Debts', and 'bad Customers (or small Custome) hath brought some of my Moones from the full, to an

---

[1] On Taylor's life and works, see Bernard Capp, *The World of John Taylor the Water-Poet, 1578-1653* (1994). Only two copies of *Taylors Travels* are known to survive today, at the Huntington Library in California and the Bodleian at Oxford. The Spenser Society republished the text in 1876, and in 1910 William McMurray printed a modernized (and incomplete) version of Taylor's list, taken from a similarly incomplete transcript in British Library MS Harley 5953, fos 66-68.

unrecoverable Wane'. Later in 1636, when Taylor extended his survey to include the counties of Berkshire, Buckinghamshire, Essex, Hampshire, Hertfordshire, Kent, Middlesex, Oxfordshire, Surrey, and Sussex, he prefaced those tours with a brief list of errors and omissions in his 'first Booke', adding another thirty-seven London establishments to his exhaustive overview of suburban taverns.[2] Yet more taverns were named by Taylor in a third handbook, the *Carriers Cosmographie* of 1637, which listed the 'innes, ordinaries, hosteries [*sic*], and other lodgings in, and neere London' where carriers and messengers from other parts of the country regularly stayed.

The later seventeenth century saw the beginnings of the London guidebook proper, often designed as a pocket-sized volume to be carried about the city.[3] One such was a 1693 French *Guide de Londres pour les estrangers*, written by Francesco Casparo Colsoni and aimed at 'voyageurs Allemands & François'.[4] Colsoni helpfully took up the problem of food and lodging in his very first paragraph, directing his readers to a Mr Block, who 'parle toutes sortes de langues', and at whose house in 'Rue Throughmortenstreet, qu'on prononce Tragmarten-stritt', they would find an *ordinaire*, or fixed-price dinner, costing only fifteen sous per head. And at the close of his little volume, among *avertissements* for businesses ranging from booksellers to telescope makers, Colsoni included puffs for the widow Marie Ortoon behind the Royal Exchange, who kept a 'Coffee-House pour les Allemands', and one Mr Savage at the sign of the Mitre behind Bow Church, who took in borders 'par Semaine à un fort raisonnable prix'; one might also find lodgings in Dean's Yard, near Westminster Abbey, at the house of Guy Miège, the émigré author of a number of popular French grammars and dictionaries.[5]

---

[2] *The Honorable, and Memorable Foundations, Erections, Raisings, and Ruines, of Divers Cities, Townes, Castles, and other Pieces of Antiquitie, within Ten Shires and Counties of this Kingdome* (1636; reprinted by the Spenser Society in 1877).

[3] For a general survey of London guidebooks from 1681 to 1799, including those published for foreigners, see Webb 1990.

[4] Again, this is a very rare book, but in 1951 it was reprinted for the London Topographical Society, with notes by Walter H. Godfrey. Colsoni's name is often given in the French form as François, rather than Francesco; his book had reached a third edition by 1697, and this was reprinted with corrections and additions in 1710 (Godfrey, p. 56).

[5] While hardly a guidebook, Miège's *Nouvelle nomenclature françoise et angloise*, included in his 1685 *Nouvelle méthode pour apprendre l'anglois*, contains several bilingual 'familiar dialogues' to help the French visitor shop or order a room or meal ('Draw me then a pint of Claret, the best you have [and] bring me a bit of cheese', etc.), as well as essays on English food and drink and 'Coffee-houses, and

By the eighteenth century several publishers were issuing popular guide-books to London, generally consisting of a brief history and lists of the principal buildings, amusements, and 'curiosities', with sometimes an index of streets or a proposed tourist itinerary. Such practical information as the location of the major stage stops or the rates charged by watermen and hackney coachmen was often included, but suggestions for suitable accommodation or a decent place to dine were almost universally lacking, no doubt in part because of the difficulty of updating such advice in subsequent editions. John Trusler's *London Adviser and Guide* (1786, 1790), directed principally to 'Strangers coming to reside in London' but 'useful also to Foreigners', is unusual in including a brief mention of hotels – that is, 'taverns or inns, under a new name, so called from the hotels in Paris, where you may be rather better accommodated than at the inns in and about London, but at a much greater expence' – and Trusler spells out the pricing differences (1786, p. 158):

> The inns, and many coffee-houses (for all the coffee-houses are now lodging-houses and taverns) will let you a lodging at one shilling or eighteen-pence a night, whereas […] hotels charge 2s. 6d. or 5s. a night, according to the goodness of the apartment; and 5s. a day for the use of a parlour or dining-room. Two shillings a day for fire, 1s. a-head for breakfast, and for your dinner according to what you order, as dear as at the most expensive tavern.

But no establishments are singled out by name, nor are they in most other late eighteenth-century handbooks. One exception is Patrick Boyle's 1799 *View of London and its Environs*, which includes, between a tally of London hospitals and a comprehensive guide to the city's Masonic lodges, a four-page alphabetical list of the 'principal coffee-houses, &c.' (pp. 314-17). Here 114 establishments are named, including several classed as taverns or hotels, but street addresses are rudimentary, and the houses are neither described nor ranked.

In fact the earliest work to attempt any kind of descriptive survey of London's taverns, coffee houses, and eating houses was not, in the strictest sense, a guidebook at all. *Roach's London Pocket Pilot; or, Stranger's Guide through the Metropolis* (1793, 1796) claimed as its purpose the 'piloting [of] unwary, and unaccustomed strangers, through the dangerous rocks and shoals, and quicksands, with which the great ocean of the universe, but more especially, the municipal vortexes thereof, is, and are, surrounded and intersected', and in the tradition of such earlier works as *The Tricks of the*

---

the Uses a Stranger may make of them', this last concluding that they are 'mighty convenient Places to meet in' and 'much genteeler than Ale-houses'.

Town Laid Open (1746) set out to expose the city's cheats and rogues and to conduct the reader 'safe to the various havens and ports where his bark may rest at anchor, with proper security' (1793, p. 1). Written by or for the publisher James Roach,[6] the *Pocket Pilot* names twenty-two coffee houses as the 'most eligible' in London (pp. 47-48), and for sixteen of them offers a few sentences of description, inviting or otherwise: we are told, for instance, that the York Coffee House in New Bridge Street has perhaps the most elegant rooms in England, with the prettiest and most obliging bar maids, but that the New Exchange Coffee House in the Strand is best avoided, for its rowdy patrons are in the habit of simultaneously farting and vomiting. Twenty-seven further coffee houses are also briefly described, with a distinction made between those 'best calculated for general accommodation' and those catering to 'foreign and domestic mercantile characters' (p. 53), and six taverns are named, together with a few inns and hotels, five eating houses, and – for those whose 'circumstances are very much constrained' – a cookshop in Salisbury Court, off Fleet Street, where four pence will provide enough roast or boiled meat for a person of 'moderate stomach', and 'for six pence a plowman may be satisfied' (p. 60).

In 1802 Richard Phillips, publisher of the *Monthly Magazine* and a profitable string of handbooks and school texts, brought out the first in a new series of pocket-sized guides, *The Picture of London*, subtitled 'a correct guide to all the curiosities, amusements, and remarkable objects, in and near London'. John Britton, writing in 1814, named the compiler as John Feltham, a native of Salisbury who had 'commenced his literary career in the Monthly Magazine, in which he produced several papers'.[7] Feltham also wrote a *Guide to All the Watering and Sea-Bathing Places* for Phillips (first edition 1803, 'by the editor of the *Picture of London*'), and claimed in the preface to that work to be the

6 Roach is often called John, a mistake that goes back to the *DNB* article of 1896, but rate books and newspaper articles consistently give his name as James. From a shop located near the Theatre Royal, Drury Lane, Roach issued song- and jest-books, poetry, plays, and volumes of theatre history from about 1787 to 1822. In 1794 he was prosecuted for publishing *Harris's List of Covent-Garden Ladies*, an annual directory of London's up-market prostitutes, and in 1795 he was sentenced to twelve months in Newgate gaol (*The Times*, 10 February); four months later, however, following the circulation of a petition 'subscribed by upwards of one hundred of the most respectable citizens of the metropolis', he was pardoned by the king (*Morning Chronicle*, 24 June 1795).
7 *The Beauties of England and Wales*, vol. 15 (1814), p. 199. Feltham died on 15 November 1803 at the age of thirty-six (*European Magazine*, December 1803, p. 487).

author of a recent guide to Paris. This last can be identified as *A Practical Guide during a Journey from London to Paris* (also published by Phillips and compiled by 'a gentleman lately resident in Paris'), which has a preface dated 1 June 1802 and includes a directory of the ten best *restaurateurs* in Paris, the most famous *pâtissiers*, and the finest of the 'at least 1000' coffee houses in the city (pp. 104-06). A second edition of the *Practical Guide* appeared less than a year later, with a much expanded section on food and drink (pp. 133-39) that includes priced lists of typical French dishes and wines: artichokes with melted butter were 10*d.*, a bottle of Romanée Conti 5*s.*, and for approximately 7½*d.* one could sample a glass of 'etherial cream of wormwood', or absinthe.

Feltham's *Picture of London* must have had an instant success – two editions appeared in the first year, one with a preface dated 31 January and the second dated 10 August – and from the beginning a regular feature of the guidebook was an extensive list of recommendations for the visitor in search of a meal, a bed, or a suburban tea garden in which to while away a Sunday afternoon. The August 1802 edition names twenty-one hotels and fifty-eight inns, alongside 129 coffee houses, the thirty 'most considerable' eating houses, and twenty-four tea gardens. For convenience both the coffee houses and eating houses are broken down into geographical subsections – east of Temple Bar or west of Temple Bar – and for the coffee houses there are further lists of those 'between the 'Change and West End of the Town' and 'between Newgate Street and the Upper End of Oxford Road' [i.e. today's Marble Arch]. For some establishments only a street name is given, but for most of the coffee houses the entries note the clientele attracted (clergy, military gentlemen, ship agents and brokers, 'literary characters', lawyers, 'gentlemen belonging to the theatre', foreigners, and so on) and often add a word about meal times and the availability of beds ('Coffee room dinner from two to five every afternoon'; 'Beds made up or procured'). A few houses are singled out for special praise ('fitted up in an elegant stile', 'very excellent', 'reasonable terms'), and there is an occasional comment about unusual features (medicinal baths, billiards, chess) or culinary specialities (turtle, boiled beef, 'excellent punch').

The *Picture* sold for 5*s.*, and could be purchased not only from booksellers but 'at the bars of the principal inns and coffee-houses' – the proprietors, perhaps, agreeing to stock the guidebook in return for a favourable mention. The lists of coffee houses and other establishments were only occasionally updated, however, so that the total number of houses named had changed little by 1812, when the *Picture* was one of several publications taken over from Phillips by the firm of Longman, Hurst, Rees, Orme, and Brown. The fourteenth edition appeared under the Longman imprint, with a preface dated January 1813 and now priced 6s. 6d., and Longman continued to publish the guidebook on a more or less annual basis through 1833, commissioning a revision by John Britton in 1826 and changing the title to the *Original Picture of London*, thereby distinguishing it from the rival *New Picture of London* published by Samuel Leigh from 1818 to 1842.

But Longman also had more ambitious plans. Almost immediately after acquiring the *Picture* they engaged Ralph Rylance, one of their regular freelance editors and translators, to put together a companion guide that would concentrate on matters of food, drink, and lodging. Writing to his friend and patron William Roscoe in early 1813, Rylance described the proposed work as 'an Epicure's Almanack on the plan of the Almanach des Gourmands published at Paris by M. Grimod de la Reynière and a jury of *bon vivants*'; as a model the publisher had provided him with seven volumes of the French *Almanach* and instructed him 'to extract the best parts and adapt them to the meridian of London'.[8] According to Rylance, the undertaking was the idea of 'Mr Peltier & Dr Buchan', most likely Jean-Gabriel Peltier, a French counter-revolutionary journalist who had fled to England in 1792, and Alexander Buchan, a London physician and medical writer.[9] The two men had assured Rylance that 'there is no doubt of its success', and Longman may have hoped to go to press within the year. But although the publisher announced the book in the April 1814 *Gentleman's Magazine* as 'speedily to be published', for reasons that will be discussed below the *Epicure's Almanack* did not appear for another year – and when it did it bore only a superficial resemblance to the French prototype.

This is not surprising, for the eight *Almanachs des gourmands* published between 1803 and 1812 were the witty and eccentric creations of a man whom few could hope to imitate without sounding ridiculous. In late 1802 Alexandre Balthazar Laurent Grimod de la Reynière (1758-1838) – today widely regarded as the inventor of the restaurant review – had set out to produce a pocketable guide both to seasonal specialities (the *calendrier nutritif*) and to the various Parisian shops and restaurants where the reader might purchase or dine on the delicacies he described (the *itinéraire nutritif* or *promenade d'un gourmand*). The resulting work, published at the beginning of 1803, was a phenomenal success, issued three times in that year and reprinted in 1810, and Grimod

[8] Letter of 3 February 1813; Liverpool Record Office 920 ROS 4309.
[9] No correspondence about the project remains today in the Longman archive (University of Reading MS 1393), and the extent of Peltier's and Buchan's input is unknown.

followed it with seven further *années* (1804-08, 1810, and 1812), gradually trans-
forming the guidebook into a platform for his extravagant observations on
all things gastronomic.[10] Thus while in the first edition the *calendrier nutritif*
occupies about two-thirds of the whole, followed by recommendations of
Parisian restaurants, cafes, and provisioners, as the *Almanach* evolved the
calendar was abandoned in favour of anecdotes, *poésies gourmandes*, occasional recipes, and – most prominently – lengthy and sometimes outrageous
essays on topics ranging from mustard to truffles, and from cooking utensils
to remedies for gout. Furthermore, in the fourth year of publication Grimod
dropped his geographical approach to eating and shopping in Paris, replacing his original *promenade* with a directory arranged not by location but by
category (bakers, confectioners, *restaurateurs*, and so on).

  In the *Epicure's Almanack*, however, the shape of the city remains central,
for the book is not merely a catalogue of celebrated eating establishments and
superior provisioners, but rather a guide through the streets and suburbs of
London, intended to help the reader discover, in whatever neighbourhood,
those places in which 'he may dine well, and to the best advantage' (page 1).
This 'Compendium of Epicurean Topography' – as Rylance calls it in his
preface – takes up eighty per cent of the *Almanack*, and follows in plan not
Grimod's *Almanach* but rather the *Picture of London*, with its lists of establishments roughly grouped by area. Where Grimod's influence is principally seen
is in the *Almanack*'s appendices, the 'alimentary calendar' and the 'review of
artists who administer to the wants and conveniences of the table', a group
including (as in the later volumes of the French *Almanach*) such retailers
as china merchants and lamp manufacturers. But again departing from the
French model, the *Epicure's Almanack* also includes a separate section on
London markets, from the grand to the obscure, directing the home cook to
the best sources for meat and fish, vegetables and fruit.

  There is no way of knowing if Ralph Rylance was given a free hand with the
project, or if the general outline of the *Almanack* was dictated by Longman, or
even suggested by Peltier and Buchan. Nor can we calculate how much of the
actual legwork was undertaken by Rylance himself: he at one point describes
a meal enjoyed by 'one of our coadjutors' (page 153), and he undoubtedly
took advice from friends, perhaps even paying out some of the fifty guineas
he earned to assistants. Indeed, tempting as it is to picture him stopping in

---

[10] The best English-language accounts of Grimod's life and work are MacDonogh
  1987 and, especially for analysis of the social and political context, Spang 2000,
  pp. 152-69.

at pastry shops and chop houses, sampling ales, and jotting down the names and addresses of innkeepers and cheesemongers, it is hard to see how one man could have found the time to visit and make notes on some 550 establishments between Marylebone and the docks, plus another hundred in his 'circumambulation of the metropolis'. But the prose is certainly Rylance's, by turns informative and whimsical (if sometimes ponderously so), and despite the circumscribed subject matter, seldom dull or repetitive. Rylance's life, too, was anything but dull, and merits notice.

RALPH RYLANCE was thirty-three when the *Almanack* appeared, and had already been in Longman's employ for several years as occasional reader, translator, indexer, and editor.[11] The son of a joiner, he was born at Bolton, Lancashire on 30 March 1782, and attended Bolton Grammar, a free school where he studied Latin, Greek, French, and possibly Italian. In 1797 Ralph left school for a brief apprenticeship with a weaver, and eventually found a commercial situation, probably in a warehouse or with a cotton broker. But by early 1806 he was unemployed, and trying to succeed as a writer. He published his first book that spring, a brief *Tribute* to the late William Pitt, and then quickly sketched out a five-act play in blank verse, taking as his theme the 1478 conspiracy to murder Giuliano and Lorenzo de Medici, as chronicled in William Roscoe's 1796 biography of Lorenzo. Tragedy in hand, Rylance travelled to Liverpool without an introduction to present his play to Roscoe, remaining in the city long enough to dash off a second drama for his prospective patron's inspection. We have no record of Roscoe's critical response to either, but the philanthropic historian and reformer was sufficiently impressed to advance Ralph twelve guineas and arrange a job for him in London, as proof-reader to his own favoured printer, John M'Creery.

Rylance moved to London in July, but lasted less than a year in M'Creery's shop, finding the work 'irksome' and the situation unconducive to the 'visits of the muse'. He was determined on a literary career in London, however, and while his schemes arose and disappeared without a trace – a handbook on 'comparative elocution', a play to be offered to the Covent Garden Theatre, a series of letters addressed to Shakespeare, and a novel based on the life of the painter Parmegiano – he supported himself with one small job after another,

---

[11] For a more extended study of Rylance's life and work, and fuller references to the quotations from correspondence included here, see Freeman 2010.

going from publisher to publisher in search of work. In 1808 he also undertook to write, at the request of Roscoe's friend Henry Brougham, a short book discussing the flight of the Portuguese government and court to Brazil following the Napoleonic invasion of Portugal; Brougham himself wrote the preface, chose the title (*A Sketch of the Causes and Consequences of the Late Emigration to the Brazils*), and corrected the main text, for which he paid Ralph £40. By then Rylance was also earning small amounts by contributing poetry and prose to magazines and newspapers, and another of Roscoe's associates, Robert Hartley Cromek, had hired him to help with a new edition of Robert Burns's *Reliques*. Although money remained tight, in April 1809 Ralph was able to boast to Roscoe that he had the prospect of enough work from Longman and another publisher to carry him through the next twelve months.

But within weeks disaster struck: as Roscoe's eldest son reported to his father from London, 'our poor Friend Ralph Rylance has taken leave of his senses & is now quite mad'.[12] Rylance's widowed mother came from Bolton to care for him, but by mid-May his behaviour was so erratic that she was obliged to place him in a private lunatic asylum. Now more than ever money was needed, and the young man's many friends promptly rallied round. Both Roscoe and Brougham offered financial help, and after his discharge Cromek helped him find work and also briefly took in both Ralph and his mother, who remained in London with her son until her death in 1831. Today it seems clear that Rylance suffered from some form of what would now be called bipolar syndrome or manic depression, but this was a condition unnamed and barely understood in his time. At its severest, during his low or melancholic periods he withdrew from correspondence, and possibly society itself, while his spells of mania were characterized by frenzied activity, grandiose plans, and sometimes abusive, malicious, or even violent behaviour. His asylum experiences can only be imagined, but they cannot have been pleasant: patients classed as manic were often physically restrained, either by a 'strait waistcoat' or special locks, chains, or hobbles, and treatment might include bleeding, purges, 'spouting' or forced feeding, and sedation with opiates.[13]

But even though he was institutionalized several times, like many other sufferers Rylance was able to function normally – and even brilliantly – for long stretches. He slowly returned to work, and in the summer of 1810 Joseph

---

[12] William Stanley Roscoe to William Roscoe, 18 May 1809; Liverpool Record Office 920 ROS 4300.

[13] See W. L. Parry-Jones, *The Trade in Lunacy: A Study of Private Madhouses in England in the 18th and 19th Centuries* (1972), pp. 192-98.

Nightingale, a friend from his days with M'Creery, hired him to help with the research for a volume in a series of the *Beauties of England and Wales*. While gathering information in Shropshire, Rylance met John Freeman Milward Dovaston, a one-time barrister who had recently inherited a small estate at West Felton, near Shrewsbury, where his orchards and beehives supported his passions for poetry, music, botany, and ornithology. The two men began a correspondence that lasted more than twenty years, and through Dovaston Ralph soon became intimate with the family of George Reynolds of Lambeth, and particularly with George's son, the budding poet John Hamilton Reynolds. Encouraged by Dovaston and Reynolds, he began a verse account of the 1403 battle of Shrewsbury and quickly completed two cantos, but like so many projects *St Magdalene's Eve* languished, and within a few years Ralph abandoned poetry altogether. Instead, he embarked on a series of romantic prose 'visions' – his own word – mostly designed to be read at the annual 'Avontide' festivities that Dovaston had initiated at West Felton to mark Shakespeare's birthday.[14]

In 1811 Rylance began supplementing his income by serving as English tutor and interpreter to several young South American diplomats, and on Henry Brougham's recommendation he and Nightingale undertook the task of indexing the first twenty volumes of the *Edinburgh Review*, of which Brougham had been a founder in 1802. Two hundred guineas were promised to the pair, but the project dragged on into 1813, when Ralph spent the entire summer in Edinburgh reading proofs and making final revisions: it is to this period that we owe our only portrait of Ralph Rylance, a 'caricature etching' by John Kay, later published in Kay's *Series of Original Portraits and Caricature Etchings* (2 vols, 1837-38). It is possible that he had begun work on the *Epicure's Almanack* project before leaving for Edinburgh, and he had certainly completed enough by April 1814 for Longman to feel confident in announcing the book. By then, however, Ralph had again entered a manic period, and after a disastrous trip to Shropshire he was placed in a London asylum in early May. But within a few months he was back at work for Longman, editing and translating, and also finishing up the *Almanack*, which finally appeared in May 1815.

---

[14] Several visions written between 1818 and 1833 were preserved by Dovaston, and are now in the Princeton University Library.

Ralph Rylance, as sketched by John Kay in 1813.

LONGMAN had gambled a considerable sum on their new guidebook. As editor Rylance received fifty guineas, and a second editor, one Mr King, was paid £5 3s. for unspecified work. Paper, printing, advertising, and miscellaneous expenses brought the total cost for 750 copies to nearly £177 before binding, giving a cost per copy of just under 4s. 8d. unbound and leaving little space for profit from a publication price of 5s. 6d. in printed boards.[15] Perhaps the most surprising of the publisher's expenses is the thirty guineas spent on advertising. Notices repeatedly appeared in all the major reviews and monthlies, stressing the fact that the work was modelled on the celebrated French *Almanach des gourmands*, and in one case even claiming that the editor had 'prepared himself, for his task, by a sedulous course of study, or rather a series of experimentary dinner-courses, during the space of three years'.[16]

Banking on the success of the *Almanack*, Longman also revised their main London guidebook in 1815, replacing the geographically arranged directories of coffee houses and other establishments in the *Picture of London* with unannotated alphabetical lists. But despite the flurry of advertisements and notices, there was little enthusiasm for their new guide to 'places of alimentary resort'. Fewer than 300 copies of the *Epicure's Almanack* had been sold by the end of 1817, when the remainder were pulped, and although the title-page announced the work as the first in an annual series, no continuation ever appeared. Clearly London was not yet ready for a dedicated 'good food guide', at least not in this form. The only review I have found was certainly lukewarm, complaining above all that the *Almanack* concentrated too much on the lesser establishments, with the result that it 'may be more frequently consulted as a guide to a *cheap dinner* than as a teacher of epicureanism'.[17] The reviewer was, perhaps, thinking of passages such as that extolling the modest Green Man public house in New Bond Street, where one could get a 'snug, neat, cheap dinner' and then emerge to mix with the fashionable mob and 'cast a smile of pity on the unthinking mortals who exhaust perhaps the entire day's pay of a subaltern over an extravagant dinner' (pages 184-85).

This was indeed a far cry from Grimod's baroque musings, and if the *Monthly Review* found the substance of the *Almanack* 'served up with rather too much affectation-sauce', other readers may have considered the sauce all too thin. Furthermore, it is not clear how the guidebook might have been used, for overall there is little sense of audience. The humble patrons of

[15] Longman Impression Book no. 5 (University of Reading MS 1393/144), fo 193.
[16] *Universal Magazine* (April 1814), p. 315.
[17] *Monthly Review* (May 1815), pp. 111-12.

Mr Epps's chain of ham, beef, and soup shops, for instance, would be unlikely even to enter the public rooms of the 'imperially magnificent' Clarendon Hotel in New Bond Street, nor would the resident guests of the Clarendon or of the nearby Pulteney Hotel need to seek out such establishments as Mr Allen's shop in Piccadilly, with its supply of sausages and 'artificial' mock turtle soup. Such juxtapositions abound – in St James's, subscription houses such as Brooks's and White's, off-limits then and now to most readers, are described alongside Tomlins's Royal Jelly House and Walker and Gother's fish emporium – but for the modern reader this diffuseness is a bonus. Instead of a dull listing of only the sumptuous and the elegant we have a truly democratic guide to each part of the city that the *Almanack* considers, giving us (in today's terms) not only the Ritz and the Ivy, but also Starbucks, Burger King, and a generous selection of neighbourhood curry and kebab houses.

With his work on the *Almanack* finished, Ralph Rylance returned to the more routine chores of revising, translating, indexing, and proof-reading. And by the beginning of 1816 he had a new medical problem, which he described to John Dovaston in June as a 'simple *ulcusculum sub glande penis*' that had been treated with mercurial ointment, a topical preparation commonly used in cases of syphilis. Whether Rylance's own 'little ulcer' was in fact the first symptom of that disease is not clear, but the 'merry madness' that he says kept him in the Marylebone Infirmary for several months was almost certainly the result of mercury poisoning, then only hazily understood. A low period followed his release, but in mid-1818 he began working for the historian William Coxe, Archdeacon of Wiltshire, assisting him in the completion of a three-volume biography of the Duke of Marlborough for Longman. Perhaps impressed with this work, on the death of George III in early 1820 the publisher commissioned from Rylance an anonymous concluding volume to Robert Bisset's six-volume *History of the Reign of George III* (1804); for this he received nearly £130, and in May 1821 he told Dovaston that he was earning around £500 a year. That summer, however, he again lost two or three months to illness, which left him exhausted and 'obliged to take lodgings out of town, for the benefit of a milk diet'. This explanation may mask another spell in an asylum, but by autumn Rylance was back at work for Longman, principally on a series of encyclopaedia articles, and in 1822 he again entered Coxe's pay, helping the now totally blind Archdeacon with what was to be his final book, *Memoirs of the Administration of Henry Pelham*. For some five years Rylance transcribed letters, ran errands, and travelled back and forth to Salisbury, and in late 1825, at Longman's suggestion, he began the job of condensing Coxe's work, which had swelled to twice the agreed length.

During the years he was working for Coxe, Rylance continued as well with other work for Longman, and seems at this time to have been acting principally as a publisher's advisor, evaluating manuscripts and making any necessary revisions. His languages continued to serve him well, and by the 1820s he was – at a minimum – able to work from French, Italian, Spanish, Portuguese, and German. He continued to act as English tutor to several Spanish-speaking diplomats and their families, charging seven shillings a lesson, and seems finally to have resigned himself to a life of such piecework, especially after an unsuccessful attempt in 1824 to obtain a post as assistant keeper of manuscripts at the British Museum. Still, new projects continued to come in from Longman, and in the late 1820s Rylance was receiving sizable payments for editorial work on Hugh Murray's massive *Encyclopædia of Geography* and the early volumes of Dionysius Lardner's *Cabinet Cyclopædia*. He and his mother moved from Soho to a house near the Regent's Park, removed from what he called 'the contamination of bricks, mortar, and cockney streetification', and here Ralph began work on a book of his own, concerned with the etymology of British place names. But this went forward slowly, frustrated by the demands of both his editorial work and his invalid mother, and when she died in August 1831 the project was abandoned.

The loss of his mother threw Rylance into a prolonged depression, and his health suffered. In late 1832 he was confined to bed for several weeks by an illness he described as 'arising from overstudy', and for a time work was impossible. On his recovery he revised a series of letters originally written to a young female correspondent seeking spiritual advice, publishing them anonymously in autumn 1833 as *Reasons for Christianity, and Hope Therein Founded*. This went into a second edition, and was followed at the end of the year by a small pamphlet of *Lessons on the Lord's Prayer*, giving Rylance hope that his 'long deferred literary career' might prove prosperous after all. But yet another spell of illness in early 1834 prevented him from completing jobs for Longman, and on 6 June 1834 Ralph Rylance died in a private asylum. Thomas Lever, a Lancashire schoolfellow living in London, sent the news to John Dovaston, reporting that 'for a fortnight prior to his dissolution, it pleased the Almighty to deprive him of his reason'. This Lever attributed to Rylance's financial difficulties, for he had debts of some £400, and only the furniture of his rooms and a few books to cover them. Lever himself arranged for Ralph's burial, but I have found no record of this, nor discovered whether Lever was successful in his attempt to raise the money for a headstone, so that he might (as he told Dovaston) 'tell who he was and where from, that so much talent might not be quite forgotten'.

By 1811, the date of the second decennial British census, inner London was home to more than a million people, with perhaps another 200,000 living in outlying areas now considered part of greater London. The *Epicure's Almanack* surveys both, adding to its principal 'trans-Thamsesian tour' of the capital (which includes the Borough of Southwark as well as Wapping and the docks) a supplementary 'circumambulation of the metropolis' that takes in towns and villages from Finchley in the north to Wimbledon in the south, and from Hampton in the west to Greenwich in the east. The following pages give an overview of the areas covered, and include some information that did not readily find a place in the notes to individual establishments. Frequent reference is made here and elsewhere to several maps of London, which are described in the bibliography and are in some cases available online; if no date is specified, references to 'Horwood' indicate that the feature is shown on both the 1799 and the 1813 maps.

The City of London

'London, strictly so called' accounts for more than a quarter of the entries in the *Almanack*, spread out over ninety-two pages and interrupted by three side trips, one north to Shoreditch and two east to Wapping and the docks. We begin at St Paul's and first move eastward, generally following Cheapside and Poultry toward the densely-provisioned area around the Royal Exchange and the Bank of England; then turn south into Cornhill, Gracechurch Street, and Fish Street Hill; and finally head north along Bishopsgate into Shoreditch, temporarily leaving the City behind. On our return to the City we first stop briefly near the two principal London synagogues in Duke's Place and Bevis Marks, visiting a neighbourhood 'chiefly inhabited by Jews' (page 40) and unsurprisingly filled with shops offering 'viands cooked according to the Mosaical ordinances'.[18] We next abruptly jump back to Long Lane near the

---

[18] Rylance's occasional unflattering comments about Jews reflect the latent anti-Semitism typical of his time, in which Jews were frequently stereotyped as 'ragged peddlars and dirty old-clothes men' and one guidebook of 1828, John Badcock's *Living Picture of London*, warned visitors 'to expect abuse, scurrility, and threats hurled at them' if they did not buy from Jewish street merchants (Todd Endelman, *The Jews of Georgian England*, pp. 106 and 183). Endelman estimates that in the early C19 the Jewish population of London was around 15,000.

West Smithfield livestock market and again travel east, this time by way of the Barbican, Beech Street, Chiswell Street, and Finsbury Square. Another leap returns us to the heart of the city and Leadenhall Market – not today's grand glass-roofed shopping arcade, opened in 1881, but a wholesale skin and leather market sharing space with stalls selling meat and poultry – and from here we again go east, passing the ancient Aldgate Pump at the junction of Leadenhall Street and Fenchurch Street and continuing into Aldgate, which later becomes Aldgate High Street and then Whitechapel High Street. This was a Roman road, once the principal approach for travellers coming into London from Colchester, and by the late seventeenth century several large galleried inns catering to travellers had sprung up along the route.

From Whitechapel we detour to the new East and West India Docks, returning to the City to survey a few establishments in avenues 'on the right and left of the principal streets' (page 51). These include taverns in the general area of the Billingsgate fish market and Lower Thames Street, and establishments in Eastcheap, Mark Lane (home to the Corn Exchange), and Mincing Lane, where in 1812 commodity traders had opened the London Commercial Sale Rooms, hoping to 'rival the coffee houses by providing a complete market for the sale of sugar, cotton, coffee, tobacco, indigo and other imported goods'.[19] Another eastward diversion into Wapping is followed by a second round-up of 'a few good houses' previously omitted (page 64), including eating houses and taverns in the Minories, Basing Lane (now Cannon Street), Aldersgate and Noble Streets, and the area between Guildhall and Old Broad Street. Finally, we set out from Temple Bar for a last City walk, travelling east along Fleet Street and up Ludgate Hill until we have once again arrived at St Paul's.

North of the City: Bishopsgate and Shoreditch

The survey of Bishopsgate as it becomes Bishopsgate Without, then Norton Folgate, and finally Shoreditch is brief, and our guide offers no real enticement, commenting at the outset that the area 'contains few places above the rank of an eating-house or a cook's-shop' (page 39). Indeed, most of the establishments named cater to the take-away trade – pastrycooks, tripe shops, 'ready-drest' ham and beef shops – although a handful boast modest eating rooms as well. But street addresses and names of proprietors are meticulously recorded, suggesting that this was perhaps the home neighbourhood of one of Rylance's 'coadjutors', who contributed to the *Almanack* the details of the shops and eating houses that he daily passed.

[19] Kynaston 1994, p. 32.

East London, Wapping, and the Docks

The bold plan to construct new, secure docks to serve the lucrative West India trade had received the Royal Assent in 1799, with work beginning the following year on the Isle of Dogs, a thumb of land projecting south into the Thames opposite Greenwich. By 1809 the massive works there were complete, and another smaller set of enclosed docks for the East India cargo ships had been erected at Blackwall, just to the east; a third, the London Dock, opened at Wapping in 1805. The new Commercial Road provided direct access, cutting across east London from Whitechapel to Limehouse, where it split into the West and East India Dock Roads. Two other well-travelled routes east also remained in use: from the Tower one could either proceed along the river-front via St Katharine's Way and Wapping High Street, or take a slightly more northerly course along East Smithfield and the notorious Ratcliffe Highway, in 1811 the scene of a sequence of murders that had shocked London and indeed the entire country.[20] The *Almanack* covers all three routes in search of establishments convenient for those who have business at the East or West India Docks or at Wapping, with its thriving shipbuilding and provisioning industries, or who are in need of safe accommodation while waiting to take passage from Wapping to Berwick and other Scottish ports.

The first tour (pages 49-50) takes us along the Commercial Road and its extensions, going as far as the East India Dock Tavern, a large and new establishment just at the gates of the docks. Closer to the West India Docks are a few taverns and eating houses near Limehouse; others are found at Poplar, a thriving community strung out along an east-west high street north of the docks. Today virtually nothing remains of the East India and London Docks, which were both closed in the 1960s, and the Canary Wharf development has utterly changed the landscape of the West India Docks, closed in 1980. Nearer the river, however, one can still occasionally step back into a previous century, and on our second trip (pages 59-62) we follow a route along Wapping High Street – probably little wider and busier now than it was two hundred years ago – as far as Gravel Lane. We then return to the City along the Highway, stopping near Wellclose Square and at the lively Rag Fair in Rosemary Lane, long the preserve of Jewish used-clothes merchants but also attracting vendors of everything from discounted day-old bread to cures for syphilis.

---

[20] See P. D. James and T. A. Critchley, *The Maul and the Pear Tree: The Ratcliffe Highway Murders, 1811* (1971).

Westminster

We begin (page 92) with establishments near Westminster Abbey, and after a detour west along Great George Street continue north into Whitehall by way of King Street and Parliament Street. In 1815 King Street ran north from Great George Street to Downing Street, but by the end of the century it had been completely absorbed by Parliament Street, created just to its east when the first Westminster Bridge was built in the 1740s. Continuing on to Charing Cross, we pass through a neighbourhood that was to change radically within a few years with the construction of Trafalgar Square. Spring Gardens, where we visit two or three establishments, still retains its earlier dogleg layout today, though minus the garden itself and now bisected by the Mall as it passes under Admiralty Arch. Just at the end of Spring Gardens is Charles Wigley's Great Promenade Room, where a shilling buys admission to a performance of J. J. Gurk's panharmonicon, a mechanical orchestra combining a set of organ pipes with all the instruments of a military band.[21] From Charing Cross we then travel east along the Strand, passing the church of St Martin in the Fields and continuing on to Temple Bar after a side trip south of the Strand into the Adelphi, developed in the 1770s by Robert Adam and his brothers.

St Marylebone, Oxford Street, and Holborn

With a 'sudden leap from Temple Bar to Tyburn' (page 118) we move to what was a newly fashionable part of London. Still a small country village at the end of the seventeenth century, by 1815 St Marylebone had been absorbed into the metropolis: the Cavendish Square area was developed in the early eighteenth century, followed by Portman Square (laid out *c.* 1765), Manchester Square (1770), and finally Montagu and Bryanston Squares (1810-17). And although grand dwellings such as Chandos House in Cavendish Square and Home House in Portman Square were designed with the very rich in mind, even the smaller squares had their sprinkling of aristocrats by the early nineteenth century.

We begin at the site of the Tyburn gallows near present-day Marble Arch, the principal place of public execution until 1783 (the Arch itself was constructed in 1827, and until 1851 stood in front of Buckingham Palace). At Tyburn two ancient Roman roads met: Watling Street, running north to St Albans (now Edgware Road and its continuations), and the Tyburn Road or Oxford Street, which continued west from this junction to Staines and

---

[21] See Altick 1978, p. 359.

Silchester. At Duke Street we turn up into Marylebone proper, returning to Oxford Street by way of Marylebone Lane and continuing east to Swallow Street – then the principal route running south to Piccadilly, but mostly lost in the building of Regent Street. Adhering to the plan of making 'the usual digressions […] right and left of the main streets', on our way toward Tottenham Court Road we also visit establishments in the Cavendish Square area, in Oxford Market, and in Wardour Street, Hanway Street, and Charles Street (now part of Mortimer Street).

St Giles's High Street, running southeast from the junction of Oxford Street and Tottenham Court Road, was (with its continuation Broad Street) the main road connecting Oxford Street and High Holborn before the construction of New Oxford Street in the mid-1840s. It was in the notorious St Giles rookery that William Hogarth had located 'Gin Lane' in his 1751 engraving, and many of the squalid tenements and narrow streets of the district had yet to be cleared away in 1815. Just before Drury Lane, St Giles's High Street became High Holborn, and east of Gray's Inn Lane (now Road), where the Holborn Bars marked the westernmost boundary of the City of London, High Holborn became Lower Holborn or simply Holborn. Again part of the Roman system, this was a principal east-west thoroughfare with large and well-established inns; it was also home to three of the ancient Inns of Chancery (Barnard's, Furnival's, and Staple), which provided preparatory training for those who would later study for the Bar at one of the Inns of Court, such as nearby Gray's Inn. Generally moving eastward, we also explore Hand Court and the Red Lion Square area north of High Holborn, and Fetter Lane to the south.

Piccadilly, Leicester Square, and St Martin's Lane

Another jump transports us to Hyde Park Corner and the subscription rooms attached to Richard Tattersall's horse and hound auctioneering business (page 141); from here we travel east along Piccadilly, which like Oxford Street had long been one of the main highways leading west out of London. The mid-seventeenth century had seen the building of several great town houses in the street (such as Burlington House, now the home of the Royal Academy), and a century later others had been added at the western end of Piccadilly, facing Green Park. Nearly two hundred years of constant rebuilding have left almost none of the buildings of 1815 standing, and the eastern end of Piccadilly was forever altered with the construction of Regent Street between 1814 and 1825.

At Haymarket the east-west thoroughfare changed its name from Piccadilly to Coventry Street, and after excursions into such byways as Arundel
Street and Rupert Street, both running north from Coventry Street, we turn
toward Leicester Square. Laid out in the later seventeenth century, over the
next hundred years the Square was home to a number of aristocratic families
as well as several artists (Hogarth, Reynolds, Copley), and – almost from
the beginning – foreign craftsmen and painters. From the continental eating
houses of Leicester Square we go east, crossing over Castle Street (widened
in the 1880s to create the Charing Cross Road) to reach St Martin's Lane,
which runs south from Long Acre to the church of St Martin in the Fields
near Charing Cross. Following detours into New Street (now Row) and Mays
Buildings (now Court) we next stop at establishments in Bedford Street and
Henrietta Street, and in King Street visit the first of the many coffee houses
located in the Covent Garden area.

A Roundabout Journey from Covent Garden to Aldwych

Covent Garden, so named from its early use as gardens and pastureland
for the Abbey (or Convent) of St Peter at Westminster, was developed by the
fourth Earl of Bedford as a residential square in the 1630s. Bedford's architect
Inigo Jones provided a new church, St Paul's, at the western end of the square,
and on the north and east sides erected tall terraces of houses, some with
vaulted arcades in the manner of Sebastian Serlio; the south side, facing the
gardens of the late-sixteenth-century Bedford House, saw little development
until the mansion was levelled in the early eighteenth century. The enclosed
paved space of Covent Garden was known as the Piazza, a term that gradually came to refer to the arcaded terraces themselves: what the *Almanack*
describes as the Great Piazza was the continuation of King Street east of
St Paul's, while the Little Piazza directly faced the church.

By the mid-seventeenth century market traders were operating in the
Piazza, and a royal charter of 1670 granted the Earl of Bedford and his heirs the
right to hold a flower and fruit market there and to levy tolls on the traders.
Soon after the demolition of Bedford House semi-permanent market booths
were erected in the central square, replaced by grander structures in 1748.
Following the opening of the Theatre Royal in the northeast corner (1732)
actors, musicians, and playwrights began to move into the area, and as wealthy
householders moved some of the empty buildings were transformed into
hotels, coffee houses, taverns, gaming rooms, or baths (*hummums* or *bagnios*,
some of them thinly-disguised brothels: see below, p. xli). The result, as John
Timbs (b. 1801) recalled, was 'a strange and shabby assemblage of shed and

pent-house, rude stall and crazy tenement, coffee-house and gin-shop, inter-sected by narrow and ill-lit footways',[22] and Ralph Rylance once described walking home after a performance as a 'ramble thro' the piazzas – running the gauntlet thro' streetwalkers & pickpockets'.[23] Eventually this jumble was cleared away, and a covered market building was erected in 1828-30. The first Theatre Royal was destroyed by fire in 1808, but its replacement, seating 2800, was open by September 1809; this too burnt down (1856) and was succeeded by today's Royal Opera House. What remained of the increasingly seedy Great and Little Piazzas was pulled down in the later nineteenth century, and were Rylance to return to Covent Garden today he would recognize little apart from Inigo Jones's church.

From Covent Garden proper (pages 159-62) we wander north along Bow Street in the direction of Long Acre and then travel northeast along Great Queen Street, essentially the continuation of Long Acre east of Drury Lane. The establishments in Serle Street and Carey Street near Lincoln's Inn, as well as those in the Chancery Lane area, are filled with lawyers, as is M'Niven's eating house near the entrance to the thriving Clare Market between Lincoln's Inn Fields and the Strand. To the west of the market we stop in at a few eating houses convenient for the Drury Lane Theatre, which had just been rebuilt, for the third time, in 1811-12. At this point we have nearly made a full circle back to Covent Garden, but instead we turn west toward Maiden Lane and end up in the area of Wych Street, an offshoot of Drury Lane that once ran east to meet the Strand near St Clement Danes, but was cleared away around 1900 for the development of Aldwych.

Bond Street, Mayfair, and St James's

We begin our tour of the 'fashionable world' (pages 181-207) at the junction of Oxford Street and New Bond Street, surveying establishments on both sides of New Bond Street and to its east and west before considering Old Bond Street and the neighbouring Albemarle, Stafford, and Dover Streets; from Dover Street we cross Piccadilly, already fully explored, and enter into St James's Street. Following a detour into Jermyn Street, filled with small hotels, we visit establishments near St James's Market, and then return to St James's Street, travelling south toward the Palace and taking note of the

---

[22] *Walks and Talks* (1865), p. 166.
[23] Rylance to John Dovaston, 2 November 1811; Shropshire Archives 1662/2/369.

many large taverns, hotels, and subscription houses, or gentlemen's clubs. Two final stops in St James's Square and in Pall Mall conclude this section.

Southwark

The 'auncient Borough of Southwerke' is our last port of call (pages 207-20) before we embark on the country tours. We begin our pilgrimage where Chaucer did, at the old Tabard Inn (renamed the Talbot by the end of the sixteenth century), and visit several other large and ancient coaching inns strung out along Borough High Street. Today only a fragment of the galleried George Inn remains, and nothing at all of the others; William Rendle and Philip Norman's *Inns of Old Southwark* (1888) and Norman's *London: Vanished and Vanishing* (1905) record their melancholy fates. From Borough High Street we travel down Kent Street toward the Bricklayer's Arms, a long-lost establishment commemorated in the name of the roundabout at the junction of what are now Great Dover Street, the Old Kent Road, the New Kent Road, and Tower Bridge Road. The *Almanack*'s direction to return to Newington Butts 'by the Grange Road' is surely a mistake: to reach the Elephant and Castle from the Bricklayer's Arms we should instead take the New Kent Road, still unnamed on the Horwood map. We then travel north on the London Road to what is now called St George's Circus – the meeting point of five thoroughfares, four of them ultimately leading back to the river, and the site of an obelisk erected in 1771. From the Circus we proceed north to Blackfriars Bridge along Great Surrey Street, but the *Almanack* also lists a few eating houses convenient for those starting at Westminster Bridge and travelling southeast to St George's.

The Country Tours: West, South, and East

'Having finished our alimentary ramble in town', the *Almanack* informs us on page 220, 'we now proceed with keen stomachs to circumambulate it'. Those in search of a Sunday walk and a visit to a country pleasure garden or tavern are given three basic options: west towards Hammersmith, Richmond, and Hampton Court; south into Surrey and then east towards Greenwich; and north towards Hampstead, Highgate, and Islington. For the first tour we set out from Hyde Park Corner, travelling west through the villages of Knightsbridge and Kensington and continuing along present day Kensington High Street and Hammersmith Road. Just past Kensington we stop at the Hand and Flower, now considerably rebuilt but still in business opposite the Olympia conference and exhibition centre, and then carry on along the High Road to Chiswick, calling in at three inns near Turnham Green and eventually reaching Kew Bridge. Here we cross the river and walk south along 'Dreary Lane', or Kew Road, to Richmond, where the well-stocked shops of provisioners furnish strong indications of the 'epicurean propensities of the inhabitants' (page 227). After sampling the fare at five taverns and inns we recross the Thames and pass through Twickenham, from whence 'a most delightful walk, or ride, of about three miles and a half' leads us past Horace Walpole's villa at Strawberry Hill and on through Bushy Park to the gates of Hampton Court and the very welcome King's Arms, still operating today.

From Hampton three return routes are suggested, the first leading north through Isleworth and Syon Park to Brentford, home to the ancient Three Pigeons Inn mentioned by Thomas Dekker and Ben Jonson and (legend has it) visited by Shakespeare; from Brentford a short walk would take the traveller back to Chiswick High Road. Our guide, however, clearly prefers the alternative southern routes, by which one might 'save at least a mile of ground, avoid the pavements in Brentford, Hammersmith, and Kensington, and be delighted with a fine diversity of scenery' (page 234) – not to mention another half dozen places of refreshment. Although his directions are vague, he would probably have walked east across Bushy Park and crossed the Thames at Kingston, where there has been a bridge since the early thirteenth century; from there the route runs along Kingston Hill, Kingston Bottom (now Kingston Vale), and Putney Vale to Putney Heath, where the eighteenth-century Green Man is still open, and on to Putney proper, with a slight detour south to take in Wimbledon. From Fulham (now Putney) Bridge the return to Hyde Park Corner along the King's Road is only four miles, easily walked 'without a single halt' after dinner; for the pedestrian 'in need of a half-way house', however, there is the Swan at Walham Green, where a brewery had been operating since the early eighteenth century. Alternatively, one could carry on south of the river through Wandsworth and 'halt nearer home' at either Vauxhall or Kennington. Today's traveller might then cross into Pimlico by way of Vauxhall Bridge, but in 1815 this was still under construction, so in default of a boat the nearest crossing was Westminster Bridge, more than half a mile down river.

From Vauxhall and Kennington the *Almanack* turns its attention to readers who 'may choose to take excursions into Surrey from the several bridges' (page 237). Here there is less sense of an organized tour as we move through towns and villages now firmly part of Greater London: Lambeth, Clapham, Balham, Streatham, Camberwell, Peckham, Norwood, Dulwich, Lewisham, Greenwich, Blackheath, and Shooters Hill. Rylance's comments on the spread of the city are worth noting. While the walk from Tooting to Streatham, with its elegant villas and old oaks that have not yet yielded to poplars, is 'one of the pleasantest in the environs of London', and from Norwood one gazes out at scenery 'with a portion of that rapture which Moses felt when he beheld the land of Canaan', a little nearer town new building has put paid to any sense of 'rural retirement' (pages 240-41):

> rows of compact boxes, with here and there a couple of porter's lodges like tea canisters; a counterpane's breadth of grass-plot, with a broad border of yellow gravel trimmed with box and studded with Michaelmas daisy, full-length windows and shade-less verandas, for the admission of road-dust and sun-shine; a wooden ruin with mock gothic casements, and in short such a heterogeneous compound of common-place and extravaganza; of wilderness and town, of trade and tillage, of shop and farm, as one would never expect to find any where but in the very limbo of vanity.

Many of the establishments named are large taverns and coaching inns, but a few tea gardens, pleasure gardens, and smaller public houses are also included. Cumberland Gardens at Vauxhall is the best-known of the pleasure gardens mentioned, but there was also Montpelier Gardens and cricket ground in Walworth, as well as smaller tea gardens at Lark Hall (Lambeth), the Half Moon (Dulwich), the Grove House Tavern (Camberwell), and the Nun's Head (Peckham). Gypsy encampments were well-established at both Norwood and Dulwich: at the Horns Tavern on Knight's Hill Common in Norwood 'ample provision [is] made for the refreshment of the many parties who come hither to have their fortunes told' (page 241), and 'gypseying parties' are seen as well at the Plough in Dulwich, where butterfly collectors also meet to exchange specimens. We conclude this tour by crossing the Thames by ferry at Woolwich and visiting two large establishments at Black-wall – the Artichoke, a popular whitebait restaurant, and the Folly House pleasure gardens.

The Country Tours: North

Far more popular with the residents of central London were the numerous pleasure gardens and taverns to the north (pages 252-64). The *Almanack* describes three routes leading north, and we begin by travelling up the last – the 'middle road at the end of Gray's Inn Lane' known as Maiden Lane (later York Road and now York Way) – to the large pleasure gardens at Copenhagen House, halfway to Highgate. One can also reach Highgate by setting out from the well-known Angel coaching inn at the junction of the New Road (now Euston Road), City Road, Goswell Road, and St John's Road. From the

Angel, Islington's Lower Road (now Essex Road) leads north to the extensive pleasure gardens at Canonbury House, from which a path runs west to Upper Street and Highbury Place. Continuing north along the latter we reach the Sluice House, or Eel Pie House, and farther on Highbury Barn, from whence a pleasant walk leads to Hornsey Wood House, whose artificial lake survives today in Finsbury Park.

Another route north from the Angel takes us first along Upper Street in Islington and then northwest on Holloway Road; a detour up what was then known as Devil's Lane (now Hornsey Road) allows a visit to the celebrated Devil's House. Past Holloway, the 'superior public house which commands an extensive view over London' (page 256), which our guide thinks is called the Prospect House, is more likely the Archway Tavern, nestled in the angle between Archway Road and Highgate Hill. Those continuing northwest from Highgate on the route now designated North Road and North Hill will soon reach the Great North Road that leads on to Whetstone and Barnet; to the northwest, along what is now East End Road, is Finchley and the Bald-Faced Stag – the northernmost point of the tour – and slightly to the east are other roads, left unexplored, that lead north to Colney Hatch, Friern Barnet, and Southgate. Having stopped at the inns on Hampstead Heath, we can descend into the village of Hampstead itself, where it is possible to catch a stage back into town; for those inclined to ramble still further, to the southwest are the pleasure gardens at Kilburn Wells, located on the site of an abandoned Benedictine priory. From there the return to the bustle of Oxford Street is easily accomplished via the old Roman road (Kilburn High Road, Maida Vale, Edgware Road). Our guide, however, prefers to return from Hampstead by way of the taverns along Haverstock Hill, from which a lane leads west to the sometimes boisterous Chalk Farm gardens, putting Camden Town within easy reach.

For the traveller who gets no farther than Highgate yet another route home is suggested. Instead of returning by way of the high road to the east (Highgate Hill, which we earlier ascended), we can take 'a beautiful shaded foot-path' that leads south to Kentish Town past Holly Lodge (page 262). Several taverns and tea gardens await in Kentish Town and farther south in Camden Town, and four more establishments bring the tour to a close: the recently relocated Jew's Harp Tavern near the Regent's Park barracks, the Adam and Eve and the King's Head at the junction of today's Hampstead Road and Euston Road, and to the northeast a second Adam and Eve, adjoining St Pancras Old Church.

Although the *Almanack* describes food sold by vendors ranging from street hawkers to West End hoteliers, its principal attention is directed to eating houses, taverns, and to a somewhat lesser extent coffee houses, licensed public houses, hotels and inns, and tea gardens. This is definitely a 'good food', rather than a 'good pub' or 'good hotel' guide, but the entries reflect both the early nineteenth-century blurring of traditional distinctions between the various types of eating and drinking establishments and the common practice of combining a range of options under a single roof ('coffee house, tavern, and hotel', 'inn, tavern, and chop house', and so on).

Perhaps the two most basic distinctions to be made are between establishments that offer lodging and those that do not, and between those that sell food only for consumption off the premises and those that provide tables or at least a stand-up bar. Rooms for the night are by definition available in inns, hotels, and lodging houses, and can also be found at many taverns and coffee houses and in some licensed public houses, but it is safe to assume that establishments described as eating houses or chop houses provide food and drink only. Usually, although not always, the *Almanack* distinguishes 'shops' (take-away only) from 'houses' – sometimes 'rooms' – in which meals are served. Customers will probably not expect to be served at table in a ham shop, tripe shop, or shellfish warehouse, nor at the simple cook's shop, although a few of the latter are singled out as also having dining rooms, such as the 'old established cook's-shop' in Red Lion Square that features 'comfortable dining rooms up stairs'. By contrast, a few steps away is Evett's ham shop, where you may purchase ham by the pound and 'if you please, put the slices thereof between the two crusts of a quartern loaf, and carry them away cool in a couple of cabbage leaves' (page 136). Allen's ham and beef shop in Piccadilly provides 'good accommodations' for eating, but at Copping's similar establishment in Oxford Street 'there are no eating-rooms attached to the shop' (pages 146, 119). Pastry and confectionery shops may fall on either side of the divide, but patrons should not always expect a full meal: sometimes, as at Tucker's pastry shop in Russell Court, you may only 'stay your stomach, if not sate it, with a variety of tit-bits in the confectionary style' (page 178).

In 1815 the words *restaurant* and *café* had not yet entered into common English usage, and 'eating house' is overall the most common designation, corresponding to what would be called 'dining rooms' later in the century; this latter term is applied to only one establishment, the Union Dining Rooms in Finch Lane, which 'come under the description and rank of an eating-house' (page 23). More specialized eat-in venues include alamode beef houses, steak or chop houses, boiled beef houses, and shellfish or oyster rooms: Mr Saunders in Piccadilly, not content with the latter designation, has conferred a 'novel title' on his business, calling it an 'oyster tavern and coffee-room' (page 146). In all these establishments the dining room itself is often upstairs, sometimes partitioned into boxes; a sampling of the dishes available is exhibited in the window or in a larder near the entrance. The display in the window of Goodhugh's, Oxford Street, is a 'tempting assemblage', 'really wonderful, both as to quantity and quality', and at the Blandford Eating House in Marylebone the 'great variety of viands' exposed in the window are 'kept warm by an improved steam apparatus' (pages 128, 124). Eating houses may also include a shop area in which food can be purchased for consumption off the premises. Here prices are usually based on weight, and in some of the eating houses *cum* cook's shops the same rule applies to food eaten on the spot, although 'per plate' prices are more common, and in a few establishments, such as the Blandford, meat is cut 'by weight or by plate'. Particularly favourable notice is given to proprietors who provide a priced bill of fare, either posted near the door or placed on the table: 'strangers and economists may thus calculate the cost ere they incur it' (page 21).

Among the grander eating houses described is John o'Groat's, near today's Piccadilly Circus, where cloths are laid and there is a priced menu on each table, along with a water decanter, goblets, and a set of castors for condiments (page 148). Wood's Eating House in Tower Street is singled out for its neat dining rooms and impressive window displays, including (in season) 'a number of fine, lively, amiable turtle', and at Anderson's, near Drury Lane, pleasant rooms combine with attentive servants, the 'primest joints', and moderate charges: 'what, in the name of conscience, reader, would you have more?' (pages 58, 175). Lower down the scale are the houses described as 'decent' or 'respectable' – often the best choice in a dodgy area – and at the bottom those dismissed as 'inferior', such as the two or three in Old Bailey whose 'principal business is to supply the poor prisoners, and those good Christians who visit them in prison', or the three 'refectories, of the humbler order' in Grub Street (pages 88, 43).

Only slightly less numerous in the listings than eating houses are the establishments described as taverns. Traditionally these specialized in wine, in contrast to the ale house or public house, but by the early seventeenth century meals could be arranged in the larger taverns, and Samuel Pepys's diaries are filled with descriptions of tavern dinners and suppers. For the author of the *Almanack* tavern is clearly a term of respect. Near St James's Market is the Tun, 'one of the meritorious houses which have risen progressively from the obscurity of a chop-house to the importance of a tavern' (page 201); a similar transformation has taken place at the Ship in Charing Cross, formerly 'considered merely in the light of a public house'. Here the proprietor has 'removed the tap to the back premises, and in its former space has fitted up a Coffee-room, with a larder displaying steaks, chops, and other light dishes' (page 100). By way of contrast, in Darkhouse Lane the grandly named Queen's Head Tavern and Antigallican Tavern are merely, 'strictly speaking, public-houses', and the Bell Tavern in Noble Street is as well '*classically* speaking a superior kind of public-house' (pages 52, 68).

The larger taverns, such as the London (Bishopsgate), the Freemason's Tavern (Great Queen Street), the Crown and Anchor in the Strand, or the Thatched House in St James's Street, boast grand public rooms suitable for public meetings and lectures, balls, concerts, and large or small dinners: one room at the Crown and Anchor is capable of accommodating as many as seven hundred diners. Even the most popular public houses – such as the Barley Mow in Salisbury Square, which is said to serve two hundred meals a day – are more intimate establishments, and many cater to particular trades or professions. The Poulterer's Arms off Cheapside is 'much frequented by gentlemen in the corn trade', while lawyers congregate at the Three Tuns in Fetter Lane and bailiffs at the Seven Stars or the Apple Tree near Chancery Lane, and Mayfair 'gentlemen's gentlemen' meet at the Goat or the King's Head in Stafford Street.

Traditional coffee houses in which hot and cold liquid refreshments are accompanied by only the lightest of snacks are still the rule in the heart of the City, where some establishments, such as Lloyd's and the Jerusalem, are essentially subscription houses. 'They dress no dishes' at the New England or the Antigallican in Threadneedle Street, we are warned (page 18), although soups and broths are on offer at the Hambro' and Edinburgh in Sweeting's Rents, and sandwiches may be had at Garraway's (Exchange Alley) and at the two coffee houses attached to the Corn Exchange in Mark Lane. At Peele's Coffee House, Fleet Street, the 'refreshments are tea, coffee, punch, wine, [and] newspapers' (page 78), the last also a staple of the Chapter in Paternoster Row, the Hungerford in the Strand, and Thomas Reid's Saloop and Coffee House, also in Fleet Street, where the 'standard magazines for the last half century' are available in bound volumes (page 82). Other coffee houses, as well as those establishments referred to as 'coffee house and tavern', provide more substantial meals, and may offer overnight accommodation. The London Coffee House at no. 24 Ludgate Hill, in business since the 1730s, is 'one of the first establishments in London; and in point of good wine, good beds, and good diet, perhaps, the very first. It is on a most magnificent scale' (page 90).

At the New Hummums Coffee House, Tavern, and Hotel in Covent Garden there are, in addition to 'dinners, suppers, and elegant lodgings', apartments 'kept under the most exact regulation, for the accommodation of gentlemen who choose only to sleep there occasionally, and who if they please may avail themselves of the warm bath' (page 162). *Hummum* or *hamman* is the Arabic term for what we would today call a sweating or Turkish bath, a treatment introduced into England during the seventeenth century. A host of bathing houses known either as hummums or bagnios (from the Italian *bagno*) opened in London during the eighteenth century, generally providing refreshments as well as baths, and by 1815 many had, like the New Hummums, evolved into coffee houses *cum* hotels. But while no scandal seems to have been attached to visiting or referring to a hummums, it was a different matter with the bagnio: from early times the word tended to imply a house of prostitution as well as bathing – the equivalent, perhaps, of today's dubious 'massage parlour'.[24]

Other hotels and inns listed in the *Almanack* include traditional coaching inns, boarding houses suitable for gentlemen on their own, small 'family hotels', and fashionable destinations such as the Clarendon Hotel in Bond Street, where 'every species of luxury, every refinement of accommodation that ingenuity can devise or money can procure, may [...] be met with and enjoyed' (page 194). Many of the inns mentioned are already ancient in 1815, and apart from a fragment of the galleried George Inn in Borough High Street all would be pulled down by the end of the century. Newer and more convenient are the hotels to be found in the West End, clustered in St James's, Marylebone, and the Bond Street area: 'much to the injury of taverns and lodging-houses', these provide accommodation for visitors wishing to 'combine all the retirement and comforts of home with the freedom of access, egress, and ingress, which one generally expects when abroad' (page 199). Although some cater only to resident guests, others have public rooms such as the 'tavern department' of Stevens's Hotel in New Bond Street, where 'dinners and other repasts are served up in the first style of elegance' (page 192).

[24] On bagnios in general, see Cruickshank 2009, pp. 215-27.

Such elegant accommodation disappears as we leave the centre of London, and the only suburban establishment dignified by the name of hotel is the 'stupendous' Star and Garter at Richmond. The outlying areas, however, were perfectly suited to another enterprise – the pleasure garden or tea garden, sometimes associated with mineral springs. In central London itself the gardens surrounding the springs at Spring Gardens, near present-day Charing Cross, had a public bowling green by 1630, and John Evelyn described two occasions on which he 'collationed' in Spring Garden (*Diary*, 11 April 1653 and 20 May 1658). By the late eighteenth century most of this prime real estate had been built over, but further afield, and still available to readers of the *Almanack*, were the mostly eighteenth-century pleasure gardens and tea gardens to the north and south of London. Some, like Kilburn Wells, capitalized on the medicinal aspects of their waters, but many more placed the emphasis on entertainment. Rooms were set aside for banqueting and sometimes for music or dancing, and at the larger establishments bowling greens were standard, with some grounds including as well facilities for trap-ball, ninepins (skittles or Dutch pins), angling and boating, rackets or fives, tennis, and cricket. A more controversial diversion was provided by the cockpit associated with the Folly House Tavern at Blackwall, while at Copenhagen House, Lower Holloway, organized dog fighting and bull baiting led to a temporary loss of license in 1816.

THROUGHOUT the *Epicure's Almanack* the emphasis is on dinner, the middle and most substantial meal of the day, and the time when readers of the guide might be likely to require nourishment away from home. In 1815 the power breakfast lay far in the future, and while private breakfast parties – occasionally lasting until early evening and often held outdoors (in their grandest form, *fêtes-champêtres*) – were enjoyed by the leisured classes, the professional man breakfasted at home or, when travelling, in his lodgings or at a coffee house. Breakfast is mentioned here in connection with only three establishments, one of them attached to a hotel (the Tavistock Breakfast Rooms) and another a City coffee house where 'the usual articles for breakfasts' are on offer. And at Billingsgate 'hasty breakfasts [...] in a superior style' are available to the fishmongers who had started work in the small hours; to these, however, 'strangers cannot gain admittance' (page 52). Undoubtedly similar arrangements prevailed at other markets such as Smithfield and Covent Garden, providing food and drink for workers making an exceptionally early start to insure that the rest of London was fed.

Many of the establishments surveyed provide a fixed-price dinner, or ordinary, sometimes eaten at a communal table. In the suburban taverns and inns catering to holiday-makers the ordinary may only be given on Sundays, popularly at two o'clock, although the host of the Angel in Islington also offers a second sitting two hours later. In town, times during the week range from half past one to as late as five, with some establishments providing two or more sittings. At the Queen's Arms, Cheapside, ordinaries are given every day at three, four, and five, and at the Feathers Tavern in Hand Court there is 'a kind of ordinary in the coffee-house style at four and five o'clock', when 'a prime well dressed joint is brought in […] and handed from box to box' (page 137). Three o'clock and later would suit brokers and bankers whose establishments typically closed at three, but other groups are also catered for: the ordinary at the Castle Tavern in Mark Lane, opposite the Corn Exchange, is generally at four, but on market days it moves to two o'clock, while at the Horse Shoe Inn in Southwark the ordinary is given at four o'clock on Mondays, Wednesdays, and Fridays, 'for the accommodation of persons attending the corn and haymarkets from various parts of Surrey and Kent' (page 214).

The most commonly mentioned time for serving hot dinners is from twelve until four, with a few establishments extending the hours to five o'clock, and a handful much later, though usually with a change in the menu. At one unnamed eating house in the Strand 'joints of meat are kept hot in succession from twelve at noon until eleven at night', and although at the modest Spital Eating House in Spitalfields the hot joints disappear at three, one can still obtain soups and alamode beef until eleven (pages 111, 44). Alamode beef, a savoury stew usually served with salad, is a popular evening offering in many establishments, along with such light dishes as Welsh rabbit, tarts, poached eggs ('seldom called for before seven or eight in the evening' at the Cock near Temple Bar), and roasted potatoes, 'served up with butter and pepper, at three-pence each' at the Dolphin Tavern off Ludgate Street (pages 76, 87). Soups are generally available all day: at the Swan with Two Necks, a bustling coaching inn, soups and 'hot and cold lunches are to be had […] at any hour', but dinners are served only 'from three o'clock until the departure of the mails' (pages 69-70).

'Lunches at any hour' may seem a contradiction in terms, but the author of the *Almanack* was in almost all cases using the noun lunch in its earlier sense of a light meal taken at any time. In the eighteenth century the hour for dinner (at least in polite society) had gradually advanced from one o'clock to four or even later, and when Rylance wrote lunch or luncheon was still evolving as a named meal to fill the resulting long gap between breakfast and dinner.[25] In his terms, a lunch is not only a smaller meal than a dinner, but also less formal, and aimed at the man on the go. In one instance he adds the adjective 'flying', and he couples the term lunch or luncheon with 'hasty dinners' four times: Williams's boiled beef shop, he conjectures, 'furnishes more hasty dinners and hot lunches to men of business, than any other house in London', and at the Bricklayer's Arms in the Kent Road travellers may be sure of 'a most comfortable repast either in the style of a hasty dinner or a flying lunch' (pages 87, 214).

In 1815, as now, the last meal of the day is supper, and proximity to a theatre often means late sittings. The Globe Public House in Bow Street provides suppers that are 'very excellent things after a mental repast at the theatre', and the 'very decent à-la-mode beef-shop' near Astley's Royal Amphitheatre is particularly busy in the evenings, 'after the close of the tremendous spectacles' (pages 163, 219). For those so inclined, things go on even later at such dubious, or at least rakish, establishments as the Finish and the School of Reform in Covent Garden, the Cyder Cellar in Maiden Lane, and the Coal Hole near the Savoy; here, the emphasis changes from eating to drinking, and the sober businessmen of three o'clock give way to young bucks and loose women.

ALTHOUGH IN PARIS it was not uncommon for women of fashion and delicacy to dine in restaurants with male companions,[26] in the London of 1815 respectable women were seldom if ever seen in chop houses, taverns, public houses, or coffee houses. They might, however, frequent confectionery and pastry shops: we read that at Farrance's in Spring Gardens 'ladies generally regale their younger friends and relatives' with bonbons, while in New Bond Street jellies, ices, and liqueurs may be had for 'yourself and the ladies' at Owen and Bentley's fruit shop (pages 104, 182). Women staying in hotels would normally have dined in their apartments, and post-theatre suppers at which women were present would have been held in private rooms. This convention changed very slowly, so that even in 1851 the author of *London at Table*, designed as a guide for visitors to the Great Exhibition, had to lament that although 'since our intercourse

[25] On meal times, see C. A. Wilson 1994 and Lehmann 2002; Wilson notes that at first lunch was primarily a meal for women and children, and that businessmen and professional men were 'unwilling to adopt the midday luncheon' because it interrupted work (p. 46). Rylance's uses of 'lunch' and 'lunching' as verbs, incidentally, predate the earliest *OED* examples by eight and 105 years respectively.

[26] See Spang 2000, esp. pp. 199-201.

with the continent, some coffee-rooms have been opened where gentle-men may take their wives and daughters', it was still hard to find a hotel or a restaurant 'where strangers of the gentler sex may be taken to dine' (p. 5; repeated virtually unchanged in the 1858 edition, p. 11).

For less genteel women – distinguished by Rylance with the somewhat contemptuous term 'females' – the rules were less rigid, although at Bushe's eating house near the Mint the landlord had found it necessary to post a regulation specifically prohibiting 'females of a certain class' from joining gentlemen at their tables. Farther from town, however, Will Nickel appeared not to discourage visits to his Surrey supper rooms by any of the 'fair frail unfortunate females' from the nearby Magdalen Hospital for Penitent Prostitutes who had attracted patrons able to arrange an exeat and pay for a meal (pages 63, 217). In general life was more relaxed in the suburbs, and couples and families taking a Sunday walk would have found that mixed company, at least in open areas, was unexceptionable at the more genteel tea gardens and riverside resorts.

A Note on Prices

Although prices are occasionally mentioned and the two sample bills of fare from the Telegraph Eating House and Pagliano's 'cheaper house' give some idea of the cost of dining in a modest establishment (pages 33, 154), the *Almanack* provides no general guide to charges. I have therefore thought it useful to summarize the information given in Longman's other 1815 guide-book, the *Picture of London* (p. 442); these charges may be compared to the figures given in John Trusler's *London Adviser and Guide* of 1786 (see above, p. xv), and for a forward comparison, one might consider the prices mentioned in Lieut.-Col. Nathaniel Newnham-Davis's series of columns on 'Dinners and Diners' that appeared in the *Pall Mall Gazette* at the end of the century.[27]

Dinners: in hotels these are charged by the dish, but in many coffee houses, inns, taverns, and chop houses the charge is per head, ranging from 3s. 6d. to 12s. In eating houses, 'every thing included', dinner costs from 1s. 3d. to 2s. 6d. Several comments in the *Almanack* suggest that a penny was considered an adequate tip for waiters in modest establishments.

Accommodation: in the more expensive hotels a guest pays from 10s. 6d. to one guinea per night for a bedroom and sitting room, with extra bedrooms

27 Collected as *Dinners and Diners: Where and How to Dine in London* (1899; enlarged and revised in 1901).

charged at 5s. each. More moderate hotels charge 4s. to 5s. per night for a bedroom and use of the coffee room, and even cheaper accommodations may be found at coffee houses (2s. 6d. to 5s.) or inns (2s. to 3s. 6d.); at these a separate sitting room may sometimes be taken for an additional 2s. or 3s. per night. 'Breakfast of tea or coffee' adds another 2s. to 3s. 6d. per day to the bill; chambermaids expect 1s. per bed per night, and waiters from 1s. to 2s. 6d. per day.

To provide a context for these prices it should be remembered that in 1815 England was just beginning to recover from the inflation brought on by the recent war with France: the cost of living had peaked in 1813, when prices in real terms were approximately double those of ten years earlier. Wages for London tradesmen were in the range of £1 10s. per six-day week for carpenters to just over £2 for skilled compositors in a London printing shop, but when the compositors' union agitated for a rise in 1810 they estimated that a family with only two children and no servants required a weekly income of at least £2 7s. Their petition usefully names a few basic 'per pound' prices: butter was 1s. 4d., cheese 11d., sugar 9d., and tea a very expensive 7s.; fourteen pounds of meat were estimated at 10s. 6d., a pint of porter at 2½d., and a standard quartern loaf of bread, weighing about four and a quarter pounds, might cost 1s. 5d.[28]

---

[28] Burnett 1966, pp. 29-50; see also Burnett 1969.

In 1862 the memoirist Rees Howell Gronow (1794-1865) looked back on life in London at the close of the Napoleonic Wars, describing in passing the 'wonderfully solid, hot, and stimulating' dinners of his youth, where in the best homes a choice of soups was followed by salmon and turbot, mutton or beef, and then 'you could take your oath that fowls, tongue, and ham, would as assuredly succeed as darkness after day'. 'French' or side dishes ('very mild but very abortive attempts at continental cooking') accompanied the main courses; vegetables came to the table unsauced and often cold; boiled potatoes were 'eaten with everything, up to the moment when sweets appeared'; and the drinks were port, sherry, and hock, all often taken to excess by men and women alike (Gronow, pp. 51-52).

It is relatively easy to reconstruct possible menus for such a private dinner party from the cookery books of the period, but less simple to deduce from the *Almanack* exactly what one might have expected to see, course by course, at the various establishments itemized. Although Rylance lovingly detailed the contents of many an eating house larder and provided two sample bills of fare, in only a few instances did he describe the substance of a meal. At Signor Pagliano's establishment in St Martin's Street, one of his informants feasted on skate, stewed rump steak, French turnips, and bread, all washed down with a half pint of porter, and considered it very good value at 1s. 6d. Roast or boiled beef with plum pudding and apple pie was 1s. 9d. at New Slaughter's Coffee House, and at Wood's 'celebrated' eating house dinners were available by the plate at prices ranging from 1s. 3d. to 3s., the latter including mock turtle soup, bread, porter, and either pudding or tart, presumably in addition to a fish and a meat course (pages 153, 156, 58). From comments throughout the book it seems safe to conjecture that a typical eating-house dinner would begin with broth or soup, continue on to fish and then a meat or poultry dish accompanied by potatoes and other vegetables (broccoli is specifically named on Pagliano's menu, and Rylance lauds the 'plentiful allowance of vegetables' at an unnamed house in Wych Street), and perhaps conclude with a sweet pudding or tart. Those seeking a bargain might opt for a lighter lunch (see above, p. xliii), or take advantage of such offers as the 'basin or soup-plate, containing a handsome mutton chop, vegetables and bread included' available for ninepence at the Ship Tavern in Water Lane (page 54).

'It is one of the heaviest charges made against John Bull', Rylance states, 'that when he intends to fare well, he cannot help crying out "roast beef"' (page 154). And indeed mentions of beef – steaks, roast, boiled, stewed, alamode, or 'ready-drest' to take away – heavily outweigh references in the *Almanack* to mutton, lamb, pork, or the various poultry and wildfowl. Along with pork and mutton chops, steaks – 'that native dish […] so much envied by the French' (page 2) – were a staple of the eating houses offering 'hasty dinners', and boiled beef was a speciality of several others, although even the boiled beef houses often gave a choice of roast or boiled. The joints set out at Anderson's eating house in Clare Court also came either boiled or spit-roasted – and truly 'roasted, not baked', unlike those in the 'inferior' houses in High Street, St Giles's, where boiled or baked joints were served with 'puddings, peas-soup, and leg of beef soup' (pages 175, 135). The popular supper dish of alamode beef consisted of thick pieces of beef – often a cut known as mouse buttock – larded with bacon and cooked for several hours with herbs, onions, and vinegar or wine, with the resulting stew served in deep dishes and accompanied by bread rolls and beet root or salad. In second-rate establishments the beef might consist of inferior cuts or scraps left over from the day's joints, and the comment that at Crish's shop in Butcher Hall Lane 'a stranger may venture to stay his stomach, without fear of being haunted by the horrible doubt as to whether the animal whose corpse he is feasting on was, when alive, an inhabitant of the stall or the stable' speaks for itself (page 6).

But although Britain was blessed with 'the primest beef, the finest flavoured mutton, the richest variety of fish, the most luxuriant crop of pulse, sallads, and table vegetables', in Rylance's opinion the British were 'comparatively novices in cookery' (page 265). It is no surprise, then, that he recommends several eating houses in which dishes were served in the French, Italian, or even German fashion. The grandest 'French' establishment named is Louis Jaquier's Clarendon Hotel in New Bond Street, later described by Captain Gronow as 'the only public hotel where you could get a genuine French dinner, and for which, you seldom paid less than three or four pounds; your bottle of champagne, or of claret, in 1814, costing you a guinea' (p. 74). This represented luxury beyond the *Almanack*'s horizons, or at least those of Ralph Rylance, and he passes over such imposing establishments quickly, concentrating instead on the various continental houses in the Leicester Square area: Monsieur Barron's Nassau Coffee House (earlier Saulieu's), Brunet's Hotel, the Huntly Coffee House run by M. Chedron, Pagliano's (formerly Sablonière's), and the Prince of Wales Coffee House and Tavern, 'a most excellent house for a dinner either in the English or in the French style' (page 151). Other continental chefs, restaurateurs, and hoteliers – all in the Marylebone or Oxford Street area – were M. Guedon in Wardour Street; Louis Mera in Oxford Street; M. Roumaingaux near Manchester Square and his neighbours the confectioners M. Parmentier and Signor Romualdo; and M. and Mme Morin in Duke Street, proprietors of Morin's Hotel, Coffee House, and Tavern.

Also in St Marylebone 'until very lately' was 'Sidi Mohammed' – Deen Mahomed or Mahomet (1759-1851), who in 1810 established the Hindostanee Coffee House in George Street, between Gloucester Place and Baker Street. Born in Patna, Deen Mahomed emigrated to Ireland in 1784 and had settled in London with his Anglo-Irish wife by 1807, working for a time in Portman Square for the Hon. Basil Cochrane, a former Madras civil servant. Cochrane had established a vapour or steam bath in his home, intending to confer its curative benefits on the deserving poor, and Mahomed's contribution to the concern was the introduction of therapeutic massage, or 'shampooing'. The Portman Square area was a hub for wealthy nabobs returned from India, and it was at this group that Deen Mahomed unsuccessfully aimed his coffee house, the particulars of which are known only from the *Almanack*'s description and the proprietor's own *Times* advertisement of 27 March 1811, which makes a point of the 'unequalled' curries and the 'Hoakha[s], with real Chilm tobacco'. But a year later Deen Mahomed had petitioned for bankruptcy, and by 1814 he was at Brighton, where he soon opened the first of several successful bath houses; he later received the royal warrant as shampooing surgeon to George IV and William IV, and published two editions of a treatise on shampooing. After the disaster of the Hindostanee no other central London restaurateur attempted to specialize in Indian food until the early twentieth century, but by the 1920s at least three Indian restaurants or cafes were in operation, including Veeraswamy's in Regent Street, opened in 1926 and still in business.[29]

Other specialities abounded in 1815. At Blackwall and Greenwich one could feast from April to September on whitebait – then considered a distinct species, but now known to be the immature fry of various fishes, notably herring and sprat – and deep-fried whitebait still features on the menus of Greenwich establishments such as the Trafalgar Tavern. Around the beginning of June live turtle began arriving from the West Indies, and some eating houses took out advertisements in the papers to assure their customers that 'turtles [are] dressed every day during the season' (*The Times*, 22 July 1813,

[29] See Collingham 2005, pp. 154 and 219, and for Mahomed's life, Fisher 1996.

with special mention of a 'fine large green Turtle, to be ready by 12 o'clock' at William Wood's eating house near the Tower). From the King's Head in the Poultry live turtle were sent out all over London, sometimes accompanied by a 'professed artist' who would undertake their preparation for a fee of one or two guineas; such turtle specialists included Mr Perry of Oxford Street, who 'on receiving an order, will go out himself, and dress turtle for families at their own houses', and Mr Wood of New Bond Street, who 'dresses turtle at home and abroad' (pages 15, 131, 186). And while today oysters are considered a delicacy, in 1815 they were ubiquitous and cheap. There were eating rooms attached to several of the oyster and shellfish warehouses described, and oysters also featured on the menus of other houses, such as the Cock in Fleet Street, where Marsh, the oyster man, 'hath the constancy of the swallow, and the dexterity of the squirrel in opening the shells' (page 76).

Venison was another seasonal speciality, arriving from the country throughout the second half of the year, and like turtle it was sometimes announced in the papers: the Worcester Coffee House in Oxford Street, for instance, advertised that 'dinners are served […] two or three times a week, from prime haunches at three shillings and sixpence each person' (page 130). Hare and game birds – pheasant, partridge, grouse, and other moor fowl – were also available both in eating houses and in markets, but those dealing in game risked prosecution and stiff penalties under various acts that went back to the seventeenth century and were only repealed in 1831.[30] The lucrative black market for game nonetheless thrived, with itinerant poultry dealers or higglers supplying wholesalers based in public markets such as Leadenhall and Newgate, where hares and partridges might be offered to the public under the code names lions and owls (pages 154, 184).

For lighter food one could visit a confectioner's shop, some of which had provision for eating on the spot; along with pastries and sweetmeats such as those listed as available at M. Parmentier's house (page 120), a confectioner might offer drinks, ices, and exotic fruit. At pastry shops more serious fare was sometimes available. Venison was 'exposed throughout the season' at Angell's pastry shop in Gracechurch Street and at Rich's in Ludgate Street, and the two specialists in turtle mentioned above, Perry and Wood, are both described in directories as pastry cooks. No pastry shop seems to have been without a supply of 'savoury patties' or tarts, and soup – particularly mock turtle – was also usually featured, alongside sweet and savoury jellies.

---

[30] See Munsche 1981, pp. 52-62.

IN SOME of the establishments surveyed by the *Almanack*, such as coffee and chocolate houses, food was less important than liquid refreshment, and in all of them beverages were included among the offerings. Spirits, wines, and ales could only be sold in licensed premises, and even coffee houses needed a license if, like Garraway's, they wished to provide 'wine or spirit and water' as well as spruce beer or soda water with their sandwiches. Non-alcoholic drinks named are (hot) coffee, tea, chocolate, and saloop, and (cold) capillaire, lemonade, orgeat, spruce and ginger beers, soda water, and mineral waters, both natural (bottled at the spa) and artificial. Saloop and capillaire were sweet eighteenth-century concoctions – Samuel Johnson is said to have sweetened his port with capillaire – and both had effectively disappeared by 1850, along with spruce beer, a weakly alcoholic small beer known from the sixteenth century and, like ginger beer, classed as a soft drink.[31] Soda water, or artificially aerated bottled water containing varying concentrations of sodium bicarbonate, was advertised as beneficial for those suffering from indigestion, gout, and stone. London's first soda-water factory had been established in 1792 by Jacob Schweppe, and by 1815 there were also warehouses in Old and New Bond Streets for the sale of 'those salubrious luxuries, the spa and artificial mineral waters' (page 192).

Spirits are mentioned infrequently and usually only in general terms: 'His liquors are of the choicest kind', or 'The malt liquors and spirits are genuine and well flavoured' (pages 126, 11). Rum and cognac get one mention each, gin and brandy scarcely more, and there are a handful of references to liqueurs – available at two fruit shops in Bond Street – and to punch. Among wines, port and Madeira are singled out, and attention is called to the quality of the claret at three establishments (one defunct), but sherry goes unmentioned, and as with spirits the comments on wine seldom stray from the general.

More specifics are provided when it comes to ale – 'this native Burgundy', as Rylance calls it (page 236). Scotch, Shropshire, 'Welch', and Windsor ales are singled out, but the most frequently mentioned of the group is Burton ale – a term now almost synonymous with Burton pale ale, but in 1815 describing a strong, sweetish, brown ale, sold by the bottle in London as early as 1738.[32] Burton ale gave its name to the Burton Coffee House in Freeman's Court, Cheapside, and several other establishments listed are described as having

---

[31] Spruce beer is mentioned several times in connection with oyster rooms, suggesting that the combination was popular.

[32] *VCH Staffordshire*, ix:65.

'Burton ale rooms': the Castle Tavern, also in the Cheapside area; the Salisbury Coffee House near the Strand; and most famously Offley's Burton Ale Rooms in Henrietta Street. Porter (or 'entire'), a dark brown brew developed in the eighteenth century, also comes in for several mentions, along with its stronger cousin, stout.

THE ALMANACK concludes with three appendices, aimed not so much at the diner-out as the housekeeper, and prefaced with Rylance's cry for a British 'culinary revolution' and a 'fundamental reform' in the kitchen (pages 264-66). The first, a 'review of artists who administer to the wants and conveniences of the table', begins with an inspection of the various new ranges, stoves, broilers, and cooking vessels available, adding notes as well on the best shops for serving dishes, knives, china and porcelain, dining tables and chairs, lamps, candles, and chandeliers. Here one finds entries for products ranging from the conjuror, a portable stove fuelled by nothing more than 'a sheet of brown paper cut into shreds and tied up as a faggot', and a very modern-sounding broiler grooved 'so as to permit the fat as it melts to flow off in all directions', to folding chairs and 'sympathetic' dining tables that 'enlarge or contract at pleasure'. Also listed are a dozen and a half Italian warehouses, where the keen cook could purchase herbal essences, spices, flavoured vinegars, rice, pasta, truffles and dried mushrooms, cheese, and a host of sauces from anchovy extract to zoobditty mutch.

    With kitchen equipped and store cupboard full, the reader is next led through London's markets, beginning with a tour of Leadenhall Market (the 'most considerable') and ending with a tribute to the incomparable fruit, vegetables, flowers, and herbs of Covent Garden. In all some twenty-five markets are described, ranging from the grandest to the 'very inferior', and including the market in Duke's Place held 'principally for the supply of the Jews'. Finally, paralleling Grimod's *calendrier nutritif*, there is an 'alimentary calendar', a month by month guide to seasonal specialities, with notes by the way on the proper choice of beef, veal, mutton, lamb, pork, poultry, game, and fish. Such 'directions for marketing' were standard in cookbooks of the day, and the tips given here for determining freshness or quality are merely abridged versions of the more extensive notes in such works as Francis Collingwood and John Woollams's *Universal Cook, and City and Country Housekeeper* (1792 ff.). Many cookery books also provided tables of foods in season, sometimes adding sample menus for each month, and again it is likely that Rylance simply followed their lead. But in putting together his monthly shopping suggestions he was not content with dull lists, and along-side the occasionally heavy-handed attempts at humour there will be found comments on such miscellaneous topics as the merits of 'barn-door' fowl versus those fattened in coops, the methods of transporting mackerel, the production of brawn, and the delights of Bartholomew Fair, with its 'raree-shows, travelling menageries, moveable theatres, conjurors, tumblers, merry andrews, toymen, pye-men, and gingerbread merchants' (page 325).

THE

EPICURE'S ALMANACK;

OR,

CALENDAR

OF

GOOD LIVING:

CONTAINING

A Directory to the Taverns, Coffee-houses, Inns, Eating-houses, and other Places of alimentary Resort in the British Metropolis and its Environs: a Review of Artists who administer to the Wants and Enjoyments of the Table; a Survey of the Markets; and a Calendar of the Meats in Season during each Month of the Year.

To be continued Annually.

————navibus atque
Quadrigis petimus bené vivere; quod petis hîc est.
HOR.

London:
PRINTED FOR LONGMAN, HURST, REES, ORME, AND BROWN,
PATERNOSTER-ROW.

1815.

PREFACE.

THE manual here offered to the Public, is formed on the Model of a Work published annually at Paris, under the title of "*Almanach des Gourmands.*" The Volumes of that Work most in request, are those which contain the Nutritive Itinerary, serving as a Guide to all the Places of alimentary Resort in Paris.[1] This consideration has induced the Editor of the present Almanack to commence it by a descriptive Tour, constituting an ample Directory to the Taverns, Coffee-houses, Inns, Eating-houses, &c. &c. in and around the British Metropolis. As a proper Sequel to this Compendium of Epicurean Topography, he has annexed a review of the Artists who administer to the wants and [iv] enjoyments of the table, by supplying the various articles, either of use or ornament, requisite in every department of domestic economy, from the kitchen to the dining-room. Then follows a Survey of the Markets, to which is added a Calendar of the Meats in season during each month of the year, with some useful Hints and Observations. An Index to the whole is subjoined, which will be found very convenient in affording the readiest means of reference to the topographical part of the Work. Thus even a perfect stranger in London, of any rank or degree, perambulating any part of it, may, by consulting this little Manual, be directed to where he may readily regale himself, according to the relative state of his appetite and his purse.

Such are the contents of this first Volume of the Epicure's Almanack. It lays great claim to that indulgence which the Public are ever disposed to afford to a new Work on a vast and important subject. The British metro- [v] polis, it must be considered, exceeds that of France in extent and population; it commands a greater supply of all articles of consumption, and contains a greater number and variety of places for public accommodation where the articles are consumed. The task here undertaken, therefore, is arduous beyond all precedent. Had the Editor been gifted with the eyes of Argus, and the palate of Apicius Celius;[2] had his organs of vision and taste been multiplied an

---

[1]   See above, pp. xviii-xix.
[2]   The references are to the mythical 'all-seeing' giant Argus and the non-existent Apicius Cælius, often named as the classical compiler of *De re coquinaria*, a book of recipes first published in 1498.

hundred fold, he must have failed to accomplish the undertaking in a single attempt. Hence, as well as from the inexhaustible variety of subjects which come within the province of the Work, arises the necessity that it should, like its prototype, be continued annually. The present Volume, it is hoped, will contain all that could reasonably be expected from it, and at the same time will tend to facilitate the Editor's future labours; for, since the design and objects of the publication will thus be clearly made known, he [vi] may expect to be favoured with those aids which he could not, in the first instance, calculate upon.

Notwithstanding the care and diligence bestowed on the Directory, he is aware that several houses of merit may have been overlooked, and that changes are continually taking place in the alimentary world, either through the formation of new establishments, or the alteration, removal, or extinction of old ones. Considering, also, that in this vast region called London, there is much *terra incognita*, he stands, in some respects, in the condition of a geographer, who has to correct and complete his general survey from accurate and authentic notices, furnished by the intelligent inhabitants of particular districts. In resuming, therefore, his peregrinations, preparatory to a second Volume, he would gladly avail himself of any information respecting the changes or omissions in question, either from the owners of the establishments themselves, or from the frequenters of them. It is [vii] very desirable, that such information should be afforded as early as possible. All letters, notes, cards, announcements, and other communications, sent to the Publishers, directed to the Editor of the Epicure's Almanack, *post or carriage paid*, will be thankfully received, and punctually attended to. [viii *blank*]

THE

EPICURE'S ALMANACK,

OR

Calendar of Good Living.

THIS book is designed to direct any man with a delicate stomach and a full purse, or any man with a keen strong stomach and a lean purse, where he may dine well, and to the best advantage, in London.

London must here be understood to comprehend Westminster, South-wark, Lambeth, Mary-le-bone, and all the districts within the cognizance or compass of Death's bills of fare – the bills of mortality.[1] We begin with London, strictly so called, on its highest [2] ground, in Pannier Court, between Paternoster Row and Newgate Street.[2] Some of our colleagues have hinted that by so doing we shall offend the Lord Mayor, aldermen, and livery of this good city; but we shall prove, in the sequel, that the point we have chosen as the centre of our survey is the proper one; and that we could not have begun with the Mansion House, that emporium of good things, without abusing the freedom of the city.

---

[1] The London Bills of Mortality, originally designed to keep track of deaths from the plague, covered the City of London, Westminster, and some other parts of Middlesex, as well as the Borough of Southwark and a few adjoining Surrey parishes. The earliest Bills date from the C16, and although they were essentially superseded by the Registrar General's returns after 1836, Bills of Mortality were still being produced in the late 1850s.

[2] Pannier Court (properly Panyer Alley) ran south from Newgate Street to Pater-noster Row, north of St Paul's. The 'Panyer Stone', showing in relief a naked boy sitting on a pannier, or basket, has been moved more than once, but is still to be seen on a wall near one of the entrances to St Paul's underground station. Dated 27 August 1688, it bears the legend 'When ye have sought the Citty Round / Yet still this is the highest Ground'.

Dolly's Chop-House.

Departing, therefore, from Pannier Court, we find, in Queen's Head Passage adjoining, a house long celebrated for giving good dinners; it is Dolly's Chop House.[1] Here is constantly kept a plentiful and very well assorted larder. The hours of dining are from two until evening; a bill of fare, distinctly and even legibly written, lies on the table, and orders are sometimes executed with commendable promptitude. Here that native dish, the beef-steak, so much envied by the French, and classed by them among their *assiettes volantes*, or *flying dishes*,[2] is dressed in the best style, and served up as hot as it should be, with all the requisite condiments. [3] The porter, wines, and liquors, are good, and the spruce beer almost unrivalled*.

* At this house the ingenious anatomist and chemical lecturer, Dr. George Fordyce, dined every day, for more than twenty years.[3] His researches in comparative anatomy had led him to conclude that man, through custom, eats oftener than nature requires, one meal a day being sufficient for that noble animal the lion. He made the experiment on himself at this his favourite house, and finding it succeeded, he continued the following regimen for the term above mentioned. At four o'clock, his accustomed hour of dining, he entered, and took his seat at a table always reserved for him, on which were instantly placed a silver tankard full of strong ale; a bottle of port wine, and a measure containing a quarter of a pint of brandy. The moment the waiter announced him, the cook put a pound and a half of rump steak on the gridiron, and on the table some delicate trifle as a *bonne bouche*, to serve until the steak was ready. This morsel was sometimes

[1] **Dolly's Chop House**, founded in the early part of the C18, was still termed a 'well-appointed chop-house and tavern' as late as 1872 (Timbs, *Clubs and Club Life*, p. 392). Just before it was pulled down in 1885 the publisher Elliot Stock announced that he would be issuing a limited edition of *The Vicar of Wakefield* 'bound in wood taken from the panels of the dining-room of Dolly's', where Oliver Goldsmith had been a regular visitor (*The Times*, 14 June 1884); according to a label in the example now in the Houghton Library, Harvard University, ten such copies of Stock's 1885 edition were indeed so bound. Virtually all of the buildings in the triangle formed by Newgate Street, Paternoster Row, and Warwick Lane were destroyed or heavily damaged by bombing on 29 December 1940, and the entire area has recently been redeveloped.

[2] The opening essay in the final volume of the French *Almanach des gourmands* (1812, pp. 1-4) surveys 'les assiettes volantes', including 'Beefteek à l'anglaise'.

[3] Fordyce (1736-1802) was an Aberdeen physician who began giving lectures in London in the 1760s and published several books, including a *Treatise on Digestion and Food* in 1791. His *ODNB* biographer suggests that his unusual pattern of dining and drinking was responsible for 'a coarseness which was reflected in his manners and careless dress'.

half a broiled chicken, sometimes a plate of fish: when he had eaten this, he took one glass of his brandy, and then proceeded to devour his steak. We say devour, because he always ate so rapidly that one might imagine he was hurrying away to a patient, to deprive death of a dinner. When he had finished his meat, he took the remainder of his brandy, having, during his dinner, drunk the tankard of ale, and afterwards the bottle of port. He thus daily spent an hour and a half of his time, and then returned to his house in Essex Street, to give his six-o'clock lecture on chemistry. He made no other meal until his return next day at four o'clock to Dolly's.

[4]

Queen's Arms Tavern, Newgate Street.

Nearly opposite to the Queen's Head Passage, in Newgate Street, is the Queen's Arms Tavern and Chop-house. Here are, a good larder, and excellent accommodations always ready. On the sign is an inscription, signifying that this is the oldest chop-house in London.[1]

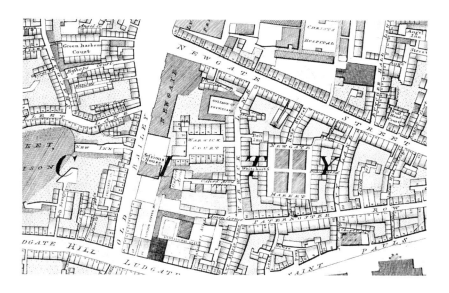

[1] The **Queen's Arms Tavern** (no. 70 Newgate Street, north side) is mentioned in an Old Bailey trial of 22 February 1716, and from the mid-C18 was a popular venue for public debates and orations, as well as meetings of musical societies. Later known as the Queen's Arms Hotel, it survived into the 1860s.

Horse-Shoe Tavern, Cheapside.

On the same side of the way, nearer to Cheapside, is the Horse-shoe Tavern (Baker). This is a licensed public-house of a superior class. It has good accommodations for lunch, and serves up dinners daily to a numerous and respectable class of customers, consisting chiefly of gentlemen who have *business* in the city.

Salutation, Newgate Street.

On the south side of Newgate Street, No. 17, is the Salutation Tavern (J. Moss), a good house up a passage, having a very *pass-* [5] *able* larder, and serving up dinners daily to a numerous and respectable company.[1]

King's Head, Newgate Street.

No. 40, on the same side of the same street, is the King's Head Tavern (kept by William May). This is a celebrated steak and chop-house, with soups always ready, and a fine exposed larder, in the passage. An ordinary is had every day at two o'clock.

[1]   The **Salutation**, sometimes called the Salutation and Cat, was at no. 17 on the south side of Newgate Street; it is marked on John Rocque's 1746 map of London, and H. A. Harben (1918, p. 453) suggested that it was the successor to the Oxford Armes Inn, shown in approximately the same place on Ogilby and Morgan's map of 1676 (ref. B35; not to be confused with a second Oxford Arms just east of Old Bailey). The Salutation was certainly in business by early 1736, when it was the scene of a literary dinner given by William Bowyer and Edward Cave (see Nichols 1812, ii:74-75), and Samuel Taylor Coleridge lodged there in the winter of 1794-95, writing poetry and apparently leaving his schoolfellow Charles Lamb to pay his bill (Lamb, *Letters*, i:5). The tavern was partly destroyed by fire on 17 April 1883 (see *The Times* of that day), but it reopened in restored premises the following year (*Lloyd's Weekly Newspaper*, 22 June 1884). The American writer Benjamin Ellis Martin, who traced 'the footprints of Charles Lamb' a few years later, was disappointed with the rebuilt Salutation, calling it a 'slap-bang City eating-house and bar' (p. 47), and although a 'lineal successor' of the old Salutation was still in business in 1909 (Shelley, p. 65), this had vanished by the time G. H. Cunningham wrote in 1927.

Minter's, Newgate Market.

Up the Three Tuns Passage, leading into Newgate Market, is a public-house (Minter's), where a fire is kept always ready to cook, and a larder is presented to you, almost always ready cooked, and presenting any chop or steak you might choose to order from the market.[1]

White Hart, Butcher-Hall Lane.

In Butcher-Hall Lane, Newgate Street, No. 1, stands Discombe's, with a larder of rump steaks, chops, and hot joints, from twelve until five o'clock. This house has an inlet from Bull's Head Court.[2]

[6]

Crish's A-la-mode Beef Shop.

At No. 20, Butcher-Hall Lane, is Crish's àl-a-mode beef shop, a very decent house, where that truly savoury viand is dressed à-l'ancienne, as well as à-la-nouvelle mode, and served up with the proper accompaniments of endive, red beet-root, and French rolls. A stranger may venture to stay his stomach, without fear of being haunted by the horrible doubt as to whether the animal whose corpse he is feasting on was, when alive, an inhabitant of the stall or the stable.

Epps's Ham and Beef Shop, Newgate Street.

At the corner of the passage leading to the Horse-shoe, is one of Epps's ham, beef, and soup shops.[3]

Before we go farther from St. Paul's on our alimentary tour, it will not be amiss to mention the houses of entertainment that immediately surround that noble structure.

---

[1] **Minter's** public house was in Three Tuns Passage (earlier Alley), which led south from Newgate Street between nos. 25 and 26 and also had an entrance into Ivy Lane; for the market, see p. 242 below.

[2] Butcher's Hall Lane is now King Edward Street.

[3] **Epps's** Newgate shop was one of several; for two others, see pp. 76 and 123.

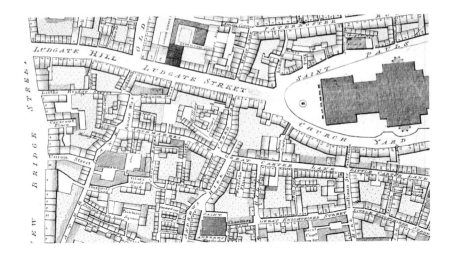

Chapter Coffee-House.

On the north side of St. Paul's Churchyard, about half way between Cheapside and Ludgate Hill, in a passage which leads into [7] Paternoster Row, is
that well-known and long-established house the Chapter Coffee-house.[1] This
place may be considered as a repository of food for the mind, as well as of the
body. Here are daily found and filed all the British newspapers, and the most
considerable monthly journals, as magazine, reviews, &c. together with all
the most popular pamphlets which appear occasionally on interesting public
questions. It may naturally be supposed that where there is so much reading
there is very little talking, except to the waiters. This is the case in every box

[1]   The **Chapter Coffee House** was at no. 50 Paternoster Row, south side, opposite
Ivy Lane; it was in business as early as 1715 and continued as a coffee house into the
mid-1850s, when it became a tavern (see the extended entry in Lillywhite). Long
patronized by booksellers, the Chapter was used by Thomas Chatterton as an
accommodation address, and Charlotte and Anne Brontë stayed there when they
visited London in 1848. Leopold Wagner claimed in 1924 that the 'Old Chapter
Coffee House' was still 'as well frequented as ever it was' (pp. 107-08), but the
building was among many in the area damaged beyond repair in the Second World
War. The conclaves mentioned here may have been nothing more than business
gatherings, but the term was also used for meetings held by booksellers after an
auction for the purpose of reselling purchases amongst themselves at advanced
prices, a practice generally known as knocking out. In the lines adapted from
Macbeth, v.3, to 'cast water' means to inspect a patient's urine as an aid to diagnosis.

except those two which are situated in the north-east corner between the door leading into the passage and the front door in Paternoster Row. These boxes have been whimsically denominated "hell."

In this house the magnificent and munificent booksellers of London hold their conclave. Whether or not there be also a board of grey-bearded reviewers, we have not hitherto discovered. Of authors, lawyers, and divines, there are plenty; of doctors of physic, several, and of doctors of state, who profess to

——————————————— cast
The water of the land; find her disease,
And purge it to a sound and pristine health,

there is daily a whole host.

[8] The usual refreshments served in this house are tea, coffee, chocolate, with muffin, toast, and pure butter, the best of wines and foreign spirits. In the evenings a petit souper may be had, of various light viands, announced by bill of fare. The curious in research will here find the principal London and provincial newspapers filed in years for a great length of time anterior to the present. There is a library, consisting chiefly of periodical works and political tracts. Any gentleman desiring to have the use of it is expected to give the waiter a small donation every Christmas – which is money very well bestowed.

Goose and Gridiron.

The Goose and Gridiron, London House Yard, St. Paul's Church Yard, is kept by Mr. Alleyn.[1] Here, if there is not always a goose ready for a gridiron, there is a gridiron ready for a goose, or for any other bird or beast of prey* which the guests order to be dressed on it. Here are also joints of all sorts,

* Not because they prey, but are preyed upon.

[1] The **Goose and Gridiron**, at no. 8 London House Yard, stood in the northeast corner of this now-vanished passage, which had two entrances into St Paul's Churchyard to the south, and a third outlet north into Paternoster Row. The tavern was long in use for Masonic meetings, at one of which the Grand Lodge of England was formed on 24 June 1717; a recent plaque nearby commemorates the event. The building was demolished in the 1890s, but the original sign, more likely representing a swan atop Apollo's lyre, survives in the Museum of London and is pictured on p. 70 of their 1999 exhibition catalogue, *London Eats Out.*

hot from one o'clock until five. At this house most of the western short stage
[9] coaches for Hammersmith, Turnham Green, Parson's Green, Fulham,
Putney, and Richmond, that go into the city, take up and set down their
passengers.

Ham Shop, London House Yard.

In another branch of London House Yard is an established shop for the
sale of ready-dressed hams, tongues, beef, portable soup, and various other
viands, all sold by weight.

Pastry Shop, St. Paul's Church Yard.

About the centre of St. Paul's Church Yard is Vanhagen's celebrated pastry
shop, where soups, savoury pies, and every description of pastry, of the best
ingredients, and after the newest fancy and device, may be found always ready.

Queen's Arms Tavern.

On the south side of St. Paul's is the Queen's Arms Tavern and Doctors'
Commons Coffee-house.[1] This is a large establishment, with excellent larder
and soups at command. Here dinners are served up in the very best style.
The proprietors, we are told, are Messrs. Leech and Dallimore, of [10] the
London Coffee-house, of whom, and of whose excellent wines, we shall have
to speak anon. They are also said to be owners of the York Hotel, Bridge
Street, Blackfriars.

---

[1]   The **Queen's Arms**, established in the early C18, was at no. 6 St Paul's Churchyard
(south side, near the west end of the cathedral), and was well known to Johnson
and Boswell. The *Almanack*'s use of the name Queen's Arms Tavern and Doctors'
Commons Coffee-house is confusing, but no more so than Lillywhite's several
entries touching on the fate of the Queen's Arms. He suggests (no. 1032) that by
the end of the C18 the tavern 'had become identified with' the St Paul's Coffee
House, also known as the St Paul's and Doctors' Commons Coffee House (Lillywhite nos. 1142-43), and there is a listing in the 1819 *New Picture of London* for the
'Queen's Arms tavern, and St Paul's coffee-house'. The establishment, later usually
referred to as the St Paul's Hotel, survived in some form at least into the 1860s.
John Leech – great-uncle to the caricaturist of the same name – and Thomas Dallimore were also the proprietors of the London Coffee House (see below, p. 81).

Horn Tavern, Godliman Street.
Mr. Lovegrove.

Turning down Paul's Chain, we come to Godliman Street, and find the celebrated Horn Tavern, kept by Mr. Lovegrove.[1] It hath a good larder; its soups are always hot and fit for the palate; and it serveth up excellent dinners at moderate charges. Here joyful heirs and sad widows promiscuously meet to take their bodily nourishment, whilst proctors and their clerks expedite the probates and letters of administration, which bring them to Doctors' Commons. Here, perhaps, faithful and faithless Exōrs and Admōrs[2] eat their own chops and steaks together in one box; whilst in another, the fond expectant bridegroom sips his soup or savoury jelly, waiting for his licence, which is to be obtained from the Prerogative Court. This soup, jelly, and licence, form the prelude to his occupancy of his (perhaps) equally impatient bride. Good easy man! he little thinks that the licence aforesaid is to rob him of his liberty for and during the [11] remainder of his, the aforesaid bridegroom's, natural life.

Let us proceed on our tour from St. Paul's, and go towards Cheapside.

Black Swan.

On the south side of St. Paul's, a little to the east of Godliman Street, is the Black Swan, a licensed public-house, which dresses dinners daily at the most usual hours.[3]

---

[1] The **Horn** was at no. 10 Godliman Street, east side, with an entrance into Knightrider Street. The tavern was in business by 1704 (*Daily Courant*, 4 December), if not earlier, and some 'very good wine' from the Horn is called for in Dickens's *Pickwick Papers*. Rebuilt in the early C19, the tavern has recently been restored and renamed the Centre Page (no. 29 Knightrider Street, near the northern approach to the Millennium Bridge). Both the Queen's Arms and the Horn would have been convenient for those with business at Doctors' Commons in Great Knightrider Street, home to ecclesiastical and other courts until 1867.

[2] Executors and Administrators.

[3] The **Black Swan** was on the corner of Carter Lane and Black Swan Alley (formerly Court), which ran north to St Paul's Churchyard; a watercolour of *c.* 1870 by J. T. Wilson shows the tavern with the dome of St Paul's behind it (London Metropolitan Archives). London directories continued to list a Black Swan at no. 6 Carter Lane into the C20, but this was damaged beyond repair in the Second World War.

Struggler Tavern and Chop-House.

A few doors on, down a passage similar to the former, is the Struggler Tavern and Chop-house, kept by Mr. Dunn, where juicy and tender steaks and chops are dressed in the most judicious style, and neatly served up. The malt liquors and spirits are genuine and well flavoured.[1]

Saracen's Head, Friday Street.

A little way down Friday Street, is the Saracen's Head Inn and Tavern, a large establishment with a good larder, and very fair accommodations for entertaining travellers. His principal guests are from the west of England.[2]

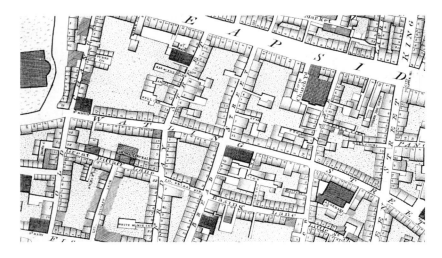

---

[1] I have been unable to identify the 'passage similar to the former' in which the **Struggler** was located, but Mr Dunn is almost certainly William John Donne, whose tavern or coffee house called the Struggler, no. 13 Bow Street, burned to the ground in the fire of 20 September 1808 that destroyed the first Covent Garden Theatre. Donne appears to have demanded and received £5000 compensation from the proprietors of the second theatre, presumably using some of the money to set up in a new location (see the *Covent Garden Journal* (1810), pp. 36-37 and 144-45, and *The Times*, 21 September 1809).

[2] The entrance to the **Saracen's Head** is shown on the Horwood map at no. 6 on the west side of Friday Street, just south of Cheapside. A building with this name is known on the site as early as 1400, but the Saracen's Head described here was pulled down *c*. 1850, and this section of Friday Street itself no longer exists.

[12]

White Horse, Friday Street.

Nearly at the bottom of Friday Street, on the right hand side of the way, is the White Horse Coffee-house and Tavern, kept by Mr. Mountain, a very considerable wine-merchant, whose stock of that beverage is equally ample and select. His larder is a paragon of neatness and abundance, and the accommodations are of the most desirable kind.[1]

Cross Keys Inn, Wood Street.

A little way down Wood Street, on the left hand, is the Cross Keys Inn and Tavern kept by Mr. William Stapler.[2] The premises are on a large scale, and there are good accommodations for travellers. The Telegraph Manchester and London stage coach takes up passengers here daily, at a quarter before three P. M.

Burton Coffee-House and Tavern, Freeman's Court, Cheapside.

In Freeman's Court, on the north side of Cheapside, opposite Bow Church, is the Burton Coffee-house and Tavern, by Mr. J. Powell, a noted place for rump-steaks, chops, and other flying dishes. Nor is it less celebrated for the high perfection of its Burton ale.[3]

[1] The **White Horse**, rebuilt after the Great Fire, was at the south end of Friday Street, west side, with the entrance shown on the Horwood map at no. 29. A later White Horse Tavern survived at no. 32 Friday Street until the Second World War, when it was damaged beyond repair by bombing.

[2] The **Cross Keys**, as shown on the 1676 Ogilby and Morgan map of London, was on the west side of Wood Street, just north of Cheapside; the name, evoking the crossed keys of St Peter, reflects the proximity of the inn to the C12 church of St Peter, Westcheap (destroyed in the 1666 fire). Stages for Great Yarmouth, Manchester, York, Chester, and other cities stopped at the Cross Keys, which according to John Timbs was taken down in 1865 (*Curiosities* (1868), p. 453).

[3] Although not named as such, Freeman's Court is shown on Horwood's map running north out of Cheapside at no. 103, just east of Honey Lane Market (for which see below, p. 245); after the Second World War the entire area, seriously damaged by bombing, was completely redeveloped. **Burton's** at no. 1 was operating as the Old Burton Coffee House into the 1920s, when it was taken over by Henekey's chain of wine lodges.

[13]

Poulterer's Arms, Freeman's Court.

In this same court, is a passage leading to the Poulterer's Arms in Honey Lane Market, kept by Mr. T. King. This is a famous public-house for good dinners of steaks and chops. Here is a good ordinary every day at three o'clock. The wine is served up in measures from the pipe, as is done at the Shades near London Bridge, a place we shall come to in due time. This house is much frequented by gentlemen in the corn trade, who make it their half-way house in going and returning to and from Mark Lane.[1]

Castle Tavern, King Street, Cheapside.

In King Street, Cheapside, at the corner of Cateaton Street, is the Castle Tavern and Burton Ale Rooms, Johnson.[2] Here is always a good larder exposed to view in front. The house is much frequented by those whom business or curiosity leads to the venerable mansion of the redoubted giants, Gog and Magog; which mansion is, in the vulgar tongue, denominated Guildhall.

Crown Tavern, Bow Lane, Cheapside.

No. 7, Bow Lane, Cheapside, is the Crown [14] Tavern, Mr. Whitfield, an old established house, having the advantage of being in the very heart of the city, yet retired from the strong current of people that daily bustles through it. Here is a plentiful larder, good wines, the accommodations are all of the

[1] The **Poulterer's Arms** at no. 2 Freeman's Court was still in business in 1937, when H. E. Popham noted that some authorities claimed it as 'the most ancient of City Inns' (p. 181). The *Almanack* never does return to the **Shades**, known from about 1750 as a tavern in Wheatsheaf Alley, adjoining the west side of the old Fishmongers' Hall and overlooking the river. With the rebuilding of the Hall the tavern moved somewhat west in 1828, and it remained in business as the Old Shades until 1882 (see Metcalf 1977). Wine from the pipe was drawn directly from the cask, rather than poured from a bottle.

[2] The **Castle**, at the corner of King Street and Cateaton (now Gresham) Street, is mentioned in an Old Bailey trial of 5 December 1744, and survived into the C20. Richards and Curl noted in 1973 that it was 'still marked by an attractive carved tablet in King Street near St Lawrence Jewry Church' (p. 120), but the site has since been redeveloped and the memorial removed. Images of the mythical giants Gog and Magog, traditional guardians of the City of London, are displayed in the Great Hall of Guildhall and carried in the annual Lord Mayor's Show.

snuggest kind, and the waiters are complete disciplinarians; their movements as quick as thought, and their way of reckoning a degree quicker than some guests can think.

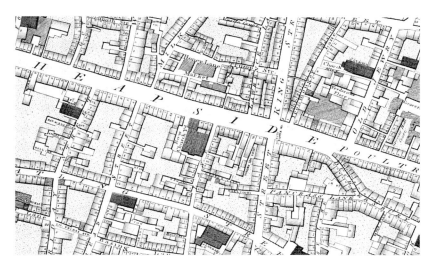

Queen's Arms, Bird-in-Hand Court, Cheapside.

In Bird-in-Hand Court, a little nearer to Bucklersbury, on the same side with the above-mentioned house, is the Queen's Arms Tavern Steak and Chop-house.[1] The landlord, Mr. Abbott, is one of the most polite hosts in the city, and that is certainly saying a great deal of him. Ordinaries are held here every day, at three, four, and five o'clock. The larder is well stored, and

---

[1] Bird in Hand Court was south of Cheapside, with the entrance between nos. 76 and 77. In November 1816 John Keats and his brothers moved into rooms on the second floor of no. 76, remaining there through the following March and no doubt frequenting the **Queen's Arms**, known from 1708 and 'partially rebuilt and enlarged' in 1811 (Wagner 1924, pp. 104-05). In late 1853 (*The Times*, 3 December) the tavern was purchased by James G. Simpson, owner of the Three Tuns in Billingsgate (see p. 50 below), and renamed Simpson's. It was substantially damaged by fire in March 1898 and rebuilt soon afterwards, remaining famous for its 'fish ordinaries' into the early 1940s, but after the war all that remained of the 'once delightful backwater' of Bird in Hand Court was a 'hideous gap of bombed and blasted masonry' (Morton 1951, pp. 34-35, also describing the pre-war ordinaries). This Simpson's should not be confused with Simpson's in Ball Court – see below, p. 28 – or with Simpson's in the Strand, which opened in 1828.

the wines are prime in quality. Add to all these well merited encomiums, the charges are reasonable.

City Coffee-House, corner of Pancras Lane and Bucklersbury.

At the corner of Pancras Lane and Buck- [15] lersbury, is the City Coffee-house, kept by Mr. Lister.[1] A good assortment of viands ready for dressing invites the passenger, and his thirst is also excited by the announcement of choice wines, spirits, and malt liquors.

Kings Head Tavern, Poultry.

The King's Head Tavern in the Poultry enjoys the distinction of being the oldest tavern in London, and the principal emporium of turtle in the whole metropolis.[2] Many city companies and public bodies have grand dinners here; the establishment is calculated to entertain large and small parties in the highest style of splendor and comfort.

Debatt's Pastry Shop, Poultry.

Adjoining the King's Head Tavern, very fortunately for ladies and beaux of delicate stomachs, stands Debatt's pastry shop, famous for sweets, soups, and savoury patties. Here the epicure, who has sacrificed too liberally to the jolly

---

[1] The City Coffee House, properly the **City of London**, was at nos. 5-6 Bucklersbury, which in 1815 ran southeast from Cheapside opposite Old Jewry and then doglegged east to Walbrook Street. Rebuilt in 1874, the coffee house was at one time known as the Bodega (*Wining and Dining in the City of London*, 1968) and later as the Old City of London Shades. This last closed in 1994, shortly before the building that housed it was demolished.

[2] The **King's Head** was at no. 25 Poultry, south side. It was originally known as the Rose, and as such was mentioned by the chronicler Henry Machyn in an entry for 5 January 1560 (see Timbs, *Clubs*, pp. 383-88, for a long but suspiciously detailed account of the early history). The Rose was renamed at the restoration of Charles II, and rebuilt after the fire of 1666. According to Timbs, 'it was long a depôt in the metropolis for turtle; and in the quadrangle of the Tavern might be seen scores of turtle, large and lively, in huge tanks of water; or laid upright on the stone floor, ready for their destination'. The building was refitted in 1852, but the King's Head had closed by the time Timbs wrote twenty years later.

god, may allay the fervency of his devotion by copious draughts of capillaire, spruce, soda, orgeat, or lemonade.

Birch, Cornhill.

Let us not pass Alderman Birch's unique [16] refectory in Cornhill, opposite the Bank of England, without a tribute to the talents, literary as well as culinary, of the worthy alderman, who having written and published on the theory of National Defence, has here illustrated his system practically, by providing a variety of superior soups and pastry wherewithal to fortify the stomachs, and stimulate the courage of all his Majesty's liege subjects. These aliments are served up in a superior style. On the tables are placed lemons, cayenne, and other condiments, with toasted French bread for the free use of the visitants. Throughout all the turtle season, is served up in positive perfection that maximum of high diet, real turtle soup. Here is also fine genuine forest venison exposed for sale.[1]

The Cock, Royal Exchange.

Immediately behind the Exchange, is the celebrated tavern called the Cock, now kept by Mr. John Locket. This house is noted for the excellence of its mock turtle and other soups, as well as for various solid viands regularly assorted and displayed. The house entertains more guests for its size than any other of the kind in the city.[2]

[1] Samuel **Birch** (1757-1841), described by *ODNB* as 'politician, playwright, and pastrycook', inherited the business at no. 15 Cornhill, south side, from his father, and ran it until 1836. H. E. Popham (1937, p. 194) reported that the shop had made the turtle soup for the Lord Mayor's Banquet 'for seven reigns', and Birch himself served as Lord Mayor for the year beginning in November 1814. Edward Callow (1899, p. 49) claimed that 'during the lifetime of Alderman Birch he ordered the savoury contents of the stock pots – the ingredients in fact, "that cost the money," of which his celebrated soups were so artistically concocted – to be taken on certain days of the week to Whitecross Street Debtors' Prison, where they were distributed among the poor and county court prisoners'. Birch's catering firm (by then Ring and Brymer) moved to Old Broad Street when the Cornhill premises were acquired by Lloyds bank in 1926, and the old shop front was at that time transferred to the Victoria and Albert Museum.

[2] The **Cock** 'faced the north gate of the old Royal Exchange' (see Timbs, *Clubs*, pp. 381-82); the address was probably no. 63 Threadneedle Street, where Robson's 1820 directory lists John Lockett as tavern keeper. The 'Cock behind the Royal

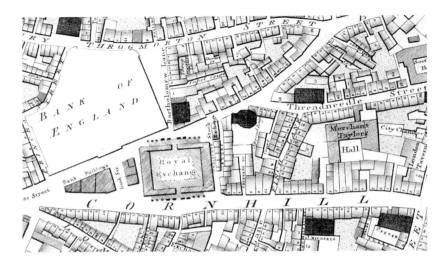

Bank of England, Threadneedle Street.

The Bank of England seems to be the [17] *magna parens* of coffee houses and taverns, at least it may dispute the honour of that pre-eminence with either of the Exchanges, Stock or Royal. Our enemies foreign and domestic have long laughed at us for being duped by paper instead of money, and for trudging on like patient asses under an increasing load of taxes. They seem to think John Bull, having broad shoulders (as the saying is,) can bear any thing; but they know not how to account for this. Let them send some spy to inspect the Bank of England and the avenues about it; John Bull may there be seen daily, waddling out of the front gate, and into one of the nearest places of replenishment, there to convert his paper into solid supplies for the service of the current day. Thus, while each new tax adds another feather to his load, he contrives to widen and strengthen his shoulders to bear it, and now he looks like the fat alderman, on the back of whose coat a wag pinned a ticket, copied from the inscription at the corner of the Old Jewry, "WIDENED at the expense of the Corporation of London."

Exchange' was listed first among eating houses in both Roach's 1793 *Pocket Pilot* and the first edition of the *Picture of London* (1802), which called it 'one of the most celebrated houses in the metropolis'. By Timbs's account the building was taken down in 1841.

New England Coffee-House, Threadneedle Street.

No. 61, Threadneedle Street, is the New England Coffee-house, kept by Mr. Clark. [18] This, and the Antigallican next door, serve coffee, chocolate, tea, soups, fermented beverages, and artificial mineral waters only. They dress no dishes.[1]

Grigsby's Chop and Steak-House.

Facing the above, in Threadneedle Street, is Grigsby's Chop and Steak-house, where they *do* dress dishes.[2] A rich larder is tastefully displayed in front, where every individual member of that *board* of health seems to say to the passer by, "for your own sake, Sir, if not for ours, pray come and try how you like us."

Antwerp Tavern.

The Antwerp Tavern, No. 58, Threadneedle Street, is kept by Mr. Butler, formerly of the Cock.[3] It being his pride and ambition to maintain the good character he gained while conducting the business of that house, he takes care

---

[1] Lillywhite records notices of the **New England Coffee House** as early as 1720; it was located on the north side of Threadneedle Street opposite the church of St Benet Fink, which was demolished in the 1840s for the building of the new Royal Exchange. The New England seems to have merged around 1839 with the **Antigallican**, next door at no. 60; the latter was in business no later than 1759, and by 1827 had become the North and South American Coffee House. In 1841 the combined leases and goodwill of the 'North and South American, New England, and Anti-Gallican Coffeehouse and Subscription Rooms' were auctioned, with the claim that 'a man of active habits would in a few years realize a large fortune' from the properties (*The Times*, 27 November), and the coffee house survived into the 1860s.

[2] **Grigsby's**, earlier principally known as a coffee and chocolate house, is recorded by Lillywhite on the north side of the street as early as 1706; it appears to have moved by mid-century, and the Post Office directory of 1813 gives the address as no. 12, on the south side. Grigsby's narrowly missed being consumed by the 1816 fire that destroyed the old Stock Exchange (*The Times*, 24 April; see below, p. 21), and seems to have survived into the 1830s.

[3] The **Antwerp**, on the north side of the street, may have been the successor of an earlier tavern of the same name, mentioned by John Taylor in his 1636 *Travels* but destroyed in the Great Fire. By June 1823 the Antwerp had been replaced by a new building housing the Baltic subscription rooms (*New Monthly Magazine*, p. 279).

to have every article of diet of the best quality, and judiciously cooked. He is celebrated for the superior goodness of his wines.

Hercules and New Stock Exchange, Threadneedle Street.

Up the passage a most inviting larder, be- [19] longing to Hercules and the New Stock Exchange, would tempt Hercules himself, if the lady from whom he turned aside were placed here as barmaid – let Madam Virtue frown as she would – though even her features would relax, when she saw in this place a whole academy of stock exchange philosophers, perusing, marking, and inwardly digesting the affairs of the nation, the fluctuating prices of the funds, and Mr. Hooper's inimitable dinners; nor would she, on a sultry day, censure the Burton, Welch, and Scotch ales on which the host honestly prides himself.[1]

Ireland's Oyster Rooms and Shell-Fish Shop.

Adjoining, in the same passage, are Ireland's oyster rooms and shell-fish shop, where spruce-beer and other fermented beverages are kept, and vended in high perfection.

Watkins's Royal Exchange Beef-Steak and Chop-House.

No. 18, in Threadneedle Street, is Watkins's Royal Exchange Beef-steak and Chop-house, where a most capital larder exhibited in front, gives token of some goodly fare within.

---

[1] Although not named on the Horwood map, Hercules Court or Passage (formerly French Court) ran northwest out of Threadneedle Street at no. 54; the site is now occupied by the Stock Exchange. The **Hercules Tavern** appears in directories into the early 1840s, but in 1842 the owner, Joseph Phillips, was declared a bankrupt (*London Gazette*, 22 November).

Stock Exchange Tavern.

As you enter Sweeting's Rents, at the east [20] end of the Royal Exchange, you cannot miss the Stock Exchange Tavern.[1] You may know it by the richly garnished livery of its sumptuous larder. Over the Old Stock Exchange are the rooms of *accommodation*,* where it is needless to say that dinners are served up in good style. Here bulls and bears roar with delight, or growl in dudgeon, over their pasture and their prey; they roar or growl according to the bargains they have made. In this establishment, if not in the larder, there is seldom or never any want of waddling ducks, whose crural defalcations are very often the subject of an anatomical or cutting-up lecture, a brief but pithy abstract of which is posted up for the benefit of the curious, and as a warning to the heedless.

* Accommodation is not here meant financially but alimentarily; though with reference to the business done here sometimes, it may have either acceptation. "Accommodated" is an excellent good word, as Bardolph says.

Edinburgh Castle Steak and Chop-House,
Sweeting's Rents.

In Sweeting's Rents, at the back of Sweeting's Alley, is the Edinburgh Castle Steak and Chop-house, kept by T. Newman. It has a good larder.[2]

[1] The old Stock Exchange was on the south side of Threadneedle Street, just to the east of the Royal Exchange, and the **Stock Exchange Tavern**, more commonly called a coffee house, was situated above the Exchange itself. When in 1802 the Exchange moved its business to new premises in Capel Court, the coffee house remained, but it was completely destroyed by fire on 23 April 1816.

[2] Sweeting's (or Swithin's) Rents and Sweeting's Alley were two narrowly separated parallel passages running between Threadneedle Street and Cornhill, just to the east of the Royal Exchange. The entire area, which had been rebuilt after the Great Fire, was completely cleared away after a January 1838 fire that destroyed the Exchange, and the site is now covered by the paved area to the east of the new Exchange. The **Edinburgh Castle** was at no. 1, with the others following in a row up to the **Hambro' and Edinburgh Coffee House** at no. 6 and the **New York Coffee House** at no. 7. The *Almanack*'s listings may reflect some confusion regarding the William Gillhams senior and junior, who respectively ran the **Red Lion** and **Joe's Coffee House**, the latter perhaps associated or identical with the establishment here called **Gillham's Chop House** (*Triennial Directory*, 1817-19).

[21]

Hope Eating-House.

No. 2, is another Chop-house, with another good larder; and No. 3, is the Hope Eating-house, (by the bye, the Hope is a singular name for an eating-house, for if there be any truth in an old adage, "he that lives upon hope shall die fasting.") It has a larder, however, that excites hopes, which Mr. Burt, the host, is always prepared to realize.

Red Lion Chop-House.

No. 4, is the Red Lion Chop-house. This is a more appropriate sign than the former, and the fare is equally good. The lion's den is well supplied, and the noble animal is pleased to share his prey with all who come.

Gillham's Chop-House.

No. 5, is Gillham's Chop-house, having a most excellent larder in front. All these houses serve by *bill of fare with the prices affixed*, a very fair and just mode of dealing, and indeed a very exemplary one. Strangers and economists may thus calculate the cost ere they incur it; and without gauging the stomach or the pocket, may, by the proper use of their eyes, be instructed how to live [22] within compass. Gillham's house is famous for the excellent dressing of its rump-steaks.

Hambro' and Edinburgh Coffee-House.

Adjoining is the Hambro' and Edinburgh Coffee-house, where in addition to the coffee and chocolate, soups and broths only are kept.

New York Coffee-House.

In the corner of Sweeting's Rents, is the New York Coffee-house, which confines its refreshments to the usual articles for breakfasts, and to wines, mixed liquors, and fermented beverages.

Cock and Woolpack Tavern.

In Finch Lane, leading from Threadneedle Street into Cornhill, are three houses for dining, lunching, and drinking. No. 6, is the Cock and Woolpack Tavern.[1] The Cock in question, occupies as authoritative a position as the Lord Chancellor, and treads *his* woolsack with almost as much dignity as his Lordship himself sits on his. Mr. Denton, the host, keeps a good larder in front, and comfortable accommodations within. Every article in the bill of fare has its price affixed.

[23]

Union Dining Rooms.

The Union Dining Rooms, No. 11, come under the description and rank of an eating-house, with shop and larder in front.

Eagle Chop-House.

The Eagle Chop-house, kept by Mr. Laming, has an excellent exposed larder; and its bills of fare are precisely priced.

New Lloyd's.

Over the Royal Exchange, you will find the celebrated coffee-house and subscription rooms, known all over the world by the name of LLOYD's. In these rooms the bustle of business for a few hours daily, is inconceivable to those who have not witnessed it. Here are kept two immensely large ledgers, in which is inserted the best information relative to the arrival and departure of every merchant ship, that adventures at sea, with the casualties attending it. In the *public* rooms are the brokers' announcements of ships wanting freight or passengers. In the subscription room, almost all the policies of insurance

---

[1] The **Cock and Woolpack** at no. 6 Finch Lane, east side, is mentioned in an Old Bailey trial of 16 February 1774, and still survives today. Thackeray described it in 'The History of Samuel Titmarsh and the Great Hoggarty Diamond' (1841) as 'a respectable house, where you get a capital cut of meat, bread, vegetables, cheese, half a pint of porter, and a penny to the waiter, for a shilling', but for Edward Callow in 1899 it was 'so renovated and altered, if not entirely rebuilt, that I fail to recognize […] the place I knew in 1845' (p. 22). Derelict in 2002, the Cock and Woolpack was relaunched two years later.

on shipping are effected. One division of the esta- [24] blishment is set apart for sales by auction of ships and their cargoes.[1]

These rooms being wholly appropriated to the transaction of business, the refreshments are merely those which belong to the coffee-house department alone. The terms of subscription are, as we learn, twenty-five guineas per annum, a sum well laid out by those whose interest it is to obtain political and commercial intelligence some hours before it transpires in the public journals.

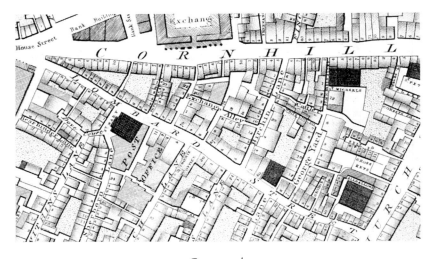

Garraway's.

Immediately opposite to the Exchange, in 'Change Alley, is Garraway's Coffee-house, where in addition to the customary coffee-house fare, there are delicate sandwiches always kept ready cut in the bar, which you may wash

---

[1]   As the *Almanack* notes, **Lloyd's** was a subscription house, including by 1815 coffee rooms both for subscribers (the Captains' Room) and for the public. It descended from a Lombard Street coffee house founded in 1691 by Edward Lloyd, which quickly became the principal meeting place of shipowners and marine insurance brokers. In 1769 the rival **New Lloyd's** opened in Pope's Head Alley, and by 1785 'old' Lloyd's had closed. New Lloyd's moved to rooms over the Royal Exchange in 1774, but was completely destroyed in the fire of 10-11 January 1838 – which may have started in its own Captains' Room (see Harding and Metcalf 1986, pp. 93-94). Lloyd's returned to the rebuilt Royal Exchange in 1844 and remained there until a further move in 1928, by which time the coffee rooms had become principally a restaurant for staff.

down with wine or spirit and water, or if you prefer it, with spruce beer or soda water. The upper part of this establishment is appropriated to sales by auction, of estates and mercantile effects of every description. Here immense possessions in the West Indies are bought and sold, which neither the buyer nor seller ever saw. Sometimes an estate of £40,000 or £50,000 value, is sold by auction by candle. The reader will of course see that we do not here mean a sale [25] by candle-light. No: business here is not done as the business of the nation is done in St. Stephen's Chapel, after dinner, and in the night time. Business is here done in the hours of open day, when the head may be supposed to be cool and fit for doing it. But at the commencement of a sale, when the auctioneer has read the description of the property, and the conditions on which it is to be disposed of, a piece of candle, usually an inch long, is lighted, and he who is the last bidder at the time the light goes out, is declared the purchaser.[1]

Let us now retrace our steps to the Mansion House, for the purpose of reconnoitring the several good houses of entertainment in the immediate vicinity of Lombard Street and the General Post Office.

Bass's, Lombard Street.

No. 85, facing the Post Office, is Bass's Eating-house, with a good shop and larder in front, and genteel accommodations up stairs.

---

[1] **Garraway's** was at no. 3 or 4 Exchange (or 'Change) Alley, a twisting series of inlets connecting Cornhill and Lombard Street; the basic outline of the passageways survives today, although completely rebuilt. Thomas Garway or Garraway was operating a coffee house in Sweeting's Rents by 1658, moving to Exchange Alley not long after it was rebuilt following the 1666 fire (Markman Ellis 2004b, p. 124); his new establishment was destroyed in the Cornhill fire of March 1748 but had been rebuilt by 1752. Garraway's remained in operation until 1873 (*The Times*, 28 January), and almost from the time it opened was the scene of auctions of goods ranging from ships and slaves to books and wine, often held 'by candle', with bidding continuing as long as the flame lasted or until the candle reached a predetermined level. With the closing of Garraway's these auctions were transferred to the London Tavern in Bishopsgate Street (p. 35 below); by 1874 the building itself had been pulled down (*ONL*, ii:172).

Ross's Oyster Rooms and Shell-Fish Shop.

Near the Post Office, are Ross's Oyster Rooms and Shell-fish Shop. This house is celebrated for dressing turtle all the season; [26] and is also noted for the maturity and briskness of its spruce beer.

Sumpter's Oyster-Warehouse, Abchurch Lane.

In Abchurch Lane, No. 6, is Sumpter's Oyster Warehouse. There is a conspicuous announcement, stating that the establishment bears date 1756. It is from hence and from other oyster shops in the vicinity, that the good citizens of London send (not a sprat to catch a herring,) but a barrel of Colchester or native oysters to ensure their Christmas turkies or chine, or, perhaps, a cargo of game from their friends in the sporting counties.

Union Chop and Steak-House, Sherborne Lane.

In Sherborne Lane, facing the back entrance to the Post Office, is the Union Chop and Steak-House, where hot joints are ready every day from twelve to five o'clock.

Lamb Eating-House.

Sherborne Lane, No. 2, Mr. Pappril of the Lamb Eating-house, serves strangers as well as his friends with hot joints and rounds of beef ready always from twelve to five o'clock. This house is much frequented by [27] persons employed in the various banking-houses.

Peto and Davis's Oyster Warehouse.

In Sherborne Lane, also, is Peto and Davis's long established oyster warehouse, whence barrels are sent to all parts of the country with the most punctual promptitude, according to order.

The Six Bells Public-House,
Dove Court, St. Swithin's Lane.

Is a good and much frequented house, for a lunch, or a hasty dinner.[1]

Evans's Eating-House.

In St. Swithin's Lane, No. 3, is Evans's Eating-house, kept now by Mr. William Trull. Here joints are always ready from twelve until five o'clock, and dinners from them are served up at a moderate price per plate.

Friend's Eating-House, Bearbinder Lane.

In Bearbinder Lane, No. 5, is Friend's elegant eating-house, having a good larder and great variety of hot joints and other dishes daily.[2] The excellent accommodations up stairs, are a model to all the rivals of this house, and a temptation to every stranger who [28] passes by it. We need scarcely add an encomium on this house, after we have stated that it entertains nearly seven hundred persons every day in the week excepting the Sunday.*

* In this house, as in some other eating-houses in the city, no bill of fare is offered; but to supply the place of one, the waiter, as soon as a guest has seated himself at table, verbally and very volubly runs over the catalogue of good things ready to be served up, and then waits for orders. A gentleman unaccustomed to this rapid style of culinary oratory, once offended the waiter here, by ordering him to repeat his nomenclature more deliberately. The waiter having sullenly complied, the gentleman made his election, then deliberately took his dinner, and afterwards hastily offered to pay. The waiter as was his custom said, "what have you had, Sir?" The gentleman, whose tongue was as glibly hung as the attendant's, replied with a very quick and happy alliteration, "Here's for pye, peas-pudding, pork, pepper, porter, potatoes, pickles, and a penny for the prig of a waiter."

---

[1] Dove Court, home to the **Six Bells** public house, ran west from the precincts of St Mary Abchurch, with entrances from Lombard Street and St Swithin's Lane.
[2] Bearbinder Lane, where **Friend's Eating House** was located, ran east from the Mansion House to St Swithin's Lane; it was later known as George Street and is now the east-west portion of Mansion House Place.

Simpson's Tavern and Chop-house, Ball's Court.

We now regain Cornhill; and resuming our tour, find Simpson's Tavern and Chop-house, in Ball's Court.[1] Its sumptuous larder and extensive premises for public accommodation, occupy nearly the whole court.

[29]

George and Vulture, George Yard.

The George and Vulture in George Yard, leading from Lombard Street through a passage into Cornhill, is an old established tavern, and has commodious dining rooms up stairs, and a complete suite of subsidiary apartments well stocked with all the requisites of good living.[2]

Africa and Senegal Tavern,
St. Michael's Alley, Cornhill.

In St. Michael's Alley, Cornhill, is the Africa and Senegal Tavern, or Cole's Coffee-house, with its admirable larder, where it is announced, that this is the only house in London for genuine rizzod haddock.[3]

[1]   Both Simpson's and the George and Vulture are still in business. **Simpson's** is located in Ball Court, a narrow alleyway that runs south from Cornhill between nos. 38 and 39, just east of Birchin Lane. Built soon after the fire of 1666, the premises were converted to a tavern in the mid-c18. *BoE City*, p. 471, notes that the present buildings 'must date from after 1748', when the Cornhill fire destroyed much of the area, and adds that 'the shopfront, looking late c18, is actually of *c.* 1900'. Simpson's was further restored in 1980.

[2]   The **George and Vulture**, in the northeast corner of George Yard (official address now no. 3 Castle Court), is on or near the site of a much older George Inn, mentioned as early as the 1470s. The original George and Vulture, erected soon after the fire of 1666, was partly destroyed in that of 1748 and was further reduced and altered in the c19. The tavern is named in the *Pickwick Papers* some dozen times and 'may be said to have been Mr. Pickwick's headquarters in London' (Matz 1922, p. 151); it has the distinction of being the only establishment named in the *Almanack* to make an appearance in the 1968 *Good Food Guide to London*.

[3]   The **African and Senegal**, located at no. 1 on the west side of St Michael's Alley, resulted from the merger of two establishments, the African and the Senegal, around 1799. The alley, a narrow passage running along the west and south sides of the churchyard of St Michael, Cornhill, was in the mid-c17 home to London's first coffee house, operated by Pasqua Rosee and Christopher Bowman on the site of what is now no. 3, but destroyed in the 1666 fire (see Markman Ellis 2004a). Rizzod or rizzared haddock is salted (and sometimes smoked) and then wind- or sun-dried.

Cock and Lion Tavern.

In the same alley, facing the Jamaica Coffee-house, is the Cock and Lion Tavern, kept by Mr. Harrison. This is in every respect a good house.[1]

Jamaica Coffee-House.

In this alley is the Jamaica Coffee-house, a very large establishment, more adapted to [30] the purposes of business than to those of relaxation or pleasure. The refreshments therefore are simply such as may be commonly found in most coffee-houses strictly so called.[2]

White Hart Chop and Eating-House, Bell Yard.

A most convenient place for rest and refreshment, from the peculiarity of its site, is the White Hart Chop and Eating-house. It has rooms up stairs for soups and dinners. It is situated in Bell Yard, leading from Gracechurch Street to St. Michael's Alley.[3]

Woolpack Tavern and Chop-House, St. Peter's Alley.

In St. Peter's Alley, leading from Cornhill to Gracechurch Street, is the noted and well accustomed house, called the Woolpack Tavern and Chop-house.[4] It is worth any thirsty man's while to walk to it from the Exchange on a hot day, only for the sake of a cool tankard of its particular porter.

[1] The **Cock and Lion**, at no. 2 on the same side, was mentioned in an Old Bailey trial of 28 June 1733, and like many other taverns served as a meeting place for Freemasons. Rebuilt after the fire of 1748 and later known simply as the Cock, it continued in some form until about 1896.
[2] At no. 12 on the east side of St Michael's Alley was the **Jamaica Coffee House**, built in 1733 on the site of an earlier establishment, the Virginia Coffee House (Ellis 2004a, p. 22, n. 87); it is not clear if references from the 1680s onward to a Jamaica Coffee House in Cornhill involve a direct ancestor. The present building, today known as the Jamaica Wine House, dates from 1885 (*BoE City*, p. 472) and has recently been completely refurbished.
[3] Bell Yard, site of the **White Hart Chop House**, is today called Bell Inn Yard, a passageway leading west from Gracechurch Street to the churchyard of St Michael, Cornhill.
[4] St Peter's Alley connects Cornhill and Gracechurch Street, forming an L-shape to the west and south of the church of St Peter. The **Woolpack Tavern** was at no. 6, and seems also to have had an entrance into Corbet Court, just south of St Peter's

No one passing through St. Peter's Alley, however, in haste, can miss casting an enamoured eye on the lovely fish reposing in the most tempting attitude on each side of him. They are all prime in their kind, and are to be had at a reasonable rate.

[31]

Jerusalem Coffee-House, Cowper's Court, Cornhill.

In Cowper's Court, Cornhill, is the Jerusalem Coffee-house, kept by Mr. Alexander Harper. This like the Jamaica, is a house of business, chiefly in the East India marine department, and the refreshments of course are not very much varied. Here as in many similar establishments in the city, the expenses are defrayed by annual subscriptions, from a large number of respectable persons.[1]

Angel's Pastry Shop, Cornhill.

At the south side of Gracechurch Street, corner of Cornhill, is Angel and Son's celebrated pastry shop, with its abundant varieties of delicious confectionery, ice creams, fruits, &c. This shop is particularly distinguished for exposing to sale the finest venison throughout all the season.

We cannot pass on from Cornhill into Leadenhall Street, without previously deviating both right and left for the purpose of inspecting several excellent and well noticed houses of entertainment, two of which are not equalled, perhaps, in the known world.

[32]

Spread Eagle Inn and Tavern, Gracechurch Street.

Turning down Gracechurch Street, on the right we soon come to the Spread Eagle Inn and Tavern, kept by Mr. Pardy. Here is a good larder, containing

---

Alley. A police report concerning illegal betting at the tavern in 1887 refers to it as 'recently rebuilt' (*The Times*, 3 November), and the new Woolpack survived into the C20, disappearing from directories about 1903.

[1] The **Jerusalem Coffee House** was at no. 3 Cowper's Court. The entrance to the Court, earlier known as Fleece Passage or Fleece Yard, was between nos. 32 and 33 on the south side of Cornhill, and there was also an entrance from Birchin Lane. The Jerusalem was a subscription house, probably founded in the 1730s and rebuilt after being destroyed in the 1748 Cornhill fire; by the late C19 it had become merely a shipping exchange, and in 1892 the premises were converted to offices (Hobhouse 1971, p. 177).

every thing of the best in its season, and affording very capital accommodations. Here the mails and principal stage coaches for Kent and other southern counties, arrive and depart.[1]

Cross Keys Inn and Tavern.

Within two or three doors of the above house, is the Cross Keys Inn and Tavern, kept by Mr. William Morris.[2] This house in point of viands, liquors, and accommodation, is worthy of its vicinity to the Spread Eagle.

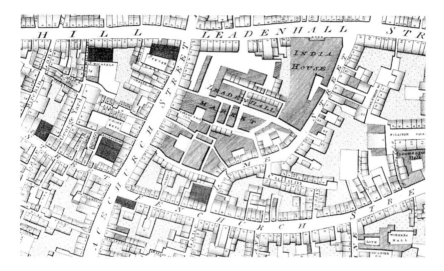

[1] A major stage stop for coaches to Kent and beyond, the **Spread Eagle** at no. 84 Gracechurch Street, east side, was built in 1671, probably replacing another establishment of the same name that perished in the Great Fire. The Spread Eagle was pulled down in 1865 and the property – by then surrounded on three sides by the new Leadenhall Market – was sold for £95,000 (*Illustrated London News*, 23 December 1865, p. 609, with a wood-engraving of the inn just before its demolition).

[2] The **Cross Keys**, another coaching inn at no. 16 on the west side, is shown on Ogilby and Morgan's 1676 map, and like the Spread Eagle replaced an earlier establishment destroyed in the fire. The first Cross Keys, a galleried inn, was by 1579 in use for theatrical performances, and may at one time have served as the winter house for the Lord Chamberlain's men, of whom Shakespeare was one (Chambers, ii:383). The later inn is still shown on Bacon's 1888 map, but in 1913 the Hong Kong and Shanghai Bank opened on the site. Today the former banking hall is home to a new Crosse Keys, part of the hotel that has replaced the bank.

Telegraph Eating-House.

Adjoining the Cross Keys Inn, is the Telegraph Eating-house, with shop and larder in front, and an entrance under the gateway to the stairs, leading to the dining-rooms. On either side of the door, is painted on a show-board the following bill of daily fare with the prices:

[33]

	s.	d.
Boiled beef, per plate	0	9
Roast beef	0	10
Roast mutton	0	10
Roast Pork	0	11
Roast Veal	0	11
Mutton Chop	0	5
Pork Chop	0	6
Rump steak	1	2
Mock turtle, per basin	1	10
Giblet soup	0	10
Gravy, or pea soup	0	6

Star Tavern, Nag's Head Court.

In Nag's Head Court, Gracechurch Street, is the Star Tavern, kept by Mr. J. Folker. This is rather a superior public-house, with a larder of steaks, chops, kidneys, and other minuter articles of refreshments. An ordinary is held here every day at two o'clock.[1]

Scarlet and Son's Ham Shop, 18, Fish Street Hill.

At No. 18, Fish Street Hill, is Scarlet and Son's celebrated shop, where hams, hung beef, tongues, and other eatables of that species, are sold by weight.

[34]

Swan Tavern.

The Swan Tavern, Mr. J. Cassidy, within three doors of Thames Street, has a good larder of joints, steaks, and chops, which being tastefully displayed, is

---

[1] The **Star Tavern** was at no. 4 Nag's Head Court (now Lombard Court), which runs out of Gracechurch Street between nos. 32 and 33 on the west side.

visible down the passage, between numbers 23 and 24 in Fish Street Hill. It is a superior public-house, and has good accommodations.[1]

Mitre Tavern and Chop-House.

Returning up Fish Street Hill, on the Monument side, we must halt for a few minutes at No. 38, the Mitre Tavern and Chop-house, kept by Mr. Clements.[2] Its inviting larder displayed in front, operates on the fasting passenger like a tacit word of command, to halt and come to quarters. On the table he will find a bill of fare, and the prices regularly affixed to each article.

Monument Tavern and Chop-House.

Any gentleman desirous of improving his appetite, may take a revolving walk up "London's column, pointing to the skies," and coming down the only safe way, (that is, the way by which he went up,) he need not stop [35] to read its inscription at the base, and consider whether it
    "Like a tall bully lifts its head, and lies;"
he may without reading that or any other inscription, proceed to the corner of Little Eastcheap and Fish Street, where he will see an inscription worth reading, every word of it being testified as truth by a variety of handsome fish and fowls, as well as by some worthy members of those noble corporations, the ox, cow, sheep, calf, and lamb, who seem to tell him they would be glad of his company to dinner in this their house in town, the Monument Tavern and Chop-house, the accommodations of which are fitted up so neatly as to correspond with the splendid alimentary display in front.[3]

[1] The **Swan Tavern** described here should not be confused with the 'Swan in old Fish streete' where Samuel Pepys enjoyed a 'fine dinner' on 15 August 1662: Pepys's Old Fish Street was further west, with the Swan on the corner of Bread Street. The passageway behind nos. 23 and 24 Fish Street Hill (west side) is shown on Horwood's map, just below a similar passage designated Globe Alley on the Ogilby and Rocque maps (later Globe Court). Apparently the descendant of the pre-Fire Swan and Bridge Inn, the rebuilt Swan described here was still in business in 1853 (Burn, p. 73), and a Swan Tavern continued in some form into the C20.
[2] The **Mitre Tavern** was on the east side of Fish Street Hill; in 1928 the Mitre Hotel was still at this address (Rogers 1928, pp. 157-59), and in 1973 the Mitre pub (Richards and Curl, p. 151).
[3] The **Monument Tavern** was also on the east side of Fish Street Hill, at no. 48, near the corner of Eastcheap; Christopher Wren's Monument to the Great Fire of London itself stands at the corner of Fish Street Hill and Monument Street (in 1815

White Lion, Talbot Court, Gracechurch Street.

Let us not forget Mr. C. Williams, of the White Lion, Talbot Court, Grace-church Street, who keeps an excellent larder in front, and hot joints within.[1] His Burton, Welch, and other country ales, draught as well as bottled, are fit for the palate and throat of the most refined toper. The fine perfume of the [36] hop in his Shropshire ale, acts on the olfactories like a veritable nosegay.

Halfmoon Tavern.

No. 88, Gracechurch Street, is the Halfmoon Tavern, by Mr. S. Kemshead. You may live through many a whole moon without finding better articles to subsist on, or better accommodations to exist in, than this house with its larder can furnish.[2]

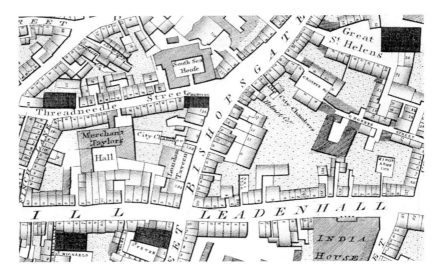

Monument Yard). Alexander Pope's lines ('Where London's column pointing at the skies,/Like a tall bully, lifts the head, and lies') refer to words added to one of the inscriptions at the base of the column in the 1680s, placing the blame for the fire on Roman Catholics; the passage was removed in 1830.

[1] Talbot Court, where the **White Lion** was located, forms an upside-down L connecting Gracechurch Street (entrance between nos. 55 and 56, east side) and Eastcheap (entrance between nos. 46 and 47, north side).
[2] The **Halfmoon**, at no. 88 on the east side of Gracechurch Street, is mentioned in an Old Bailey trial of 8 December 1773. It was rebuilt in 1881 and, now called the New Moon, remains open at the corner of Leadenhall Market.

London Tavern.

We will now with the permission of our readers, and those coachmen and draymen who so frequently jam up the way, cross Cornhill again, and enter Bishopsgate Street. On the left hand side, we immediately enter that magnificent establishment, the London Tavern, commanded for the benefit of the public service, by Messrs. Hale and Co. This house is on a truly great scale in all its departments, being capable of entertaining the most numerous of those associations and public bodies, for whose use it is generally in requisition.[1]

City of London Tavern.

A little farther on, in Bishopsgate Street, [37] on the opposite side of the way, is another monument of the wealth and magnificent spirit of the citizens of London, called the City of London Tavern.[2] This splendid edifice was begun a few years ago, and completed in the astonishingly short space of four months. The citizens baptized it "The City of London," to distinguish it from "The London." These titles remind us of the Archbishops of Canterbury and York; the one primate of England, the other of all England. But the rival houses in question contend for the prize of convivial preference, to be awarded not only by the City, or by Westminster, and all the metropolis, but by the universal British nation, her allies, friends, and even enemies, at home and abroad.

[1] The **London Tavern** is prominently shown on Horwood's map at what is today no. 3 Bishopsgate, just above Cornhill on the west side. It was built in 1767-68 on the site of an earlier tavern, the White Lyon, and in the early C19 was used not only for public dinners but also for concerts (see King 1986). The London Tavern was demolished in June 1876, when the property was acquired by the Royal Bank of Scotland; the tavern owners then took over the King's Head in Fenchurch Street (see below, p. 44).

[2] The **City of London** was set back in a small alley at no. 17 on the east side of the street, opposite the church of St Martin, Outwich; it had opened only a few years earlier, and was described by David Pugh ('David Hughson') in 1817 as 'the shewy rival of the Old London Tavern' (p. 48). In 1839-40 the disused tavern was converted to the Wesleyan Centenary Hall, with a new facade by William Fuller Pocock.

Bull Inn and Tavern.

The Bull Inn and Tavern, No. 93, Bishopsgate Street, is kept by Mr. Walde-grave, in a style worthy of himself and of his frequent guest Mr. John Bull, who, as our readers very well know, can no more resist the temptation of a well-stocked larder, a foaming pot of porter, and a bottle of particularly curious old port, than a Jew can resist the temptation of cent per cent.[1]

[38]

Marlborough Tavern and Chop-House.

The Marlborough Tavern and Chop-house, No. 97, in Bishopsgate Street, is a very comfortable and reasonable dinner house.

Vine Inn.

The Vine Inn, No. 70, in the same street, is built on a large scale, and we hope that, as it hath no bush in front, its wine is so good as to need none. The larder, we understand, is worth seeing.[2]

Four Swans.

The Four Swans, No. 83, Inn and Tavern, have good accommodations, principally for travellers.[3]

---

[1] The **Bull Inn** was at no. 92 on the west side of Bishopsgate; although it is shown on Ogilby and Morgan's 1676 map and the 1746 Rocque map as the Black Bull Inn, it was known simply as the Bull in the late C16 when it was in use as a public theatre (see Chambers, ii:380-81). The inn was torn down in 1866 for the building of Palmerston House (Cunningham 1927, p. 47), and today the site is occupied by the City's second-tallest building, Tower 42, formerly the NatWest Tower.

[2] The Vine Inn, the Four Swans, the Green Dragon, and the White Hart are all indicated on the 1676 Ogilby and Morgan map (Bishopsgate, west side), and the first three are named by John Taylor in his *Carriers Cosmographie* of 1637. The **Vine Inn** was just below Wormwood Street, but by 1866 the site had been covered over by an office block known as Ethelburga House.

[3] The galleried **Four Swans** was described by Thornbury in 1874 as 'just pulled down' (*ONL*, ii:161). According to Wagner (1924, p. 54), it was 'considered to be the most perfect and best preserved of all the City inns, having three gallery tiers on one side and two on the other'.

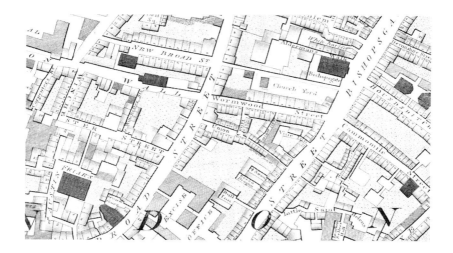

Green Dragon.

The Green Dragon Inn and Tavern, No. 86, Bishopsgate Street, has an excellent larder, and some of the very best accommodations.[1]

White Hart, Old Bethlehem.

The White Hart Tavern, at the corner of Old Bethlehem, is kept by Mr. Ankers, a wine-merchant, who of course, we should [39] suppose, is too good a judge of the blood of the grape, to offer his guests any of that impure, sophisticated, adulterated, deleterious, abominable mixture, for which foreigners so often reproach the tavern-keepers of this metropolis.[2]

[1] The **Green Dragon** closed in 1877 and was demolished the following year, when it was remembered by a *Times* correspondent as a 'relic of old London', with its 'curious inn-yard, forming a quadrangle, surrounded by wooden balconies […] and its quaint old dining-room, cut up into separate boxes by dark and high partitions' (13 May 1878).

[2] Somewhat north of the preceding three was the **White Hart**, an ancient establishment described by John Stow in 1598 as 'a fayre Inne, for receipt of travellers' (p. 127). It was situated next to the parish church of St Botolph, and the date 1480, which appeared on the front of the old inn, may have indicated the year in which the structure was rebuilt. It underwent considerable alterations around 1790, and was again improved in 1811, but when Old Bethlehem Street was rebuilt and widened to form Liverpool Street in 1829, the inn was torn down and replaced with a successor of the same name. The new White Hart continues in business at no. 121

Hilliard's Eating-House.

At No. 12, down Old Bethlehem, is Hilliard's Eating-house, long ago established, and always noted for hot joints daily, from twelve to four o'clock. There is a decent dining-room up stairs.

BISHOPSGATE WITHOUT.

Bishopsgate Without being rather beyond the sphere of good living, is a "region scarce of prey" to the epicure,[1] and contains few places above the rank of an eating-house or a cook's-shop: a very summary notice will therefore suffice. No. 35 is the long established shop of Messrs. Yates and Hayward, pastry-cooks. No. 130 is Nichols's ready-drest ham and beef-shop, with Bologna and dried German sausages and other prepared meats. No. 100 is Wilson's pastry-shop. No. 107 is Owen's tripe-shop. In Worship Street, one door from Bishopsgate, is Taylor's eating-house.

[40] In Shoreditch, at No. 239, is a ready-drest ham and beef-shop, with the usual accompaniments of tongues, sausages, &c. No. 210 is Valenduke's tripe-shop. No. 203 is Portlock's eating-house, or rather cook's-shop, with hot joints from twelve till four. No. 154 is Cheshire's eating-house and cook's-shop. No. 115 is Bolton's pastry-shop. In Kingsland Road, No. 7, is Macklew's eating-house, a very good establishment. Returning into Shoreditch, we find, at No. 108, Stedall's ham and beef-shop. No. 93 is Alliston's tripe-shop, a superior establishment of the kind, where pickled tripe can be had for exportation to the East and West Indies.

Turning down Church Street, we find, at No. 3 from Shoreditch, Ray's eating-house and cook's-shop, which serves hot joints from twelve to four.

The whole district, from St. Mary Axe to Houndsditch, and from Aldgate to Bevis Marks, is chiefly inhabited by Jews. Almost every shop has some eatable or other for sale. Here are Israelitish butchers, fishmongers, and cooks. The latter exhibit in their windows fish fried, or rather, perhaps, boiled in oil, until they look brown and savoury. In the interior of Duke's Place, and in many of the avenues, is held an open market daily (with the exception of the Jewish [41] sabbaths and fasts), for the sale of viands cooked according to the

---

Bishopsgate, the street having been renumbered in 1911 to eliminate the 'within' and 'without' distinction. Adulteration of wine was common after the end of the C18, when duties were raised and 'almost all descriptions of wine – port, claret, Rhenish, Malaga and others – were faked by unscrupulous merchants, druggists and tavern-keepers' (Burnett 1999, p. 147).

[1] The reference is to Milton's *Paradise Lost*, Book III.

Mosaical ordinances.[1] Here are stalls of dried and fresh fish; pickles of several sorts, among which are very large Turkey cucumbers. Merchants, both male and female, attend with fires, for the purpose of boiling eggs, and of keeping grey peas, lentils, and other pulse, hot. Large quantifies of passover biscuit, as well as confectionery and foreign fruit, are to be had here. From this neighbourhood, the itinerant retailers of fruit, fish, and confectionery, sally forth into the city, during change hours. In Duke's Place there is annually held, in the autumn, a Jews' fair, which continues a week: this being one of the few occasions on which these money-getting people lay down their cares and amuse themselves, gives rise to a scene at once grotesque and humourous.

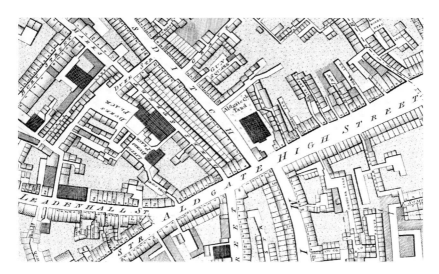

Brick Lane is a sort of market street, for supplying Bethnal Green, Mile End Old Town, and part of Spital Fields.[2] It has several eating-houses and tripeshops. Here are also several Jewish manufactories of sugar-sticks and peppermint-drops. Several manufacturers also of *real* Banbury cakes, mutton

[1] For the market in **Duke's Place**, see below, pp. 246-47. The fish described here may have been some version of the battered fish fried in olive oil popular among Sephardic Jews, often named as an ancestor of today's fish and chips (see Roden 1997, p. 100).

[2] **Brick Lane**, today the heart of London's Bangladeshi community, was earlier home to Huguenot refugees and, by the early C19, a growing Jewish population. The market itself was established by the C17.

and eel pies, &c. reside here, who supply most of the tossing-up piemen that attend executions, fairs, boxing-matches, and other polite assemblies.[1]

[42] The Blind Beggar of Bethnal Green is a very good house of entertainment: the officers of the second regiment of the Tower Hamlets militia for some years held their mess-dinners at this house.[2]

Judging that some of our readers might possibly be induced to proceed to White-chapel *viâ* Smithfield, we have perambulated that route through Long Lane, Barbican, Beech Street, Chiswell Street, through Finsbury Square into Sun Street, and thence down Union Street, Spital Fields.

In Long Lane, at No. 39, is a ham and beef-shop, where also savoury meat pies are vended: 66 is Budd's eating-house: 90 is Walton's eating-house, with good accommodations, neatly fitted up.[3]

At No. 34, Barbican, is Plympton's pastry-shop, presenting a very tasteful assortment of sweet and savoury compositions.

Golden Lane contains a noted brewery and several refectories of the humbler sort.[4]

Looking into Old Street, we find, at No. 119, north side, among the new buildings, a very neat ham and beef-shop, kept by Mr. Taylor. In Featherstone Street, at No. 30, is a decent eating-house. No. 9, Beech Street, is Cooper's pastry-shop, of rather a superior class.

[43] In Chiswell Street, at No. 73, is the Finsbury Eating-house, kept by Mr. Evans, where hot joints are to be had from twelve till four o'clock. No. 16 is the eating-house of Mr. Powell, formerly a disciple of Mr. Butler, at the

---

[1] A customer could 'toss the pieman' by throwing up a penny and waiting for the vendor to call heads or tails. If the customer won, the pie was free, but if the pieman called correctly he pocketed the money without handing over the pie; see Mayhew, *London Labour and the London Poor*, i:196.

[2] The present-day **Blind Beggar** at no. 337 Whitechapel Road – famous as the pub in which Ronnie Kray murdered George Cornell in 1966 – is a late-Victorian successor to the establishment mentioned here, which according to Leopold Wagner (1924, p. 166) was a 'timbered tavern' located at the point where the Whitechapel Road becomes Mile End Road. In 1808 the landlord, Richard Ivory, built the Albion Brewery next door to his tavern; this closed in 1979, but the Grade II listed building still adjoins the new public house.

[3] **Long Lane** leads east from Smithfield, then an open market for the sale of livestock (see below, p. 246). Much of the neighbourhood between here and Old Street was devastated in the Second World War.

[4] The Genuine Beer Brewery, shown on the 1813 Horwood map, had taken over the Golden Lane premises of Combrune's Brewery in 1804, remaining in business until 1826.

Exchange. In Grub Street there are no fewer than three refectories, of the humbler order, which, considering that the more eminent inhabitants of this haunt of the muses generally pursue that "spare fast, which oft with gods doth diet," are amply sufficient for the population in general.[1]

Crossing the bottom of Finsbury Square, we find, at No. 73, Sun Street, a respectable and commodious eating-house, kept by Mr. Oxley. Not far from this house, Long Alley intersects Sun Street: it well deserves its name, for it extends from the bottom of Moor Fields to the Curtain Road, and contains about 150 houses, one-third of which may be said to be inhabited by persons who vend eatables and drinkables to the neighbouring population. Long Alley has obtained the name of Little Cheapside. Its principal eating-house is the Peeping Tom, kept by Mr. Sadgrove.

At No. 78, Sun Street, is Morris's shell-fish shop, which does a great deal of business.

[44] Crossing Bishopsgate Street, into Union Street, Spitalfields, we find, at No. 9, Barton's eating-house, with accommodations up stairs, and a good display of meats in the window.

In Paternoster Row, at No. 22, is the Spital Eating-house, where joints are kept hot from noon till three o'clock, and soups and à-la-mode beef until eleven at night.[2]

King's Arms Inn and Tavern, Leadenhall Street.

We now proceed to Leadenhall Street, and stop at the Old King's Arms Inn and Tavern, for a moment. Here is an ordinary every day, at a convenient hour for people in business.[3]

[1] **Grub Street**, famous from the late c17 as the home of impoverished writers, ran north from Fore Street to Chiswell Street; in 1830 it was renamed Milton Street (commemorating a local builder, not the poet), and is now partly under the Barbican development. The 'spare fast' tag is from Milton's *Il Penseroso*.
[2] These last two stops in Spitalfields, Union Street and Paternoster Row, are now combined in Brushfield Street.
[3] The **King's Arms** at no. 122 Leadenhall Street, north side, is shown on the Horwood map, as well as on Rocque's of 1746 and Ogilby and Morgan's of 1676, justifying the *Almanack*'s use of Old in the name. The tavern closed in 1844 or 1845 and a new building was erected on the site to house the offices of the Peninsular and Oriental Steam Navigation Company.

Lamb Tavern.

Just look over the Skin Market, in Leadenhall Street, and you will see the Lamb Tavern, kept by Mr. Pardy. This is a large house, recently built on the site of the old one.[1] The larder is capital, and the rooms of accommodation extensive, being principally [45] resorted to by skin-salesmen, tanners, and leather-sellers, men who have generally a hearty constitution, and a good twist for roast and boiled; and who consequently love elbow-room, when they play a knife and fork.

East India House.

We need not remind our readers that in Leadenhall Street there is a very neat commodious tea-warehouse and draper's shop, kept by a company or corporation of mercantile men trading to the East Indies. We are told they are good people, and though much in debt, yet always in capital credit. They seldom meet upon the business of settling accounts, giving or taking orders, sending out ships or receiving cargoes, without having a good dinner together. We believe the City of London Tavern is the house they commonly use.

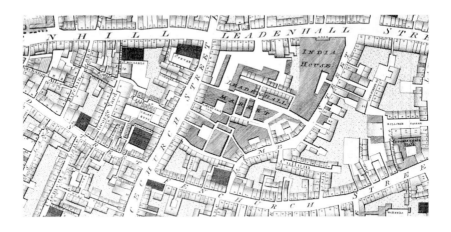

[1]   Several sources give 1780 as the foundation date of the original **Lamb Tavern**. Its successor remains, part of the glass-roofed Leadenhall Market designed by Horace Jones and completed in 1881, but the 'skin-salesmen, tanners, and leather-sellers' of 1815 have given way to underwriters from the nearby Lloyds Building, built on the site of the old **East India House** (demolished 1862).

Crown and Anchor Tavern.

On the right hand of the way in Leadenhall Street is No. 43, the Crown and Anchor, kept by J. Mackintosh. The larder is excellent, and the place is noted for giving particularly good dinners.[1]

[46]

Ship Tavern.

The Ship Tavern, kept by Mr. Henry Adams, stands immediately facing the India House.[2] Its excellent larder, always ready with soups of the best quality, and its good accommodations, render this a house of very good resort. At and from this tavern most of the gentlemen belonging to the India House are occasionally entertained.

No. 87, Leadenhall Street, is a shop long noted for selling bears' hams, foreign tongues, &c. The most illiterate and untravelled guest may very soon be proficiently conversant with these foreign tongues. A course of three lessons will make him an adept.

East India Coffee and Chop-House.

No. 66, on the right hand side of the India House, is the East India Coffee and Chop-house, in front of which is a well-displayed larder of fish, flesh, and fowl.[3] This house is famed for good soup, particularly mock turtle: several tureens of it may be seen in one of the windows, constantly ready for sale, with half a dozen fine calves' heads with lemons in their mouths, seeming to

---

[1] The **Crown and Anchor**, still in business in 1882, may have been a descendant of the Crown Tavern mentioned by Strype in 1720 as 'large and of a good trade' (1.2.82).

[2] The **Ship Tavern** at no. 129 Leadenhall Street, north side, was popular for Masonic meetings from the mid-C18. By the 1840s it was known as the Ship and Turtle, and several writers remark on the excellence of its turtle. A descendant of the original was still in business when H. C. Shelley wrote in 1909, and the Ship and Turtle name was later used for a public house in the 1960s P&O building at no. 122, now demolished.

[3] No. 66 Leadenhall Street, the address given in the *Almanack* for the **East India Coffee and Chop House**, can in no way be described as 'on the right hand side of India House', and must be an error. In the mid-C18 the coffee house operated at no. 10, adjoining East India House to the west (to the right as one faced the building), and although Lillywhite suggests that it had removed to no. 153 by 1800, this description indicates it had not.

utter defiance to the West Indian heterogeneous intruder, with his callipash, callipee, and gout.

[47]

Aldgate Pump and Co.

We now arrive at Aldgate, where we shall halt for a few minutes, not to receive a draught at the famous pump there, but to direct any person who may arrive at the same place of resort through Fenchurch Street.[1]

King's Head Tavern, Fenchurch Street.

He will find good refreshments at the King's Head Tavern in that street, facing Ironmongers Hall. It is kept by a gentleman named Cannon, and has long been famed for the excellence of its larder, and for sending out of it good things, well cooked, to the tables of its guests.[2]

Stickwood's.

No. 68, Fenchurch Street, is Stickwood's Eating-house, a very diminutive establishment.

Saracen's Head.

Being again at Aldgate, we see an immense Saracen's head staring on us, and seeming ready to shout that this is an inn fit for the Soldan himself to choose for his hostel.[3] Attached to it very intimately is the Aldgate [48] Coffee-house

---

[1] The **Aldgate Pump**, shown on the Horwood map at the junction of Aldgate High Street with Leadenhall Street and Fenchurch Street, was a late C18 stone pump, built on the site of a medieval well. It was modified and slightly moved a century later, but is today inoperative.

[2] The **King's Head** was on the northwest corner of Mark Lane at its junction with Fenchurch Street (no. 53 Fenchurch Street). A popular anecdote names the King's Head as the inn at which Princess Elizabeth dined after her release from the Tower in May 1554, but Lillywhite found few records of the tavern before the C18. Completely rebuilt in 1877 and renamed the London Tavern, it was destroyed by bombing in the Second World War.

[3] The entrance to the **Saracen's Head** is shown on the Horwood map between nos. 3 and 6 on the south side of Aldgate High Street (now simply Aldgate). It was a well-known terminus for coaches to Norwich as early as 1681, and the yard of the

and Tavern, kept by S. Freeman. Here soups are always ready, and dinners are speedily drest. The larder down the inn yard is very conspicuous.

Three Nuns, Aldgate High Street.

Let us now pay a chaste and not intemperate visit to the three Nuns, in High Street, Aldgate, just past the church. These three Nuns are in keeping of Mr. William Webb. Their inn and tavern is large as their consciences, and as they never fast, the refectory is always well stocked, and their soups are always ready.[1]

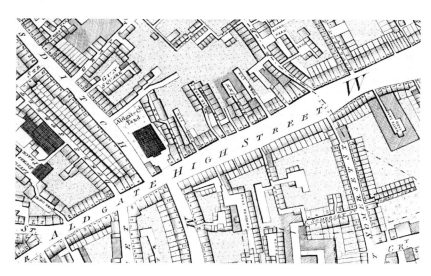

Crown and the Magpye.

Mrs. Ann Bruce keeps the Crown and the Magpye, a few doors from the Three Nuns, whose credit and fair fame never suffers from the loquacity of that tell-tale bird. Indeed, the magpye seems to be placed there for no other purpose but to invite the passers-by to this very considerable tavern, and to tell them they will here find one of the amplest larders in London,

galleried inn was apparently still intact as late as 1887 (Norman 1905, p. 82). The **Aldgate Coffee House** adjoined it to the west, at no. 2.

[1] The **Three Nuns** was at nos. 11-12 on the north side of Aldgate High Street; like the Saracen's Head it was a galleried coaching inn, but in 1877 it was entirely rebuilt as a hotel, derelict by 1973 (Wagner 1924, p. 162; Richards and Curl, p. 170: 'next to Aldgate Underground Station').

comprehending the principal genera and species of fish, flesh, and fowl, which are registered (if we may so say) and displayed in puris naturalibus, on either side of a long entrance, which if you once pass, you can- [49] not well repass, without the guilt of having been accessory to the destruction of the said fish, flesh, and fowl. The accommodations are of the best, and the wines are excellent.[1]

Bull Inn and Tavern, Aldgate.

A few doors on, in High Street, Aldgate, Mrs. Ann Nelson keeps the Bull Inn and Tavern. The guests are principally travellers and strangers from the eastern parts of England.[2]

Proceeding to the Commercial Road, we find, soon after turning down by Whitechapel Church, the East London Coffee and Chop-house.[3] About half way down the road, on the left-hand, is a large public-house, called the Half-way House, where chops, steaks, or any other kind of hasty dinner, may be had.[4] Nearly opposite Limehouse Church is another establishment of the same kind, situated at the foot of the bridge, over Limehouse Cut. This house is very convenient for persons who have business at the East or West India Docks.[5]

[1] The **Crown and Magpie** was also on the north side of Aldgate High Street; Lilly-white places it at no. 20.

[2] The **Bull** or **Black Bull** was at no. 25 on the north side. Another 'Pickwickian' inn – the journey to Ipswich began here – the Bull 'began to decline when the railway was opened in 1839, and in 1868 it was demolished' (Matz 1921, p. 121).

[3] In 'turning down by Whitechapel Church' to reach the new Commercial Road, our guide was travelling south along either White Church Lane, west of the church, or Union (now Adler) Street, and the **East London** was presumably in one of the two.

[4] The **Halfway House** considerably predated the new Commercial Road, and is shown on Rocque's map of 1746 and on Cary's 1786 *Survey*, as well as on Horwood's original map of 1799. The Halfway House site is now occupied by a Victorian public house, the George Tavern (no. 373 Commercial Road, at the junction of Jubilee Street).

[5] The large public house described as 'nearly opposite' St Anne's, Limehouse, was very likely the **Britannia**, shown on the Horwood map just west of the complex marked 'White Lead Works'.

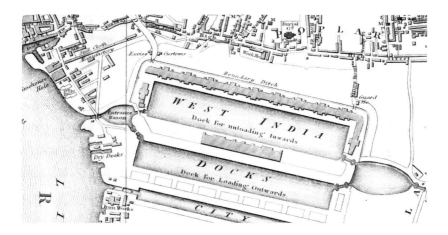

On the right-hand, near the West India Docks, is Putman's Commercial Eating-house, a kind of superior cook's-shop. Almost facing it, is the Blue Posts and West India Dock Tavern, &c. kept by Mr. John Perkins. Here dinners are drest for parties, or single persons, having business at the Docks.[1]

[50] The West India Commercial Coffee-house and Tavern, at the corner of the entrance into Poplar, is a large house with good accommodations.[2] This and the other establishments of the kind in the vicinity of the Docks are much frequented, as no cooking is allowed on board while the ships are in Dock. A little way into Poplar is the White Horse, where a chop or hasty dinner may be had.[3]

[1] **Putman's** (or possibly Putnam's) Eating House would have been on the southwest side of West India Dock Road, south of Back Lane (now Ming Street). The **Blue Posts and West India Dock Tavern** was on the northeast side of the road, at no. 73. In the c18 the tavern stood on the south side of Limehouse Causeway, at the intersection with Pennyfields and Back Lane, but with the construction of the West India Dock Road it moved to a new three-storey brick building. The premises were expanded in 1876 but demolished in 1987-88 (*SL* 43, p. 117).

[2] The **West India Commercial Coffee House** was possibly the ancestor of the Commercial Tavern at no. 1 Pennyfields, north side; still in business as late as 1944, the tavern, along with most of the other buildings in the street, was demolished in the 1960s (*SL* 43, pp. 112-13).

[3] The **White Horse** was at no. 279 Poplar High Street, north side (later renumbered as no. 11); the site was long in use as a tavern, with the name known at least since 1690. The White Horse was rebuilt *c.* 1868-70, about the same time the street was renumbered, and again in the late 1920s, but this, the final public house on the site, was demolished in 2002 (see *SL* 43, p. 61, and Sygrave 2004).

Close by the gates of the East India Dock is a very large establishment, called the East India Dock Tavern and Hotel, kept by Messrs. Duff and M'Intire.[1] This house is amply provided with conveniences for giving dinners in the most comfortable style; and on the arrival, as well as during the unloading of the fleets, is much frequented. On a post adjoining is a direction to the Orchard House Tavern, whence there is constantly a ferry to Greenwich.[2]

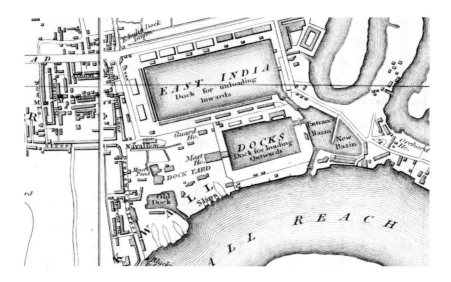

[1] The **East India Dock Tavern** stood on the northeast corner of East India Dock Road and Quag Lane (now Brunswick Road). The tavern, a large establishment with lodgings, opened in 1808 but had closed by 1816; a slightly later Dock House Tavern at no. 293 East India Dock Road, established in 1818 and shown on William Faden's *Plans*, was also sometimes known as the East India Dock Tavern. The original tavern building later served as a Custom House and as Poplar Hospital, but was demolished in 1981-82 (*SL* 43, p. 147).

[2] The **Orchard House**, located on a spit of land between the Thames and Bow Creek, is indicated to the east of the docks on the map above. In use as a public house from the early C18, it closed in the 1860s and was pulled down in the following decade (*SL* 44, pp. 646-48); the name survives locally in Orchard Wharf and Orchard Stairs.

Blue Boar Inn, Aldgate.

On our return we notice the Blue Boar Inn, Aldgate, kept by Mr. Belling-ham. The tavern and coffee-room department are in front. The larder, and the cheerful apartments, and the good accommodations thereof, are always at the guests' command, and they are well worth commanding.[1]

Having now reconnoitred the chief esta- [51] blishments in this direction, we shall fix upon Temple Bar as our next point of departure, but shall first make a circuit for the purpose of directing those whom pleasure or business may lead through the city, by avenues on the right and left of the principal streets.

UPPER THAMES STREET.

In Upper Thames Street are two or three inferior cook's shops to be met with. Though they be not of a description that may either invite or entertain an epicure, yet the porter is good, being of quick draught, that is, frequently called for. The guests are of that class of personages who eat to live, and live to labour.

Almost as soon as you enter Lower Thames Street, you find, on the left hand, No. 121, Old Sir John Falstaff. He is now maintained by E. Williams, a descendant of mine host of the Garter at Windsor, and formerly of the Gun Tavern, Billingsgate. Here are soups, lunches, and dinners daily.

Bell Tavern, Lower Thames Street.

Almost facing the aforesaid fat knight is the Bell Tavern. Here steaks and chops are announced on the shew-board, but the landlord seems to attend more to his bar for liquor, than to his bars for broiling.

[1] The entrance into the yard of the **Blue Boar Inn** was at no. 30 Aldgate High Street, north side. The inn appears on both the 1676 Ogilby and Morgan map and Rocque's map of 1746, but the Horwood map wrongly places the entrance between nos. 34 and 35 (this was in fact Black Horse Yard, also shown by Rocque, and later by Bacon). In 1855 J. G. Waller described the Blue Boar as 'very dilapidated', and by mid-1859 it had been levelled (*The Times*, 4 June, advertising property that included a plot of some 10,000 square feet, 'formerly the site of the Blue Boar Inn').

[52]

Howard's Eating-House, Dark-house Lane.

In Dark-house Lane, No. 6, is Howard's Eating-house, where, notwithstanding the darkness of the house and lane, you may see dinners eaten, and see to dine yourself, any hour of the day.[1]

Queen's Head and the Antigallican.

At the two corners of Dark-house Lane, next the river, are the Queen's Head Tavern and the Antigallican Tavern. The Queen's Head is kept by Mr. C. Clark, and the Antigallican by Mr. Goddard. These houses are strictly speaking, public-houses.[2]

Immediately in the fish-market are the Three Tuns,[3] and two other houses where they will cook a steak or a chop, or any kind of fish you can catch and bring. Here is no want of good living, even when persons are mostly in bed asleep. The hours of entertainment are regulated by the markets and the tides, and the meals are served principally to guests going and coming by the tide-

[1] Writing in 1817, David Pugh noted (p. 30) that Dark House Lane, 'the turning immediately joining Billingsgate to the west, contains a number of public-houses, used by watermen, fishermen, females, and others: here, from the confined situation, candles are necessary all day, particularly in winter. As some of these houses are open all night, to accommodate persons waiting for the Gravesend boats, beds may be had for *all*, whether really going to Gravesend, or only pretending so to do. Strangers who act prudently will avoid the mixed company in a place like this, especially such as wish to escape the fangs of those called *kidnappers*, or East India crimps.'
[2] Both the **Queen's Head** and the **Antigallican** are named in Old Bailey proceedings of the 1760s, and both were still in business at least into the 1870s; the Queen's Head was at no. 6, and the Antigallican at no. 5.
[3] In Billingsgate Market itself (for which see below, pp. 245-46) was the **Three Tuns**, dating from the early C18 and according to one source located 'beside the river at the bottom of Bell Alley' (Wagner 1924, pp. 102-03). The traditional date of founding by one Simpson is 1723, and the Three Tuns remained in that family until 1853, when James G. Simpson sold it and moved to the Queen's Arms in Bird in Hand Court (pp. 15-16 above); by 1856 the tavern was owned by Richard Phillips (advertisement in *The Times*, 9 June). There is a description of the Three Tuns, probably written by Peter Cunningham, in *Fraser's Magazine* for April 1846, pp. 453-54; it was still being recommended – 'for gentlemen only' – as late as 1889, when the two-shilling 'fish ordinary' was described as consisting of fish, meat, and cheese (Baedeker's *London*, p. 15).

boats. Early in the morning hasty breakfasts are made at one or two of the houses, in a superior style, to the fishmongers and salesmen, whose coffee or tea is served up in silver mugs. To these breakfasts strangers cannot gain admittance. During the season in Dark-house [53] Lane, great abundance of Gravesend asparagus is exposed to sale at reasonable prices; as are also frequently fine mushrooms, from the Kentish marshes.

Around this spot are several shops for the sale of shell-fish, either alive and not dressed, or dead as mutton and dressed. Such as buy them in their life-time may have them boiled very expeditiously, at a very trivial charge, in coppers wherein water is kept constantly on the boil, during market hours. In these shops may also be purchased salted cod, either barrelled or dried. Salmon, and herrings, preserved, either way, are vended in retail quantities at wholesale prices.

The clearing of a site for the new Custom-house, since the late conflagration of the old one, has occasioned the destruction or annihilation of many good houses of entertainment, particularly the celebrated Gun Tavern, whither epicures, singly or in parties, frequently resorted, for the purpose of eating fish in its highest state of perfection.[1]

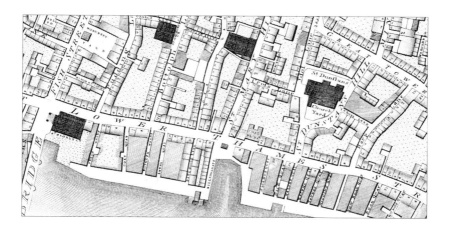

[1] The C18 riverfront **Custom House** at the eastern end of Lower Thames Street was destroyed by fire on 12 February 1814 and replaced by the present building just to the west, completed in 1817 but already under construction before the fire. A **Gun Tavern** at Billingsgate – perhaps identical with or an ancestor of the one named here – was mentioned by Daniel Defoe in *The History … of Col. Jacque* (1722).

ST. MARY'S HILL.

The only houses now remaining immediately in this vicinity are the Newcastle Tavern and Chop-house, William Ingram, master; and the Anchor Tavern, George Wall; both cruizing off and on St. Mary's Hill, facing [54] Billingsgate. At both these houses, fish, rump steaks, and chops, are dressed very comfortably, and as comfortably served up.[1]

The Ship Tavern, in Water Lane, simply speaking, is a most excellent house: it stands facing the ruins of the Custom House; and here numerous persons, whom business led to that important fountain of national revenue, were regaled. Here, among many other good things, a basin or soup-plate, containing a handsome mutton chop, vegetables and bread included, is served up for ninepence.[2]

From the improvements making in this neighbourhood, there is little doubt that in some future edition of this Directory we shall have to put on record some large establishments which, phœnix like, will rise from the ashes of the conflagration around the new office now rapidly erecting.

Coal Exchange Eating-House, Little East-cheap.

Such as pass hither by way of Little East-cheap, will find, at No. 13, in that street, the Coal Exchange Eating-house, kept by Mr. Winmill, with a good larder, cheerful accommodations, and very reasonable charges. The coal-traders may here exchange a modicum of their profits on black diamonds for very substantial garniture to the stomach.[3]

---

[1] The **Newcastle Tavern and Chop-house** is probably identical with the Newcastle Coffee House listed by Lillywhite at no. 21 St Mary at Hill. The Anchor was properly the **Blue Anchor** at no. 25 or 26, mentioned in an Old Bailey trial of 4 April 1733; a public house of that name continued at the address into the C20.

[2] The **Ship Tavern** was at no. 15 Water Lane, which ran north from Lower Thames Street to Great Tower Street but was 'swept away' in the 1960s (*BoE City*, p. 513). The Ship itself, mentioned by Strype in 1720, had been taken down by 1872 (Timbs, *Clubs*, p. 5).

[3] In 1815 'Little Eastcheap' denoted the stretch of modern Eastcheap between St Mary at Hill and Fish Street Hill; all three of the establishments named here would have been on the south side of the street, between Pudding Lane and Botolph Lane. The **Coal Exchange** in Lower Thames Street, built in 1770, was one of the first specialist trading floors; another was the Corn Exchange in Mark Lane (1749).

[55]

Sun Tavern and Chop-House.

No. 10, is the Sun Tavern and Chop-House, kept by Mr. S. Taylor. It is a good house; its exhibition of provisions is very judiciously disposed; and the throats of the thirsty are here to be relieved with Burton, Welch, and Scotch ales, in high perfection.

Union Eating-House.

No. 7, is the Union Eating House, a very decent and reasonable establishment. It announces its contents on the title page, or frontispiece of the house.

Mark Lane, Corn Exchange.

Proceeding on from Little East Cheap to Tower Street, on the left we find Mark Lane, up which is the Corn Exchange. Here on the Monday, Wednesday, and Friday of every week a market is held, in which wheat and flour, barley and malt, oats and tick beans, with other kinds of grain and pulse are sold by sample. Here quakers gravely commune with themselves and each other about smut, short crops, and small supplies. Water and windmillers may be found drawing on two of the elements for apologies to their extortions. [56] Here dry souls complain of wet seasons, and souls which are tenants of well moistened clay talk about dry souls.

From this mart not only the metropolis but its environs, for several miles round, are principally supplied. The amount of money here turned over, and changing hands every market-day, is almost inconceivable. Those sums that revolve on mere speculation are truly astonishing.

Corn Exchange Coffee-House,
and Corn-Factors' Coffee-House.

Up a flight of steps, on either side of the Corn Exchange, are 1. The Corn Exchange Coffee-House; and 2. The Corn-Factors' Coffee-House. The former is kept by Mr. James Smith, the latter by Mr. William Carter. The business of both is very brisk on market-mornings for a few hours. The refreshments are coffee, chocolate, tea, and sandwiches, with mixed liquors and fermented beverages. After market-hours there are ordinaries for the country factors, masters of coasting corn-vessels, and other persons of that class and rank in life.[1]

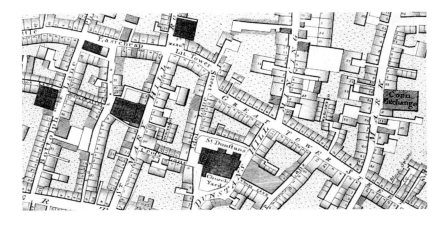

Castle Tavern.

No. 31, immediately facing the Corn Exchange, is the Castle Tavern.[2] Here are soups, [57] a larder of cold joints, and an ordinary on market-days at two-o'clock, and on other days at four o'clock.

MINCING LANE.

In Mincing Lane, attached to that noble edifice lately erected for the sale of all colonial produce, is a coffee-house. Since the proprietors of it have accommodated the commissioners of the customs with these premises for a

[1] The *Almanack*'s description of the **Corn Exchange Coffee House** and the **Corn Factors' Coffee House** (sometimes known as **Jack's Coffee House**) as 'up a flight of steps, on either side of the Corn Exchange' was echoed by David Pugh in 1817: the Exchange was 'a plain building two stories high, containing two coffee-houses, to which there are ascents by a flight of handsome stone steps on each hand' (pp. 38-39; the stairs can be seen in a 1753 engraving of the Exchange (London Metropolitan Archives)). In the late 1820s a new Corn Exchange was built next to the old one, which was itself extended and partly rebuilt in 1827, but the coffee houses seem to have survived the renovations (see Lillywhite nos. 299 and 301).

[2] The **Castle Tavern** would have been on the west side of the street, facing the Corn Exchange.

temporary Custom-House, the tavern business is added to that of the coffee-house for the accommodation of persons attending at that office.[1]

TOWER STREET.

No. 54, in Tower Street, is Wood's justly celebrated Eating-House. The dining-rooms are fitted up in a remarkable neat style. Perhaps the best proof of the superiority of the fare served up in them, is the great number of guests who daily resort thither. Some hundreds of respectable gentlemen belonging to the Custom-House, the Auxiliary Excise on Tower Hill, the Office of Ordnance, and other departments in the Tower itself, form the main body of its customers; a body that perhaps could no where so conveniently, and [58] so fully be fed as here. The joints, with vegetables, are served up per plate. A good dinner may be had here at fifteenpence and upwards, to three and sixpence. The latter price would include mock-turtle, bread, porter, pudding or tart. Mr. Wood is particularly celebrated for his mock-turtle; several tureens full of it are constantly to be seen in his window exposed, and on sale. In another shew-window are drest hams, tongues, and other eatables of that class; and round his shop, or rather library, the epicure may amuse himself by looking over a series of real dairy fed pork of the latest edition during the season. In summer Mr. Wood is particularly fortunate in having an attentive waiter, his brother-in-law, we believe, who conducts and regulates the dining manœuvres with the least possible bustle.* In that sweet season of love, also, Mr. Wood exhibits in his window a number of fine, lively, amiable turtle – fit to draw even the car of Venus with four insides, Cupid, Bacchus the jolly god, old Vulcan, and Jove himself.[2]

* His diligence does not go unrewarded, as his annual perquisites are supposed to exceed £500.

---

[1] The 'edifice lately erected' in Mincing Lane was the London Commercial Sale Rooms, built in 1811 to provide a venue for the sale of sugar, cotton, and other colonial produce, and destroyed by enemy action during the Second World War. The establishment described here is presumably Lillywhite no. 750, the **London Commercial Coffee House**, at no. 36 Mincing Lane, east side.

[2] **Wood's Eating House**, at no. 54 Great Tower Street, north side, was run by William Wood, who advertised his 'fine large green' turtle in *The Times* (see above, pp. xlix-l).

New Excise Coffee-House.

At the corner of Water Lane, Tower Street, is the New Excise Coffee-House, where soup and other refreshments are to be had.[1]

[59] Commencing our progress into Wapping from the Tower, we come to a decent house, facing Iron Gate Stairs, which is called the Iron Gate Eating-House, kept by Mr. Keates, from the Antwerp Tavern. Here, as at other places of entertainment in this quarter, hot dinners are to be had from noon till four o'clock.[2]

Within a few doors of this is the Tower of London Eating-house, with dinner at the usual hours, and soups always ready. Here are good accommodations up stairs.

Soon after passing Hermitage Bridge,[3] we come to the Blacksmiths' Arms Tavern and Coffee-house, No. 28, Mr. G. Edey. Here is an ordinary daily at half-past one, and accommodations for passengers by the Berwick and other Smacks.

No. 26, near Burr Street, is Surguy's Eating-house, with a decent public-room up stairs.

At the Cock and Lion, facing Goodwyn's Brewhouse, repasts are dressed to order, and a family dinner is served up daily at two o'clock. Here also are accommodations for passengers by the smacks to Scotland.

[1] I have found no record of a **New Excise Coffee House** at the corner of Tower Street and Water Lane, but it is possible that the *Almanack* was referring to the King's Head Tavern and Excise Coffee House at the corner of Tower Street and Tower Hill (Lillywhite no. 688).

[2] Iron Gate Stairs lie just under the late C19 Tower Bridge; the 'decent' **Iron Gate** eating house was probably on the north side of St Katharine's Way, and the **Tower of London** a few doors farther along the same street.

[3] From St Katharine's Way the *Almanack* makes a quick detour into Lower East Smithfield, just north of the large brewery marked on the 1799 Horwood map as Goodwyn, Skinner & Thornton's Brewhouse and on the 1813 map as the Red Lion Brewhouse. Here we find the **Blacksmiths' Arms** (possibly later known as the Albion Tavern), **Surguy's Eating House**, the **Cock and Lion** (still operating in 1891), **St Andrew's Tavern**, and the **Inverness Arms** (both still in business in 1841). Much of the nearby area, including more than a thousand houses and the C12 church and hospital of St Katharine, was cleared in 1825 for the building of St Katharine's Dock (closed 1968; now St Katharine's Marina); the timber frame of the brewery, reused in a later warehouse building, survives as the Dickens Inn of *c.* 1974-76 (see *BoE East London*, p. 505).

The St. Andrew's Tavern, No. 93, has similar accommodations; and commands a pleasant prospect of the river from its principal [60] rooms. Here dried fish may be had in great perfection.

No. 8, on the other side, is the Inverness Arms, where also passengers by the smacks are accommodated with bed and board.

Three public-houses, respectively denominated – the King of Denmark, the Duke of Argyle, and the Ship and Pilot, situated within a few doors of each other, all announce bed and board for passengers and sea-faring persons. At the Duke of Argyle's there is a billiard table.[1]

Near the church is a house called – the Town of Ramsgate Ale and Chop-house, where soups or a hasty dinner may be had. Below the church, No. 103, is the Gun Tavern, a house of similar description.[2]

No. 251, is the Dundee Arms Tavern, &c. an excellent house, where a larder is kept, and dinners are to be had in comfortable style. This house the opposition tilt-boats sail from, and arrive at, every tide. Here are several pleasant rooms, and awnings next the river, with a convenient jutty-head for embarking or landing.[3]

Turning up Gravel Lane we come to Ratcliffe Highway, where at No. 123, near the church called St. George's in the East, is Lee's Eating-house, which is of rather a superior class, having a good exposed larder on [61] one hand,

[1] Having returned to St Katharine's Way, our guide crossed the bridge over Hermitage Basin (the beginning of a small canal leading north to the new West India Docks) and entered Wapping High Street, where he visited the next six establishments mentioned. On the north side were the **King of Denmark** at no. 24 and the **Ship and Pilot** at no. 27, with the **Duke of Argyle** probably between them.

[2] On the south side of the High Street the c18 **Town of Ramsgate** at Wapping Old Stairs (no. 288; now no. 62) still remains, as does another establishment overlooked by the *Almanack*, the **Prospect of Whitby**, rebuilt in the c18 on the site of a c16 tavern. Pub historians tend to identify the Town of Ramsgate as the successor to the Red Cow, where the famous 'hanging judge' George Jeffreys was captured in late 1688, but that establishment seems to have been in Anchor and Hope Alley, near King Edward's Stairs (see *ONL*, ii:136). It is also sometimes suggested that the Town of Ramsgate was earlier known as the Prince of Denmark, but this may result from a confusion with the King of Denmark. The **Gun Tavern** at no. 103 (now no. 75) on the north side of the street, facing Gun Dock, survived into the c20.

[3] The **Dundee Arms** – farther east, at no. 252 on the south side – is known as a Masonic meeting place in the mid-c18. Tilt boats were large rowing boats covered by a tilt, or canopy, used for transporting passengers and goods between London and Gravesend.

and hot joints on the other.[1] Farther onwards to Wellclose Square is the Ship and Eight Bells Public-house, No. 131, kept by Mr. Mansell, where chops and steaks are drest to order, and an appropriate dining-room is kept.

No. 147 is a respectable eating-house, having in its window a good choice of cooked hams, poultry, and other viands.

Near St. Dunstan's in the East, and nearly facing the gates of the London Docks, is the Dog and Shepherd Tavern.[2] Beneath it there is a Subterranean Tap and Gin Dispensatory, frequented by sailors of every nation, and by lady abbesses and nuns from St. Catherine's, with eyes of every hue. Stillness is certainly not among the characteristics of this retreat, and, whatever be the fare up stairs, the guests who repair thither to partake of it, must expect now and then to be greeted with the distant murmurs of a storm in these lower regions of smoke and darkness.

In Ship Alley, a very considerable thoroughfare leading into Wellclose Square, is the London Dock Eating-house, kept by Messrs. Wilson and Co. Facing this long-established and well-conducted house, is a very respectable pastry-shop.[3]

In Grace's Alley, leading from the opposite angle of Wellclose Square into Wells Street, [62] are two contiguous rival houses, where good dinners and other refreshments may be had. The first (Wallis's) called the Royalty Eating-house and Stranger at Home, has an excellent larder of meats and poultry, with soups, tarts, &c. always ready. Tea and coffee may also be had

[1] Leaving Wapping High Street, our guide travelled north along Old Gravel Lane (now Wapping Lane) and turned west into the Ratcliffe Highway, later described by Thomas De Quincey as then 'a most dangerous quarter', where 'every third man at the least might be set down as a foreigner' and 'manifold ruffianism' was the rule ('Three Memorable Murders', 1854). **Lee's** eating house was at the top of Old Gravel Lane, just below the church of St George in the East; the **Ship and Eight Bells** was a few doors to the west, and the 'respectable house' at no. 147 still farther west, just past Cannon Street.
[2] In locating the **Dog and Shepherd Tavern**, the *Almanack*'s St Dunstan is a slip for St George; 'nearly facing the gates of the London Docks' suggests something south of the Highway, perhaps along Old Gravel Lane or Pennington Street. The Dog and Shepherd – or at least its Subterranean Tap and Gin Dispensary – was clearly a dubious establishment: abbesses and nuns were cant terms for procuresses and prostitutes.
[3] Ship Alley ran northwest from the Highway to the respectable **Wellclose Square**, home to a number of sea captains; Grace's Alley left the square at the northwest corner and led into Well Street (now Ensign Street).

here.[1] The business of the other house, No. 6, is rather confined to drest hams, tongues, beef, &c. In this alley there is also an excellent pastry-shop, and a shell fish and oyster warehouse.

On turning out of Wells Street into Rosemary Lane we enter upon the precincts of the celebrated Rag Fair,[2] which is held at the end of this lane nearest the Tower every afternoon, almost every house being either a second-hand clothes shop, or a victualling shop, except here and there a domicile occupied by an artist who shaves, bleeds, and extracts teeth on the easiest terms, or perhaps by one of the many rivals of Dr. Cerf, the Hermes of Rag Fair. The symbol of these medical practitioners, is a blind Cupid holding in one hand a wounded heart, and in the other a box of Mercury's antidotes, the

[1] The **Royalty Eating House** undoubtedly catered to the patrons of the Royalty Theatre in Well Street, which opened in 1787 and burned down in 1826.

[2] At the junction of Well Street and Cable Street our guide turned back toward the City, travelling along Cable Street as it became Rosemary Lane (since 1850 Royal Mint Street). Near the Tower – just west of modern Mansell Street, then called Little Prescot Street and earlier Rosemary Branch Alley – he came upon **Rag Fair**, principally known as a secondhand clothes market. Here, among the dubious surgeons and 'ambulating tailors', one could purchase pies, soup, puddings, and other portable foodstuffs; those who preferred to sit down could call in at the eating house in nearby Queen Street – or, nearer the new Mint (opened in 1809 on the site of a former tobacco warehouse), visit **Bushe's**.

pil. hydrarg.[1] Among the singular groups in Rag Fair, are to be seen ambulating tailors and mantua-makers, as well as peripatetic restaurateurs, of whom may be purchased hot soup, baked faggots, grey peas boiled, and peas-pudding. The flying pyeman [63] also occasionally attends with his tarts and his pudding, which he serves out at a penny a slice hot. Bakers attend the fair with stale loaves, which they sell at a considerable discount from the assize price. In short, this is the place where one half the world may form some idea as to how the other half lives.

In Queen Street, adjoining Rag Fair, there is an Eating-house for the accommodation of those who choose to sit down to dinner rather than take it walking or standing.

Facing the New Mint is Bushe's long-established Eating-house, which continues to be much frequented by a company rather numerous than select, as may be inferred from the tenour of a regulation put forth by the host, which prohibits females, and of a certain class, from dining at the gentlemen's tables, and enjoins them to take away whatever viands they purchase.

No. 72, Minories, is a very neat, cleanly, and long-established Tripe-shop, where all the usual articles belonging to this branch of trade are sold. No. 56 is a large Cook's-shop and Eating-house, which has for years maintained the reputation of selling good provisions.

[64] Returning into the city we direct our readers to a few good houses for dining, and which we before omitted, merely because they did not lie immediately in our track or course.

Clement's Lane, Frederick Wolf.

In Clement's Lane, at No. 17, lives Frederick Wolf, Cook, from Mr. Birch's of Cornhill. In sallad time you will here be reminded of Æsop's comical fable of the wolf and the lamb. The shewboard announces that turtles also, and made dishes are cooked, whether they be abroad or at home, or, again, they are sent out to order.

---

[1] Three broadside advertisements for Dr Cerf's services survive from the last decade or so of the c18: living near Tower Hill, he claimed to be able to cure all kinds of diseases, including the 'secret disease', or syphilis, which was commonly treated with mercury pills (pil. hydrarg.).

Hine's Ham, Beef, and Tongue-Shop.

At No. 14, in Clement's Lane, is Hine's Ham, Beef, and Tongue Shop. Here, therefore, if you like to lay in a supper while dining, you may hold your tongue while you eat your ham. The ham, beef, and tongues, are to be had either dressed, or in the simple state of nature. Here are Westphalia hams, with reindeer's and other foreign lingoes; some of them speak good Russ, and other High Dutch. This is a pleasant way of acquiring the power of conversing with our continental allies, for [65] you at the same time imbibe their taste, and gratify your own.

Basing Lane, Gerard's Hall.

Gerard's Hall Inn and Tavern, in Basing Lane, (kept by James Watts, from that celebrated university the London Coffee-House) has a larder and accommodations dedicated to, and constructed chiefly for, the use of travellers and factors from the western parts of England, who deal in woollens, gloves, and other commodities, the produce of that famous part of the British empire. This is one of the oldest inns in London.[1] The effigy affixed at the door, and some internal remains (some intestines, professionally speaking) of the original hall, or *salle à manger* as the French say, have furnished subjects for prints, wherewith to enrich the cabinets of antiquaries, and impoverish their pockets. They have also operated as inducements for the curious to visit the premises. If the curious be disappointed in their hope of satisfying their cravings after antiquities, it will be their own fault if they go away with the additional craving for a good dinner.

[66]

Bush Lane, Cannon Street.

In Bush Lane, Cannon Street, is an establishment on a plan rather novel. Gentlemen are, to a certain limited number, accommodated with a good family dinner every day, with the exception of Sunday, at the moderate rate of twenty pounds per annum, or, at a proportionate charge, by the month or

---

[1] **Gerard's Hall Inn** at no. 3 Basing Lane, near Bread Street, was built on the foundations of an ancient hostelry destroyed in the fire of 1666, which John Taylor referred to as 'the Crowne (or Jarrets Hall)' in his *Carriers Cosmographie* of 1637. The inn had been rebuilt by 1676, when it was shown on Ogilby and Morgan's map; it closed in 1852 and the superstructure was dismantled prior to the extension of Cannon Street.

week. That the party may be kept select, none are admitted without an introduction by one or more of the boarders.

Having passed through the city by the principal streets and the avenues on the right-hand side of those streets; we do now, for the benefit of those who may choose to take the left, also take that part, having left it expressly with this very design.

Some choose bye passages to avoid the bustle of the high street, or in hot weather to avoid the sun; or again on the supposition of stealing a march on old time, and distancing him.

We begin this tour by turning down St. Martin's Le Grand, which parish, by some quirk or old usage, or fiction of law, though an integral part we might suppose of the city of London, belongeth to that of Westminster, and sends voters to Covent Garden, at a general election.[1]

[67] A little way down is an Eating-house, with dining-rooms up stairs, where meat is served up at moderate price per plate.

Aldersgate Street, Castle and Falcon.

The Castle and Falcon Tavern, Coffee-House and Hotel, No. 4 and 5, in Aldersgate Street, is a large establishment in front of the street. It is distinct from the Inn, and has every thing requisite for giving the very best entertainment.[2]

FALCON SQUARE.

Facing Noble Street, Falcon Square, is a decent, long-established eating-house, with a dining-room up stairs. Here roast and boiled meats are served up by the plate on reasonable terms.[3]

[1] The next two establishments were north of St Paul's, in St Martin's Le Grand and its continuation Aldersgate Street.
[2] The **Castle and Falcon** was on the east side of the street, just north of the junction with present-day Gresham Street; the inn behind the coffee house is shown on maps from Ogilby and Morgan onward, but had disappeared by Thornbury's time (*ONL*, ii:227).
[3] The now-vanished Falcon Square was just east of Aldersgate Street, at the north end of Noble Street.

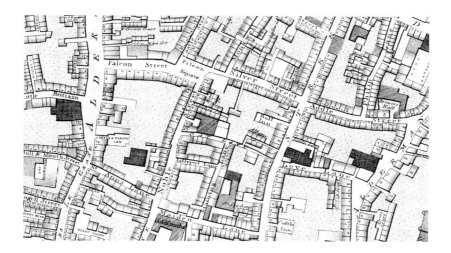

No. 28, Noble Street, Spanish Chocolate.

At No. 28, Noble Street, Spanish Chocolate, warranted to be manufactured by a native, is sold by Mrs. Severin.

Bell Tavern Inn, Mr. J. Linfett.

At the Noble Street-corner of Oat Lane, Mr. J. Linfett keeps the Bell Tavern, an old [68] established and good house for steaks and chops.[1] It is, *classically* speaking, a superior kind of public-house, famous for ales, &c. A few years ago, a company of *sober* citizens met here to drink their wine or ale. They called themselves the knights of the square caps. Round the room hung a number of square caps, like those worn by students at the universities, with gold tassels. To be entitled to the honour of wearing one of these caps, the candidate must take hold of a massive ring that hung in the centre of the room from the bell. He must swing it round in a certain direction, and hang it three successive times on a cloak-pin in the wainscoat. Having achieved this, he was admitted a member. With some, a course of a month or two's practice was requisite to acquire dexterity for the feat.

[1] **Mrs Severin's** Spanish chocolate emporium was at the top of Noble Street, and the **Bell Tavern** farther south, at the corner of Oat Lane. There are numerous references to the tavern in Old Bailey proceedings, the earliest being 12 October 1743, but it too was gone by the time Thornbury wrote.

WOOD STREET.

In Wood Street, near Maiden Lane, is the Angel and Crown Tavern and Chop-House, kept by J. Birmingham. Here are soups always ready; an excellent larder and good accommodations. There is an entrance to the house from Maiden Lane.[1]

[69]

LAD LANE.

We will now pay our respects to Mr. Dewhurst, the proprietor of that far-famed establishment the Swan with Two Necks, Lad Lane.[2] All persons who recollect the deplorable disorder of things during the time of Williams, his predecessor, will, on contrasting it with the neatness, regularity, and comfort, which are now diffused throughout every department of the hotel, pronounce Mr. Dewhurst as well worthy of an equestrian statue in the centre of the yard, as king William the Third was of that in the pond in St. James's Square. The Swan with Two Necks is now a first rate tavern, hotel, and coffee-house; its bills of fare comprehend the best of every thing in season, and its port and claret are worthy of being called superb. The numerous mail and stage-coaches which put up here, though they necessarily cause a little annoyance at times, constitute in other respects one of the greatest conveniences of the place; and the situation, in the very heart of the city, is certainly not one of the least. The establishment is on such a scale that it can accommodate parties of any number, from two persons to three hundred. The coffee-room is spacious, well lighted, and tastefully fitted up; soups, hot and cold lunches [70] are to be had here at any hour; dinners to order, from three o'clock until the departure of the mails. There are two detached rooms beyond the bar, the one called the Liverpool; the other the Manchester: in the latter many natives of the county palatine of Lancaster meet to pass their evenings.

---

[1] The **Angel and Crown** was on the west side of Wood Street, at the corner of Maiden Lane (now part of Gresham Street), and again we find a 1743 Old Bailey reference to the tavern.

[2] Modern Gresham Street has absorbed Lad Lane, where at no. 10, on the north side, was the **Swan with Two Necks**, a well-known coaching inn built shortly after 1666 to replace the C16 establishment destroyed in the Great Fire. In the early C19 it was one of the most important starting points for mail coaches leaving London, with underground stabling (added 1825) for some two hundred horses. The Swan was demolished in 1856, and today the site is occupied by Barrington House, nos. 59-67 Gresham Street (see Charlton 1987).

Baptist's Head.

The head of St. John the Baptist stands near the corner of Aldermanbury, and of course invites you into a tavern, where you may feed on something more to your palate than the produce of the desert. There is another entrance in a passage connecting Cateaton Street with the court before Guildhall.[1] This is a good house, and is well frequented by gentlemen of the law, and by merchants. The commissioners of bankrupt, in most of their summonses for private examinations of bankrupts, appoint this house as the place of meeting.

Guildhall Coffee-House.

The Guildhall Coffee-House is much upon the same scale, and of the same character as the preceding. Merchants as well as lawyers frequent it.[2]

[71]

Old Jewry Eating-House.

In Cateaton Street, at the corner of Old Jewry, is the Old Jewry Eating-House.[3] It is a licensed public-house, with an excellent larder attached to it, and good accommodations up stairs.

Three Tuns, Coleman Street.

The Three Tuns, No. 37, Coleman Street, kept by Mr. F. Lench, is a large public-house, with dining-rooms up stairs. Its larder has a constant supply of steaks and chops, with joints occasionally.[4]

---

[1] A little north of Lad Lane, at no. 2 Aldermanbury, west side, was the **Baptist's Head Coffee House** (also known as the **Aldermanbury Coffee House**), in business at least since the 1750s. I have found no listing for it after 1834.

[2] The **Guildhall Coffee House** stood on the northeast corner of King Street and Cateaton (now Gresham) Street, just south of Guildhall and facing the church of St Lawrence Jewry. The coffee house was known as early as the 1690s, but from the 1830s was listed as a tavern; it is prominent on the Ordnance Survey map of 1873 and there is an early C20 photograph in the London Metropolitan Archives.

[3] The **Old Jewry Eating House** would have been on the south side of Cateaton Street.

[4] The **Three Tuns** was just at the bottom of Coleman Street on the west side, with **Newman's** opposite it.

Newman's.

No. 44, Coleman Street, is Newman's Beef-Steak and Chop-House, a small, but very decent establishment, very civilly conducted.

Lothbury, Black Swan.

In Whalebone Court, Lothbury, the Black Swan Chop and Dinner-House is kept by Mr. R. Derrill. It is a large house, with good accommodations.[1]

THROGMORTON STREET.

Immediately adjoining the Auction Mart is the Auction Mart Coffee-House, in Throg- [72] morton Street, kept by Mr. Holdsworth. The coffee-room is large, and fitted up in very neat style. Here soups, and the usual coffee-house refreshments, are served up.[2]

Excise Coffee-House, Broad Street.

In Broad Street, No. 56, directly facing the Excise Office, is the Excise Coffee and Chop-House.[3] This house gives hasty dinners and luncheons to persons who belong to the Excise Office, and others who have business there. During the three or four days following each quarter day, this house does a wonderful deal of business; as all the officers and clerks then receive their salaries, and at this house arrange their personal affairs. For the prevention of any inconvenient association and confusion, there are an inner and an outer room.

[1] The configuration of the neighbourhood in which the **Black Swan** was located changed radically with the building of Moorgate (begun 1835), but in 1815 Whale-bone Court was a narrow inlet running north from Throgmorton Street, just east of Token House Yard.

[2] The **Auction Mart**, on the southeast corner of Throgmorton Street and Bartholomew Lane, was designed to take over some of the auction business previously conducted in coffee houses. It opened in March 1810 and the coffee room was in operation from the start, but seems to have disappeared by mid-century; there is an illustration in John Papworth's *Select Views of London* (1816). The Auction Mart itself – where in 1847 Shakespeare's Stratford house was sold – moved to new premises in Token House Yard in 1866.

[3] In Old Broad Street the **Excise Coffee House** was on the west side, a few doors south of Great Winchester Street; the Excise Office itself moved to Somerset House around 1848.

TEMPLE BAR.

We commence our examination of that part of the city which lies west of St. Paul's, at Temple Bar, near which, at No. 16, Fleet Street, south side, we find the neat shop of Messrs. Groom and Pellat, who manufacture and sell every requisite article of confectionery, for deserts [*sic*] and rout-entertainments. All the [73] articles are good, and of the most novel device, as the reader or passenger may judge, (if he will not take our word) by a mere glance of his eye at the window as he passes.[1]

Mitre Tavern, Mitre Court.

Proceeding on the south side of Fleet Street, we turn down Mitre Court, and there find three houses of entertainment for gentlemen. The first is the Mitre and Hope Chop House and Tavern. Its good things (and its window contains many, and very novel ones every day) are served up by bill of fare, from box to box, at the regular dining hours for gentlemen in an afternoon, or to order when gentlemen please. Need we here say that Dr. Johnson and Boswell were, at one period of their lives, every evening "at the Mitre." (See Boswell's Life of Johnson).[2]

---

[1] The **Groom** family were established at no. 16 Fleet Street, south side, by the late C18, if not earlier, and by 1850 the confectionery shop had expanded into a coffee house, still popular with lawyers and journalists in the 1930s (Burke 1937, p. 63). The narrow premises were damaged in the Second World War, and since 1945 have housed a succession of bookshops.

[2] Mitre Court (now Old Mitre Court) runs south out of Fleet Street west of Serjeant's Inn, with the entrance between nos. 44 and 45. Described by Strype in 1720 as 'a pretty open Place […] much taken up by Publick Houses' (1.3.277), it takes its name from the C17 **Mitre Tavern** that stood in Fleet Street between Mitre Court and Ram Alley just to the east (= Ram Court on the Horwood map). This Mitre, famous as the haunt of Johnson and Boswell, ceased to function as a tavern in the late C18, and was pulled down in 1829 for the expansion of Hoare's Bank; a plaque marks the site at no. 37. A different Mitre, usually referred to as a coffee house, is known from 1702 (see Lillywhite no. 827), and may be represented by the Mitre Tavern shown by Rocque in 1746 on the west side of Mitre Court. The *Almanack's* **Mitre and Hope Chop House and Tavern**, however, is neither of these – and certainly not the scene of Dr Johnson's dinners – and I can find no other mention of it.

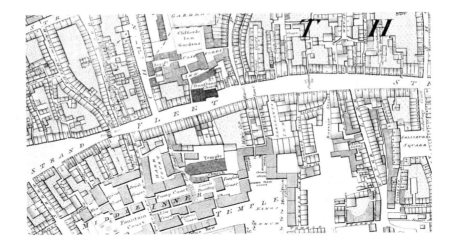

Joe's Coffee-House and Tavern,
Brown's Coffee-House and Tavern.

Lower down in Mitre Court are the other two houses we mentioned: Joe's, and Brown's.[1] Each is a coffee-house and tavern. Joe's is kept by Mr. Scriven, and Brown's by Mr. Maskin. Both houses keep good soups and a larder; and each is conducted on the same [74] plan as the taverns in Devereux Court, which we shall enter upon, when we are called to the Bar (Temple Bar), and thence to the said Devereux Court, and all the higher courts in Westminster, where either justice or a dinner is administered. These taverns are frequented by Templars and others, to whose chambers a dinner, or any other repast, if ordered, will infallibly be sent; with a waiter (a dumb one if required) and every other article or noun *substantive*, signifying or importing comfort and refreshment.

[1]   **Joe's Coffee House** at no. 8 Mitre Court was in business before 1744, and was still listed in directories in 1833. Most authorities agree that not long after the 1829 demolition of the Mitre in Fleet Street Joe's took over the old name; this 'spurious "Mitre Tavern"', as Thornbury calls it, seems to have continued into the C20 (Rogers 1928, p. 132, noting that it 'still exists'). **Brown's Coffee House** at no. 7 is known at least from the 1690s, but was probably out of business by the 1830s.

Clifford's Inn Passage.

The Crown Tavern and Chop-House in Clifford's Inn Passage, is kept by Mr. Bowen, late of the Cock, near Temple Bar. Here is an ordinary daily at four o'clock, which is in general very well attended by gentlemen attached to the profession and execution of the law, and by others who have legal business to transact. The house is noted for its wines, spirits, and Burton ale, as well as for its good cooking. A steak or chop may be had to order, at almost any hour of the day. Whether or not this tavern be a rendezvous for the red-tail knights and their esquires, we cannot state, and are not at all interested in ascer- [75] taining; that being a matter entirely beyond our province.[1]

Three Tuns, Fetter Lane.

The Three Tuns, in Fetter Lane, must not be passed unnoticed, for it is a superior public-house, long famed for giving good dinners. It is frequented chiefly by gentlemen in the law. An ordinary is announced every day at two o'clock. It faces the gateway into Clifford's Inn, and its larder is seen in the passage.[2]

Horse Shoe and Star, Fleet Street.

Just after passing St. Dunstan's Church in the west, we are struck with the Horse-Shoe and Star; therefore, being kicked and planet-struck, we must halt perforce. Geoffrey Chaucer, when a Templar, was fined two shillings for beating a Franciscan friar in Fleete Streete, nigh unto this hostel. The two shillings we hope was spent by the poet and the frere together at the Crown and Star. Perhaps the pardoner was of the party. It continueth to be famous for cooking, and serving up rump-steaks, chops, cutlets, kidneys, and sausages. The house is much frequented by respectable company. Here is held Lodge No. 2, of the knights of Trafalgar.[3]

---

[1] Clifford's Inn Passage, the site of the **Crown**, runs north from Fleet Street on the west side of St Dunstan's Church; the Inn itself was the first of the London Inns of Chancery, but most of the buildings were demolished in 1934.
[2] The **Three Tuns** was on the east side of Fetter Lane, facing the gateway into Clifford's Inn.
[3] The **Horse Shoe and Star** was on the north side of Fleet Street, just west of St Dunstan's. The Chaucer story, almost certainly an invention, derives from Thomas Speght's 1598 biography of the poet.

[76]

Cock, near Temple Bar.

How we came to think of the Cock, at Temple Bar, by daylight, we cannot tell. It has the best porter in London, fine poached eggs, and other light things, which are seldom called for before seven or eight in the evening. There are two good reasons for this: 1stly. The room at mid-day is almost as dark as Erebus, so that the blazing-faced Bardolph himself would hardly be able to quaff a tankard by the light of his own countenance. 2dly. The situation of the Cock is just half way between the heart of the city and the purlieus of Covent Garden and of Drury Lane, where there are two Theatres Royal for the enaction of plays by his majesty's servants. One box at the end of the room is occupied by a knot of sages, who admit strangers into their fraternity on being presented with a crown bowl of punch. Mine host of the Cock used to smoke his pipe among them nightly. Marsh, the oyster-man, attends here the whole season with his Native's, Milton's, and Pyfleet's: he hath the constancy of the swallow, and the dexterity of the squirrel in opening the shells.[1]

[77]

Richard's Tavern and Chop-House.

No. 8, Fleet Street, almost facing Chancery Lane, up a passage, is Richard's Tavern and Coffee-House. It is a very retired, comfortable, and highly respectable place; and is frequented by gentlemen of serious dispositions from the universities, on their occasional visits to town. Here sequestered they almost

---

[1]   The original **Cock Tavern** was in operation well before the Great Fire of 1666, and may go back to Elizabeth's reign; many of the furnishings, including a Grinling Gibbons overmantle, survived the fire and were incorporated in the rebuilt tavern at no. 201 Fleet Street, north side. The Cock was mentioned by Strype in 1720 as a 'noted Publick House', and its 'plump head-waiter' was immortalized in verse by Tennyson ('Will Waterproof's Lyrical Monologue', 1842). In 1924 Leopold Wagner (b. 1858) recalled the tavern as 'snug and comfortable to a degree […] with a very low ceiling, saw-dusted floor, tiny window panes, and boxes or pews topped by green curtains' (p. 86); the pews and curtains are clearly shown in John Crowther's watercolour of 1881 (London Metropolitan Archives). The Cock closed in April 1886, when the premises were acquired by the Bank of England and the building demolished; the original furnishings were saved from the wreckers and moved across the street to a new Cock Tavern at no. 22 Fleet Street, but in 1990 fire again destroyed part of the interior, and the establishment (now 'Ye Olde Cock') has since undergone yet another extensive refurbishment.

forget the *fumum et opes, strepitumque Romæ,* and transport themselves in fancy to the groves of Isis and of Cam.[1]

Rapsey's.

No. 41, South side of Fleet Street, is Rapsey's Shell-Fish Shop, with its oyster-rooms. Brawn is to be had here during the season, and an abundance of spruce, ginger-beer, soda, and other beverages.

Thomas's Eating-House, No. 33, Fleet Street, serves hot joints daily from twelve to five o'clock.

Peele's Coffee-House.

No. 177 and No. 178, Fleet Street, near Fetter Lane, form that large establishment universally known by the name of Peele's Coffee-house. It is much frequented by gen- [78] tlemen of the long robe and by travellers, as well as by advertisers in the public papers. Its refreshments are tea, coffee, punch, wine, newspapers, London and provincial, which are filed. These files may be referred to for years back by any gentleman, on paying to the waiter a moderate fee, not smaller than sixpence.[2]

Red Lion, Red Lion Court.

Up Red Lion Court is the chop-house of that name; a snug house, with a larder constantly good.[3]

[1] **Richard's** (or **Dick's**) Coffee House on the south side of Fleet Street was established in 1680, and a deed of that date, now in the Folger Shakespeare Library, provides a brief description of the property and names the founder as Richard Turver. Dick's continued in business as a coffee house *cum* tavern until 1885; later a restaurant, the building was demolished in 1899 (Chancellor 1912, p. 253). The Latin tag, which may be translated as 'the smoke, the grandeur, and the din of wealthy Rome', is taken from an ode by Horace.

[2] **Peele's Coffee House**, on the opposite side of the street, was established in 1715 and was particularly known for the newspaper files mentioned here, much consulted by writers and politicians, but sold off in 1878. Latterly usually listed as a hotel, Peele's was described by Thornbury in 1873 as having 'within the last few years […] been entirely rebuilt' (*ONL*, i:52); it seems to have closed around 1928.

[3] The entrance to Red Lion Court is between nos. 169 and 170 on the north side of Fleet Street, and the 'snug' **Red Lion** chop house may have been a descendant of the C16 tavern that gave the passage its name.

Golden Head, Three King's Court.

At the Golden Head, in Three Kings' Court, is a manufactory of portable soups, from meats of the best quality.[1] These soups are warranted to keep good for any length of time in any climate. This article of diet is very convenient for soldiers, travellers, domestic cooks in small families, old maids, and old bachelors. We are told that the French soldiers on a forced march, when they have not time to get hot water to melt their soup, and dissolve their biscuit, put a lump of their tablette into their mouth as a quid, and subsist upon it for an astonishing length of time.

[79]

Cheshire Cheese, Wine Office Court.

The first house on the right, in Wine Office Court, is the Cheshire Cheese,[2] kept in high order by Mr. John Calton, who now as host, reposes from his labours as waiter, which office he for many years filled in this house, with amazing dexterity and precision, to the universal satisfaction of all comers. Customers who have long *used* the house, meet of course with greater attention than strangers. The moment you enter, you give your order to the waiter, he calls to the cook below with the voice of a Stentor. So great is the afflux of diners to this house, between noon and six in the evening, that many persons find it convenient to call and order their dinner an hour or two beforehand, go out to transact business, and then on returning, their dinner is instantly served up smoking, and their porter foaming. The brandy, rum, and rack, vulgarly called gin, of this house, are pure and genuine: so is the wine.

[1] Three Kings Court, home to the **Golden Head**, is still used as an address by firms operating from the building at no. 150 Fleet Street, north side. For the portable soup described, see the Glossary.
[2] Wine Office Court runs north from Fleet Street between nos. 145 and 146; the tavern and chop house, expanded in the 1990s and still in business today as **Ye Olde Cheshire Cheese**, replaced a late C16 establishment destroyed in the Great Fire. *BoE City*, p. 501, notes that it 'originated as a pair of small late C17 houses, amalgamated and heightened probably in 1755', and adds that the bar, while 'most atmospheric', contains 'largely early to mid-C19 fittings'; Brandwood and Jephcote 2008 remark that 'some of the woodwork in the old bar […] might conceivably go back to […] the late 17th century' (p. 20). The tradition that Samuel Johnson was a regular customer can be traced back no further than hearsay of the 1820s (it is perhaps significant that the *Almanack* does not mention him), and certainly there is no foundation for believing that 'Dr Johnson's favourite chair', prominently displayed, was ever sat in or even seen by him.

Bolt in Tun, Bouverie Street.

A little way down Bouverie Street, on the right hand, will be found some very extensive modern built premises, attached to the Bolt [80] in Tun Inn, Fleet Street. These premises have acquired the title of the Bolt in Tun Tavern Hotel and Sussex House, and are kept by Mr. Croome.[1] Here is a larder constantly stored with the best things in season, with soups, and excellent restoratives to the stomachs of travellers and loungers.

Cooper's.

A few doors lower in Bouverie Street, is Cooper's Hotel and Tavern, with excellent accommodations for families, as well as single persons.[2]

Bird's Eating-House, Salisbury Square.

Lower down Fleet Street, we turn to the right into Salisbury Square, and then on scenting Bird's Eating-house, we cannot refrain from joining the strong current of customers who pour into it. In front is the larder and kitchen, where are constantly seen three or four men cooks busily employed. Simpson, who formerly kept this house, had a rider or forager, as we may call him, constantly travelling in quest of roasting-pigs and barn-door fowls.

Barley Mow.

Next door is the Barley Mow Public-house, [81] which some years ago, began cooking dinners in opposition to its neighbour, and on a cheaper plan. It is now become so noted, that two hundred or more persons dine in it daily.[3]

[1] The ancient **Bolt in Tun Inn**, a busy coach terminus, stood on the corner of Fleet Street and Bouverie Street; the establishment described here is listed in slightly later directories as occupying nos. 17-18 Bouverie Street, east side, under the name **Bolt in Tun Tavern and Sussex Hotel** (later simply the Sussex Hotel). The hotel had been pulled down by early 1883 (*Morning Post*, 8 January).

[2] **Cooper's** Hotel and Tavern at no. 15 Bouverie Street, east side, continued in business at least through 1838.

[3] Salisbury Square is just west of St Bride's church. At no. 135 was the **Barley Mow**, which in 1871 became the headquarters of the Society of Cogers, a convivial debating club founded in 1755; they continued to use the premises (completely rebuilt in 1937) until the pub – by then also called the Cogers – closed in the late 1960s.

Some time ago, a musical wit, accustomed to recruit his body here diurnally, reproved the waiter in the following distich, which was left for him on the table, and which the waiter picked up in lieu of his usual "penny-fee:"

"All is good that here they cater,
"But each guest is himself the waiter."

Crown and Sugar Loaf, Fleet Street.

The Crown and Sugar Loaf, near the bottom of Fleet Street, No. 99, on the right hand side, has greater claims on the notice of the passenger, than its humble ensign appears to assert.[1] You go up a passage into a small court, bounded on two of its sides by the bar and the coffee-room windows. Go in, and leave your orders as you pass the bar, proceed into the coffee-room, which is elegantly fitted up and well furnished with the daily papers. The host has rooms up stairs for clubs and private parties; and very quiet neat bed-chambers for travellers and sojourners. His liquors and wines are good; add to which, [82] he is a rising young man, and deserves encouragement.

Great Bell of Oxford.

We omitted to mention the Great Bell of Oxford, a few doors above, formerly kept by Mr. Hallam, and now by Mrs. Garnet. This is a licensed public-house which dresses dinners to order; the beverages are good, and the charges moderate.[2]

[1] The Sugar Loaf, presumably the ancestor of the **Crown and Sugar Loaf**, is mentioned by Pepys and appears in a 1668 list of victuallers who 'doe sell Ale and Beere' (Rogers 1928, p. 148). Around 1846 the Crown and Sugar Loaf changed its name to the Punch Tavern, reflecting the popularity of the magazine of that name (founded 1841), whose staff were regulars at the establishment. Rebuilt in what *BoE* calls 'Neo-Jacobean' style in 1894-97 (*City*, p. 499), the pub has recently been divided into two distinct establishments, one facing Fleet Street and still known as the Punch Tavern and the other, opening into Bride Lane, refurbished in high Victorian style and renamed the Crown and Sugarloaf.

[2] The **Bell** is at no. 96 Fleet Street, south side, and since about 1840 has been known as the Old Bell; the *Almanack*'s 'Great Bell of Oxford' seems otherwise unrecorded as a name. *BoE* dates the front of the public house to 'shortly after 1897' (*City*, p. 499), but the rear of the building is late C17.

Saloop Shop and Coffee-House. Reid.

A few doors below is the noted Saloop and Coffee-house, where sober politicians may entertain themselves over their "cups which cheer, but do not inebriate," by perusing the daily papers, and the standard magazines for the last half century, which are here preserved in volumes.[1]

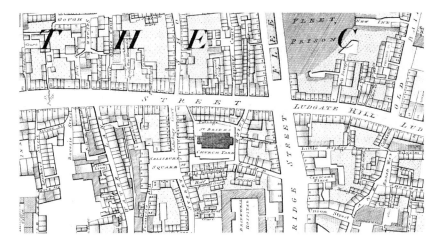

Anderton's.

We must now take a turn, and begin where we left off on the north side of Fleet Street. Anderton's Coffee-house claims our first regard.[2] It is an excellent house for a good dinner, ordered either from larder or by bill of fare; or again from prime joints sent round [83] from table to table at the ordinary

---

[1]   Thomas **Read's Saloop Shop** (no. 102 Fleet Street, south side) is described by Charles Lamb in his essay 'The Praise of Chimney Sweepers' (1822); for the drink itself, see the Glossary, but note that the 'cups that cheer but not inebriate' in William Cowper's poem 'The Task' contained not saloop, but tea. The saloop house seems to have been founded as Mount Pleasant by one Lockyer in the early c18 (see Lillywhite no. 848); later known simply as Read's Coffee House, it closed around 1833.

[2]   **Anderton's Coffee House** had established itself at no. 90 on the south side of Fleet Street by 1702, and in the 1790s moved across the street to no. 162, once the site of the ancient Horn Tavern. Anderton's was rebuilt in 1879 as a hotel, but this closed in 1939 and the building was then demolished; the site is now occupied by Hulton House (*The Times*, 22 April 1954 and 15 February 1957).

afternoon hours. The wines and accommodations are of the best. Many gentlemen from Scotland reside here during their visits to this southern metropolis of the empire.

Globe Tavern.

The Globe Tavern, No. 133, Fleet Street, is kept by Messrs. Tuckey and Bolt.[1] The edifice stands on the site of one of the oldest taverns in the city of London, and deservedly maintains the character of being a most excellent house. Here are soups and a larder at command. Joints of prime meat are sent round at the stated ordinary hours in the same style as at Anderton's.

Lynn's Oyster Rooms.

No. 145, Fleet Street, on the north side, are Lynn's Shell Fish Shop and Oyster Rooms. The best accommodations are up stairs. The beverages are excellent.

Epps's Ham and Beef Shop.

No. 117, is another of Epps's establishments for vending drest hams, tongues, rounds and flanks of beef, mock turtle soup in a port- [84] able state, Epping sausages, Bologna puddings, and other viands of that stamp and consistency. This is an excellent place of supply for any independent traveller, who going by mail or stage coach, does not like to depend on inns on the road, and dreads the heavy charges attending them. He may here lay in a stock, which though it scarcely occupies one pocket of his upper Benjamin, will serve him a day or two's journey with the help of some slight beverage, or tea occasionally.[2]

---

[1] The **Globe**, also on the north side of the street, is known as early as 1629 and was named by John Taylor in his 1636 *Taylors Travels*; it was destroyed in the fire of 1666 and rebuilt soon afterwards. The tavern is mentioned in Samuel Pepys's diary, and in the C18 Oliver Goldsmith is known to have frequented the Globe. The premises were altered and the entrance moved to Shoe Lane in 1829 (*The Times*, 21 March), but by 1873 the tavern was 'only a memory' (*ONL*, i:61).

[2] For **Epps's** shop, see above, p. 7. An upper Benjamin was an overcoat.

York Hotel, Bridge Street, Blackfriars.

In Bridge Street, Blackfriars, on the right hand side, at Nos. 10 and 11, is the York Hotel for gentlemen and families; nearly over the way, is the York Hotel and Coffee-house.[1] They are, we suppose one concern, and constitute a kind of chapel of ease to that metropolitan establishment, the London Coffee-house on Ludgate Hill, of which we shall soon have occasion to speak. As to the York Hotel we need not add, that the wines are peculiarly good, the accommodations in the first style, and the waiters well-bred. Many very respectable strangers, of course, board and lodge here, the situation being quite central in London.

[85]

FLEET MARKET.

On the east side of Fleet Market, there is a middling sort of eating-house, which serves hot joints from twelve to four o'clock.[2]

No. 53, on the West side of Fleet Market, is Munn's old established ready drest ham and beef shop. Its hams have a delicate appearance, for they are stripped of their rinds, and the knuckles are left on.

Rich's Pastry Shop.

On the south side of Ludgate Street, adjoining the Albion Fire Office, is Rich's famous Pastry Shop, where soups, savoury patties, and jellies, with ices in season, and pastry of every kind, are constantly supplied in the highest and most inviting condition. Mr. Rich is a considerable dealer in venison, and exposes at the proper season some of the finest forest haunches for sale.

Belle Sauvage.

You may dine well at either of the two excellent houses up the yard of the Belle Sauvage Inn. One is called the Bell Tavern, and the other the Belle Sauvage Tavern. [86] Mr. Shaw and Mr. Edwards, the respective landlords, vie with each other in exhibiting a well stocked larder. Both are well attended

[1] Opposite each other in New Bridge Street were the **York Hotel** (west side) and the **York Hotel and Coffee House** (no. 39 on the east side). The coffee room of the latter was particularly recommended by *Roach's London Pocket Pilot* (1793, p. 48) as 'the most elegant perhaps in England'.

[2] **Fleet Market** was removed in the late 1820s, and the site is now occupied by Farringdon Street (see below, pp. 243-44).

by travellers from many parts of the kingdom; and, perhaps, the better attended by some persons not travellers, because both these houses have the convenience of being within the rules of the Fleet Prison. The readers will understand, that persons who are obliged to make it convenient to take up their residence within those precincts, called rules of the Fleet, are themselves dignified by the title of rulers; not because they rule, but because they are ruled. We understand that the old sign of a savage, with a bell in his hand, is very properly pulled down; but the proper sign of a beautiful wild nymph, hath not hitherto been substituted. Numbers, however, of nymphs of that description, do nightly haunt the purlieus of Ludgate Hill.[1]

Dolphin Tavern and Chop-House.

We meet with a great variety of odd fish in London. Over the way here, on the south side of Ludgate Street, a Dolphin stares us in the face, and invites us up Dolphin Court into the Dolphin Tavern and Chop-house.[2] Its convenient accommodations and variety of provisions, attract a great number of custo- [87] mers, particularly from among the rulers of the Fleet Prison. In the winter evenings roasted potatoes are to be had here, served up with butter and pepper, at three-pence each.

[1] Like the original Cross Keys in Gracechurch Street, the galleried **Belle Sauvage** (or Bell Savage) Inn served as a theatre in the late C16; see Berry 2006, and for the later history of the property, Nowell-Smith 1958. The name most likely commemorates an early owner named Savage (a tenement known as 'Savagesynne', alias 'le Belle on the Hope', i.e. Hoop, is known on the site from the mid-C15), but popular histories continue to link the 'savage belle' with Pocahontas, who – at least in a C20 work of fiction – stayed there with her husband John Rolfe in 1616. The original Belle Sauvage was destroyed in the 1666 fire, but rebuilt by 1676 (Ogilby and Morgan map); the entrance was through an arch on the north side of Ludgate Hill, near present-day Limeburner Street, and Rocque's map shows the inn as abutting the back of the Fleet Prison. By the early C19 the Belle Sauvage was an important stage terminus, but it was almost derelict by mid-century and after 1857 had no license. Much of the site had by that time been developed as Cassell's publishing works; with the expansion of these in the 1870s the inn was pulled down, and the works themselves were destroyed by bombing in May 1941.

[2] Dolphin Court ran south from Ludgate Hill between nos. 11 and 12, and was described by Strype in his 1720 *Survey* as 'but small, having but one House, which is an Ale House, and hath the Sign of the Dolphin' (1.3.277). The **Dolphin Tavern** had disappeared by 1906, when J. Percy Simpson published what he described as 'a photograph from the [Edmund Garrett] Gardner Collection as it stood just prior to its demolition' (p. 22).

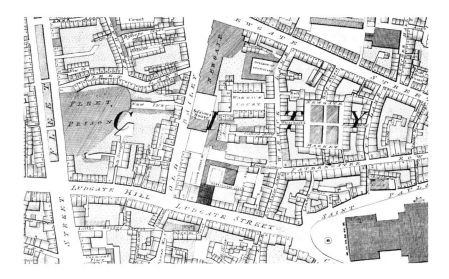

Williams, Old Bailey.

Let us no longer delay our visit to the celebrated boiled beef shop, No. 4, Old Bailey, formerly Mascer's, now Williams's.[1] So constant is the supply, and so uniformly good is the beef, so regular is the concourse of eaters, between the hours of one and five each day, and so punctually and speedily are they served, that the following motto, a little altered from Magna Charta, might very well serve for this refectory: *Nulli negabimus,* OMNIBUS *vendemus, nulli differemus repletionem stomachi.* Here small buttocks and flanks of beef, with vegetables, peas and rice puddings, fruit pies, &c. are in hot succession, and in quick cut, throughout the hours noted above. Perhaps this house furnishes more hasty dinners and hot lunches to men of business, than any other house

---

[1] In Old Bailey, the c18 Sessions House stood to the south of the old Newgate Prison; both were demolished in 1902 and replaced by the present Central Criminal Courts building. **Williams's** – whose boiled beef was 'renowned throughout Europe' according to G. A. Sala (*Things I Have Seen* (1894), ii:205) – was on the east side of the street, **Wheeler's** and the **Sessions' Eating House** on the west. Ralph Rylance's proposed Latin motto for Williams's establishment (roughly 'we will deny no one, we will sell to everyone, we will not delay the satisfaction of anyone's stomach') is adapted from a clause in Magna Carta: 'Nulli vendemus, nulli negabimus aut differemus, rectum aut justitiam', i.e. 'to no one will we sell, to no one deny or delay, right or justice'.

in London. An additional suite of rooms has lately been fitted up, where a variety of meats, roast as well as boiled, are to be had.

Wheeler's, late Oram's.

Wheeler's, late Oram's, stands opposite to [88] Williams's, and is opposed to it in rivalry as well as locality. Here roast as well as boiled is served, and the calf and sheep, as well as the ox and cow, are immolated to Epicurus, and distributed among his disciples. The charges at both these houses are very moderate.

Sessions' Eating-House.

Facing the Sessions House in the Old Bailey, is the Sessions' Eating-house, kept by the widow Milne. In the window may constantly be seen a plentiful supply of joints, roast and boiled, as well as pigs and sometimes geese, with pies and puddings. There is a decent room up stairs, in which is consumed a large quantity of the provisions above cited, particularly during the sittings of the criminal court. The passenger will not fail to observe on some of the panes in the shop window, masonic symbols and devices, painted with the following very legible and intelligible inscription underneath, in the name of the widow, "I deal on the square, I charge within compass, and we part on the level."

There are in the Old Bailey two or three more eating-houses, of and for the inferior order and lower class. Their principal business is to supply the poor prisoners, and those good Christians who visit them in prison.

[89]

Blue Last, Cock Court.

Opposite to the street, called Old Bailey, in Cock Court, leading from Ludgate Street in Broadway, Blackfriars, is the Blue Last Public-house, kept by Mr. Barker. A few years ago, this house supplied the famous Boiled Beef Shop in the Old Bailey with porter. Some misunderstanding arose between the landlord and mine host of the Blue Last, probably because the latter violated the adage, "*Ne sutor ultra crepidam.*" Mine host commenced cook in opposition to the boiler of beef, and being determined to keep him in hot water, converted his own upper rooms into a dining saloon, and soon succeeded in acquiring a considerable run of business, notwithstanding the start which the other had got. Dinners and lunches are here served up on moderate charges.[1]

London Coffee-House.

As we are no respecters either of houses or persons, Messrs. Leach and Dallimore of the London Coffee-House, will take it for granted that we mean no disparagement in mentioning them after two such humble caterers for the public, as those last mentioned. Our's is a court of justice, and we must adhere as strictly to the order of our circuit, as their lordships in the courts above. This London Coffee- [90] house is one of the first establishments in London; and in point of good wine, good beds, and good diet, perhaps, the very first. It is on a most magnificent scale; the accommodations elegant, and the company numerous and respectable. In the coffee-room dine a great number of small parties and single gentlemen daily. Up stairs the most sumptuous entertainments are frequently served up to large parties. To those persons who rarely visit such establishments, it is scarcely possible to conceive the quantity of plate, china, and other essentials, requisite for the conducting of this vast concern. The number of cooks, waiters, and domestics, as well as the order that reigns among them, are equally surprising and admirable. Almost all the British newspapers, and the most popular monthly journals are taken in; and the greatest facilities are afforded to the stranger for pursuing any plan he may conceive, either of business or pleasure, access and egress being available at all hours by the guests. In fact, you can no where so soon effectually domesticate yourself, so as to feel perfectly at home. At the bar of this favourite tavern, Rowley's British cephalic snuff has for many years been sold.[2]

[1] Cock Court (later St Martin's Court, then Ludgate Court, and now Pageantmaster Court) runs south from Ludgate Hill between nos. 18 and 19, just opposite Old Bailey; it feeds into Ludgate Broadway, and the address of the **Blue Last** is often later given as no. 1 Broadway, suggesting that it was a corner house. Known from the early C18, the Blue Last survived into the C20 in rebuilt premises, but was destroyed by enemy bombing in 1940. The Latin tag may be translated as 'Cobbler, stick to your last', meaning in this instance the selling of porter rather than the providing of hot dinners.

[2] The **London Coffee House**, prominent on the Horwood map at no. 24 Ludgate Hill, north side, was established in 1731 by James Ashley and was much used for Masonic meetings in the later C18; for Leech and Dallimore, see also p. 10 above. The coffee house quickly gained a reputation as one of the finest establishments of its kind, and in the C19 was particularly popular with Americans. It was closed in 1867 and demolished in 1872, being replaced by Ye Olde London public house,

AVE MARIA LANE.

At the corner of Ave Maria Lane, you [91] may halt a moment, and take a glass of capillaire in the old established pastry-shop, where soups, mock turtle, savoury patties, ices, and confectionary, in all their glory and splendour, with custards of the greatest delicacy, are daily offered up to the Hebes and Junos of the city.[1]

Crown Tavern, Stationers' Court.

In Stationer's Court, is the Crown Tavern and Chop-house, kept by Mr. J. Gadd.[2] It has an excellent exposed larder in front. You here regale yourself with chops, steaks, soups, broth, and as it is a licensed house with excellent porter and curious ales, all which good things derive additional relish from the civility and promptitude with which they are served up to you.

STATIONERS' HALL.

The Worshipful Company of Stationers have a large fair hall in Stationers' Court, where they meet and commune together on literary matters.

Sun Tavern, Ludgate Hill.

On the north side of Ludgate Hill, near St. Paul's, is the Sun Tavern and Literary [92] Chop-house. Why it should be called a literary chop-house, unless the terrible and venerable company of reviewers meet there to cut up books as well as chops, we know not. Mr. Twallin, late of the *Bell* Savage, who keeps it, perhaps does know; but of this we are doubtful, because reviewers,

---

which – after a brief incarnation in the early c21 as a gothic theme pub called the Bell, Book, and Candle – has recently returned to the Olde London name. Cephalic snuff was a 'medicinal' snuff, intended to cure or relieve disorders of the head.

[1] The pastry shop at the corner of Ave Maria Lane (no. 28 Ludgate Street, north side) was run by James and/or Thomas **Farrance** (see below, p. 92); for capillaire, see the Glossary.

[2] Stationers Court (earlier Stationers Alley, now Stationers' Hall Court) runs north from Ludgate Street – since 1865 part of Ludgate Hill – to the hall of the Worshipful Company of Stationers. The **Crown Tavern** at no. 7 should not be confused with another Crown in Ludgate Hill, known from the c18: this was further west, near Horseshoe Court (earlier Sword and Buckler Court).

like other great men, when on *private* business, are always *incog*. There is a *back* entrance into the Sun, from Stationer's Court, for the accommodation of those authors, who not having the fear of reviewers before their eyes, but possessing copy-money in their pockets, may boldly enter and challenge a chop with the great G— himself.[1]

We shall here terminate our city tour, leaving unexplored for the present, those secret and sacred haunts of the Muses, which are hallowed by their proximity to Paternoster-Row, Avemaria Lane, Creed Lane, and Amen Corner.

WESTMINSTER AND MARYLEBONE.

We arrive at St. Peter's Abbey in Westminster, and departing thence, we shall, as we did at St. Paul's, first notice the houses of refreshment in the immediate vicinity of this noble pile, and then proceed from it through [93] the principal streets, noticing their tributary streetlets to the right and left.

Exchequer and Oliver's Coffee-Houses, Westminster Hall.

Attached to Westminster Hall, are two old establishments, uniting the functions of coffee-house and tavern, the one called the Exchequer Coffee-house; the other Oliver's.[2] They vie with each other in the display of the larder. The

---

[1] The entrance to the **Sun Tavern** was up a passage at no. 31 Ludgate Street, north side, unnamed on the Horwood map, but referred to as Sun Tavern Court in an Old Bailey trial of 10 July 1805. The Sun was in use for Masonic meetings from 1740, and is usually described as a coffee house; it was still in business as late as 1853 (trial, 31 January). The 'great G—' mentioned here was almost certainly the powerful William Gifford, editor of the *Quarterly Review* from 1809 to 1824.

[2] The **Exchequer Coffee House** and **Oliver's** were located in New Palace Yard, the open area between Bridge Street and Westminster Hall. Both establishments at one time abutted the north wall of the Hall itself, but were moved to new premises in or adjacent to Bridge Street around 1793, when some of the buildings on the south side of the yard were demolished during improvements (Saunders 1951, p. 286). The Exchequer, known from the 1730s, was by the mid-C19 more often referred to as Fendall's Hotel (the *Almanack's* 'Tendall' is an error); Dickens mentioned the Exchequer in *Our Mutual Friend* (1864), but it was pulled down later in the same year, during improvements to the Westminster Bridge approaches (*The Times*, 25 August and 25 November). Oliver's was probably established at the end of the C17, and was still in business as late as 1857 (*The Times*, 31 October, 'foot of Westminster-bridge').

accommodations in both are excellent; so are the wines. The Exchequer is under the government of Mr. Tendall, and Oliver's is subject to Mr. Hillier. Their guests are numerous during the sittings of the courts of law and the high court of parliament. Here a private gentleman who has attended morning service in the abbey, after praying that all the nobility may be endued with grace, wisdom, and understanding, may say grace for himself over some of the best things, that bounteous heaven provides for our vile bodies. Before the improvements were executed in the avenues to the two houses of parliament, these two establishments were situated in front of Westminster Hall, and by their incongruous protrusion concealed some of the beauties of that venerable structure. It is a fact not generally known, that the stone effigy of one [94] of our Saxon kings was displaced, and the niche converted into a cupboard for bread and cheese. The head of another monarch, with its round and top of sovereignty, and the shoulders also, were unceremoniously knocked off to make headway and shoulder room up a strait staircase.

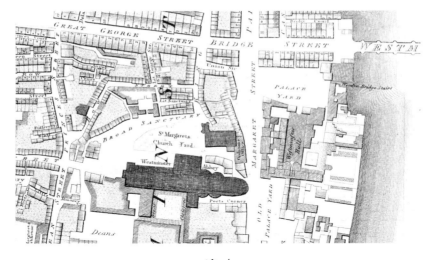

Alice's.

A passage at the farther end of the hall leads to Alice's Coffee-house, where according to the vulgar idea, most gentlemen of the long robe put on *some* of their wisdom with their wigs. The refreshments had here are limited to that simple diversity which is obtained in most coffee-houses. Up stairs are apartments exclusively devoted to the use of such members of parliament, as choose to regale there when off their legs. In the good old times, three houses of refreshment were attached to the hall, severally denominated Heaven, Hell, and Purgatory.[1] In the first, those litigants who had gained a cause, exultingly ate their dinners; whilst the losers grumbled in dudgeon over the good things in Hell. The desert [*sic*], mayhap, consisted of better fruit than those fair apples filled with dirt and ashes, which Satan's crew "with spattering noise rejected." They again, who waited the issue [95] of their causes, were promiscuously entertained with hopes, fears, and good cheer, in Purgatory. Over this latter house was suspended a large bell, which the landlord, on receiving a fee, would cause to give tongue and warn the lawyers to deserve their fees by using their tongues and lungs well for the cause of their clients, when it came on.

Bellamy and Kew.

In some apartments attached to the House of Commons, Messrs Bellamy and Kew, the housekeepers, have splendid apartments for the accommodation of the members or their friends.[2] Here may be had genuine delicacies of every description, hasty dinners, hot lunches, and evening beverages of tea and coffee. It is needless to say that the wines are of supreme quality, since Messrs. Bellamy and Kew are known to possess one of the amplest and best stocked caves in England.

King's Arms, Palace Yard.

The King's Arms, fronting Westminster Hall, has an entrance in Bridge Street, and another on the terrace in Palace Yard. It is a most respectable and old established house, where an excellent larder and a fine variety [96] of soups constantly invite the visitor. During the sessions of the courts, it

---

[1] **Alice's** seems to have been on the south side of Westminster Hall, in Old Palace Yard; it was established by the beginning of the C18, and was still in business in the mid-C19. Alehouses on the sites of **Heaven**, **Hell**, and **Purgatory** were in existence as early as 1485 (see *OEC*, pp. 7 and 9). 'Hell', where the author trusts that the food was superior to the ash-filled fruit eaten by the demons in Book 10 of *Paradise Lost,* was certainly known as a tavern as early as 1619, but was demolished during the improvements of 1793. A meal at 'Heaven' is mentioned in Samuel Pepys's diary entry for 28 January 1660; the building, along with that housing 'Purgatory', was pulled down around 1741, during the building of Westminster Bridge.

[2] Lillywhite suggests that **Bellamy's**, adjoining the House of Commons in Old Palace Yard, was established before the end of the C18; it had 'passed away' by 1875 (*ONL*, iii:502).

has much business. It has long been a custom here, that on every first day of term, a baron of beef be roasted, and cut from the spit during the sitting of the court. On this solemn occasion, many unlearned in the law, become solicitors at the bar for a slice, by way of imparting a glibness to the tongue; and many expectant baristers [sic] swallow now and then a morsel to keep the back bone from touching the merry-thought. The business of Mr. Henderson, the host, is not confined to the well-being of the lawyers; he has some very considerable parochial dinners holden and eaten in his house.[1]

Swan Tavern, Bridge Street.

The Swan Tavern in Bridge Street, Westminster, is a long established house, deservedly celebrated for the excellence of its fare.[2] It also has its share of the parochial and electioneering entertainments; and is much frequented by persons from the country and resident in Westminster, either on parliamentary or law business.

To demonstrate its capability of giving good cheer, suffice it to say, that the Right Honourable the Lord Mayor of London, holdeth here annually a court of conservancy.

[97]

Parliament-Street Coffee-House.

Parliament-street Coffee-house is, and has long been frequented by the inhabitants of the good city of Westminster, for the sake of its good dinners, and its well-flavoured wines.[3]

---

[1] The **King's Arms**, with entrances in New Palace Yard and Bridge Street, was in existence at least from 1743 to 1864, and was much used for political and Masonic meetings; there are two late-c18 illustrations of the house in *OEC*, p. 8.

[2] The **Swan**, at no. 10 Bridge Street, north side (corner of Canon Row), was built around the time of the opening of Westminster Bridge in 1750. It was a starting-point for post coaches to Dover and Canterbury, and was used for Masonic and other meetings during the c18. The Swan was rebuilt as St Stephen's Tavern in 1875; after being saved from demolition in the early 1990s the building was empty until December 2003, when the tavern, refurbished in high Victorian style, reopened.

[3] The **Parliament Street Coffee House**, mentioned in an Old Bailey trial of 13 April 1768, was at no. 16 Parliament Street, west side, just south of King Charles Street. It was later known as Holmes's Hotel and Harris's Hotel, but disappears from directories in the late 1830s.

Storey's Gate Coffee-House.

Near the entrance of St. James's Park, by Storey's Gate, is the Storey's Gate Coffee-house, a convenient place of resort for persons having business at the public offices in the vicinity, and for others who may have been inclined to view the monuments in the Abbey.[1]

KING-STREET, WESTMINSTER.

At each end of King-street, Westminster, is an Eating-house, established and carried on according to the usual plan of cutting from hot joints at a certain charge per plate, which is very reasonable. That at the end nearest the Abbey is perhaps one of the oldest Eating-houses in town.[2]

In accomplishing the late improvements in Westminster, the masons, or their pioneers, have swept away several houses of good fame and notoriety for good living. The Mitre Chop-house, in Union-street, is now no more; [98] and the Horn-tavern, in Palace-yard, has also succumbed.[3] It was for many years considered one of the best houses in Westminster. Our companion on this western tour once heard the following extraordinary order given as a supplement to a general dinner-order, on an occasion so melancholy that we must conclude that grief, which is generally allowed to make people dry, may occasionally whet the appetite for solid food also. A violent and sudden pull at the bar-bell brought out a waiter, who was despatched to the butcher's, in a stewing haste, to order ten pounds more of rump steaks for

[1] Until 1854 Storey's Gate stood at the west end of Great George Street, closing off the entrance to Bird Cage Walk; today Storey's Gate refers to the Princes Street of 1815, running south from Great George Street to Tothill Street. The **Storey's Gate Coffee House** is mentioned in an Old Bailey proceeding of 21 February 1753; Lillywhite records the address in the late 1830s as no. 26 Princes Street, west side.

[2] At this time King Street ran north from Great George Street to Downing Street (see above, p. xxx); *BoE Westminster*, p. 11, notes that there were some fifty-eight taverns in the street in the mid-C16, and it is possible that the establishment referred to here as 'one of the oldest Eating-houses in town' had its foundation in that century.

[3] Union Street, site of the lost **Mitre Chop House**, is shown on the Rocque map as connecting King Street with New Palace Yard. The **Horn Tavern** in Palace Yard is named in an advertisement of 1711 (*Daily Courant*, 20 September), and burnt down in 1797 (*True Briton*, 4 November; see also *OEC*, p. 7); the funeral of Benjamin Cooke, organist and master of the choristers at Westminster Abbey, took place on 21 September 1793.

Dr. Cooke's mourners. The mystery was, on enquiry of the lady at the bar, instantly solved. The good, the lamented, the harmonious Dr. Cooke, who for years had conducted the musical department in the choir of the Abbey, had himself been recently summoned to assist the celestial choir, and to hear "the lark at heaven's gate sing," while angels chaunted his far-famed canon *Amen*. His body was on this day to be interred. The gentlemen of the choirs of St. Peter and St. Paul had been invited to attend the funeral. The choristers of Windsor being also desirous to shew their respect to the remains of the amiable Doctor, had unexpectedly arrived to join in the dirge, and the Doctor's house being too small to entertain them, they adjourned to the Horn [99] tavern; and hence the extraordinary demand for rump steaks, which doubtless would be followed, since their grief was profound, with no ordinary order for port wine.

BUCKINGHAM-COURT, ADMIRALTY.

In Buckingham-court, near the Admiralty, there is an established and well-known shell-fish and oyster shop, with very commodious rooms for customers.[1]

Salopian Coffee-House.

The Salopian Coffee-house, near Charing Cross, is a most respectable and ancient establishment.[2] Its larder has meats of various kinds and soups always ready, and its cellar furnishes excellent wines and liquors. On account of its proximity to the War-office and the Admiralty, it is much frequented by officers in the army, navy, and royal marines, who generally make it head quarters when their affairs call them to Whitehall. Army and navy lists, with all the pamphlets relative to either service, are to be seen here. An entrance into it from Spring Garden obviously adds to the convenience of the place in

---

[1]   The vanished Buckingham Court was a short passage running west from Whitehall to Spring Gardens, just north of the old Admiralty offices.

[2]   The Salopian and the Ship were both on the west side of Charing Cross (now part of Whitehall). The **Salopian**, at nos. 41-42, a few doors north of the old Admiralty offices, was established by the mid-c18; as the *Almanack* mentions, it was much used by military men, and it was also popular with engineers, serving as Thomas Telford's residence and headquarters from 1800 to 1821. The Salopian is named by Tallis in 1840, but disappears from directories after 1844.

many exigencies. Since the commencement of this tour, Mr. Horseman, the host, has paid the debt of [100] nature, and the business is conducted, with admirable fidelity, by his widow.

Ship Tavern.

A few doors nearer to Messrs. Drummond's is the Ship-tavern. Until of late this concern was considered merely in the light of a public house. The present proprietor has removed the tap to the back premises, and in its former space has fitted up a Coffee-room, with a larder displaying steaks, chops, and other light dishes. He has done this purely for the accommodation of persons going or coming by the numerous short stages which draw up at the door. He also takes care to have an outlet into Spring Garden.[1]

---

[1] The **Ship Tavern** at no. 45 Charing Cross, west side, shared a name with at least two other nearby establishments, and is sometimes confused with them, as well as with a tavern known as the Rummer, which gave its name to the Rummer Court shown on the Rocque map at approximately the location of the later Ship. No. 45 was built about 1765, and was listed in the rate books as 'ye Ship' by 1771; for a time after 1825 the tavern also occupied no. 46 (*SL* 16, p. 92). Later known as the Ship Restaurant, the establishment continued into the 1920s but was cleared away for the building of the Whitehall Theatre in 1929-30. The 'outlet into Spring Garden' mentioned here is probably the narrow passage shown on the Horwood map between nos. 3 and 4 Spring Gardens, the latter of which was occupied by the portraitist Robert Dighton from 1810 until his death in 1814.

Eating-House.

Immediately facing the last-mentioned Tavern is a celebrated Eating-house and A-la-mode Beef shop. It was formerly Dighton's, the celebrated caricaturist. The rooms upstairs are very comfortable. In the shop are daily to be seen, from one o'clock in the afternoon until five, a fine assortment of hams, rounds of beef, with other hot joints and poultry in succession, which are served up, or out by weight, or by plate. In the evenings à-la-mode beef sallads, and the cold contents of the larder are served until midnight.

[101]

Golden Cross.

Perhaps there could not be named another house in the known world so generally known as the Golden Cross, Charing Cross. If you were in Paris, and enquired where it was, Monsieur would politely beg you to go by way of Calais to Dover; or were the same question asked in Holland, Mynheer would instinctively point towards Harwich. Its fame has spread from the pillars of Hercules to the Ganges, from Nova Zembla to New Zealand, from Siam to California. Of late years the concern has become so extensive, that it has been found necessary, as it once was at a great house in Downing Street, to separate it into two departments; and now the inn is detached from the tavern. The latter has been recently repaired, fitted up, and decorated with a new front. It possesses almost every convenience; and Mr. Stratton, the proprietor, caters for his guests in the most assiduous manner the best viands his money or his credit can procure, with the aid of his judgment and experience.[1]

[1] The site of the **Golden Cross** described here is now under Trafalgar Square (Popham 1937, p. 114, specifies the spot 'now occupied by the lion at the south-eastern corner'). Following Nash's redevelopment of the area, the establishment moved a stone's throw away in 1832 to a building demolished a century later for the construction of South Africa House; today an office block at no. 8 Duncannon Street preserves the Golden Cross name. The original Golden Cross was a well-known coaching inn serving southern England, and it figures in so many works by Dickens that B. W. Matz devoted a whole chapter to it in his *Inns and Taverns of 'Pickwick'* (1922).

Most of our town readers will call to mind the stale hoax played off on the Tony Lumpkins of former days, by a letter of recommendation to Charles Stuart, with an assurance [102] that they would see him on their arrival at this famous house.[1]

We cannot commence our intended march up the Strand without reminding our readers that there are several houses in the vicinity of Charing Cross, where most of the good things of this life are to be obtained in a style of superior comfort. This quarter was indeed noted for substantial and savoury cheer even in the time of Henry IV., if we may credit the testimony of one Mr. Shakspeare, who declares that one of his men, named Gadshill, overheard a carrier at an inn so called in Kent, say, that he had a gammon of bacon and two rases of ginger to be delivered as far as Chearing Cross.[2] The testimony may be taken like the bacon, *cum* GRANO *salis*, for Gadshill at the best was a suspicious character, or rather a character to be suspected.

Cannon Coffee-House.

Facing Spring Garden Mr. Charles Hodges keeps the Cannon Coffee-house, well charged with ammunition for the stomach.[3] His larder and soups, his waiters and cooks, are like our hearts of oak, "always ready." In the vaults below this arsenal may be seen a range of stoves well manned, and the fumes which arise are as delightful (almost) to the nose of [103] a militaire affamé, as those of gunpowder itself, "the incense offered to the god of war."

[1] A Tony Lumpkin (from the character in Goldsmith's *She Stoops to Conquer*) was a country bumpkin, and the Charles Stuart that he would have seen on his arrival at the Golden Cross was the equestrian statue of Charles I, erected at Charing Cross in 1675; for another version of this 'stale hoax' see Macmichael 1906, p. 80.

[2] Shakespeare, *1 Henry IV*, II.i. A rase or race of ginger would today be called a ginger root.

[3] The **Cannon Coffee House**, at no. 1 Cockspur Street, north side (corner of Whitcomb Street), is known from the late 1720s, but seems to have been out of business by 1821 (see Lillywhite). In 1824-27 Sir Robert Smirke erected a new building on the site, which survives today, somewhat altered, as Canada House.

Spring Garden Coffee-House, Tavern, and Hotel.

The Spring Garden Coffee-House, Tavern, and Hotel, is worthy of its neighbourhood to the Cannon. Mr. Barnet, the host, takes care that the accommodations and the fare shall be in every respect equal to those of Mr. Hodges.[1]

Farrance's.

Farrance, the Pastry Cook, lives at the corner of Spring Garden, or rather his numerous friends may be said to live there; for so much does he attend to the gratification of their appetites, that he seldom has time to think of his own. In point of magnitude, and of the excellence and cheapness of its articles, this long celebrated shop has no superior, perhaps, in the world. Here are exquisite soups, highly flavoured tarts, savoury patties, and delicious pastry and confitures. Fruits and ices throughout the whole extent of their season, good and in great variety. Need we say that in this temple Pomona and Ceres hold daily a levee of beauty and fashion; and that you may observe at all hours in the forenoon a [104] whole nidus of little Cupids and Psyches feasting in terrene nectar and ambrosia. In plainer terms ladies generally regale their younger friends and relatives here with the incomparable bon-bons of Monsieur Farrance.

Park Passage.

There is a pastry-shop on a small scale in the narrow passage leading by the Panharmonicon Rooms in St. James's Park.[2] It is very convenient for sedate persons who do not like to be seen lounging in a pastry-shop, and who prefer smuggling a few trifles to munch on the benches in the Park. They may here be served very discreetly, and with very good things.

[1] The **Spring Garden Coffee House** was known as early as 1730, moving sometime after 1759 to the southernmost of three new houses built on the eastern side of the short segment of Spring Gardens running south from Cockspur Street (see *SL* 16, p. 145); the northernmost of the houses, at the corner of Cockspur Street, was occupied by the pastrycook Thomas **Farrance** (cf. p. 82 above).
[2] The **Panharmonicon Rooms** mentioned here were properly Charles Wigley's Great Promenade Rooms (see above, p. xxx).

The British.

The British is one of the oldest taverns in London. Its eatables and drinkables have been too long and too judiciously tasted to need any commendation from us. The excellence of its wines is almost proverbial. Foreigners from the vine-covered hills and vales of the continent, admit them to be equal in flavour to any produced in their own lands, and on their own tables at home. Messrs. Morley, the hosts, with the laudable design of accommodating families as well as single [105] gentlemen, have of late greatly extended their premises.[1]

Strand, Northumberland Coffee-House and Tavern.

We will not proceed any further westward at present, but with our reader's leave, which we take for granted, we will return to Charing Cross, and without hesitation proceed boldly up the Strand, passing the mansion of the Duke of Northumberland, whose ancestor, a great epicure and lover of venison in his day, once vowed to God that he would take three days pleasure in the woods of Scotland. Our vow binds us to a three days ramble among the more prolific haunts of *plaisaunce* in the capital of England, where we hope to find a greater variety of good cheer, without any of the perils that attended the mighty hunter of the north.[2]

[1] The establishment at no. 27 Cockspur Street (opposite Great Suffolk Street), although described by the *Almanack* as a tavern, was more commonly known as the **British Coffee House**. It came into existence in the early years of the c18 and was rebuilt to Robert Adam's design in 1770, shortly before the lease was sold to the first of the Morley family to run the business (*SL* 16, pp. 148-49). Also known as the British Hotel and sometimes Morley's British Hotel, it was demolished in 1886-87; a second Morley's Hotel, occupying the entire eastern side of Trafalgar Square, was built around 1830 (sold to the South African government in 1920 and demolished for the building of South Africa House).

[2] The reference is to the famous 'Ballad of Chevy Chase', telling the story of an early Duke of Northumberland whose three-day hunting party in the Cheviot Hills was interpreted by the Scottish Earl of Douglas as an invasion of Scotland.

Northumberland Court Coffee-House and Tavern.

In Northumberland Court will we make our first stand, and there recon-noitre the Coffee-House and Tavern of that name.[1] Its excellent larder is constantly in view, and the viands thereof are served by bill of fare. The proprietor has just added to it some pretty [106] extensive premises fronting into the Strand. They are neat and commodious.

Army and Navy Coffee-House and Tavern.

The Army and Navy Coffee-House and Tavern, No. 2, St. Martin's Lane, has a larder and soups constantly at command.[2]

The Craven, in Craven Street.

The Craven Tavern, in Craven Street, which debouches into the Strand, was formerly called the Globe, and is an establishment of very ancient date.[3] The host, Mr. Stevenson, dresses dinners for large and small parties, with equal alacrity and exactitude. He even sends out dinners to the several lodging-houses in his own neighbourhood. This is the only tavern remaining in the parish of St. Martin's in the Fields since the demolition of the Standard Tavern, which occupied the site of the Panorama, in Leicester Square;[4] we

[1] The Jacobean mansion of the Duke of Northumberland was demolished in 1874 to make way for Northumberland Avenue. I find no mention of a coffee house in Northumberland Court, but *SL* 20, p. 11, places the **Northumberland Coffee House** at the corner of Northumberland Street and the Strand (no. 4 Strand, south side). Lillywhite records mentions of the establishment from the 1780s, but it was apparently lost in the construction of Trafalgar Square.

[2] The **Army and Navy Coffee House** was just north of the Strand, at no. 2 St Martin's Lane, east side. Although Lillywhite found no record of the establishment earlier than 1818, an article in *The Times* of 24 June 1822 refers to it as 'an old established tavern, hitherto we believe of very good repute', adding that it had not long previously closed down 'in consequence of the failure in business of the then landlord'. The Army and Navy reopened under new management later that year, and is listed in directories through 1833.

[3] At this time Craven Street, built in the 1730s, ran southeast from the Strand all the way to the river; the **Craven Tavern** was at nos. 45-46, on the north side. Known as the Globe until about 1800, the premises were later enlarged and more usually referred to as the Craven Hotel (still in business into the 1970s).

[4] The **Standard Tavern** was known as early as 1719 (*Original Weekly Journal*, 24 October), and was sometimes called the Royal Standard.

say the only tavern which can boast of a large room, capacious enough for parochial and election feasts. Here the munificent Duke of Northumberland treats his fellow-parishioners annually with venison – the fat bucks of Chevy no doubt. At this house we may say, without fear, is held the largest senior bucks' lodge.

[107]

Hungerford Coffee-House.

The Hungerford Coffee-House, No. 470, Strand, is another ancient establishment, famed for the goodness of its fare and accommodations.[1] This is one of the few houses that take in, and carefully preserve, the newspapers. Here the literary antiquary and compiler of history will find complete series of all the papers now publishing, as well as those which, having expired, are laid on the shelf of oblivion. Go any where else, except to Peele's and the Chapter Coffee-house, and he will be disappointed in the hope of such a complete assortment.

Yeates's.

Nearly opposite the Hungerford, at No. 23, Strand, is Yeates's Ham and Beef-shop, containing also tongues, smoaked puddings, both of Bologna and Germany, and portable cold mock-turtle soup. These articles are vended by weight and taken out.[2]

Church Court.

Opposite Hungerford Street is Church Court, and in that court is the Oxford Eating-house.[3] Well was it so called, for since Ox- [108] ford supplies the church with divines, an eating-house should be provided near the church to supply the congregation with something as solid as a sermon, to peruse,

---

[1] The **Hungerford Coffee House**, mentioned in an Old Bailey proceeding of 24 October 1770, was at no. 470 on the north side of the Strand, facing the entrance to the C17 Hungerford Market.

[2] In 1865 John Timbs described **Yeates** as a confectioner, noting that the house, 'with a wooden front, which must have been built in the seventeenth century', had been removed in 1863 during improvements to the Strand (*Walks and Talks*, p. 159).

[3] Church Court, home to the **Oxford** eating house, ran north from the Strand, just east of the Hungerford Coffee House.

mark, and inwardly digest. Joints hot from twelve to five o'clock form the afternoon service here each day. The meats are cut at a reasonable rate per plate.

Some years ago the courts immediately surrounding St. Martin's Church were so thronged with eating-houses, that the district was denominated Porridge Island. At one of these humble refectories the rich and eccentric Sir Gregory Page Turner dined daily for many years. The cook accidentally discovered his rank, and by that lost his custom.[1]

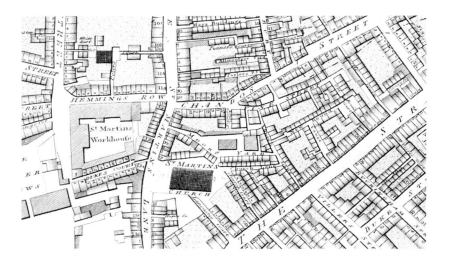

Wheatsheaf, Strand.

This was a superior public-house in the days of Mr. Dewhurst, who a few years ago removed hence to the Swan with Two Necks, Lad Lane, and raised that establishment to an unprecedented height of popularity and splendour.[2]

---

[1] **Porridge Island** is described in Grose's 1785 *Classical Dictionary of the Vulgar Tongue* as 'an alley leading from St. Martin's church-yard, to Round-court, chiefly inhabited by cooks, who cut off ready dressed meat of all sorts, and also sell soup'. Sir Gregory Page Turner, 3d baronet, was well-known for his eccentricities, which included hoarding a vast number of gold guineas, discovered after his death in 1805.

[2] The **Wheatsheaf** was at no. 433 Strand, north side, not far from Bedford Street. Lillywhite records a mention of the Wheatsheaf in 1806, and directory listings from 1809 to 1827; like many establishments it was used for Masonic meetings.

His successor preserves the credit and fame of the house unsullied. Though a public-house merely, it displays an excellent larder, which entirely occupies the front window. It is particularly noted for rump-steaks, chops, and other articles that constitute what men of [109] business call a hasty dinner. Mr. M'Niven, of whom we shall have occasion to speak in the sequel, established its fame, which, we again say, is worthily maintained by the present proprietor, Mr. M'Jaggar.

Castle Court, Tea and Coffee-House.

Proceeding past two or three doors, we come to Castle Court, where, facing the private door of the British Fire Office, we find a snug house that supplies tea and coffee at one shilling a head, and soups at a rate proportionably moderate per basin. The design of this economical retreat is to afford sober politicians a quick opportunity for reading most of the morning and evening newspapers.[1]

DURHAM STREET.

One door down Durham Street, facing Bedford Street, Strand, will be found the Salisbury Coffee-house, and Burton ale-rooms. Here is a handsome exposed larder of fish, steaks, chops, kidneys, hearts, and other small dishes, all calculated to give a zest to Mr. Ireson's native Burton ale.[2]

New Exchange Coffee-House.

The New Exchange Coffee-house, No. 69, Strand, has been long established, and [110] maintains the character of a prime house for a comfortable

---

[1] Castle Court, with its 'moderate' tea and soup shop, ran northwest to Chandos Street from the British Fire Office (no. 429 Strand).

[2] At this date Durham Street (now Durham House Street), home to the **Salisbury Coffee House**, had an entrance into the Strand between nos. 64 and 65, nearly opposite Bedford Street. On the 1746 Rocque map this area is designated Durham Yard, the name deriving from the old residence of the Bishop of Durham, demolished at the end of the Civil War. Horwood's identification of the dogleg Durham Street as 'William Street' and 'James Street' suggests that he was under the impression that Durham Yard had been renamed for William and James Adam, two of the brothers responsible for redeveloping the area in the mid-C18.

dinner.[1] Next door, No. 70, is a pastry-shop, well worth the attention of those delicate persons who are seldom hungry, but often, what the cits call *peckish*.

Cecil Coffee-House.

The Cecil Coffee-house has been established for upwards of fifty years, and is a great favourite both in its coffee-house and tavern capacity. Its dinners are excellent.[2]

Beaufort's Buildings.

Down Beaufort's Buildings is the Plough, a very respectable public-house, kept by the facetious Mr. Burridge. Under the sign it is announced, that joints are kept hot every day from twelve to three o'clock. It is well known that they are of good meat.[3]

Coal Hole, Fountain Court.

Be not afraid, gentle and timid reader, of venturing into a mine of black diamonds. Here is nothing brilliant in the Coal Hole of Fountain Court but the fire of the cook, and the wit and guineas of the guests. Notwithstanding the blackness of its name, this house is noted for its cleanliness and propriety of [111] arrangement. Its whimsical title was bestowed upon it by a club of coal merchants, or, as they called themselves, black diamond merchants, who some years ago frequented the house, which was erst called the Fountain. This is reversing the order of nature. Old coal mines generally subside into

---

[1] Lillywhite notes references to the **New Exchange Coffee House** in the 1730s; the building was pulled down in 1924 (*SL* 16, p. 98). *Roach's London Pocket Pilot* of 1793 was hardly flattering, complaining that the New Exchange was 'crowded with young men of fashion', who 'having taken in a surcharge of the best port and claret, […] often disgorge it to the general use' (p. 51).

[2] The **Cecil Coffee House** at no. 84 Strand, south side, on the corner of the now-vanished Cecil Street, was also known as the Cecil Street Coffee House; it was in business at least since the late 1730s but seems to have disappeared after its last owner, Ebenezer Charles Cox, was declared a bankrupt in March 1816 (*London Gazette*, 17 August).

[3] Beaufort Buildings, site of the **Plough** (no. 16), ran south from the Strand, with the entrance between nos. 95 and 96.

wells of water, but we never hear of a fountain being petrified into a coal mine.[1]

Exeter 'Change.

At No. 365, Strand, near Exeter 'Change, there is an Eating-house, with comfortable rooms up stairs. Its joints of meat are kept hot in succession from twelve at noon until eleven at night.

Oxford Coffee-house and Tavern.

Gentlemen from the universities frequent the Oxford Coffee-House and Tavern, on account of its excellent dinners and wines, as well as of the comfort and good order which prevail in the house. Other guests of unobtrusive character and retired habits choose this for their town retreat, as a kind of *rus in urbe*.[2]

ADELPHI.

In the Adelphi are three celebrated hotels and two boarding-houses. In Adam Street, [112] Adelphi, is Hudson's (late of the Grand Hotel, Covent Garden); a few paces further is Osborne's hotel. It occupies the corner house

[1] Fountain Court (now Savoy Buildings) also ran south from the Strand, just west of the Savoy, and there is a reference to 'the **Coal Hole**, a public House just by the Savoy' in an Old Bailey proceeding of 24 February 1742. Popular with actors and singers, the Coal Hole was listed among London's private theatres by J. G. Burton in 1819, with the note that it 'musters a grand assemblage of the Sock and Buskin every Saturday evening, among which, are frequently some well-known musical characters' (*The Critic's Budget*, p. 49). From 1814 to 1817 it was a particular haunt of the actor Edmund Kean, founder in 1815 of the Wolf Club, a rowdy drinking society that met in the tavern, and in the 1840s the establishment became even more disreputable under the lead of the impresario Renton Nicholson (cf. the Garrick's Head and Cyder Cellar, pp. 144 and 156 below). The Coal Hole was relaunched as the Occidental Tavern in 1872, but was torn down for the building of Terry's Theatre (opened 1887, demolished 1923). In 1904 a new Coal Hole – still in business today – opened at no. 91 Strand.

[2] The *Almanack*'s 'Oxford Coffee House' was by 1815 the **Oxford and Cambridge Coffee House**: the Oxford was at no. 105 Strand, south side, from the early c18, but seems to have merged with its next door neighbour around 1809 (see Lillywhite nos. 958 and 960).

of John Street and the two houses adjoining. A little further on is Sheffield's.[1] The business of these three mansions is such as strictly belongs to the hotel department; and so good are the accommodations that, during the season, they are always full. We mean the London winter season, which commences when the sun enters Aries, and terminates soon after the birth-day of our sovereign lord the king.

The terms and regulations of Mrs. May's, No. 8, and of Mrs. Laver's, No. 19, Adam Street, Adelphi, can be had on application by any gentleman desirous of becoming a whole or half-boarder by the week, month, or year.[2] We know not whether it was here that

> Will Waddle, whose temper was studious and lonely,
> Hired lodgings that took single gentlemen only;
> But Will was so fat he appeared like a tun,
> Or like two single gentlemen roll'd into one.

Turk's Head, Canada, and Bath Coffee-House.

The Turk's Head, Canada, and Bath Coffee-House and Tavern, a tremendously incongruous title, which might be mended by altering it to the Turk, Chickasaw, and Bladud's Heads, [113] thus making a Cerberus of it, is at No. 141, Strand, kept by Mr. Whitehead. The situation is a happy one since it fronts Catherine Street, and is at a very short distance from both the theatres, and St. Paul's Church, Covent Garden. Mr. Whitehead exposes his larder in handsome style, and describes his fare by bill, which is always ordered to lie on the table. The different clauses are generally agreed to without any

---

[1] Sometime before 1780 the Osborn family took over the Adelphi New Tavern and Coffee House at nos. 1-2 John Street (now John Adam Street), south side, corner of Adam Street, and the establishment was subsequently sometimes known as **Osborn's Adelphi Hotel**. It features in Dickens's *Pickwick Papers* and included among its more unfortunate guests the Queen of the Sandwich Islands (Hawaii), who died there in 1824. The hotel was considerably enlarged in 1906 but was demolished for offices in 1936, and should not be confused with another Adelphi Tavern at no. 18 Adam Street, now incorporated in the Royal Society of Arts building. **Sheffield's Hotel**, at nos. 6-7 John Street, had become Tetsall's Hotel by the early 1820s.

[2] According to *BoE Westminster*, p. 327, no. 8 Adam Street, east side – the former **Mrs May's** boarding house – survives intact, but the house once occupied by **Mrs Laver** (no. 19, west side) went in the 1936 demolition. The humorous quatrain is from George Colman the Younger's 'Lodgings for Single Gentlemen' (from *My Night-gown and Slippers*, 1797).

amendment, and the bill passes. His lodgings and accommodations are very pleasant.[1]

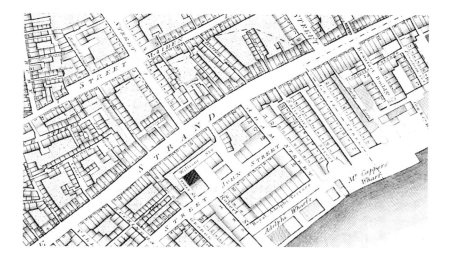

Holyland Coffee-house and Hotel.

The Holyland Coffee-house, Tavern, and Hotel, No. 150, Strand, kept by Mr. Williams, can frequently boast of as jovial a company of pilgrims, as that which Sir Geoffry Chaucer joined at the Taberd in Southwerke. It is a superior house, and the devotee, who lodges there, might go farther and fare worse, even if he trudged as far as Jerusalem.[2]

---

[1] The **Turk's Head, Canada, and Bath Coffee House** at no. 142 Strand, south side, was well established by 1763, when James Boswell's journal records visits with Samuel Johnson; it was rebuilt around 1838 and had been pulled down by the end of the C19.

[2] **Holyland's Coffee House** and hotel was at no. 150 Strand, south side, two doors west of the entrance to Somerset House; it was established by the late 1780s, and was described in 1793 as elegant if expensive (*Roach's London Pocket Pilot*, pp. 49-50). It had closed by 1826, when the 'spacious premises' were fitted up for use by a firm of gentlemen's outfitters, also using the name Holyland's (advertisement in *The Times*, 9 February). Holyland's Family Hotel at no. 10 Norfolk Street, east of Somerset House, may have been a successor to the original Holyland's.

Somerset Coffee-house and Tavern.

Near Somerset House is the Somerset Coffee-house and Tavern.[1] Mr. Saunders, the host, uses every exertion to give *eclat* to his establishment, and this with a view to obviate [114] any disappointment that might accrue to a stranger, who should mistake this for the two last mentioned houses. Such are the accommodations and the fares; though he must be a cynic indeed who would not call such a mistake a lucky misfortune.

Betty's Chop-House.

On the other side of the way behind the New Church in the Strand is an old established eating-house, known by the name of Betty's Chop-house, where a good dinner may be had at a very easy charge.[2]

Navy Coffee-House and Tavern.

The Navy Coffee-house and Tavern, in Newcastle Street, is well frequented by gentlemen belonging to the several offices in Somerset Place, and by officers in the navy, who have business at the Navy Office. Its viands are generally very good.[3]

[1] The **Somerset Coffee House** at no. 162 Strand, south side, stood opposite the church of St Mary le Strand; it is recorded as early as 1744 and mentioned several times by Boswell. Known as the Somerset Hotel by 1827, it was still in business in the mid-C20.
[2] **Betty's Chop House**, also known as Old Betty's, is sometimes confused with Clifton's eating house in Butcher Row, called Betty's by several writers: this was frequented by Samuel Johnson but pulled down with the rest of the Row shortly before the *Almanack* appeared. Our Betty's was at no. 315 Strand, north side, behind the 'new' church of St Mary le Strand, the first of fifty modern London churches built in accordance with an act of 1711. The establishment continues in directories until the late 1860s.
[3] The **Navy Coffee House** at no. 4 Newcastle Street, west side, was in business by 1787 (advertisement in the *World*, 2 June), and is recorded in directories through 1833; the street, which ran north from the Strand behind St Mary's, disappeared with the building of the Aldwych crescent, opened in 1905.

Spotted Dog, Holywell Street.

The Spotted Dog, in Holywell Street, has long been a celebrated dining-house. Its terms are very moderate, and its larder is particularly neat and curious.[1]

[115]

Crown and Anchor, Strand.

The Crown and Anchor Tavern in the Strand, we were going to say, is one of the largest and best houses in London.[2] By its magnitude and magnificence it ensures to itself a great number of the public festivals, anniversary as well as special. Here are three saloons: in the largest, an area of 2969 square feet, covers are frequently laid for five hundred, and even for seven hundred guests. The second contains 1200 square feet; and the third 1500, which is called the Apollo, or South Room, generally used for grand concerts, balls, and masquerades. In this room the celebrated Anacreontic Society held their rational meeting. So characteristically and tastefully is the room fitted up, that it might form no unworthy temple of the god whose name it bears, or at least it might pass for that which he sent Polyhymnia to prepare for the sons of harmony. Here are numerous elegant rooms for small parties; and the larders, cellars, and offices, correspond in excellence with the other parts of

[1] Holywell Street, home to the **Spotted Dog**, ran parallel to the Strand to the north, between St Mary le Strand and St Clement Danes; it too was lost in the building of Aldwych. In 1764 William Pitchford announced that he had 'removed from the Spotted Dog in the Strand to the House late the King's Arms (now the Spotted Dog) in Holy-well Street, near the New-Church', and advertised 'Neat wines, Brandy, Rum, &c.' (*Public Advertiser*, 6 November). The tavern and coffee house, more commonly called simply the Dog (later the Old Dog), remained at no. 23, north side, until about 1863; it is praised in James Smith's poem *The Art of Living in London* (1768, pp. 9-10) as a place where 'we're serv'd with decency at small expence', though readers are cautioned to avoid the tempting early vegetables, 'else, by magnific skill / They'll stand against you in th' approaching bill'.

[2] The **Crown and Anchor** at no. 189 Strand, south side, is shown on Horwood's map at no. 38 Arundel Street, east side. As the *Almanack* notes, this important tavern, built in the late c17 and reconstructed in 1790, was much used for lectures, dinners, and meetings – often with a radical thrust, such as the dinner held to celebrate the fall of the Bastille – and both amateur and professional musicians performed in the rooms (the Anacreontic Society mentioned here was an amateur musicians' society formed in the c18). The Crown and Anchor ceased to trade in 1847, and the building was destroyed by fire eight years later; see Macfie 1973.

this mansion of Comus. One of the partners in the concern is a considerable importer of wines, and of course takes care to supply his friends with the very best.

[116]

Temple Chop-House.

Adjoining the Unitarian Chapel, in Essex Street, there is a recently established house called the Temple Chop-house.[1] The most listless lounger must be struck with the tasteful display of good things in its window, and with the announcement that soups and a-la-mode beef, with sallads, are always ready.

Nearly opposite to it, is the Blucher's Head, a very recent establishment.[2]

George's.

No. 213, Strand, is George's Coffee-house and Tavern, which enjoys an established reputation for good dinners and other repasts. Its soups are very excellent, and the wines undeniable. There is an entrance into it from Devereux Court as well as one from the Strand. Mr. Sterling, we believe, has recently succeeded to the management of it.[3]

[1] The **Temple Chop House** was on the west side of Essex Street and adjoined the Unitarian Chapel, opened at nos. 2-3 in 1778, four years after Theophilus Lindsey first held Unitarian services on the site. The building that once housed the chop house was presumably destroyed by the same flying bomb that hit the chapel in July 1944, and the site is now occupied by the modern Essex Hall, the new Unitarian headquarters of 1958.

[2] The **Blucher's Head** opposite the chop house would indeed have been a 'very recent establishment', for the name commemorates the Prussian Field Marshall Gebhard von Blücher (1742-1819), who supported the British in the Napoleonic wars and visited London in 1814. Writing in the *Quarterly Review* in April 1815, John Wilson Croker mentions in passing the 'Blucher's Head at the corner of Essex-street' (p. 199), but I have found no other reference to the establishment.

[3] **George's Coffee House** was at the corner of Devereux Court (no. 213 Strand, south side); it was in business by 1735, and by the mid-C19 was usually described as a tavern and hotel. There is still a George public house on the site, with a Victorian mock-Tudor facade added to the original C18 building (Markman Ellis 2009, p. 19).

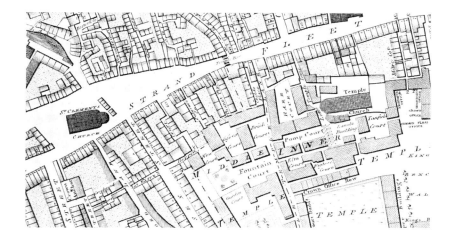

Grecian Coffee-House.

The Grecian Coffee-house and Tavern in Devereux Court is a very ancient and most excellent house, much frequented by Templars, students as well as barristers. Dinners of any compass and variety are daily sent [117] hence to their chambers to order. In front of the house is a bust of Robert Devereux, the famous Earl of Essex.[1]

Robinson's, Pickett Street.

We may now cross over to Pickett Street, and visit No. 2, a very superior eating-house, kept by Mr. Robinson.[2] Here is all day long a wonderful display of good things, such as hams, rounds of beef, and a great variety of joints,

[1] Devereux Court, home to the **Grecian Coffee House**, runs south from the Strand just east of Essex Street, with an outlet into that street, and is now a pedestrian passage. The coffee house was established not long after 1676 by George Constantine, a Greek who had earlier had establishments at Wapping and in Threadneedle Street (Ellis 2004b, pp. 107-08); often mentioned by Addison and Steele in the *Tatler* and *Spectator*, it was frequented by a wide range of writers, antiquaries, and scientists. The coffee house closed in 1843 and the site was converted to chambers, or bachelor lodgings (*OEC*, p. 97), but the later Devereux public house at no. 20 considers itself a direct descendant of the Grecian.

[2] Pickett Street, where Mr **Robinson** had his eating house, was the name of that portion of the north side of the Strand just behind St Clement Danes, built on the site of the former Butcher Row shortly before the *Almanack* was published.

roast and boiled, pigs, poultry, tarts, and other light provisions, all cooked at home. The dining rooms up stairs are commodiously fitted up. The articles are vended by weight, or per plate, at prices announced on the bill of fare. Mr. Robinson was regularly bred to the profession under his relative, Mr. Anderson, of Drury, whose establishment will be distinguished with a proper eulogium in the course of our tour.

TEMPLE BAR.

Adjoining Temple Bar, is a fishmonger's shop, long celebrated for vending venison and brawn, during the season.

BELL YARD.

We just step through the Bar to pay our [118] respects to the Haunch of Venison in Bell Yard, the first house on the right. It is a public-house, but dinners are daily drest here. Its poached eggs and Welch rabbits we can recommend, as well drest and served up in a peculiar style.[1]

ST. MARY-LE-BONE.

Our readers will not be alarmed if we take a sudden leap from Temple Bar to Tyburn, for the execution, not of them or ourselves, but of a tour from that spot down Oxford Street, St. Giles's, and Holborn, with the usual digressions to a certain extent, right and left of the main line of streets.

Hyde Park Coffee-House.

No. 242, on the north side of Oxford Street, is the Hyde Park Coffee-house, Hotel, and Tavern, kept by Mr. Humbert. This house formerly bore the name of General Wolf. The cheer is good, and the apartments in both senses of the word cheerful, as they command extensive views of Hyde Park, and the hills of Surrey.[2]

---

[1] Bell Yard runs north from Fleet Street, just east of the late-C19 Royal Courts of Justice; the **Haunch of Venison** at no. 1 was the first house on the east side. It is mentioned in an Old Bailey proceeding of 11 July 1781, and was still in business at the beginning of the C20.
[2] None of the Oxford Street establishments named here remains, and the street itself was renumbered in 1880. The **Hyde Park Coffee House** at no. 242, north side,

Heard's Eating-House.

Heard's Eating-house, No. 222, same [119] side as the above, supplies such soups as are generally to be had in cook's-shops, with joints of almost all sorts hot, from twelve until four o'clock in the afternoon. The accommodations are decent.[1]

Copping's Ham and Beef-Shop.

No. 178, same side, is Copping's Ham and Beef-shop, a good mart for purchasing those articles, and tongues ready drest, by weight, to carry away with you, which you must do, since there are no eating-rooms attached to the shop. Mr. Copping has acquired great fame by the sale of his excellent plum puddings.

King's Arms Inn, Tavern, and Chop-House.

No. 262, on the south side of Oxford Street, is the King's Arms Inn and Chop-house. The larder is well stocked and tastefully arranged, and the public rooms are particularly neat.

We now deviate a little, for the purpose of directing our readers to a few good houses of entertainment in the neighbourhood of Manchester Square. Turning up Duke Street, we find at the first house on the right hand a shell fish and oyster-shop, where various light [120] beverages, such as spruce beer, ginger-beer, and soda water, are sold as proper accompaniments to the viands.[2]

Poole's.

A little higher up, on the same side, lives Mr. Poole, an established pastry-cook, at whose shop all the usual produce of such establishments are made of

survived as the Hyde Park Hotel into the C20; the site is now occupied by the 1930s Cumberland Hotel.

[1] **Heard's** eating house, at no. 222, was one door west of Portman Street; **Copping's**, at no. 178, was three doors west of Duke Street (Selfridges department store covers the site); and the **King's Arms**, at no. 262, was on the southwest corner of Oxford Street and North Audley Street, just opposite today's Marks & Spencer.

[2] The unnamed shellfish and oyster shop and Thomas **Poole's** pastry shop at no. 10 would have been on the east side of Duke Street, facing the present-day entrances to Selfridges.

the best and most genuine materials; of course the prices are conscientiously moderate.

Parmentier.

Three doors from Duke Street, on the north side of Edward Street, at No. 9, lives Monsieur Parmentier, the celebrated confectioner to the Prince Regent and the Dukes of York and Kent. Here every article is perfected in the true Parisian style of excellence. You find eau de Cologne, pâte de guimauve, cachou à la rose, cachou à l'orange et à la violette, papillottes avec devises. Here are to be had preserves and conserves, wet and dry, jellies, jams, coloured transparent pastes, fruits dried or preserved in French brandies, comfits, lozenges, drops of every colour and flavour, superior macaroons, and rout cakes of the most fanciful forms, with ices and [121] creams. From this emporium and from that of Signor Romualdo, No. 29, Duke Street, the nobility in the neighbouring squares order supplies for their entertainments.[1]

It will not here be improper to state, that in many streets of this fashionable quarter of the town, there are china and glass-shops, the proprietors of which undertake at a few hours notice, to furnish a splendid equipage for a tea and turn out, as well as all the moveables and ornaments for large rout parties. Chairs, tables, china, glass, knives, forks, extra plate, looking glasses, mirrors, girandoles, chandeliers, wax lights, and candelabra, transparent lamps, Aurelian shades, transparencies, vases, and other decorative appendages for a complete suite of rooms, together with exotics and greenhouse plants for verandas, and a corps of artists to embellish the floors with coloured chalk. It was by means of this almost magical aid, that the Earl of Shrewsbury gave a few seasons ago, his magnificent house-warming to the Haut Monde, in his splendid new mansion in Bryanstone Square, which was at that time in so unfinished a state, that the walls in many of the apartments were not even plastered. To the astonishment and delight of all the noble guests, the whole was thrown open, and every room was found furnished and decorated in [122] the most perfect splendour. The principal drawing room appeared one blaze of light, the flames of the lamps and lights being reflected

[1] Edward (or Edwards) Street is now part of Wigmore Street; the Marylebone rate book for 1815 lists **Fortunate Parmentier** at no. 9 on the north side, just east of Duke Street. The *Triennial Directory* for 1817-19 lists '**P. Romoaldo**, confectioner' at the Duke Street address (two doors north of Edwards Street, on the west side next to Morin's Hotel), and the rate books for 1815 and 1816 give him as 'Romaldo Flato'. For the confections mentioned, see the Glossary.

many times by looking-glasses of large dimensions, that rendered it equal, in a mortal's conception, to the hall of Pandæmonium. As a contrast to this, there was another room, which in sombre gloom resembled an Arcadian grove. It was filled with orange and lemon trees in full bearing, myrtles, and a great variety of odoriferous shrubs and plants, in part natural and in part artificial, tastefully disposed and arranged in gradins. The amusements consisted of a dramatic representation, a concern performed by the first rate vocal and instrumental professors, a dress ball, a masquerade, and lastly, what is most in our province, a most magnificent supper. At two o'clock, the rooms appropriated for this essential part of the entertainment were thrown open. Covers were laid for three hundred, and we believe fully that number were regaled to their hearts' content, with every delicacy which the season, and the season to come, could naturally produce. These elegant festivities cost the noble host several thousands.[1]

Morin's.

Morin's Hotel, Coffee-house, and Tavern, [123] Nos. 27 and 28, Duke Street, on the west side, is a very considerable establishment, that happily combines the three departments above-mentioned. The dinners are cooked by French artists, who are at stated times carefully physicked and dieted, in order to preserve their palate in all its original delicacy of tact. This is a most essential precaution, not sufficiently attended to by our English Amphitryons, as their frequent chagrins over dinners overdone or underdone, palpably demonstrate. The wines are excellent, Monsieur and Madame Morin being natives of France.[2]

---

[1] The Bryanston Square ball described here is completely imaginary, and the passage should probably be seen as Ralph Rylance's whimsical tribute to his Shrewsbury friend John Dovaston.

[2] **Morin's Hotel** in Duke Street was sometimes called Morro's, and was later known as Hake's Hotel. The building is now no. 4, marked with a blue plaque commemorating the fact that Simón Bolívar lodged there in 1810. In his *Recollections of Paris* (1806), John Pinkerton stated that some Parisian families insisted that their cooks 'regularly take medicines, in order to preserve the fineness of their palate, and of their sauces' (ii:209), but Rebecca Spang has called his claim 'otherwise unsubstantiated' (Spang 2000, p. 303, n. 83). An amphitryon is a generous host: in 1808 Grimod de la Reynière published a *Manuel des amphitryons* that included sample menus and advice on etiquette for both hosts and guests.

Roumaingoux.

At No. 69, George Street, Manchester Square, lives Monsieur Roumain-goux, by profession a cook.[1] He serves up dinners in the French style on very moderate charges. Many of the noblesse of France, during their residence in this country, did Mr. Romaingoux the honneur to partake of his refreshments.

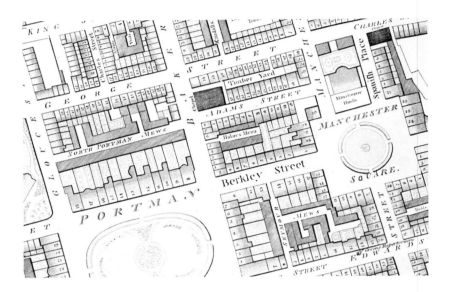

At the corner of George Street, there was until very lately an establishment on a novel plan. Mohammed, a native of Asia, opened a house for the purpose of giving dinners in the Hindustanée style, with other refreshments of the same genus.[2] All the dishes were [124] dressed with curry-powder, rice, Cayenne, and the best spices of Arabia. A room was set apart for smoking

---

[1] The Marylebone rate books for 1813-14 list a Peter **Roumaingaux** at this address.

[2] Deen Mahomed opened his **Hindoostanee Coffee House** at no. 34 George Street, north side, in 1810, and advertised in *The Times* of 27 March 1811, promising 'Indian dishes in the highest perfection', choice wines, and 'Hoakha[s], with real Chilm tobacco'; his venture is discussed more fully above, p. xlix. The site of the Hindoostanee – now renumbered no. 102 and part of a C20 office block – was marked in 2005 by a green Westminster City Council plaque honouring Mahomed and 'London's first Indian restaurant'. At least one earlier attempt to market Indian food in London had been made by 'the Mistress of Norris street Coffee-House, Haymarket', who advertised in 1773 that she not only sold 'true Indian curey paste',

from hookahs with oriental herbs. The rooms were neatly fitted up *en suite*, and furnished with chairs and sofas made of bamboo canes. Chinese pictures and other Asiatic embellishments, representing views in India, oriental sports, and groups of natives decorated the walls. Either Sidi Mohammed's purse was not strong enough to stand the slow test of public encouragement, or the idea was at once scouted; for certain it is, that Sidi Mohammed became bankrupt, and the undertaking was relinquished.

Blandford Eating-House.

In Blandford Street, there is an eating-house of rather a superior kind. It has great variety of viands, which are exposed in the window, and all kept warm by an improved steam apparatus. They cut here by weight or by plate.

Wheeler's.

Wheeler's Eating-house and Cook's-shop is a decent house, where hams, tongues, and joints, are kept hot from one o'clock until four in the afternoon. Here may be had a-la-mode beef and sallads at night.

[125]

Manchester Arms.

The Manchester Arms Tavern, Hotel, and Coffee-house, Manchester Street, is a respectable establishment, nearly approaching the rank of tavern.[1] Here rump-steaks, chops, and other ready dishes are served up at a cheap rate and very comfortably. Some very intelligent persons pass an hour or two here every evening. Mr. Lloyd, the host, is very much respected.

Le Fevre's Hotel.

At the corner of South Street, Manchester Street, is Le Fevre's Hotel, which, though but a small establishment, unites the functions of a tavern, coffee-house, and hotel. It is fitted up in very genteel style; and is attended by a very respectable company of customers.

but would 'at the shortest Notice, [send] ready dressed Curey and Rice, also India Pilaws, to any Part of the Town' (*Public Advertiser*, 6 December).

[1] The *Almanack*'s Manchester Arms is presumably identical with the **Manchester Coffee House** at no. 14 Manchester Street. By the 1840s this had become Ford's Hotel, later expanding into nos. 13, 15, and 16 and surviving for another century.

George's.

George's Pastry-shop, No. 6, Blandford Street, is a very superior concern. Its soups, as well as its savoury and sweet articles, are compounded according to the most exact rules of the art culinary; and it produces delicious ices throughout the season.

[126]

Crown, Cavendish Street.

The Crown at the corner of Henrietta Street, Old Cavendish Street, kept by Mr. Williams, is a public-house of the first rate, with a larder of steaks, chops, and whole joints, which are comfortably served up in a coffee-room on the first floor.[1]

King's Head – Buckland's.

Mr. Buckland, of the King's Head, Old Cavendish Street, is one of the most civil landlords and honest men in London.[2] He dresses any hasty dish, such as a steak, a chop, or broiled sheep's heart, or a basin of peas-soup, in the most expeditious and satisfactory way to order. His liquors are of the choicest kind. A club of harmonious gentlemen meet here every Tuesday evening in the winter, to which club any respectable person, introduced by a member, is eligible on paying a shilling. The money is well spent, for some of the best singers from both the Theatres Royal, often visit the rooms, and delight the company by their vocal effusions. The utmost decorum prevails.

The first house on the left in Old Cavendish Street, is a very superior shell-fish shop, [127] with oyster-rooms up stairs. It is one of the best establishments of the kind in London. All the usual beverages are to be had here, in high perfection.

[1] The **Crown** was still listed at no. 22 or 23 Henrietta Street (now Place) into the 1840s.

[2] I can find no other mention of a **King's Head** in Old Cavendish Street, and suspect that the *Almanack* erred in naming the tavern run by Mr Buckland. The *Triennial Directory* of 1817-19 places him instead at the **Red Lion** (later the Old Red Lion); this was still in business at no. 5 Old Cavendish Street in the 1930s, but today the John Lewis department store covers the site.

Mr. Smith's Eating-House.

After this deviation we shall direct our course toward Oxford Street by way of Mary-le-bone Lane, for the purpose of indicating to all real epicures an eating-house, which is, perhaps, the very best in London. It is situated within three doors of Edward Street, on the east side of Mary-le-bone Lane. Mr. Smith, the master, became master of his art, in the kitchen of his present Majesty, where his father was for many years master cook, and Mr. Smith himself held the same important situation in the household of his Royal Highness the late Duke of Gloucester. Every dish that is taken in Mr. Smith's house or out of his shop, is guaranteed to be composed of the best meat, and cooked in the most scientific manner, at the most reasonable prices. Collared beef, veal, pig, larded beef, and veal cakes, are all sold at two shillings per pound. There is also always ready an excellent raised pie of large dimensions, built with alternate strata or layers of ham and veal, the interstices being filled with a highly fla- [128] voured, well seasoned, transparent jelly. Half a pound is sufficient for a moderate eater, and the charge for that is only one shilling. Mr. Smith's rounds of beef and his hams are, as may be expected from his judgment in buying, and his management in cooking, super-excellent. The neighbouring gentry avail themselves of Mr. Smith's larder, when entertaining their friends; and its contents serve for either a cold collation or a *petit souper*.

Hinton's.

Hinton's Eating-house is in Mary-le-bone Lane, within two doors of Bulstrode Street, a very decent refectory, with hot joints from twelve until four o'clock, and a-la-mode beef at night. The saloon is up stairs.

Goodhugh's.

We are now again in Oxford Street, where at No. 290, the inquirer will find Goodhugh's Eating-house, a very respectable establishment, with good accommodations.[1] The display in the window, morning, noon, and night, is really wonderful, both as to quantity and quality. It is not uncommon to see among this tempting assemblage, a whole jury of roasting pigs, all ready, not

---

[1] Richard **Goodhugh's** eating house, on the south side of Oxford Street, is shown in Tallis's 1839 view of the street; Bond Street station occupies the site today.

to be impan- [129] nelled but impaled on the spit. Mr. Goodhugh provides daily for three hundred customers within and without.

Stratford Tavern and Hotel.

No. 160, on the north side of Oxford Street, is the Stratford Hotel and Tavern.[1] It adjoins Stratford Place. It is a regular tavern, with larder and soups always ready, and almost always called for, as it is very well attended. Immediately facing Stratford Place, is Freeman's Cook-shop, one part of which is appropriated to the exhibition and sale of drest hams, rounds of beef, joints of pork, and other solid meats, all sold by the pound to take out.

At the corner of Mary-le-bone Lane, Oxford Street, is an established pastry-shop, kept many years by Tupp.[2] It has long enjoyed the well earned reputation of vending excellent soups, savoury patties and pies, with pastry and ices in the most abundant variety.

Ibbetson's Hotel and Tavern.

In Vere Street, between Oxford Street and the Chapel of Vere Street, is Ibbetson's Hotel and Tavern, a first rate house with the best accommodations, an amply stocked larder and [130] rich soups. This house is much frequented by military officers of rank, English as well as foreign.[3]

Fladong's.

No. 144, Oxford Street, is Fladong's Hotel, now kept by Mr. John Morris. It is a house of the first class, and has recently been repaired and fitted up

---

[1] The **Stratford Hotel** was at no. 160 on the north side, one door west of Stratford Place; it was in use for Masonic meetings in the 1780s, but disappears from directories in 1835.

[2] **Tupp's** pastry shop was just to the east of the Stratford Hotel on the same side (corner of Marylebone Lane), and Mr **Freeman's** establishment was probably near the corner of South Molton Street.

[3] Ibbetson's (properly **Ibbotson's**) Hotel was at no. 3 Vere Street, on the east side; in his memories of London hotels of 1814, Captain Rees Gronow described it as 'chiefly patronized by the clergy and young men from the universities' (*Reminiscences* (1862), p. 75). By 1849 Ibbotson's had become the Oriental Hotel, but this too was gone by 1860 (*The Times*, 14 November 1859).

with every accommodation for good dinners and elegant entertainment in general.[1]

As we would much rather come up Bond Street than go down, we shall leave that thoroughfare of the fashionable world for the present, and consider it as tributary to Piccadilly and St. James's Street.

Worcester Coffee-House.

At the corner of Swallow Street, Oxford Street, stands the Worcester Coffee-house, Tavern, and Hotel.[2] Here Messrs. Goddard and Bailey keep a larder and soups always ready. When the venison season commences, they announce in the papers, that dinners are served here two or three times a week, from prime haunches at three shillings and sixpence each person. Many of the western and midland mails and stages take up and set down passengers and parcels here.

[1] **Fladong's Coffee House** was on the north side of Oxford Street, opposite Shepherd Street; Gronow described it as 'chiefly frequented by naval men' (p. 75).

[2] The **Worcester Coffee House** was on the south side, at the corner of Swallow Street (now Swallow Passage, leading into Swallow Place). In 1815 Swallow Street was the principal north-south route between Piccadilly and Oxford Street, but apart from the most southerly portion and this short fragment just west of Oxford Circus, it disappeared in the building of Regent Street.

[131]

Woodley's.

Woodley's shell fish and oyster-shop adjoins the Worcester Coffee-house, and is a [sic]good mart for the various fish that supply the tables of our gentry as any in London. Here are the usual beverages in very vivid condition.

Moody's.

Adjoining the coffee-house last mentioned, down King Street, is Moody's Eating-house, where hot joints are cut from noon till four by the plate.[1]

Perry's.

No. 336, at the corner of Argyle Street, on the south side of Oxford Street, is Perry's Pastry-shop, fitted up very tastefully in the rural or grotesque style. All the articles are of the best, Mr. Perry being a professed cook. He dresses dinners to send out; and on receiving an order, will go out himself, and dress turtle for families at their own houses.[2]

Mera's.

No. 93, Oxford Street, north side, formerly was held by Mr. Escudier, the pastry-cook.[3] His worthy successor, Mr. Mera, is [132] extolled for his excellent soups and savoury patties. Here, during all the fashionable season, is a great variety of articles, cooked in a decidedly superior manner, and decorated for side-board dishes, cold collations, dejeunés, &c.

[1] King Street, also lost in the construction of Regent Street, closely paralleled the route of Swallow Street to the east; the two met in a point at Oxford Street, which explains how **Moody's** eating house in King Street could 'adjoin' the Worcester.

[2] Although the *Almanack* describes George **Perry's** pastry shop as being on the corner of Argyle Street, no. 336 was in fact a few doors west.

[3] Louis **Mera**, successor to John Escudier (see below, p. 126), was on the north side of the street at the corner of Market Court, leading into Oxford Market; he is presumably the James Louis Mera who declared himself insolvent in 1827 (*London Gazette*, 15 May).

Oxford Market.

In Market Street, Oxford Market, there is an old established eating-house, which produces hot joints from noon until four o'clock. It is a convenient lunching place on your way to the park.[1]

Cray's, Wardour Street.

Mr. Cray, the proprietor of the Kentish Larder, in Wardour Street, one door from Oxford Street, a true Kentish man, and one of the best carvers in the United Kingdom, has raised this establishment to a high pitch of popularity. He has made the tour of Europe, and his house is much frequented by respectable foreigners, as well as Englishmen. Roast and boiled beef, mutton, lamb, pork, and veal, in constant succession throughout their respective seasons, send forth each day, from noon till night a fragrant steam, which no man, whose stomach and purse are in good plight, pass without feeling a sudden irresistible sti- [133] mulus to his appetite. Peas-soup and other dishes for lunch or evening repast, are to be had here all day, and in the evening.

Guedon's.

We may as well walk down Wardour Street, a few doors lower, to pay our respects to Monsieur Guedon, Restaurateur, of whom you may of course have an excellent dinner, cooked in the French manner, at a very small charge.[2]

York Chop-House.

Almost facing St. Anne's Court in Wardour Street, is the York Chop-house, kept by Mr. Clark.[3] The house is very neatly fitted up, and the handmaids are in general very neatly dressed, which circumstance, added to the goodness of the cheer, constitutes no small temptation to youth of sanguine temperament and vigorous digestive organs. The beef steaks and chops here are capitally cooked.

[1] Market Street, now the lower portion of Great Titchfield Street, led north from Oxford Street to Oxford Market, a c18 arcaded marketplace east of Great Portland Street that was demolished in 1880 (see below, p. 249).
[2] The 1816 *Picture of London* described **Guedon's** as 'Guidon's French Eating-house', and located it on the corner of Portland Street and Poland Street.
[3] Christopher Clark's **York Chop House** was at no. 96 Wardour Street, west side (the entrance to St Anne's Court was between nos. 30 and 31).

Cambridge Coffee-house.

At the corner of Newman Street, Charles Street, is the Cambridge Coffee-House, formerly kept by Mr. Bellchambers. You may get a tolerably good dinner here, and very [134] passable wine; but the waiters are not so brisk and active as they might be.[1]

HANWAY STREET, OXFORD STREET.

In Hanway Street, two doors on the left from Oxford Street, is a small neat eating-house, where joints roast and boiled, as well as a-la-mode beef may be had at the usual hours, in a comfortable room up stairs.

Boar and Castle Coffee-House, Oxford Street.

Mr. Sanderson, of the Boar and Castle Oxford Coffee-house, No. 6, Oxford Street, near the end of Tottenham Court Road, has soups always ready, and a larder pretty well supplied. Here are convenient rooms, and a coffee-room,

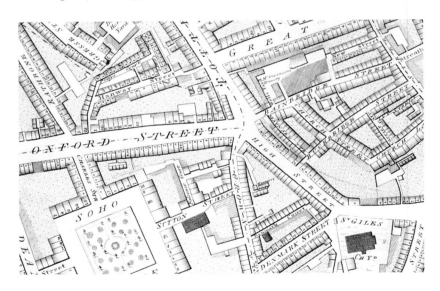

[1] The **Cambridge Coffee House** was at no. 47 Newman Street, at the corner of Charles Street (now part of Mortimer Street); it is mentioned in an Old Bailey trial of 11 July 1787. Ralph Rylance lived at no. 34 Newman Street from 1809 until about 1816, and undoubtedly knew the Cambridge well.

for dining large or small parties. The greatness of the establishment is such, that the charges are necessarily rather high; and here, as well as in most places, the merit of the wine is progressive; videlicet, from *good* to *very* good.[1]

HIGH STREET, ST. GILES'S.

In High Street, St. Giles's, there are two decent eating-houses of the inferior order, [135] both on the right hand side, one near Oxford Street, the other near the Church of St. Giles.[2] The daily fare sold and eaten in them is boiled and baked joints, with puddings, peas-soup, and leg of beef soup. You can hardly miss your hour, for the cloths are laid from noon till an hour before midnight.

The region of St. Giles is very well stocked with eating-houses of an inferior kind, but they cannot be said to afford much to entertain the epicure.

At our entrance into Holborn, we find on the left hand side an eating-house and ham and beef-shop, where the usual articles of diet are sold by weight or plate. The victuals must be cheap and good in quality, for the customers are numerous.

George and Blue Boar.

To that very considerable inn, called the George and Blue Boar, is attached a tavern on a very large scale, with a well stored and well supplied larder, and all the various soups.[3] Here St. George himself, and the damsel whom he

[1] The **Boar and Castle**, on the north side of Oxford Street, was an ancient galleried coaching inn near the junction with Tottenham Court Road; the site was later taken over by the impresario Charles Morton, who in 1861 converted it to the Oxford Theatre, a popular music hall.
[2] St Giles's High Street, running southeast from the junction of Oxford Street and Tottenham Court Road, was in 1815 the principal route connecting Oxford Street and High Holborn
[3] The **George and Blue Boar** was at no. 270 High Holborn, south side. Rocque's map of 1746 shows the site simply as the George, locating the Old Blue Boar Inn directly opposite on the north side of the street; an amalgamation presumably took place sometime before 1774, when the George and Blue Boar is named in an Old Bailey proceeding of 13 April. The building was demolished in 1864 and replaced by the Inns of Court Hotel (later Emmeline Pankhurst's London base), and the site is now occupied by the British Telecom Archives. Rylance's recollection of the *Decline and Fall of the Roman Empire* was hazy, to say the least: Edward Gibbon, who identified the fourth-century George of Cappadocia with St George (a theory

freed from the fangs of the dragon, might dine in as good array as in any hotel in the country that owns him her patron. It is very odd that Mr. Gibbon, the historian, should have called St. George a swineherd, but we suppose he [136] had better authority than *hoc signum*, the George and Blue Boar.

Queen's Arms Eating-House, Red Lion Passage.

Let us turn up Red Lion Street, and we shall find in Red Lion Passage, just at the entrance of Red Lion Square, the Queen's Arms Tavern and Chop-house. We were on entering just thinking of a new Anglo-Gallic version of the French celebrated song:

Où peut on être-mieux, than in the Queen's Arms.

This is a public-house regularly licensed, and contains some good Burton ale. The larder and accommodations are very admirable, and the waiters particularly civil.[1]

Evett's Ham-Shop.

In the same passage, you may purchase any quantity of ham by the pound at Evett's, and by way of being economical, you may, if you please, put the slices thereof between the two crusts of a quartern loaf, and carry them away cool in a couple of cabbage leaves.[2]

Leading into the north side of Red Lion Square, there is an old established cook's-shop [137] and eating-house, with comfortable rooms up stairs. Dinners are served here from hot joints daily, at noon and until five o'clock.

now rejected), referred to him not as a swineherd, but as having had a commission to supply the army with bacon.

[1] Red Lion Square is just north of High Holborn. The passage described here led into the square from Red Lion Street, just above Eagle Street, but was completely destroyed in the Second World War; a **Queen's Arms** had survived at no. 10 until about 1915. The popular French song mentioned, which properly begins 'Où peut-on être mieux qu'au sein de sa famille' ('Where better to be than in the bosom of one's family'), was written by André Grétry in 1769.

[2] This form of 'green' packaging is also mentioned by G. A. Sala, who in 1894 recalled businessmen purchasing a chop or steak at a butcher's, handed to them 'neatly wrapped up in a fresh cabbage-leaf' and ready to take to a chop house for cooking (*Things I Have Seen*, ii:201).

Wheatsheaf, Hand Court.

Returning into Holborn, through Hand Court, we find two famous houses of entertainment.[1] The first is the Wheatsheaf Tavern, where a good larder is exposed in front. This house is famous for home-brewed ale; and in the winter, it is announced by placard in the window, that every evening at eight o'clock, prime Irish fruit is ripe and ready to be served up. No native of the British Isles need be informed, that prime Irish fruit are fine kidney potatoes, roasted in a stove. They are served up with a pat of butter for threepence each.

Feathers.

Immediately adjoining, is the Feathers Tavern, kept by Mr. Goodman. This is a greatly celebrated Burton Ale-house, where all the requisites of a hasty or deliberate dinner are at command. Here is a kind of ordinary in the coffee-house style at four and five o'clock. A prime well dressed joint is brought in at each of those hours, and handed from box to [138] box. Suppers are got to order. The wines and foreign spirits are of the first quality, and of course the guests are mostly respectable, and all more or less men of *sense*.

In this court are also two celebrated shell-fish and oyster-shops, which attract many customers from among the gentlemen, who visit either of the houses above mentioned.

White Hart.

The White Hart Tavern, at the corner of Warwick Court, Holborn, facing Chancery Lane, is kept by Messrs. Walker and Wingfield.[2] It is a very respectable and ancient establishment. The situation is at a convenient vicinity to the principal inns of court.

---

[1] Hand Court ran north from High Holborn with the entrance between nos. 67 and 68; it is now a pedestrian passage. The **Feathers** was frequented by Charles Lamb in the 1790s when he lived in nearby Little Queen Street, but by 1890, when B. E. Martin traced 'the footprints of Charles Lamb', the 'dirty, dingy, delightful' Feathers had been replaced by a 'modern something' (p. 48).

[2] The **White Hart** at no. 39 High Holborn, north side (corner of Warwick Court), was used for Masonic meetings as early as 1775; a public house of the same name continued at the address until 1941, when it was destroyed in the Blitz.

Belcher's.

A little farther on is the Lancashire House, formerly kept by the noted Robert Gregson, who after bravely sustaining several fistic defeats, laid down the cœstus, and took up the corkscrew. He has also occasionally exercised his manly fingers on the lyre for the entertainment of the heroes who dined at his house, and in celebration of their respective achievements. His successor here is Mr. T. Belcher.[1]

Queen's Head.

Mr. Millington deserves a place in the ca- [139] binet, for the good order in which he keeps the Queen's Head, at the corner of that emporium of good counsel, Gray's Inn.[2] Some of the cavities of this sensorium may be seen from the passage, which is lined with linings for the stomach, such as steaks, chops, kidneys, beef, veal, mutton, and delicate fish. The lawyers digest the fees of their clients by the help of Mr. Millington's Port and Madeira.

Gray's Inn Coffee-House.

Gray's Inn Coffee-house is at the other corner of the gateway, leading into Gray's Inn. Here every article of the primest kind of food and beverage is kept for the sustenance of the learned and learning gentlemen of Gray's Inn.[3]

[1] The public house referred to by the *Almanack* as the **Lancashire House** was the **Castle**, at no. 25 on the north side. Both Thomas Belcher and Bob Gregson (the 'Lancashire Giant') were noted pugilists, and the latter's nickname was informally attached to the tavern, which was also sometimes known as Bob's Chop House (see Pierce Egan's *Book of Sports and Mirror of Life* (1832), pp. 65-77). Belcher was landlord from 1814 to 1828, during which time the Castle was 'virtually the headquarters of the sport' (*ODNB*); he was succeeded by the bare-knuckle champion Tom Spring (d. 1851), but by 1855 the house was known as the Napier, a name that continued in directories into the first decade of the C20.

[2] The **Queen's Head**, at the northwest corner of the entrance into Gray's Inn, is known as early as 1720 (*Daily Post*, 24 September), and James Boswell records visiting the tavern with his publisher and printer in 1763 and 1788. I have found no listings for it after 1830.

[3] The **Gray's Inn Coffee House** at no. 20 High Holborn, north side, was earlier known as Abington's (1730) and sometimes as Lowe's or Low's, from the name of the proprietor in the 1790s; it is described in chapter 59 of *David Copperfield*. The coffee house later became a hotel, and was replaced around 1870 by a block of offices known as Gray's Inn Chambers.

Epps's Ham and Beef-Shop.

At Holborn Bars, No. 5, we smell before we see one of Epps's shops for the sale of beef, tongues, and portable mock turtle soup.[1] At No. 29, over the way, there is a shell-fish shop.

Furnival's Inn Coffee-house is much of the same stamp as those that lead into Gray's Inn.[2]

The reader will hardly expect that we should examine and report the *fare* which is eaten by "Inn's of Court-men," (as Justice [140] Shallow hath it), on their way to the bar. We never expect to be called to the bar, and therefore shall trouble never a bencher of the whole jurisprudential body.

Barnard's Inn Coffee-House.

Barnard's Inn Coffee-house, formerly Seagoe's, stands almost facing Furnival's Inn, and comprehends most of the functions of the last-mentioned house.[3]

---

[1] For **Epps's** shops, see p. 7 above. The Holborn Bars near the Gray's Inn Road marked the boundary of the City of London: east of the Bars High Holborn became Lower Holborn, or simply Holborn.

[2] Lillywhite records mentions of the **Furnival's Inn Coffee House** at no. 139 Holborn, north side, as early as 1744; by 1836 it was also known as Brett's Hotel, and in 1875 the premises were offered for sale (advertisements in *The Times*, 13 May 1836 and 23 August 1875).

[3] **Seagoe's Coffee House** at no. 20 Holborn, south side, is known from the early c18, and seems to have changed its name to the **Barnard's Inn Coffee House** shortly before the *Almanack* appeared. The establishment survived under that name into the c20, but was replaced by an office block, Halton House, in 1907.

Bell and Crown.

On the north side of Holborn, a little eastward of Furnival's Inn, is the Bell and Crown Coffee-house, an accessory to the inn of that name, from whence many of the western and south-western stages depart. Here is a larder and dining apartments, neatly fitted up, and very good dinners are daily served up to the strangers who sojourn there.[1]

White Horse, Fetter Lane.

Fetter Lane, formerly called Faitor Lane, from the number of idle rascals who infested it, debouches into Holborn, nearly opposite the position above mentioned. Near its mouth stands the White Horse Inn, at which, [141] among many coaches to different parts of the kingdom, arrives the Royal Telegraph, from Manchester. Attached to this well-known inn is Richard's Tavern and Hotel. Its business is chiefly confined to the entertainment of those numerous passengers per coaches who arrive at the inn.[2]

In Fetter Lane there are also two eating-houses, of moderate charges and accommodations.

Old Bell.

We again cross Holborn, and sound the Old Bell, which answers with its "iron tongue and brazen mouth," that within you may subdue your hunger and thirst, even though you had the throat of a furnace and the stomach of a cormorant. Many western coaches depart from and arrive at this inn.[3]

[1]   The **Bell and Crown** coaching inn just east of Furnival's Inn (no. 133 Holborn, north side) is named on the Horwood map, and in 1838 Tallis showed it as the Bell and Crown Hotel. It was torn down in 1898 for the expansion of the Prudential Insurance building.

[2]   The **White Horse** was at no. 88 Fetter Lane, west side, behind Barnard's Inn. It was an ancient inn, shown on Ogilby and Morgan's 1676 map of London, and an important stage stop; by the time the *Almanack* was published much of the fabric dated from the C18, but portions of the earlier wooden structure remained (Norman 1905, pp. 165-66). The inn was demolished in the late 1890s and replaced by a White Horse public house, now also gone.

[3]   At no. 123 Holborn, north side, was another ancient establishment, the Bell or **Old Bell Inn**, described by Philip Norman (1905, pp. 153-61) as 'the last galleried inn on the Middlesex side of the river'. Norman notes that a messuage with a garden called the Bell was known as early as 1538; the structure may have been rebuilt about 1720. In September 1897 the furniture and fittings were sold at auction and

We shall now transport our readers to Hyde Park Corner, and conduct them along Piccadilly, Coventry Street, Leicester Square, Covent Garden, Clare Market, Lincoln's-inn-fields, and the parts adjacent, proceeding thence towards St. Paul's, occasionally turning to the right and left.

Tattersal's.

At Tattersal's there is a coffee-room, where [142] various refreshments are served to a medley of characters. Sometimes you may observe a privy council, composed of peers, gentlemen, jockies, and grooms. At this house is kept a registry of bets of the turf; and a high court is held here for determining the legality or illegality of debts of honour. All questions that come before this court are, we suppose, decided according to the laws of honour; and if the decisions prevent, in any case, that dernier resort, the pistol, the institution of such a court does honour to the jockey-lords, and bucks of England. Here sometimes a sum, large enough to be a fortune for a man of moderate views, is given for a colt not yet foaled, or for a filly, with half a score of connubial engagements into the bargain. It is no uncommon sight here to see a steak and a stake at the same table, and perhaps taken up at the same time. You may sometimes behold a right honourable selling a well-bred puppy, with a pedigree longer even than his own will be for generations to come. On a settling day, after a spring or an October meeting, this place bears no faint resemblance to the Stock Exchange, even on such a day after a series of hoaxing and gambling speculations.[1]

[143]

Pulteney Hotel.

That magnificent edifice, the Pulteney Hotel, was built, or rather begun, by the ingenious Novoselski, for the residence of the late eccentric Lord Barrymore, whose premature death is fresh in the recollection of some of

'shortly afterwards it was levelled with the ground'. There is a photograph of the Old Bell as it appeared in 1885 in Hermione Hobhouse's *Lost London* (1971), p. 198.
[1] **Tattersall's** was at Hyde Park Corner, where Richard Tattersall had set up as a horse and hound auctioneer just behind St George's Hospital (now the Lanesborough Hotel) in the mid-1760s, adding subscription rooms for refreshments in 1780. Initially available only to members of the Jockey Club, these were expanded by his son Richard in 1815 and were universally recognized in fashionable London as the centre for turf wagering. When the lease ran out in 1865 Tattersall's moved to Knightsbridge, and today the firm operates chiefly from Newmarket.

our readers. After that event, it remained for a considerable time in a dilapi-dating state: at length, by a union of purses and talents, it was finished on a very extended scale.[1] We believe the concern is in shares, under a committee of management. The direction of the furnishing department rests principally with Mr. George Oakley, of Bond Street. The cellar department is assigned to the care and cure of a very considerable wine-merchant. That department which properly comes under our cognizance, the dispensation of viands, is conferred by charter (as large as the largest bill of fare) on Monsieur Escudier, formerly cook to the Right Hon. the Earl of Cholmondely, afterward confi-seur in Bulstrode Street, and subsequently in Oxford Street, at the refectory now kept by Mr. Mera. The above prefects of the above departments last year enjoyed somewhat very like a sinecure, as the Duchess of Oldenburg, and her imperial brother took a fancy to the whole hotel. [144] It was in this elegant mansion that the late lamented Duchess of Gordon paid the debt of nature.

Gloucester Coffee-House.

The Gloucester Coffee-house Tavern and Hotel is conducted by Mr. Puls-ford, who, we believe, has shoulders quite valid for the burden of this triple concern, which is no small praise to him, for the business in each branch is immense. It is the last and first house at which all or most of the western mails and stages, short and long, stop. A most excellent dinner, or any other repast, is to be had here; the lodging rooms also are very commodious and pleasant. The larder and soups are always at command.[2]

[1]   The **Pulteney** opened in May 1810, occupying a mansion on the western corner of Bolton Street, facing Piccadilly and Green Park (*Morning Post*, 7 May, describing it as a 'superb pile of building', with ten suites of rooms); the original architect was Michael Novosielski (*c.* 1747-1795). One of the most fashionable hotels of the day, it was chosen by Emperor Alexander I of Russia and his sister as their residence when the Allied Sovereigns visited London in June 1814 to celebrate the abdica-tion of Napoleon. Although John Escudier advertised in the *Morning Chronicle* of 15 April 1822 that he and his son had just 'newly and elegantly furnished' the hotel and made other improvements, a year later the Pulteney removed to no. 13 Albe-marle Street (*Morning Chronicle*, 24 April 1823, advertising the sale of the contents of the old hotel). The Piccadilly building was later replaced by Bath House, built for Alexander Baring, later 1st Lord Ashburton. For Oakley, see below, p. 238.

[2]   The **Gloucester Coffee House and Hotel** at no. 77 Piccadilly, north side (east corner of Berkeley Street), was a major terminus for coaches from Bath, Bristol, and other points west, and is mentioned as such in a 1765 Post Office notice (see Lillywhite). It was succeeded by a series of later hotels, including the St James's

Attached to that repository for luggage and game of all feather and hair, longs and shorts, the White Horse Cellar, is a most excellent accommodation house, which affords great variety of comfortable refreshment. It is situated on the south side of Piccadilly, between Park Wall and Arlington Street.[1]

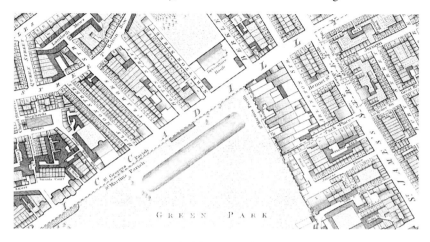

Nichols's Pastry-Shop.

No. 75, immediately opposite, is Nichols's Pastry-shop: the proprietor acquired the rudiments of his art under that celebrated [145] professor Mr. Perry. We need not confer any eulogium, therefore, on the productions of this accomplished confectioner and cook.

Hatchett's.

Hatchett's Hotel, at the corner of Dover Street, Piccadilly, has, like its neighbour, the Old White Horse, a cellar for the reception of parcels and luggage for the western stages: in fact, the hotel establishment rose from this

(later called the Berkeley) and the Bristol, built in 1971 and now the Holiday Inn Mayfair.

[1] Today the Ritz Hotel stands on the site of the old **White Horse**, a major coaching inn that was the starting point for journeys to the west. By 1876 (*ONL*, iv:261) the White Horse had moved to the north side of the street, next to **Hatchett's**, which stood on the eastern corner of Dover Street (the address was sometimes given as nos. 1-3 Dover Street); both had been pulled down by the end of the C19 (Norman 1905, p. 167).

humble cellar, and now it is a upper [*sic*] and tavern of the first-rate, where capital dinners and suppers are served to a numerous and respectable set of customers.

Bachelor's, George Court.

In George Court, facing St. James's church, is Bachelor's Eating-house, where joints of all sorts, with vegetables, as well as the minor essentials, puddings and pies, are hot and eatable, by the plate, every day, from noon until four o'clock.[1]

Fletcher's, Little Vine Street.

Close at hand to the above house, at No. 13 Little Vine Street, is Fletcher's Eating- [146] house and à-la-mode beef-shop. This place may be classed among the cook's-shops.[2]

Black Bear.

The business of the Black Bear Inn depends chiefly on passengers by the numerous western stages which stop here.[3]

Allen's.

No. 332, south side of Piccadilly, is Allen's Ham and Beef-shop. Mr. Allen is a relative of the almost omnipresent Mr. Epps, whose hams, soups, sausages, and puddings, regale our noses wherever we roam. Here are good accommo-

[1] George Court, home to **Bachelor's** eating house, can be seen on the Horwood map running north from Piccadilly to Little Vine Street, with the entrance between nos. 40 and 41; it was renamed Piccadilly Place in 1862.
[2] With the building of Regent Street, Vine Street proper disappeared and the former Little Vine Street took over its name. **Fletcher's** would have been located on the north side near the Little Vine Street watch house shown on the 1813 Horwood map, an ancestor of the recently demolished Vine Street police station.
[3] The entrance to the **Black Bear** is shown on Horwood's map between nos. 13 and 14 Piccadilly, north side; the inn also appears on Rocque's 1746 map, and in 1733 was named as the starting point for a coach to Bath (*Daily Post*, 25 October). It was taken down around 1820, during the development of Regent Street and Piccadilly Circus.

dations for eating famous mock-turtle soup, of which article there is a good display in the window, both artificial and natural. It is rather an Iricism to say natural mock-turtle; but any Englishman will understand us here to mean calf's head.

Saunders's Shell-Fish and Oyster-Shop.

No. 334 are Saunders's Shell-fish and Oyster-rooms. Mr. Saunders has conferred a novel title on the establishment; he calls it an oyster tavern and coffee-room. A private [147] passage leads up the stairs to the apartments allotted to the guests.

White Bear.

At the White Bear, No. 335, near the Hay-Market, Mr. Holmes keeps a larder, with soups and other refreshments. The accommodations are good.[1]

George's, Coventry Street.

George's, in Coventry Street, is a celebrated coffee-house and tavern, now kept by Mr. J. Curt, and mostly frequented by officers of the British army.[2] Here much valuable information, respecting the actual state of military affairs, may be had. The viands and wines are worthy of the heroes who feast upon them, and the accommodations form a complete and pleasing contrast to those of a Spanish camp or a bivouac on the Pyrenées. A few years ago, the then head waiter retired upon a fortune realized by lending money to officers, and acting as broker in the sale and exchange of commissions.

[1] The **White Bear**, at no. 235 Piccadilly, south side (not 335: this and the preceding two addresses are off by one hundred), is named in an advertisement of 1719 (*Daily Courant*, 12 May) and shown on Rocque's 1746 map. Like the Black Bear it was a busy coaching inn, but by the 1860s it had become 'the resort of Sporting characters' (*SL* 29, p. 254), and in 1870 it was demolished. The site is now occupied by the Criterion Theatre, which opened in 1874.
[2] Before the building of Piccadilly Circus, the east-west thoroughfare changed its name from Piccadilly to Coventry Street at Haymarket; **George's** was at no. 16 Coventry Street, north side.

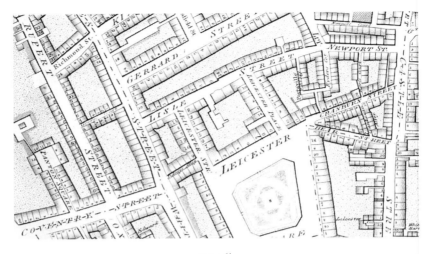

Wood's.

At No. 2, Arundel Street, on the right from [148] Coventry Street, is Wood's Hotel, Tavern, and Coffee-house, a very genteel place of resort, and well supplied with refreshments belonging to each of the three departments.[1]

John o'Groat's.

No. 58, Rupert Street, on the left from Coventry Street, is that famous eating-house, known by the name of John o'Groat's. The neatness of its eating-rooms is really exemplary: cloths are laid in them, and on each table is a bill of fare with prices, a decanter of water with goblets, and the castors with the customary condiments. At two o'clock the first supply of joints commences, and a succession of them is kept up with great spirit until five o'clock, when the cook's fire slackens, and at length entirely ceases. Whole corps of beef, mutton, lamb, veal, pork, as well as many light divisions of pies, puddings, peas, sallads,

[1] Arundel Street, earlier known as Panton or Panton's Square, ran north from Coventry Street with the entrance between nos. 12 and 13; the street was razed in 1920 (*SL* 31, p. 42), and the Trocadero Centre occupies the site today. **Wood's Hotel**, at no. 2 on the east side of Arundel Street, was substantially damaged in a fire of 1 June 1833 (*Morning Chronicle*, 3 June, noting that Wood had unfortunately allowed his insurance to lapse), and it was taken over not long after by George Gregory, owner of **John o'Groat's**, which abutted it to the rear. Gregory renamed the establishment the Arundel Hotel, and seems eventually to have amalgamated the two properties.

vale-royal Cheshire cheese, Gloster [*sic*], single and double, are cut to pieces, and, as the French used to say, annihilated; torrents of porter, ale, and stout, overwhelm their remains, and by seven in the evening the field of destruction is completely cleared. Among the respectable and tried gourmands who daily repair to this scene of action, the most conspicuous and staunch [149] in doing execution are those who come latest; the corps of students from the lectures that are given all the campaigning or slaughtering season in the late Dr. Hunter's theatre of surgery, in Windmill Street. These enterprising youths display equal dexterity with the knife and with the scalpel.[1]

The Hope.

The Hope, formerly the Black Horse, at the corner of Coventry and Whitcombe Street, is a good public-house, where is daily exposed in the front a larder, garnished principally with prime steaks and chops. The room in which they are eaten is very commodious.

LEICESTER SQUARE.

Now, reader, after toiling down Piccadilly, if your appetite be either sharp-set, or delicately urgent, be you peckish or half famished, only go with us through Sidney Passage, and a field shall burst on your view to which the Elysium of the Heathens has nothing fit to be compared. Leicester Square! how many noble and right honourable bowels yearn at the sound! Leicester Square! once the residence of the great Sir Isaac Newton, now the theatre of Miss Linwood's incomparable [150] talent for picturesque needle-work, the spot where Catalani's seraphic or rather *angelical* notes and trills have consecrated! Leicester Square! the mirror in which the great cities, islands, sieges, battles, bombardments, sea-fights, and volcanoes, have been panoramically represented. Leicester Square! the very stones of which have trembled and turned pale under the marshal tramp and Tartarian mustachios of Ferdinand

[1] The **John O'Groat's** eating house was on the west side of Rupert Street, at the corner of Coventry Street; the address is more usually given as no. 61 and later as nos. 60-62. By 1874 the property had become Challis's Hotel (sometimes called Challis's Royal Hotel, and later Challis's Restaurant), which was replaced in 1909 by the first Lyons Corner House (closed 1970). William Hunter's medical school occupied no. 16 Windmill Street (now Great Windmill Street), just west of Arundel Street.

Baron Geramb, as he strode into the hotel à-la-Sablonière, curling up the said mustachios, and uttering a peremptory and irrevocable decree for dinner and wine, *selon le bulletin de son excellence le restaurateur.*[1]

Four Nations, Nassau Street.

Let us pause awhile before we enter the square itself; and for this purpose, eat we some bouilli at the tavern of the Four Nations, kept by Monsieur Barron, the restaurateur, at the corner of Nassau and Gerrard Streets, Soho.[2] Here dishes are cooked equally well, after the English, French, Italian, and German culinæ, and are constantly ready to be served up to the order of any individual of any of those four nations. The kitchens for cooking these various dishes being directly under the salle à manger, or eat- [151] ing-room in front, the effluvia of the hot viands cannot fail to invite the passenger, though the savoury steams suffer a little from being combined with the mephitic vapour that escapes from the charcoal used to keep them hot. The charges at this house are not extravagant.

Prince of Wales.

At the corner of Leicester Place, Lisle Street, stands the Prince of Wales Coffee-house and Tavern, a most excellent house for a dinner either in the English or in the French style, every article being of the best; and the wines choice and curious. At this house, those who choose, may regale themselves

[1]   By the early C19 **Leicester Square** was synonymous with popular entertainment: see Altick 1978, pp. 229-31. Mary Linwood's gallery of 'needlework paintings' opened in 1809 and attracted visitors until her death in 1845, when the collection was sold at auction (Altick, pp. 400-41); the Italian soprano Angelica Catalani lived and performed in London from 1806 to 1814; the 360-degree views displayed in the Leicester Square Panorama, opened in 1794, gave visitors the illusion of being within the picture portrayed (Altick, pp. 128-40); and the adventurer François Ferdinand, Baron de Geramb (1772-1848), who lived in London for several years in the early C19, was noted for his outlandish dress and particularly for his enormous black moustaches.

[2]   The *Almanack's* **Four Nations** does not seem otherwise to be known as such: the establishment referred to is properly the **Nassau Coffee House** at no. 3 Gerrard Street, corner of Nassau Street (now Gerrard Place). The first proprietor, Francis Saulieu, occupied the premises from 1793 to 1802, and the establishment continued to be referred to as Saulieu's Coffee House for some time afterward (*SL* 34, p. 387). The renovated C18 building is now in the heart of London's Chinatown.

with the *coup-d'après* of any elegant liqueur, such as Noyau, Tokay, or Maras-quin, or again with a very capital cup of coffee.[1]

Huntly Coffee-House.

At the north-east corner of Leicester Square, at the termination of Bear Street, is the Huntly Coffee-house and Tavern, directed by Monsieur Chedron, Restaurateur. It is a remarkably neat house, where soups, lunches hot or cold, and dinners may be had in the domestic or foreign style, and where orders are taken by bill of fare.[2]

[152]

Brunet's.

On the east side, about half way down, is Brunet's Hotel, the largest house in the Square, and fitted up in the most elegant and appropriate manner for the business of a tavern and hotel.[3] The larder contains every thing in season, and the wines are excellent. Many foreigners of high distinction in the military or diplomatic line, make this their temporary residence, doubtless, because care is taken to assimilate the attention of the domestics as much as possible to the natural habits and wants of the guests, be they of what nation they may.

[1] The **Prince of Wales**, at no. 10 Leicester Place, west side (corner of Lisle Street), opened in the late C18; Charles Dickens gave a famous dinner there in 1837 to celebrate the completion of *The Pickwick Papers*. The site was later occupied by the French Hospital and Dispensary, established in 1867 for the medical relief of French-speaking foreigners.
[2] The **Huntly Coffee House** was at no. 17 Leicester Square, corner of Bear Street. Later known as Chedron's Hotel, by 1835 the business had passed to another Frenchman, André Picnot, who continued it for a few years as the Bedford Arms.
[3] **Brunet's Hotel** at nos. 24-26 Leicester Square, east side, was founded in 1800 by Louis Brunet and quickly became a centre for French exiles in London; as the business prospered he extended the establishment north and south from his original house at no. 25. From 1815 until 1838 the hotel was run by Brunet's half-brother Francis Jaunay, but by 1839 the houses were empty and soon after 1840 they were demolished. The Royal Panopticon of Science and Art opened on the site in a new, Moorish-inspired building in 1851; in 1858 this gave way to the Alhambra Palace, a theatre that burned to the ground in 1882, and today the site is occupied by the Odeon Cinema (*SL* 34, pp. 490-93).

Pagliano's.

A few door from Brunet's, there is a large establishment rendered conspicuous by the following label in staring capitals, SABLONIERE, which inscription is an obvious absurdity.[1] La Sablonière is the name of a once famous cook in Paris, whose performances on the spit, gridiron, and kitchen-dresser, were so much admired, that his rivals and followers, by way of obtaining a share of his custom, used to announce that they gave dinners *à la Sablonière*. Such was the an- [153] nouncement here; but some John Bull of a house-painter retrenched the article at the expense of propriety, and for the sake of brevity. This house is now kept by Signor Pagliano, who is himself, perhaps, as good a cook as the noted La Sablonière. Make the experiment, and you will at all events find his establishment to be a most excellent and reasonable house for getting a good dinner, either in the French, English, or Italian style. Mr. Pagliano has another and a cheaper house near at hand, in St. Martin's Street, which house was the very identical residence of our great Sir Isaac Newton.[2] His observatory is still to be seen on the roof. One of our coadjutors, by way of experiment did penance here, (as the Spaniards say when they make a feast of a dinner,) by bill of fare, at the following moderate expense.

[1] Rylance was unaware that the original owner of **Pagliano's**, at nos. 30-31 Leicester Square, east side, was indeed named La Sablonière. The hotel was operating from no. 29 as early as 1788, and in 1790 expanded into no. 30 (earlier the residence of William Hogarth from 1733-64, and of his widow until her death in 1789); a further expansion into no. 31 took place in 1792. By 1796, when Antoinetta La Sablonière was declared a bankrupt, no. 29 was no longer part of the hotel, and by 1799 the lease of nos. 30-31 was in the name of Louis Jaquier. An 1844 reference by Charles Dickens to 'Paganini's' has been taken by the editors of his letters as 'probably a joking variant for Pagliano's, i.e. the Sablonnière [*sic*] Hotel in Leicester Square' (*Letters*, iv:59). The hotel was pulled down in 1870 for the building of Archbishop Tennison's school. At that time the manager was Charles Joseph Pagliano, presumably a descendant of the Pagliano named here; for further discussion and a drawing of the hotel, see *SL* 34, pp. 502-03.

[2] **Pagliano's cheaper house** was at no. 35 St Martin's Street, east side, just above Orange Street. Newton lived in the house from 1710 to 1727, and in the late C18 it was occupied by Charles Burney and his family. The building became part of Bertolini's Hotel in the later C19, but was taken down in 1913; the site is now occupied by the Westminster Reference Library.

	s.	d.
Plate of fish (skate)---	o	6
Stewed rump steak and French turnips----------------------	o	9
Bread; and porter (half pint) ---------------------------------	o	3
	1	6

Subjoined is one of Pagliano's bills of fare:

[154]

	d.		s.	d.
Soups.		Beef, with turnips ----	o	6
Vermicelli -----------------	6	Do. with radishes ----	o	6
Herb soup -----------------	4	Mutton à la mode ----	o	8
Broth ---------------------	4	Omelette---------------	o	8
		Fried liver--------------	o	6
Fish.		Boiled fowl ------------	1	6
Boiled skate---------------	6	Maccaroni -------------	o	8
—— holibut--------------	9	Roast beef -------------	o	6
—— cod ------------------	8	Roast fowl -------------	1	6
—— salt fish -------------	6	Sallad ------------------	o	6
Fried fish -----------------	8	Brocoli------------------	o	6
		Potatoes----------------	o	2

It is one of the heaviest charges made against John Bull, that when he intends to fare well, he cannot help crying out "roast beef." We caution him, that when at this or any other house, he sees announced in the bill of fare, a stewed lion, or a roasted owl, he do hold his tongue, preserve every muscle in his jolly countenance undistorted, lift not up his bushy eye-brows, but quietly order up some of the lion or owl. He will find either dish excellent fare; the one as like hare and the other as like partridge as gold is like to gold.[1] But he must not say aught for or against game-laws or poachers; he must use his teeth and hold his tongue; he must not as Pistol did, and as *he* sometimes used to do, [155] when bad news annoyed him, "eat; and eat; and swear." *Verbum sat sapienti,* Johanni.

---

[1] See p. l in the introduction for a discussion of laws concerning the sale of game; and for the terms used here, the Glossary.

Finch's.

Passing from Leicester Square to St. Martin's Lane, through St. Martin's Court, we find at the corner, one of the oldest and best ham and beef repositories in London. It has belonged to the family of the present Mr. Finch for many years; during which two ample fortunes have been made at it. In addition to rounds and flanks of beef, and to hams, here are also fillets of veal and tongues kept ready dressed. If you want beef marrow, you will be sure of a supply here. Yorkshire and Westmorland supply hams to Mr. Finch; and of Mr. Finch, if any one buy hams, he may in Mr. Finch's capacious coppers have them boiled.[1]

ST. MARTIN'S LANE.

Opposite New Slaughter's Coffee-house in St. Martin's Lane, there is a shop famous for vending prime York and Bath Cream cheeses, fresh twice a week.[2]

New Slaughter's.

No. 82, near the top of St. Martin's Lane, is New Slaughter's Coffee-house, now kept [156] by Mr. Robertson.[3] The good dinners of this tavern have gained it great reputation among gentlemen of the army and navy, as well as among private gentlemen, and functionaries in the public offices. At the back entrance to this house from St. Martin's Court, there is a hot and cold larder, which serves in some sort as a chapel of ease to the main refectory. You may dine here on prime roast and boiled, with plum-pudding and apple-pie for one shilling and nine-pence.

---

[1] St Martin's Court, home to **Finch's** ham and beef shop, is today a pedestrian court connecting the Charing Cross Road (earlier Castle Street) and St Martin's Lane.
[2] The cheesemonger on the east side of St Martin's Lane was very possibly **T. Marshall**, listed in Johnson's 1817 directory at no. 64, almost directly across from Slaughter's.
[3] Located at no. 82 St Martin's Lane, west side, **New** (or Young) **Slaughter's Coffee House** opened shortly after the death in 1740 of Thomas Slaughter, proprietor of another coffee house a few doors away. In 1837 the premises were taken over by Augustine Fricour, who directed an advertisement in *The Times* to 'the amateur of French cooking', promising that at the Hotel Fricour and Restaurant he would find a 'real French dinner' (26 October). The site was later occupied by the Westminster County Court, built in 1908-09 and converted to restaurant use in 1996.

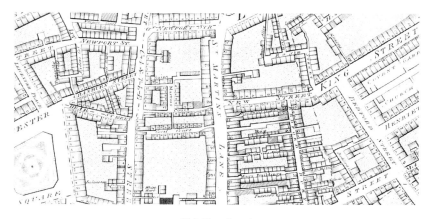

Old Slaughter's.

No. 74 and 75, St. Martin's Lane, constitute Old Slaughter's Coffee-house, which also is a very excellent house. Very large additions have of late years been made to the hotel department. It may not be unworthy of remark, that for many years previous to the time when the streets of London were all completely paved in the present improved style, Slaughter's was called the 'coffee-house on the pavement' in St. Martin's Lane.[1]

Perryman's.

Perryman, at No. 53, near New Street, keeps a decent shell-fish shop and oyster-rooms, with good accommodations up stairs.

[157]

Sawyer's.

No. 125, near Church Street, St. Martin's Lane, is another shell-fish and oyster-shop, kept by Messrs. Sawyer and Co. It is one of the largest concerns of the kind in London, for the sale not only of shell-fish, but also of pickled and dried salmon, spruce beer and other beverages.

[1] The original Slaughter's Coffee House at nos. 74-75 St Martin's Lane, west side, was founded by Thomas Slaughter in 1696, and with the opening of New Slaughter's the original establishment promptly adopted the name **Old Slaughter's**. Before the foundation of the Royal Academy in 1768 it was a popular meeting place for artists, and in the early C19 was much frequented by the painter Benjamin Robert Haydon. The coffee house continued in business until it was pulled down in 1843 for the building of Cranbourn Street.

NEW STREET, COVENT GARDEN.

In New Street, Covent Garden, within two doors of St. Martin's Lane, there is a considerable cook-shop, the window of which is very temptingly filled with hams, tongues, joints of beef, veal, pork, poultry, and with pies, plum-puddings, tarts, and sausages. The accommodations are neat, but the space for them is rather circumscribed.

Swan Tavern.

The Swan Tavern in New Street, is a long established house, well known for the excellence of its fish, flesh, and fowl, which are served up in the best style of cookery by bill of fare daily, to a respectable and numerous company of guests.[1]

[158]

Sutherland Arms.

In May's Building, St. Martin's Lane, is the Sutherland Arms Tavern, a house of a decidedly superior class, and noted for possessing the best waiter in London. Its larder in many points is unrivalled; its cooking department ably and spiritedly conducted; its bar replete with the best liquors; and its dining-room decorated and preserved in the neatest order. An exclusive apartment in this house is occupied by the Illustrious Society of Eccentrics, who meet at least three hundred and sixty-five nights in the near [sic].[2]

---

[1] The **Swan Tavern** at no. 14 New Street (now New Row), south side, was in exist-ence from at least 1733. It was later known as the White Swan, and for a time as Moth's, and is now part of the 'Irish' pub chain O'Neill's (*OEC*, p. 79).

[2] May's Buildings (now Mays Court, a pedestrian passage) reflects the name of Thomas Mays, who in 1738 granted building leases on property that had been left to him by a relation. The entrance to May's Buildings was between nos. 40 and 41 on the east side of St Martin's Lane, and the **Sutherland Arms**, opened in 1739 by Benjamin Sutherland, was at no. 7 (*OEC*, p. 81); it vanished with the building of the Coliseum Theatre in the first years of the C20. The convivial Society of Eccentrics was founded around 1796 and is well-described in the first edition of the *New Picture of London* (1818), p. 367. Any stranger might attend if introduced by a member, and would immediately be admitted to membership on contributing three shillings to a charitable fund. 'The chair is taken by a respectable member of the society between nine and ten o'clock, and some subject, exclusive of politics and religion, is regularly discussed.'

Constitution.

The Constitution in Bedford Street, has its sign painted symbolically, and represents Westminster Hall and Westminster Abbey, which the learned say, mean Church and State. Be that as it may, the constitution of John Bull will never be in jeopardy, while he has money and appetite for the good things offered to him at this house, especially if he take moderately a plentiful potation of the peerless punch for which the Constitution is renowned.[1]

Otley's Burton Ale Rooms.

In Henrietta Street, No. 2, are Otley's [159] (formerly Field's) Burton Ale Rooms. So exquisite is this ale considered by many gentlemen, that they frequently dine here for the sake of drinking it, taking a rump steak or a chop by way of giving a zest to the tankard or bottle. Mr. Field and his son sell the article wholesale in the stores below. It is taken medicinally by many delicate ladies of quality.[2]

[1]   Lillywhite records that the **Constitution**, at no. 32 Bedford Street, east side, was in use for Masonic meetings as early as 1767; the tavern, later rebuilt, survived until the 1870s and was 'noted as the resort of working men of letters, and for its late hours; indeed, the sittings here were perennial' (Timbs, *Walks and Talks* (1865), p. 179).

[2]   There are two mistakes in this entry: the address was no. 23 Henrietta Street, north side, not no. 2, and the house was **Offley's**, not Otley's. William Cornelius Offley (formerly of Bellamy's) established his tavern and eating house in 1807, and it quickly became famous for the quality of its Burton ale and for its thick chops, served with shredded shallots. Mentioned by Dickens in 1835 ('Love and Oysters', published in *Bell's Life in London*), Offley's was particularly known for its convivial amateur musical evenings, with songs offered by both the host and his diners. W. C. Offley himself was dead by 1841 – see the whimsical 'Horæ Offleanæ' by Percival W. Banks in *Bentley's Miscellany* for March of that year – and by 1851 the establishment had become Brookes's, which advertised 'Wine, Stout, Rare Bits, Steaks, Chops (with the Chalots [sic]), on the fine old plan of Offley's', as well as 'Singing, Science, and Sentiment – Fun without offence' (the *Era*, 4 May 1851). By 1856 Brookes's had closed, and the house was taken over as offices by the Board of Works, but on the night of 18 July 1856 the building 'fell with a tremendous crash', weakened during construction on the adjoining property (*Daily News*, 21 July).

Rainbow Coffee-House.

In King Street, No. 2, on the east side of Covent Garden, is the Rainbow Coffee-house and Tavern.[1] Its dinners and wines are in high repute, and there is no lack of good things in its larder. It would be a shame if there were, considering its contiguity to Covent Garden Market, and its vicinity to those of Newport and of Clare.

Richardson's.

The first house under the arcades, commonly called the Piazza, is Richardson's Hotel, very celebrated for its viands, and particularly in the turtle season, for that highly prized luxury, turtle.[2]

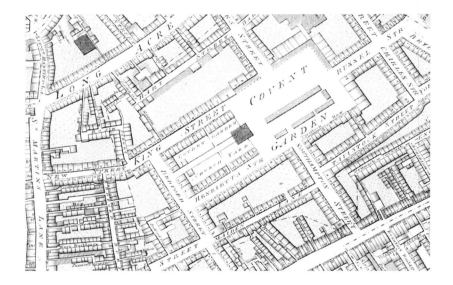

[1]   The *Almanack* gives the number of the **Rainbow Coffee House** as no. 2 King Street, south side, which is not among the various addresses recorded by Lillywhite; the most likely address is nos. 3-4 King Street. The establishment was known as early as 1766, and recorded as late as 1855.

[2]   **Richardson's Hotel** was at no. 1 Great Piazza, Covent Garden, adjacent to no. 43 King Street; for the layout of Covent Garden, see above, p. xxxii, and for all of the following establishments, *SL* 36. Richardson's was earlier known as Wood's Hotel (from 1779), and was taken over by Charles Richardson in 1796; it remained in business, later under the name Clunn's Hotel, until 1876, when the building was demolished.

JAMES STREET, COVENT GARDEN.

The Covent Garden Eating-house is in [160] James Street. A great stroke of business was formerly done here, but on the death of the last proprietor, the successor thought proper to expend, over and above seven or eight hundred pounds for the goodwill and fixtures, a considerable sum in genteel accommodations. These embellishments which were expected to attract, rather tended to dismay the plain dealing market gardeners and others, who were, as we may say, the real strength of the house; and on their secession, no better or more polite company of customers was formed, as the host expected.

Tavistock Breakfast-Rooms.

As you enter the second piazza from James Street, you find Mr. Harrison's establishment, called the Tavistock Breakfast-rooms, where besides the essential refreshments of tea and coffee, you may take excellent soup of various kinds, served up with great neatness.[1]

Piazza Coffee-House.

The Piazza Coffee-House is one of the most extensive and splendid establishments in town.[2] The premises occupy a considerable portion of space over the piazza, and are connected with a great pile of back building as [161] far as Prince's Place. Here dinners for large and small parties are served up in the most consummate style of elegance.

Bedford Coffee-House.

The Bedford Coffee-house, Tavern, and Hotel, is a very large establishment. The tavern department is under the superintendence of Mr. White,

[1] The **Tavistock** coffee house and hotel at nos. 6-7 Great Piazza, Covent Garden (just past James Street) was established in 1801 by Thomas Harrison, and by the time of his death in 1841 had expanded into the greater part of nos. 8-10. It continued in business until the lease expired in 1928, and the buildings were then demolished.

[2] The **Piazza Coffee House** (nos. 10-12 Great Piazza) was founded by the actor Charles Macklin in 1754, and although he was declared a bankrupt four years later the establishment survived and remained popular with patrons from the world of the theatre. The buildings were demolished in 1858 for the building of the Floral Hall and the new Opera House.

who discharges the duties of his station with honour to himself and satisfaction to his customers. Mr. Joy, the wine merchant, who attends to the other functions, is a worthy coadjutor to Mr. White. His dealings in wine are very considerable.[1]

Russel Coffee-House.

The Russel Coffee-house, at the corner of the Piazza and Russel Street, was formerly a common public-house, where a chop was occasionally broiled for the customers, and from that small beginning, its progress to the rank and dignity of a tavern has been rapid. Some apartments under the piazza, formerly called the Piazza Chambers, have been added to it; and in these the hotel business is carried on.[2]

New and Old Hummums.

The New Hummums Coffee-house, Ta- [162] vern, and Hotel, is a most respectable house for dinners, suppers, and elegant lodgings. Like its neighbour, the Old Hummums, it has numerous apartments, kept under the most exact regulation, for the accommodation of gentlemen who choose only to sleep there occasionally, and who if they please may avail themselves of the warm bath.[3]

[1] The **Bedford Coffee House** at no. 14 Great Piazza dated from 1726, and in 1785 expanded into no. 15; the hotel at nos. 16-17 was opened in 1801. In the C18 the coffee house was the particular haunt of actors, actresses, and wits, and in 1763 the *Memoirs of the Bedford Coffee-house* (by 'A Genius') was published. The Bedford continued in business through most of the C19, but all of the houses were pulled down in 1887-88 during the expansion of Covent Garden Market

[2] A coffee house called Sam's operated at nos. 18-19 Great Piazza from 1745, and later a similar establishment known as the Hat and Beaver. Philip Salter, who was the licensee of the Red Lion public house at no. 13 Russell Street, adjoining the coffee house, took over the lease in 1801, and the **Russell Coffee House** was sometimes known as Salter's Hotel. Both the hotel and the public house were demolished in 1887-88.

[3] Nos. 1-2 Little Piazza, Covent Garden, formerly run as a bagnio by Matthew Lovejoy, were taken over in 1781 by Thomas Harrison, who later founded the Tavistock Hotel on the north side of the Piazza; by 1790 he had expanded the **New Hummums** into the corner building at no. 11 Russell Street, south side (on bagnios and hummums in general, see above, p. xli). In 1885 the buildings were demolished, and a newly-built Hummums Hotel opened on the site two

British Imperial Hotel.

The British Imperial Hotel and Tavern, adjoins the Old Hummums. It was formerly called the King's Arms.[1] Its extensive larder is constantly supplied with every delicacy in season; and Mr. Kinsey, the proprietor, who is a considerable importer of foreign wines and spirits, piques himself on the goodness of the stock in his caves.

BOW STREET.

In Bow Street, No. 37, facing the public office, is an eating-house of the usual description, with this addition, that when the hot joints for dinner have been served up until five o'clock from mid-day, a repetition of that fare, together with *à la mode* beef for suppers, commences in the even-tide, and continues until midnight; so that the culinary fire at [163] this house is like that of the vestals, it never is quenched.[2] These suppers are very excellent things after a mental repast at the theatre, and a cheering glass after, fortifies the mind against the attacks of those blue devils that ply at the play-house as regularly as link-boys; and when you come out from a blaze of beauty and a roar of fun, those imps accompany you through the cold damp dark streets to your gloomy, chilly fire-side, and put you to bed between the wet blankets of melancholy. These fiends attend also at routs, balls, and masquerades. Many a young lady will recollect, that after the last tender, lingering, sorrowful "good night", (which these infernal tormentors take as their signal of onset,) she has slipped into bed in the most tristful hurry, her closed eyes still dazzled with the lustre of wax lights, candelabra, and coloured lamps; her ears tingling with

years later, but by 1909 this had failed. The hotel building, now known as Russell Chambers, was for some time used as a warehouse by market traders, but since the closure of the fruit and vegetable market one part of it has returned to use as a brasserie and wine bar. The **Old Hummums** at no. 3 Little Piazza, adjacent to the New Hummums, was established some time after 1769, when a disastrous fire necessitated the rebuilding of the Little Piazza buildings. By 1813 James Hewitt had taken control of the Hummums, and it remained in his family until 1865, when it closed; the building was demolished in 1885.

[1] The **British Imperial Hotel** at no. 1 Tavistock Row was formerly the Bedford (not King's) Arms tavern. The premises were converted to a hotel around 1800 by John Stacie, and the British Imperial survived until 1859-60, when it was demolished to make way for a temporary flower market.

[2] A victualler was known at no. 37 Bow Street as early as 1682 (*SL* 36, p. 187); today the rebuilt premises are occupied by the recently refurbished **Globe** public house and restaurant.

the never to be forgotten strains of Vaccari, and the heart melting tones of the horns of Herren Schunke. Then she has, like a disconsolate Ophelia, repeated the desponding ejaculation of Hamlet,

> How weary, stale, flat, and unprofitable,
> Seem to me all the uses of this world.

All this she may be assured arises from the [164] vapours, brought by these blue devils from the stagnant pools of Erebus.

> "We never mention Hell to ears polite."

A splendid breakfast will dispel them. The hiss of the tea-urn, the crackling of the coffee berries, and the *cliquetis* of cups and tea-spoons, will put the whole legion to flight. *Experto credite Roberto.*[1]

There is a house on the south side of Covent Garden, called the Finish; and another called the School of Reform, whither many of our choice spirits retire from the noise and confusion of midnight, and joyously await the levée of Aurora.[2]

Garrick's Head.

Garrick's Head very properly faces the main front of Covent Garden Theatre. That head belongs to a tavern and chop-house, which concern has

---

[1]   The violinist Francesco Vaccari of Modena gave several London concerts in 1815, and returned in 1823; the brothers Johann Michael and Johann Gottfried Schunke or Schuncke, considered the greatest horn players of their time, toured England in 1814. Alexander Pope mocked preachers who 'never mention hell to ears polite' (*An Epistle to the Right Honourable Richard, Earl of Burlington*, 1731); *experto credite Roberto* may be translated as 'trust Robert, who speaks from experience'.

[2]   The **Finish** was notorious as an unsavoury after-hours establishment serving both men and women, and the **School of Reform** – possibly taking its name from Thomas Morton's enormously popular play of 1805 – was presumably another such. The Finish, originally Carpenter's Coffee House, was nothing more than a wooden market shed at the bottom of Covent Garden, facing the New Hummums; it was established in the early 1760s and was sometimes known as the Queen's Head. West's *Tavern Anecdotes* of 1825 records that the building was then occupied by a 'vendor of coffee and tea, hot rolls and butter' serving the market traders, and Timbs (*Clubs*, p. 341) says that it was 'cleared away' in 1829. Another source gives it a much longer life: Larwood and Hotten fittingly conclude their 1866 *History of Signboards* with an account of the Finish, describing it as 'pulled down recently' and saying that 'down to a recent date it was a gloomy disreputable coffee-house', where 'in interdicted hours, beer and spirits could be obtained when all the public-houses were closed' (p. 511).

been established many years; and is occasionally frequented by performers of both theatres. It was kept for a long time by the late Mr. Spencer, the celebrated jumping harlequin. We use the term jumping, because many performers in that nimble walk, confine their efforts to terrene exploits. But Mr. Spencer was as notorious for high bodily [165] leaps, as his name-sake, the poet, was for intellectual soarings; therefore his house was called the jump, and it formed, as astrologers would say, a trine with the Go and the Finish, two other planets that are sunned by the Apollo of Drury.[1]

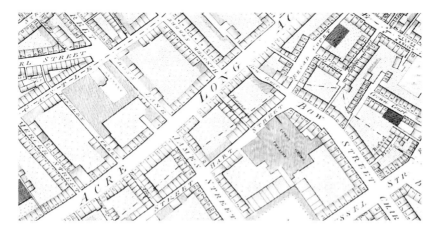

Queen's Head.

   Turning out of Bow Street by the last house, we come to Duke's Court, and there salute the Queen's Head. What Queen's Head? you say. We know no more than you; but look at the larder, English reader, and the occiput and sinciput of a calf there, shall make you forget all the crowned heads in Europe. When Mr. Jupp kept this house, it was called the Go. It might have been as properly called the Stay, in consideration of the good things that

[1]   The former landlord of the **Garrick's Head**, at no. 27 Bow Street, east side, was William Barber (1757-1803), who used the stage name Spencer; well known as an actor, dancer, and acrobat, he retired from the stage in 1791 and is mentioned as landlord in an Old Bailey trial of 16 February 1791. In the mid-C19 the Garrick's Head was home to the bawdy 'Judge and Jury Society', in which the impresario Renton Nicholson presided over mock trials, usually involving crimes of a sexual nature (cf. the Coal Hole, p. 98, and the Cyder Cellar, p. 156); it was demolished for the building of the Bow Street Magistrates' Court (opened 1880). For the **Go**, see the following note.

tempt one to do so. This is the origin of the Go. Mr. Jupp was one of the first publicans who served spirits to his parlour guests, in small pewter measures; the requisite sugar and water was always left on the table for the gentlemen. One customer, who seldom quitted the company without taking the contents of several measures, (half quarterns), always gave his order in these words: "One more and then I'll go." A gentleman hearing this one day, for, perhaps, the fifteenth time, said to the waiter, "Bring [166] me a double quantity for I mean to stay." Thenceforward the half quartern measure, and the quartern measure, were baptized in spirits by the names of the Go and the STAY. A Go of white was *gin*, a Stay of yellow was brandy; the new names circulated all round the Garden; and the Go became quite the Go.[1]

New Chapter Coffee-House.

Facing the Queen's Head in Duke's Court, is the New Chapter Coffee-house, which is literally a coffee and tea-house, where those articles only, with muffins, bread, toast, and cold bread and butter, are served up at very easy charges. Here most of the morning and evening papers are taken in and filed.

Wrekin, Broad Court, Bow Street.

The Wrekin in Broad Court, Bow Street, has progressively become a tavern of great note, chiefly on account of its dinners.[2] Few houses can exhibit a better larder, and the accommodations are particularly good. That great and

[1] Duke's Court ran east from Bow Street at no. 27, and the site of the **Queen's Head** (named in an Old Bailey trial of 1758) was also absorbed by the Victorian police station and magistrates' court. In the 1811 *Lexicon Balatronicum* the term 'Go Shop' is specifically defined as referring to the Queen's Head, 'frequented by the under players: where gin and water was sold in three-halfpenny bowls, called Goes'. A quartern measure equalled a gill, or one quarter of a pint.

[2] The **Wrekin** was at no. 22 Broad Court, on the east side of Bow Street; it was particularly popular with actors, including John and Charles Kemble. Walford notes that 'from 1842 "The Wrekin" began gradually to decline, and within the last few years its declension was so rapid that by the end of 1871 the ancient hostel was levelled with the ground, and its position occupied by a block of new houses' (*ONL*, iii:274).

genuine actor, George Frederic Cooke, at one period of his life, used to dine here daily; and the place is now frequented by many respectable theatrical gentlemen.

[167]

Mollard.

In this catalogue of culinary curiosities, it would be injustice to pass by the name of an artist, whose work has caused an impressive sensation among the amateurs of refined repast. As long as good digestion waits on appetite, and health on both, the name of Mollard will be fondly remembered; he will be regretted when his spit stands still, and his fire is extinguished by the economy of his female partner. As an author he is eminently distinguished, and as a practical artist he is without a rival. If commendation could add to the celebrity of the host of the Old Drury Tavern in Brydges Street, and of the Crown and Sceptre at Greenwich, the most respectable encomiums would be lavished by the members of the Committee of Taste, a club consisting of philosophers, anatomists, and metaphysicians, who hold their session under the roof of Mollard.[1]

The middle avenue leading into Broad Court, nearly opposite the Wrekin, connects this court with Long Acre, whither we shall now hasten. We have no sooner passed the third door round the corner, than we come to a decent eating-house, which keeps its viands hot from noon to four o'clock. If you prefer a simple basin of à-la-mode beef to a dinner [168] in form, you may have one at a house on the same side of the way, between James Street and Bow Street; there is a public-house hard by, where you may precipitate the deglutition of your spiced porridge, with a tankard of truly galvanic Meux's entire. We say galvanic, because the chemists have proved that porter taken out of a pewter pot, is slightly galvanized, and therefore is much more salubrious than porter served up in a vessel of clay.

[1] John Mollard's **Old Drury Tavern** was at no. 23 Brydges Street, east side, just below Drury Lane Theatre, which at one time owned the premises. Brydges Street was renamed in 1872, yielding the new address no. 50 Catherine Street; the tavern closed around 1894 and the building has since been replaced. Mollard also ran the Crown and Sceptre at Greenwich (see below, p. 214); his *Art of Cookery Made Easy and Refined* first appeared in 1801, and had gone through four editions by 1808.

Freemason's Tavern.

Before we perambulate the hundreds of Drury, we cross its far-famed Lane, for the justifiable purpose of contemplating the Freemason's Tavern and Hall, in Great Queen Street, Lincoln's Inn Fields.[1] We have no design to scrutinize the symbolical arcana of masonry; we can see no use in a silver trowel, except as a substitute for a fish spoon; the masonic hammer seems to us most fit for breaking a marrow bone; or the armour (total gules) of a lobster; the white apron would in our way of thinking, serve only for a napkin; and we deem none of all their other symbols half so significant as the Bacchic corkscrew; the capacious tankard; the sacred shrine of the ancient baron of beef, who suffers as a [169] martyr in his country every Christmas and Easter tide; that venerated relique, the pope's eye; and last and dearest of all, that noted type in ornithological augury, the merry-thought.

We never go the hall of the free-masons, except to eat, drink and be merry, and we are told that many good masons believe that so to do is the fulfil a very essential part of their masonic duty. We may regard as convincing proofs of this assertion, the comely looks, the portly habit, the constant good humour, and the glorious passion for music, which form the characteristics of some distinguished members of this mystic fraternity.

The good cheer served up at this tavern, is celebrated all over the world. We will not particularize it, because there are probably none of our readers who have not once in their lives at least, either partaken of a public dinner at this house, or heard as well as read the description of one in the journals of the day.

Hercules' Pillars.

Opposite the Free Mason's Tavern, stand the Pillars of Hercules, between which you pass on (*plus ultrà,* according to the motto on the pillars stamped on the Spanish dollars) [170] to a very superior public-house, where a heca-tomb of fish, flesh, and fowl, is kept ready at command, on which Hercules

---

[1] The **Freemason's Tavern**, opened in 1776, occupied the front portion of the lodge's grand hall in Great Queen Street (south side, just east of Queen's Court) and was, as noted here, extensively used for public dinners and meetings. The tavern was expanded in the early C19 and rebuilt in the 1860s; today the site is occupied by London's largest permanent banqueting facilities, the Connaught Rooms (opened 1905).

himself would not disdain to regale, after the accomplishment of the last of his labours.[1]

In continuing our tour, we pass diagonally the great square, called Lincoln's Inn Fields, the area of which is said to be equal to that of the base of one of the Egyptian pyramids. Having crossed this area, we find ourselves once more in the awful haunts of the gentlemen of the long robe, barristers as well as serjeants, learned in the law, on whose heads the law allows a black patch, or coif, to be stuck, lest genius and wit should make their escape thence (as Minerva did from the brain of Jove) without a fee. Our readers may remark, that whenever we and they approach any of the inns of court, we invariably find them fortified with superior houses of entertainment, which stand like outworks to defend these citadels of jurisprudence. The fact is, that the law being a dry study, those gentlemen who profess it are instinctively addicted to the juice of the grape, or rather they have a perpetual thirst for it. They love good fare, solid as well as liquid, especially when their clients defray the costs, it being one of the articles of their belief, that,

[171]   To hear, see, and say nothing —
          To eat, drink, and *pay* nothing —
are essentially necessary to legal advancement.

Will's.

The first house we enter at the close of this remark is Will's Coffee-house, at the corner of Serle Street and Portugal Street, which is now kept by Mr. Green. It stands most invitingly, facing the passage that leads into Lincoln's Inn, New Square. This is indubitably a house of the first class, which dresses very desirable turtle and venison, and broaches many a pipe of mature port, double-voyaged Madeira, and princely claret; wherewithal to wash down the dust of musty law-books, and take out the "inky blots" from "rotten parchment bonds;" or, if we must quote and parodize Will's, "hath a sweet

---

[1] The Pillars of Hercules at the entrance to the Mediterranean, once considered the boundary of the known world, were said to have borne the warning *Nec plus ultra*, meaning 'nothing further beyond'; in the Spanish coat of arms the Pillars appear with the more positive motto *Plus ultra*, encouraging exploration beyond traditional limits. The 'very superior' **Pillars of Hercules** described here is mentioned in an Old Bailey proceeding of 17 December 1766, and the Hercules Pillars name has continued in Great Queen Street to the present: today's public house is part of a 1960s office block, but remains popular with Freemasons.

oblivious antidote which clears the cranium of that *perilous* STUFF that clouds the cerebellum."[1]

Serle's.

Almost directly facing Serle Street is Serle's Coffee-house and Tavern, kept by Mr. Hewit, who takes constant care to have his larder well replenished, and his stock pots temptingly filled with excellent soup. The house and its [172] accommodations are of the first order and respectability.[2]

Nor are the inferna membra of the law, sheriffs' officers and their obedient humble followers, without their favourite houses of resort. These body-snatchers, as they are vulgarly called, may be seen at all hours of the day waiting for prey (in two senses of the word); watching, and either praying or swearing, at the following houses: Ꞓo Ꞷit, The Seven Stars in Carey Street, the Apple Tree in Cursitor Street, and the Serjeants' Inn Coffee-house in Chancery Lane; where the gridirons and frying pans are in constant service of these red-tail knights. Here do they chivalrously repose after making a caption, may-hap of a redoubtable Irish baronet, or waiting four or five hours on a frosty morning to trap a shy cock; which, truth to say, is more tedious sport than setting springes for woodcocks.[3]

[1]   **Will's Coffee House** at no. 7 Serle Street, west side (corner of Portugal Street) is not to be confused with the older Will's Coffee House in Bow Street, Covent Garden. The Serle Street establishment opened in the early C18, and was known as Green's Hotel by 1825; today the Land Registry Office occupies the site. Rylance ends this entry with two allusions to Shakespeare: the 'inky blots and rotten parchment bonds' occur in *Richard II*, and in the final act of *Macbeth* the title character seeks some 'sweet oblivious antidote' to the 'perilous stuff' that weighs on his wife's heart.

[2]   **Serle's Coffee House** was at no. 4 Carey Street, south side, and is mentioned as early as 1711. It continued in business until the mid-1840s, when it was converted to chambers; the site was cleared for development as office blocks in the 1890s.

[3]   The **Seven Stars** at no. 53 Carey Street, north side, celebrated its 400th birthday in 2002, although the building itself probably dates from the 1680s (Brandwood and Jephcote 2008, p. 18). It was originally known as 'The League [later corrupted to 'Leg'] and Seven Stars', a reference to the seven provinces of the Netherlands and a reminder that the original clientele included Dutch sailors who had settled in the area. Today it faces the rear entrance to the Royal Courts of Justice, and, recently expanded, is still much frequented by members of the legal profession. Located at no. 30 Cursitor Street, south side (opposite the entrance to Took's Court), the Apple Tree – properly the **Apple Tree and Mitre** – is mentioned in Old Bailey proceedings as early as 1767, and was still in business in the early 1940s.

M'Niven's.

Turning again, and shaping "our course toward Cyprus," for Drury may be so called in allusion of the Cyprians who inhabit there, we pass along Portugal Street, and in Gilbert's Passage that leads into Clare Market, we find M'Niven's commendable and much commended Eating-house.[1] This establishment [173] serves up most delicious lunches, dinners, and suppers. No fewer than half-a-dozen able bodied men-cooks, and perhaps as many neat handed maid-cooks are on permanent duty there. In their respective seasons the forest buck, and the turtle, come hither "like sacrifices in their trim," and are offered hot and smoking to the gods of jollity. Turtle soup is sent out to order, at the not-to-be-grudged price of twelve shillings per quart. Mr. M'Niven for many years went the home circuit, for the purpose of holding his session of oyer and terminer at the assize dinners; his office being to hear and determine by the capacity of the lawyers and justices of fair round bellies, with good capon lined, what should be the daily fare of their lordships and their learned friends. Mr. M'Niven also had for a great length of time the contract for the dinners taken in by the Lord Mayor, the Judges, Mr. Recorder, Mr. Common Serjeant, and others of the body corporate, forming the court, pending the trials of the Sessions House in the Old Bailey. Of the sumptuous fare on these solemn occasions an estimate and opinion may be formed (we would much rather form a dinner of it), by any one who chooses to take the trouble and enjoy the amusement of reading Sir Richard Phillips's letter to the Livery of London. In that letter, among other im- [174] portant matter, the learned bibliopolist, philanthropist, and *jurist*, gives a schedule of monies taken, or disbursed out of his pocket, during his shrievalty for Middlesex. The charges for the aforesaid dinners make no minute item in the aforesaid account of expenditure.[2]

The **Serjeant's Inn Coffee House** was at no. 4 Chancery Lane, east side, just at the entrance into Serjeants' Inn, which accommodated barristers and dated back to the reign of Henry IV (demolished *c.* 1910; *BoE City*, p. 337). The adjoining coffee house figures in an Old Bailey trial of 10 December 1735, and is mentioned in *The Pickwick Papers* (chapter 43, published July 1837), but seems to have disappeared when the Inn was rebuilt in the late 1830s.

[1] Gilbert's Passage, home to **M'Niven's** (or McNiven's) eating house, led from Portugal Street into Clare Market, now the site of the London School of Economics, but in the C19 a thriving market located between Lincoln's Inn Fields and the Strand (see below, p. 247).

[2] Richard Phillips, *A Letter to the Livery of London, Relative to the Views of the Writer in Executing the Office of Sheriff* (1808).

Thomas's and Johnson's.

As soon as we have passed the many good things exhibited in Clare Market, and feasted our eyes thereon, we will proceed down Blackmoor Street, for the purpose of entering Clare Court; there to recognise two of the best à-la-mode beef-houses in London – The Old Thirteen Cantons and the New Thirteen Cantons, both regularly licensed as public-houses.[1] The former is kept by Mr. Thomas, and the latter by Mr. Johnson. The beef and liquors, at either house, are equally good, and the attention of all who pass is attracted by the display of fine sallads in the windows, which display is daily executed with great ingenuity, and comprehends a variety of neat devices, in which the fine slices of red beet root are pleasingly conspicuous. Mr. Johnson was the master of the famous dog Carlo, who once enacted so capital a part on the boards of Old Drury. The sagacity of this animal was so famous, [175] that it brought as many customers to Mr. Johnson as did the excellence of his fare. At length, unhappily, a report was spread that the faithful animal had been bitten by a mad dog, and Mr. Johnson was reluctantly compelled to sign his death-warrant.

Anderson's.

At the other corner of Clare Court, Drury Lane, we find Mr. Anderson's long and justly celebrated Eating-house, which, for variety and for the goodness of the articles served up in it, is not excelled by any establishment of the kind in all London. The primest joints, as well boiled as roasted (and roasted,

[1]   Clare Court ran northeast from Drury Lane, and had an outlet into Blackmoor Street just to the east (the New Thirteen Cantons, later Jaquet's, is sometimes described as being at no. 21 Blackmoor Street). The names of the two beef alamode houses located in the Court refer – for whatever reason – to the cantons of the Old Swiss Confederacy; for the dish itself, see above, p. xlviii. It was presumably the **Old Thirteen Cantons** that was mentioned in an Old Bailey trial of 26 May 1757, and named in a poem attributed in 1763 to William Woty (*The Beauties of the Magazines Selected*, ii:341), but it was the **New Thirteen Cantons** that Charles Dickens remembered visiting as a boy of twelve or fourteen: having brought his own bread with him, 'wrapped up in a piece of paper like a book', he confidently marched into Johnson's and ordered a plate of alamode beef to go with it (John Forster, *The Life of Charles Dickens* (1872), i:34). The theatrical Newfoundland dog Carlo, owned by George Johnson of the New Thirteen Cantons, had 'starred' in the 1803 hit play *The Caravan, or The Driver and His Dog*, in which he rescued a drowning child on stage, and is commemorated in Eliza Fenwick's book for children, *The Life of Carlo, the Famous Dog of Drury Lane Theatre* (1804).

not baked, we believe every joint so announced really is); these, as well as prime fowls, geese, ducks, pigs, tongues, puddings, and tarts, with the suitable vegetables, are to be seen and to be had here all day; and to a late hour at night, for the benefit of persons returning from the theatres. There are a pleasant room and good accommodations up stairs: the servants are attentive, and the charges are moderate. What, in the name of conscience, reader, would you have more?

Langley's.

Before we cross Drury Lane we shall direct our readers to two other houses higher up in [176] Drury Lane. The first is Langley's Eating-house, directly opposite the old stage door, a very good refectory, with large rooms up stairs. You may dine here very well and cheaply. The second is still higher up in Drury Lane, on the west side, near Brownlow Street. This is a Cook's-shop, where joints are kept hot from noon till four o'clock, and cut by weight, or plate, to be eaten there or carried away at the discretion of the purchaser.[1]

---

[1] Brownlow Street ran southwest from Drury Lane and was renamed Betterton Street in 1877, honouring the C17 Shakespearean actor Thomas Betterton.

Egg Shop, Russel Court.

We now turn into Russel Court, and as soon as we enter discover an Egg Mart, which has maintained for many years its reputation for eggs, warranted fresh, but not to keep for any length of time in any climate. Every variety of edible egg may be had; those usually in request are the speckled plover egg, and the delicious ovum of the guinea fowl.

G. P. R.

The next house is an à-la-mode beef-shop; and the proprietor, in imitation of his other next door neighbour who deals in similar viands, has adopted for his sign the three charming letters G. P. R., which we presume mean George Prince Regent. If the Prince [177] of Wales should ever deign to send his commands to this loyal à-la-mode artist, his Royal Highness might depend on being served with a delicious olla (olio *vulgariter*). We think the man's name is Carrill.[1]

Cheshire Cheese, Read.

Turning up what was formerly called Vinegar Yard, near Woburn Street, facing the old pit door, is the Cheshire Cheese, a famous house for ales and brown stout. Chops and kidneys are at sundry times and in divers manners taken therewithal as a relish.[2]

[1] Russell Court, home to the **G. P. R.**, was a passage leading from Drury Lane into Brydges Street (now Catherine Street); the entrance from Drury Lane was between nos. 74 and 75.

[2] Vinegar Yard was the old name for the passageway leading southwest from Drury Lane between nos. 70 and 71; on the 1799 Horwood map this is named Marquis Court, continuing as Wooburn [*sic*, for Woborn] Street. Plans of the old theatre, destroyed by fire in 1809, show that the 'passage to the pit' – presumably the 'old pit door' opposite **Hudson's** cook shop – was about halfway along the southern side of the building. The **Cheshire Cheese** in Vinegar Yard is mentioned in an Old Bailey proceeding of 4 December 1741. By the 1820s the address was being given as Marquis Court, and for a while it is listed at no. 10 Cross Court (shown but not named on Horwood's map, and identified on the Rocque map as the passage between Vinegar Yard and Russell Court: presumably the establishment was on a corner). Not surprisingly, by 1858 it had become the Old Cheshire Cheese, but within five years the name disappears from directories.

Hudson's.

Near the old pit door is Hudson's, a Cook's-shop of the common order; the customers are mostly from among the carpenters, scene-shifters, and lamp-trimmers, belonging to the Theatre Royal Drury Lane.

Finch's.

We find it difficult to get out of Russel Court, it being occupied by the Jews as a strong hold, and in this respect resembling the *Rue de la Friperie* at Paris; from whence you cannot come unclad if you be without a coat on your back and have money to buy one.[1] Here [178] is Finch's celebrated O. P. and P. S. Tavern, where Jews and Christians may dine to their heart's content. O. P. and P. S. are misinterpreted by a loyal serjeant in Sheridan's Farce of the Camp into Old Pretender, and Pretender's Son. We believe the equivoque to be founded on fact. Finch displays an excellent larder in front, and accommodates his guests in very handsome style within. Two tables d'hôte are announced daily; the one at three, and the other at five o'clock, which are well attended by provincial managers and theatrical candidates. The pleasantries of these and other knights of the sock and buskin, some of them of the highest "tire of metropolitan admittance" who frequent this house, are strong temptations to strangers, who seldom leave the table of Mr. Finch without having cause to thank him for a feast of reason and a flow of soul.[2]

[1] Drury Lane was one of several areas named in Henry Mayhew's *London Labour and the London Poor* as home to the trade in old clothes, principally in the hands of Jewish merchants (Mayhew 1861, ii:27).
[2] The initials O. P and P. S. in the name of **Finch's** refer to 'opposite prompt' and 'prompt side', traditionally stage right and stage left from the actor's point of view. The owner of the tavern, John Charles Finch, was declared a bankrupt in 1816 (*London Gazette*, 20 February), and by 1819 the establishment had become the Kean's Head; for several years kept by the songwriter and publisher Thomas Hudson, this was usually listed in directories at no. 21, but disappears around 1850. In both incarnations the tavern was popular with actors and theatre-goers: Finch himself hosted occasional 'theatrical dinners', offering 'Mirth with Music, Wit with Wine' (*Morning Chronicle*, 9 June 1814; tickets were 6s. each), and in 1819 J. G. Burton included the Kean's Head in a list of London private theatres (*The Critic's Budget*, p. 49).

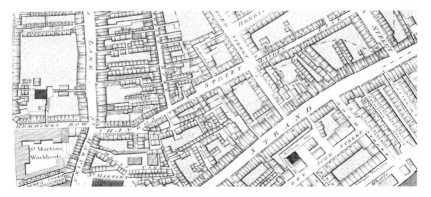

Tucker.

Facing Finch lives Tucker, a noted Pastry-cook, where you may stay your stomach, if not sate it, with a variety of tit-bits in the confectionary style.

Bedford Head.

We again deviate for the sake of reminding those who choose to pass by a sort of mid- [179] way between Covent Garden and the Strand, that in Maiden Lane stands the Bedford Head, a superior public-house, with a good larder, kept by Mr. Garden. Many gentlemen attached to the marine of the Hon. East India Company frequently assemble here.[1]

Munday's.

In this same Maiden Lane is Munday's Coffee-house and Tavern, a very old establishment, now kept by Mr. Robinson. It has of late years been considerably improved and enlarged. It now ranks high as a dinner and supper house.[2]

Here is also the famous cyder-cellar, noted as the cavern, where a celebrated Greek professor for a long period used to take his nightly potations of

[1] The **Bedford Head** public house at no. 41 Maiden Lane, north side, was established about 1740 (*SL* 36, p. 241); rebuilt in the early 1870s, it is now the Maple Leaf, London's only Canadian pub.
[2] **Munday's Coffee House** had opened by 1720 in New Round Court, a few blocks southwest of its later location, and moved to no. 20 Maiden Lane, north side, around 1770-72; the building was pulled down some time before the widening of the street in 1872. It cannot be proved that some member of the family associated with today's **Rules Restaurant** at no. 35 had already established a business in

diluted cogniac [*sic*].[1] Alluding to queer fellows generally in the company, and the *free* maids who perambulate Maiden Lane, an observer might have said

> Bacchum remotis carmina rupibus
> Vidi docentem, credite posteri!
> Nymphas que discentes, et aures
> Capripedum satyrorum acutas.

Chandos Street.

Turn the key in Chandos Street, we mean by all means turn from the Key, for you may [180] repent if you turn in.[2] There is for the benefit of the public a long-established Cook's-shop and Eating-house in Round Court in this

---

Maiden Lane by 1815. Directories show that Thomas Rule was operating a barrelled oyster warehouse at no. 52 Minories into the 1820s, but by 1830 he is listed at no. 38 Maiden Lane, where his son Benjamin first paid rates in 1828. The younger Rule later moved his business to no. 36, and in 1873 built new premises for his oyster rooms at no. 35; in the mid-C20 the restaurant expanded into no. 34, built in 1875-76 and originally occupied by a maker of chemical apparatus (see *SL* 36, pp. 250-51).

[1] The **Cyder** (or **Cider**) **Cellar**, no. 20 on the south side of Maiden Lane, is mentioned in *Adventures Under-Ground*, an anonymous satire of 1750, and was probably older. The 'celebrated Greek professor' was Richard Porson (1759-1808), a regular visitor towards the end of his life, and the lines from one of Horace's odes (II.19) speak of glimpsing the god of wine in a remote location, teaching songs to nymphs and goat-footed satyrs (Rylance may have been alluding here to the three satirical letters on the 'Orgies of Bacchus' that Porson published in the *Morning Chronicle* in 1793, under the pseudonym Mythologus). A somewhat later habitué of the Cyder Cellar was B. W. Procter ('Barry Cornwall'), who in 1820 described the Cellar of 'a few years ago' as being a single basement room furnished with several tables and arm chairs, seldom frequented until nine or ten in the evening. The food was plain and cheap ('Welch rabbit' and poached or boiled eggs), and the principal attraction was the political and literary talk and, after midnight, the singing of catches and glees. By the mid-C19 the entertainment had become racier, especially after Renton Nicholson took over the management in early 1858, advertising 'poses plastiques and tableaux vivans' at 7:30 and after the theatre, and mock 'Judge and Jury' trials at 9:30 (the *Era*, 31 January; cf. the Garrick's Head, p. 144 above). The Cyder Cellar continued in the same vein after Nicholson's death in 1861, but in 1863 complaints led to its closure (the *Era*, 6 September 1863), and by 1867 no. 20 had been absorbed into the Adelphi Theatre (*SL* 36, p. 249).

[2] The **Key Hotel** in Chandos Street (now Chandos Place) was sometimes known as the Key Bagnio, a good indication of its status as a quasi-brothel; it was described as 'a most infamous house' in an Old Bailey trial of 10 January 1798, and included

street, where you cannot possibly take any harm unless the good things tempt you to overlay your stomach, and thus superinduce dyspepsy, cachexy, or perhaps apoplexy.[1]

White Lion.

Come back with us to Drury Lane, and we will thence proceed toward Temple Bar through Wych Street. At the White Lion, in Wych Street, you may have a chop, steak, or cutlet, at three minutes warning. It is a licensed and famous house for ales.[2]

Almost opposite is a very good Eating-house, noted for its plentiful allowance of vegetables to every plate of meat.

Sol's Arms.

Near the bottom of Wych Street is the famous Sol's Arms and Shakspeare Chop-house. Here is always a tempting bill of fare and a larder to match it. The house is much frequented by the society whose badge of distinction forms part of the sign, and by many theatrical gentlemen. Mr. Rees, the proprietor, for many years trod the comic walk [181] at Covent Garden Theatre, and is still celebrated for giving imitations of most performers of the old school. Mr. Rees is no niggard of his humour, and frequently entertains his guests with a specimen of his mimetic powers.[3]

---

in the fascinating 1828 *How to Live in London; or, The Metropolitan Microscope and Stranger's Guide* (written by 'Two Citizens of the World') among houses 'where women are not farmed or regularly lodged, but which are kept open for casual calls' (pp. 117-18). The Key was rebuilt after burning to the ground in June 1806, and demolished in 1830 for the building of the Royal Westminster Ophthalmic Hospital.

[1] Old and New Round Court were two of the many now-vanished alleyways in the area between Chandos Street and the Strand.

[2] Wych Street, running southeast out of Drury Lane as it approached the Strand, was destroyed for the building of Aldwych, opened in 1905. The **White Lion** 'in Wytch street near Drury Lane' was named as a Masonic meeting place as early as 1725 (Lane 1889, p. 170); by 1875 the site was occupied by a carpenter's shop (*ONL*, iii:34).

[3] The **Sol's Arms** is mentioned in Old Bailey proceedings of 1794 and 1817, one confirming that it was at 'the bottom of Wych Street'; J. Holden MacMichael (*Notes and Queries*, 22 February 1908, pp. 154-55) identified the establishment with

Angel Inn.

At the end of Wych Street, facing St. Clement's Church, is the Angel Inn, a house where all travellers, and particularly navy officers, landing in London from the Portsmouth stages, are entertained with good fare and excellent lodgings.[1]

THE FASHIONABLE WORLD.

In our walks along Piccadilly and Oxford-street, we purposely forebore to enter upon Bond-street, and those streets and squares which being morally, physically, and locally connected with it, form as it were a world of themselves of which it is, if we may so say, the axis.

Blenheim, New Bond-Street.

On entering New Bond-street, from Oxford-street, the first house to our purpose is the Blenheim Coffee-house, Tavern and Hotel, kept by Mr. Fosbury; the title-page of [182] his epicurean compendium, in the shape of a label in front, announces that dinners are dressed here, and that mock turtle, and other soups are constantly ready.[2]

Opposite the Blenheim, is Owen and Bentley's Fruit-shop, at which are to be had all early produced fruits, exotic, as well as indigenous. You may also

the later **Shakespeare's Head** (no. 31 on the north side of the street), also popular with actors and for a time kept by Mark Lemon, later the editor of *Punch*. The landlord named here, Thomas David Rees, was a well-known mimic, actor, and ventriloquist, regularly seen at Covent Garden between 1790 and 1800.

[1] The venerable **Angel Inn** was at no. 34 Wych Street, north side, facing St Clement Danes church. A galleried inn known as early as 1503, with a large yard extending north from the point at which Wych Street met the Strand, it appears on Ogilby and Morgan's map of 1676 as well as on the later Rocque and Horwood maps. The Angel was a noted coaching terminus, with stages to Dover and Portsmouth; it closed in 1853 and the building was demolished the following year.

[2] The **Blenheim Coffee House** – earlier Tavern and later usually Hotel – was on the northwest corner of Blenheim Street at no. 87 New Bond Street (renumbered no. 94 by the mid-1820s). The Blenheim Tavern was in operation no later than 1788, and the establishment continued as a hotel through most of the C19; by the late 1870s it was the Blenheim Restaurant (with billiard rooms attached), and in 1904 this was transformed into the Blenheim Cafe, part of the Lyons empire (closed 1921).

regale yourself and the ladies here, with jellies, ices, and liqueurs. It is actually a temple of Pomona.

Green Man.

Do not disdain to take a peep at the humble public-house a little below the Blenheim, called the Green Man.[1] It was, until lately, kept by the eccentric George Steevens, a fellow of infinite jest, though at times too whimsical and too independent to submit to the restraints of civilized life. He died a year or two ago, in full possession of his mental faculties, regretted by all to whom his soundness of principle and honest kindliness of disposition were known. His son we believe has succeeded him, and conducts the establishment in a very respectable manner. You may here get a snug, neat, cheap dinner, of plain roast and boiled, and be quite incog. – When you come out, you of course mix with the lounging well-dressed mob, and not a soul [183] will surmise that you have not dined at a sumptuous table d'hote. Thus having kept your head clear and spared your purse, you may cast a smile of pity on the unthinking mortals who exhaust perhaps the entire day's pay of a subaltern over an extravagant dinner; and if you can recollect this wise remark of our English Horace, you may repeat it.

> "He that dines at a guinea a head,
> "Will ne'er by his head get a guinea."

Henster and Co.

At the corner of Brook-street, we observe the successors of Phillips the Fishmonger – Messrs. Henster and Co. They have the honour to be fishmongers to his Majesty and the Royal Family. Here is daily the finest possible display of every sort of edible fish, from the gudgeon to the sturgeon. The shop is decorated with some exquisite portraits of very handsome goodlooking trout, carp, tench, jacks, and other tenants of the seas, ponds, and rivers.

---

[1] The **Green Man** public house at no. 101, west side, was listed in directories through the 1880s. The lines quoted are from 'The Bill of Fare' in Horatio and James Smith's 1813 *Horace in London*.

Gover's.

No. 3, in Brook-street, is Gover's Coffee-house and Tavern. Excellent dinners, and very tasty soups are served here. In the house [184] adjoining, Mr. Gover keeps an extensive assortment of very curious ales.[1]

Phillips, Fishmonger.

On the west side of Bond-street, No. 121, is Mr. John Phillips's emporium of fish. He removed hither from the corner of Brook-street, and came thither from Carnaby market. His renown is, that of being perhaps the first fish-monger in the world. On the day we inspected his tray, there was a display of ray, turbot, cod, and skate, at which a true epicure would have been enchanted. There were turbots of various bulk, from the weight of four pounds to that of the largest ever landed at Billingsgate; these turbots were set off by some brilliant lobsters placed about them, who looked like a guard of honour round some fat foreign prince just invited from Russia or Germany by John Bull. Here are also fine proportioned salmon of all sizes, red gurnets, soles, whiting, mackarel, and John Dories. The race of John Dories, we are told, has greatly ennobled itself since Quin's time.[2]

Barker, Confectioner.

No. 106, on the west side of Bond-street, is Barker's Repository of Confectionery in all [185] its branches. All the sweets of both the Indies, without a particle of the bitter alloy, seem to be concentrated in this spot, at least you would say so, when you saw a bevy of your fair countrywomen tasting them, which they love to do, much to the detriment sometimes of their pearly teeth. Mr. Barker has the warrant for supplying their Majesties and the Royal Family with sweet articles.

[1] **Gover's Coffee House and Tavern** at no. 3 Brook Street, north side, was presumably run by James Gover, landlord of the 'house adjoining', the **Haunch of Venison** (no. 4; after the renumbering of Brook Street in 1867, no. 26). The latter survived in some form into the early C20, leaving its name on Haunch of Venison Yard, now best known for its art galleries.

[2] Many anecdotes are told concerning the actor James Quin (1693-1766) and his love of this fish, and he is often credited with having remarked that 'delicate Ann Chovy' married well with 'good John Dory'.

Molloy's.

No. 129, is the Tower Hotel, Tavern and Coffee-house, kept by Molloy. "Where shall we dine to day," said a facetious Irish captain to our companion on this tour, and a Spanish Don of his acquaintance. Then throwing himself into the attitude of Cooke in Richard, he mused some moments with a curious "lack lustre eye," and muttered, "The Tower? ... Aye the Tower." To the Tower they went; and although the Don could talk very little English, and the Captain hardly any thing but Irish, they dined, drank wine, and took coffee in a very joyous style, and retired perfectly satisfied with their entertainment, and the charges for it. The dinner was at the Captain's expense, who took this mode of laying siege to the impenetrable and impregnable heart of the Don, he having a rich post abroad [186] in his gift, that was much coveted by the Captain. How different therefore were our companion's evening reflections, from those of Gil Blas, when he went out of the Inn at Penaflor, *en donnant à tous les diables, le parasite, l'hôte et l'hotellerie.*

By way of apology to Mr. Molloy, and our readers for this digression, we shall conclude our descant on the Tower, by saying, that it is well governed, and well provided with every thing that one can reasonably expect in a tavern. The waiters are, or at least were, a brisk set of fellows.[1]

Wood's Pastry-Shop.

No. 43, on the east side of Bond-street, is Wood's Pastry-Shop, where savoury patties, pies, soups, and pastry of every sort are vended. The announcement of the shop states that the proprietor dresses turtle at home and abroad. This phrase if interpreted in its utmost latitude, might signify, that Mr. Wood sometimes takes a trip to the West Indies, to serve Johnny

---

[1] Henry Molloy's **Tower Hotel, Tavern, and Coffee House** on the west side of New Bond Street had become the Grosvenor Hotel or Coffee House by 1818; the latest directory listing I have found is 1835. Writing in *Fraser's Magazine* in July 1860, A. V. Kirwan claimed that Molloy – 'a very popular landlord' – was an Irishman who had been 'servant to the gallant Sir Thomas Picton' (p. 122). The Irish captain was imitating the recently deceased actor George Frederick Cooke in his most famous role, Shakepeare's Richard III; in *Gil Blas*, the popular picaresque novel by Alain-René Lesage, the eponymous hero damns the inn, the innkeeper, and a parasitic admirer who has conned him into paying for his meal.

Newcome with callipash and callipee from the shores of his own estates, the native country of that amiable amphibe the turtle.[1]

[187]

Waud.

Kings, Lords, and Commons, laud Mr. Waud, for his celebrated confectionery and pastry. The Prince Regent and the Duke of York, have honoured Mr. Waud with an appointment to serve them with *bon bons;* and have thus placed him in the via lactea of preferment. In almost all public masquerades, Mr. Waud is a part proprietor, and undertakes to supply the suppers and refreshments. So established is Waud's reputation, that you may taste and satiate yourself with any article warranted from his ovens, with the same confident composure in which Alexander the Great swallowed the bowl of physic, while his old doctor stood by reading Parmenio's letter, which accused him of a design to poison the son of Jupiter Ammon.[2]

[1] Johnny Newcome was a nickname given to a newcomer, or new military recruit; for callipash and callipee, see the Glossary.

[2] Charles **Waud**, later confectioner to Queen Victoria, was at no. 38 on the east side of New Bond Street; the butchers Paul **Giblett** and Son were at no. 110 on the opposite side. The story of Alexander the Great would have been familiar to any schoolboy of the day: having received a letter from his advisor Parmenio that warned him of a plan by his doctor to poison him, Alexander swallowed the doctor's medicine nonetheless, giving him Parmenio's letter to read as he did so.

Hickson's.

At No. 134, is another Pastry Shop of the first class, kept by Messrs. Hickson and Co.

Giblet and Son.

The admiration and wonder of all foreigners on visiting the Butchers' Shops in London may well be in the extreme. The precise [188] neatness in which they are kept, and the delightful order in which they are set out, are such that they resemble rather the dissecting-room of an accomplished lecturer on anatomy, than the shambles of a butcher. Messrs. Giblet and Son are in the highest degree exemplary in this respect; eulogies on the mutton, veal, and beef, of Messrs. Giblet, would be as superfluous as gold lace to a patriot, double fees to an honest lawyer, claret to a clergyman, or money to a Jew. Blessed indeed are those noble and right honourable stomachs which digest the mutton of Messrs. Giblet and Son.

We ought to have noticed, when we were in Brook-street, three Hotels of the first class. We should be guilty of taking an unwarrantable liberty, if we even hinted at a preference. Therefore since our printer cannot perhaps arrange his types for this paragraph in the form of a Round Robin, we do here protest, that in mentioning Mr. Mivart's the first, we mean no disparagement to the other twain. Mivart's is at No. 44; Caulson's, No. 45, and Kirkham's, No. 48. All three are endowed with the most splendid accommodations, and replete with fare the most sumptuous. It is in these and similar establishments, that families of rank during a temporary sojourn in town enjoy all the comforts of the Dulce Domum.[1]

[1] Mivart's Hotel and Coulson's [not Caulson's] share a complicated history, not helped by the renumbering of Brook Street in 1867, which has transformed the numbers on the south side from the consecutive nos. 41-49 of 1815 into the odd-numbers-only nos. 57-41, given here in square brackets. The original proprietor of **Mivart's** at no. 44 [51] is sometimes named as a 'M. Mivart', a French chef, but the *Survey of London* volume covering Brook Street shows him to have been one James Edward Mivart (1781-1856), who was set up in business by Lord William Beauclerk in 1812 (see *SL* 40, pp. 23-29, for all three Brook Street hotels). By 1838 Mivart had acquired the adjoining houses nos. 41-43 [53-57], as well as the corner house at no. 48 Davies Street. Almost from the start the hotel was aimed at a fashionable and exclusive clientele, and it is frequently mentioned in novels. Mivart's neighbour and rival at no. 45 [49] was **Coulson's Hotel** (originally Wake's), which opened in 1806 and operated under the Coulson name from 1812 until 1853, when it was acquired by William and Marianne Claridge. The Claridges then quickly

[189]

Mount Coffee-House.

In Grosvenor-street, two or three doors on the left from Bond-street, is the Mount Coffee-house and Tavern, kept by Mr. Read; this house has been long celebrated for its sumptuous larder and its mature wines.[1]

Thomas's.

We turn up Bruton-street, for the purpose of noticing the elegant establishment in Berkeley-square, known by the name of Thomas's Hotel, into which if guests enter in the expectation of enjoying the best possible fare, bed and board, we can only assure them they will not be disappointed. That widowed wife, the amiable Countess of Westmorland, for several seasons honoured this house by making it her town residence.[2]

Gunter's.

We could not, if we would, leave Berkeley-square without paying a tribute to the merit of Mr. Gunter, as a cook, confectioner, and fruiterer, if not the

---

acquired Mivart's as well, connecting it to Coulson's and running it under their own name. In 1893 the hotel was sold to a limited company, who demolished the c18 houses and erected a new Claridge's, opened in 1898. Directories and guides list the next hotel variously as Kirkham's or Kirkman's, but while Lillywhite felt that Kirkman was the correct form, the *Almanack*'s Kirkham is confirmed by the records quoted in *SL*, which names **Kirkham's Hotel** at this address from 1802 to 1832. It was the first of a series of hotels at no. 48 [43], followed by Scaife's, Patterson's, Lillyman's, and finally Buckland's; after the First World War the premises, by then amalgamated with those at no. 49 [41], housed the Guards Club, which was succeeded in 1959 by the Bath Club.

[1] The **Mount Coffee House** at nos. 79-80 Grosvenor Street, south side, had been completed by 1721 (*SL* 40, p. 56), and was mentioned by James Boswell in 1772; only a few years before the *Almanack* appeared the establishment had been under the management of John Westbrook, the father of Shelley's first wife Harriet. The Mount continued as a hotel until around 1850 but had been demolished by 1852.

[2] **Thomas's Hotel**, at no. 25 on the north side of Berkeley Square, was established by Tycho Thomas in the late 1790s, and like Mivart's quickly acquired a reputation for quality. By 1826 John Britton's *Original Picture of London* listed the hotel as 'Bailey's (late Thomas's)'; it was demolished in 1904 and replaced by a block of luxury flats, now the headquarters of Cadbury Schweppes plc (*SL* 40, pp. 65-66).

first, as Goldsmith says of somebody else, in the very first line. Mr. Gunter has had for many years the high honour of supplying the Royal Family with [190] articles from his shop. Some of the Royal Dukes condescend occasionally to give Mr. Gunter a call for the purpose of tasting his pines, as if in gratitude for the many sweet repasts furnished to them from Mr. Gunter's Shop during their juvenile days. Neither a native Greenlander, nor a Highlander from the remotest part of Caledonia, nor yet a Norwegian would easily calculate the value of the ice in Mr. Gunter's cellar. He has at Earl's Court, Kensington, a most luxuriant garden, from whence, during the season, strawberries, pines, raspberries, and other delicious offerings from Pomona to her votaries, arrive fresh gathered twice a day in Berkeley-square.[1]

Prince of Wales.

We will now cross Bond-street into Conduit-street, and there at the left hand corner of George-street, will we do homage to that truly elegant and very extensive establishment, the Prince of Wales Hotel and Tavern.[2] It has for many years been conducted ably, and we trust successfully, by Mr. Limmer,

---

[1] James **Gunter's** famous confectionery and ice cream shop at no. 7 Berkeley Square, east side, descended from an earlier establishment opened at the Sign of the Pineapple by the Italian pastrycook Domenico Negri in the late 1760s (see Elizabeth David 1994, pp. 310-15, and *ODNB*). Gunter joined his brother-in-law Negri's business in 1777, and also had a shop in New Bond Street; the business was continued by his son Robert, and 'Gunter's ices' remained fashionable for more than a century. Gunter himself died a wealthy man in 1819, having built up the 'luxuriant gardens' mentioned here into a substantial estate at Earl's Court, later developed by his son and grandsons. The shop – latterly principally a catering firm – remained in Berkeley Square until the 1930s, when it removed to nearby Curzon Street.

[2] The **Prince of Wales** at the corner of George Street (now St George Street) and Conduit Street was known as a tavern at least since 1773, and seems to have been under Limmer's management from about 1805. I can find no evidence for Lillywhite's statements that Limmer had a *second* coffee house and hotel, also on the corner of Conduit Street, and that this merged with the Prince of Wales about 1825 (see Lillywhite nos. 722 and 1018); it seems more likely that all references to **Limmer's** and to the Prince of Wales are to the same establishment. Limmer's Hotel was described as an 'evening resort for the sporting world' by Captain Gronow, who remembered it as 'the most dirty hotel in London', though 'in the gloomy comfortless coffee-room might be seen many members of the rich squirearchy, who visited London during the sporting season' (*Reminiscences*, p. 74). Rebuilt in the late C19, the hotel remained in business until 1903, when the

who is perhaps the most active man in London of his age, being as we have heard him say, somewhat older than his present Majesty. It is no derogation to his merit or his repu- [191] tation for wealth to say, that industry alone has raised him to the station of master of this almost unique Hotel. Forty-six years ago Mr. Limmer officiated as principal waiter at the New Exchange Coffee-house in the Strand. So large is the concern he now manages with such great ability, that including cooks and scullions, waiters and drawers, house-maids and chamber-maids, hair-dressers and boot-cleaners, cellar-men and porters, bar-women and grooms of the chamber, Mr. Limmer does not retain fewer than thirty domestics, the expense attending whom, together with that of the large supplies of coals, candles, linen, and other articles of constant consumption is very great indeed; and this consideration should of itself operate as an ample justification of the apparently high charges which Mr. Limmer and other Hotel keepers of his rank and degree are necessarily compelled to make.

In Conduit-street, a little about George-street, are two others Hotels; No. 22, kept by Mr. Weizall, and that opposite to it, No. 42, kept by Mr. Warner. At No. 93, Mr. Collings, from the Prince of Wales, keeps also an Hotel. These are all respectable establishments, and of course well attended during the season.[1]

[192]

Lambe's.

Returning again into New Bond-street, we find a celebrated mineral water warehouse, kept by Mr. Lambe, who is purveyor to the Royal Family, for those salubrious luxuries, the spa and artificial mineral waters.

premises were purchased by the piano manufacturers John Broadwood and Sons and converted to showrooms.

[1] Continuing along Conduit Street, the *Almanack* mangles the names of all three of the next hoteliers mentioned. Thomas **Weigall** was in partnership with Matthew **Warne** in 1809, when they issued a joint advertisement thanking their neighbours for help during the 'dreadful conflagration at their hotel on Sunday last' (*The Times*, 7 February). The partnership was dissolved in 1818 (*Times*, 26 October), and Weigall is listed alone at no. 42 in an 1820 directory, with Warne's Hotel advertising for trade at no. 22 in the same year (*Times*, 19 April). The hotel kept by John **Collins** was at no. 19 (not 93) Conduit Street, north side, but seems to have disappeared in the 1820s. As headwaiter at Limmer's, he is sometimes credited with having invented the Collins cocktail, transformed from a John Collins into a Tom Collins when sweetened Old Tom gin replaced the original genever.

Stevens's.

Within one door of Clifford-street, at No. 17, New Bond-street, is Stevens's Hotel and Tavern, kept by Messrs. Scot and Towesland. This is a very elegant establishment, and comprehends a tavern department, where dinners and other repasts are served up in the first style of elegance. It is needless to say, that they consist of the best fare.[1]

Long's.

Long's Hotel, at the corner of Clifford-street, is a similar establishment, and perhaps more spacious if we consider the premises which extend up Clifford-street. At this and similar resorts of fashion, the gentlemen who lead the ton in dress and amusement philosophize their hours. In an evening they are generally entertained by bands of Savoyard Pandeans with their music-mills, who grind [193] and puff away in the porches, for the entertainment of the mobs without, as well as the nobles within.[2]

Nerot's.

At No. 13, Clifford-street, is Nerot's Hotel. The business of this very respectable house was carried on for many years in King-street, St. James's.[3]

[1] **Stevens's Hotel** was on the east side of New Bond Street, near the junction with Clifford Street; it was most commonly listed as no. 18, and there was also an entrance into Clifford Street. According to Gronow, Stevens's was 'supported by officers of the army and men about town' and 'it was not an uncommon thing to see thirty or forty saddle-horses and tilburys [light carriages] waiting outside this hotel' (p. 75). In later years Stevens's became 'scarcely more than an annexe to Long's Hotel' (*The Times*, 3 October 1911), and by 1865 it had closed.

[2] **Long's Hotel** was on the corner itself (later numbered no. 16 New Bond Street); the premises were rebuilt in 1887-88 and the hotel closed in 1911 (*The Times*, 3 October). Itinerant musicians with music-mills or hurdy-gurdies (and sometimes monkeys) were known both as Savoyards and Pandeans, but a Pandean band would also have employed mouth organs resembling pan-pipes.

[3] **Nerot's Hotel**, at no. 13 Clifford Street, south side, was earlier at nos. 23-24 King Street (1776-1811). The grandson of the founder advertised in 1832 that 'the charges are moderate, the wines are old and of the first qualities' (*The Times*, 1 May), but the hotel vanishes from directories in the mid-1840s.

Blue Posts, Cork-Street.

We turn down Cork-street, for the express purpose of noticing that very superior house of entertainment, the Blue Posts, kept by Mr. Stapleton.[1] Though rigorously speaking, it must be termed a public house, yet its principal room up-stairs is frequented by guests the most respectable. No where perhaps in London can a more intelligent and select company be found. The port of this house is capital, and its Burton and Windsor ales would of themselves ensure it a preference over many establishments of the same class.

Jaquier's.

In Bond-street, No. 169, is the Clarendon Hotel, and Jaquier's Coffee-House and Ta- [194] vern.[2] We do not aim to do perfect justice in this slight work, to an establishment so imperially magnificent. In a word we may say, that every species of luxury, every refinement of accommodation that ingenuity can devise or money can procure, may here be met with and enjoyed.

OLD BOND-STREET.

At No. 20, in Old Bond-street, is Hawkins's (late Wade's) warehouse, for the sale of mineral and spa waters.

[1] The **Blue Posts** in Cork Street was famed for its steaks and chops, and was one of the few establishments singled out in the 1851 *London at Table* ('a very snug place during the winter for a dinner of four, in the small private parlour on the ground floor', p. 4). The house, at no. 13 on the west side, is mentioned by Dickens in a letter of 10 January 1856 (*Letters*, viii:18), and was described by Edward Walford in 1876 as 'for several generations a favourite dining-house for bachelors' (*ONL*, iv:309). Rebuilt about 1881 after a fire, the premises were taken over around 1903 by the Halcyon Club, an organization for professional and artistic women.

[2] At no. 169 New Bond Street, west side, the **Clarendon Hotel** occupied a mansion built on a portion of the gardens that had formerly belonged to Clarendon House, pulled down in 1683; the proprietor was Louis Jaquier (sometimes given as Jacquier or Jacquiers). Captain Gronow described the Clarendon as 'the only public hotel where you could get a genuine French dinner, and for which you seldom paid less than three or four pounds' (p. 74), and in 1849 Peter Cunningham said that it was 'generally spoken of as the best of its kind, and is much resorted to by persons desirous of entertaining friends in the best style, and to whom expense is no object' (*Handbook for London*, i:xxiii). The Clarendon closed in 1870, and was demolished soon after.

No. 19, is Chapman's, a celebrated Fruit-Shop, where jellies, ices, marma-lades, cakes, liqueurs, and other delicious things are sold in the highest state of perfection.

At No. 4, is the shop of Lyne, the confectioner, who supplies routs and balls with the multifarious produce of his ovens.

At No. 45, Mr. Others has long kept a princely repository long noted for the finest forest venison.

No. 166, Piccadilly, facing Old Bond-street, is the Shop of Messrs. R. and J. Taylor, who style themselves Fish Salesmen. Perambulate all London, and you will no where find so splendid a display of fine fish.

[195]

Gordon's Hotel.

We now proceed to Albemarle Street, and find, at No. 1, Gordon's Hotel for gentlemen and families: we suppose it may rank among the many respectable establishments of the same kind in this fashionable part of the town.[1]

Grillon's.

A few doors on is Grillon's Hotel, which was honoured by being chosen as the temporary residence of Louis XVIII. during his stay in London, after his recal [*sic*] to the throne of his ancestors. The gout had long had possession of his majesty's lower extremities, and certainly his majesty could not have come

---

[1] Byron stayed at **Gordon's Hotel** (no. 1 Albemarle Street, east side) for several weeks in the summer of 1807; his publisher, John Murray, was nearby at no. 50.

to a worse place than this luxurious establishment for the purpose of getting rid of so troublesome a compagnon de voyage. He came hither, we believe, from his noble friend's residence in the delightful vale of Aylesbury: if we may apply a culinary proverb, on so dignified an occasion, it was leaping out of the frying-pan into the fire. Many gouty SUBJECTS, as well as kings, lame as they are, too often take such leaps, and thus become lamer than before. But who would grudge a fit of the gout as the *peine forte et* [196] *dure* of being feasted by Grillon! As well might Marshall Marmont repine at that wound in the arm which marked him for life with the distinguished honour of having been carbonadoed by the Duke of Wellington.[1]

London Hotel.

Opposite Grillon's is the London Hotel, occupying two contiguous mansions, and superintended by Mr. Hitchcock.[2]

York Hotel.

At the corner of Stafford Street, in Albemarle Street, is the York Hotel, kept by Mr. Cook.[3] This large and magnificent house was formerly conducted by a person of foreign extraction, who took French leave of his creditors, after having been declared a bankrupt, and has ever since taken especial care to keep out of their company. We rather suspect that he dislikes the retreat they have kindly provided for him during his embarrassments. Mr. Cook, the present occupant, will, we trust, so improve upon the system of his predecessor, as to render any offer on the part of his friends, for a change of residence, unnecessary.

---

[1] The fashionable hotel at no. 7 Albemarle Street, east side, was founded by Alexander Grillion in 1803, but was almost universally miscalled **Grillon's**. It flourished at this address until 1860, when it removed to nos. 19-20 in the same street. No. 7, which dates from 1721, was later the headquarters of the National Book League; for the building itself, see *BoE Westminster*, p. 495. The 'residence in the delightful vale of Aylesbury', where Louis XVIII and his court lived in exile between 1809 and 1814, was Hartwell House, Bucks., now a hotel.

[2] The **London Hotel** (no. 44 Albemarle Street, west side) continues in directories until 1864.

[3] The **York Hotel** was on the east side of the street, at no. 10; it later expanded into nos. 9 and 11, but seems to have disappeared after it was advertised for sale in 1925 (*The Times*, 4 April).

[197]

DOVER STREET.

In Dover Street are two respectable hotels, well attended during the season: Batts's, No. 43, and Cook's, No. 45.[1]

The Goat and the King's Head.

Daniel Defoe's distich, in the True Born Briton, describing the consequent proximity of the devil's chapel to the Lord's house (we do not mean the most distant hint at any chapel near any house in Westminster), this distich we say, is susceptible of a close parody in relation to life above and below stairs; as thus —

> Where'er my lords appoint their house of call,
> The servants duly fix their audience hall.

Certain hotels may appositely be denominated houses of call for lords, and the tap-room of the nearest ale-house may, with equal felicity of metaphor, be termed the audience hall of many a silver-tagged and scarlet-breeched lord-duke, and Sir Harry.

There are two mansions for entertaining persons of this distinction in Stafford Street; the Goat, kept by Mr. Kime, who serves up an ordinary to the grooms in waiting, daily at two o'clock; and the King's Head, in the [198] custody of Mr. Vickery, whose cold larder is ever at the service of gentlemen's gentlemen.[2]

---

[1] **Batt's Hotel** at no. 43 Dover Street, west side, was still in business as late as 1942; **Cook's Hotel** had become the Lisbon Hotel by 1827, and Raggett's Hotel by 1835. Ten years later the hotel was virtually destroyed in a fire that killed the proprietor, William Raggett, his daughter, and two guests (*The Times*, 27 May 1845).

[2] The **Goat** was at no. 3 Stafford Street, north side. In 1957 L. T. Stanley suggested that the Goat 'probably dates from the original building of the street' in 1683, adding that 'with the exception of the ground floor, the structure is unaltered' (*Old Inns*, p. 51). A year later the pub was demolished and rebuilt, with the plan of the new Goat Tavern, which is still in operation, following that of the old (*OEC*, p. 25). The **King's Head** was on the southeast corner of Stafford Street and Albemarle Street (now no. 10 Stafford Street). The original premises at no. 8 Albemarle Street were licensed in 1710, and in 1869 the pub was rebuilt and the next-door property at no. 10 Stafford Street incorporated (see *OEC*, p. 38, and *BoE Westminster*, p. 495). From about 1845 the establishment was known as the King John's Head; later, during the time it was owned by Frederic Shelley (1861-87), it became known

York Coffee-House, St. James's Street.

We now cross Piccadilly, and enter St. James's Street, where we find, on the left-hand side, No. 46, the York Coffee-house, kept by Mr. Parker: here dinners are drest to order, and soups served at all hours. The accommodations are good, and the charges moderate.[1]

Opposite this, stands a subscription house, where the subaltern officers of the guards, and other hopeful shoots of fashion, wage perpetual war against time, either by the slow tactics of the Roman lounger Fabius Cunctator, or *selon* the more dashing manœuvres of the modern Attila – by *killing* the enemy *off:* – with billiard balls.

White's, now Martindale's.

Between the York Coffee-house and the end of Jermyn Street is that magnificent mansion long celebrated by the name of White's Chocolate-house, and now called Martindale's Subscription-house.[2] Here, and at similar establishments during the parliamentary session and season, noble lords and honourable [199] gentlemen pass their forenoons in skimming over the newspapers, pamphlets, and other ephemera, and in making their senatorial arrangements. In the evenings, nights, and mornings, cards and dice succeed to motions and amendments.

We now enter Jermyn Street, and descry a whole range of hotels of the same generic character, and of course dismissible with one general description. All the articles of consumption are of the best; and the accommodations, much

as Shelley's, a name officially adopted in 1957. It has now once again become the King's Head.

[1] The **York Coffee House** at no. 46 St James's Street, east side (just south of Picca-dilly, on the corner of the now-vanished Villiers Court) was known as early as 1776 but disappears from directories in the 1830s; the proprietor in 1815 was Mr Parkes, not Parker. The subscription house at no. 49 on the west side was the **Guards' Club**, founded in 1813 and transferred to no. 70 Pall Mall in 1849; the Roman general Fabius Maximus Cunctator was famous for his delaying tactics during the Second Punic War.

[2] South of the York Coffee House was **White's** clubhouse. Originally known as White's Chocolate House (founded 1693), by the end of the c18 White's was a completely private club; in 1755 it moved to nos. 37-38, where it continues today. The building, parts of which may date back to 1674, was successively owned by John and Benjamin Martindale in the period just before the *Almanack* appeared, and although the latter was declared a bankrupt in 1812 the Martindale name continued to be associated with the house for some time (see *SL* 30, pp. 450-58).

to the injury of taverns and lodging-houses, combine all the retirement and comforts of home with the freedom of access, egress, and ingress, which one generally expects when abroad. Having said this, we shall merely indicate them in the order of locality: – Reddish's, 61, north side of Jermyn Street; Blake's, 56, north side; St. James's, 83, south side; Miller's, 87, south side, with roomy premises, extending into Duke Street;[1] British Hotel, kept by Mr. Hickinbottom, a very considerable wine-merchant, 89 and 90; Topham's, late Beale's, 42 and 43, north side. At the time we were making our tour, the business of the Albion was in a course of removal to No. 5, Cleveland Row, St. James's.

[200]

Walker and Gother's Fish Shop.

At No. 126, in Jermyn Street, is Walker and Gother's Fish-shop, which contains daily a very fine and varied display of the choicest fish in season. We noticed, with peculiar pleasure, on the day we inspected this establishment, among other estimable subjects in ichthyology, two royal sturgeons exposed. Messrs. Walker and Gother, as well as all first-rate fish-dealers, have ice stores, for the purpose of preserving their fish during hot weather.

Gun Tavern.

Opposite this emporium of fish is the Gun Tavern Chop-house and Coffee-house, No. 17, kept by Mr. J. Tooke: the house is also well known by the name of the Shades, on account of its subterraneous apartments, tastefully fitted up, into which there is a descent from the street, and in which are served various refreshments; in particular, a select series of curious ales. The house has a good larder.[2]

---

[1] In 1836 **Miller's Hotel** at no. 87 Jermyn Street, south side, became the Cavendish Hotel, which (rebuilt in 1964-66) still survives, now numbered no. 81. In 1902 the hotel was purchased by Rosa Lewis (1867-1952), whose life served as the basis for the popular 1970s television series *The Duchess of Duke Street*. The **British Hotel** at nos. 88-89 (by then the André Hotel, renumbered no. 82-83) became part of the Cavendish in 1911, along with nos. 18-20 Duke Street.

[2] The **Gun Tavern** at no. 17 Jermyn Street, north side, is known as early as 1743 (*Daily Advertiser*, 13 August); it was levelled in 1816, during the general improvements to the area (*European Magazine* for April, p. 368).

Turning out of Jermyn Street, into Market Street, St. James's, we find an excellent tavern and chop-house, designated The Tun.[1] [201] This is one of the meritorious houses which have risen progressively from the obscurity of a chop-house to the importance of a tavern. If report may be credited, it owes its first rise to an accidental circumstance. The late Charles Bannister, of facetious memory, having, for some time, occasionally *used* the house, and by his wit and inexhaustible humour, attracted a crowd of company, the honest host thought fit to fix this magnet by crying quits for bed and board as long as Mr. Bannister continued his guest. The terms we believe were accepted, and the contract terminated only with the life of the comedian. Mr. Bannister, for many years after his retirement from the stage, took an annual benefit at the Little Theatre in the Hay Market, at which his son dutifully volunteered his powerful assistance, and the company frequenting the Tun always ensured a bumper.

St. Alban's Tavern.

In making the tour of St. James's Market, we come to St. Alban's Street, in which we find the St. Alban's Tavern, an establishment that has for more than a century maintained the character of a first-rate. Of late years it has been rebuilt, and dignified with an elegant [202] front, to correspond with its elegant interior. It is now kept by Mr. Richold.[2]

---

[1] The *Almanack*'s 'Tun' was properly the **One Tun Tavern** at no. 107 Jermyn Street, behind St James's church (not, as described here, in Market Street). The actor Charles Bannister (1741-1804) was well known at the One Tun, and a good description of the tavern *c.* 1800 appears in John Adolphus's biography of Charles's more famous son (*Memoirs of John Bannister, Comedian* (1839), ii:64-65). Popular with sporting men, the One Tun survived until about 1834.

[2] The St Alban's Street of 1815 was lost in the development of Regent Street, and today's street of that name was formerly part of Market Lane, one of the boundaries of the market itself (see *SL* 29, pp. 215-20, for the complicated renamings, and for the market itself, pp. 249-50 below). The **St Alban's Tavern**, established near the end of the C17, was much used for Masonic and other meetings in the C18, and it was here that the first dinner of the bibliophilic Roxburghe Club was held in 1812. The tavern seems later to have moved around the corner to Charles Street, where an establishment of that name (later called a hotel) is known at no. 12 between 1822 and the 1850s.

Charles Street Rooms.

Over the way, in Charles Street, are the celebrated Charles Street Subscription Rooms. They extend through two houses, and are principally used as card-rooms. Here are refreshments of all sorts, served to subscribers only.[1]

In Carleton Place, St. Alban's Street, at No. 3, lives M. Augero, the successor to Onorati, and chocolate-maker to the Royal Family.[2] Here are chocolate-rooms, where that nutritious beverage is served up in its utmost perfection. M. Augero proclaims on his shew-board that he is always at the command of any noble family, as professor of cookery and confectionery, to officiate at their dinners and routs.

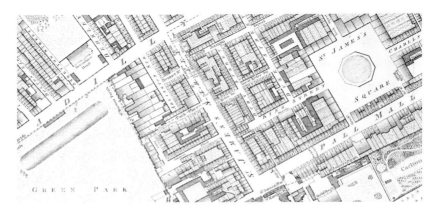

Boodle's.

We will now resume our progress down St. James's Street, at the point where we turned off into Jermyn Street. No. 31, on the east side of St. James's Street, is that splendid mansion known by the name of Boodle's Subscription House.[3]

[1] The area around St James's Square was home to many card rooms and gaming houses, but I have been unable to identify the one described here.

[2] Carlton Place, where M. **Augero** had his chocolate shop, was a turning west out of St Alban's Street, just north of Pall Mall.

[3] **Boodle's Club**, previously in Pall Mall, moved to no. 28 (not 31) on the east side of St James's in the 1780s; the building itself was built for the Savoir Vivre Club in 1775-76 (*SL* 30, pp. 441-49).

[203]

Jordan's.

On the west side, No. 57 and 58, is Jordan's Hotel, which, on account of its superb and complete accommodations, is worthy of its site almost on the very verge of the court.[1]

Brookes's.

A door or two lower is another elegant subscription house, called Brookes's: none but subscribers are admitted; and those subscribers are gentlemen of the highest rank and fortune in the kingdom.[2]

Cocoa Tree.

No. 64 is the celebrated house called the Cocoa Tree, that sign having been transferred hither from the house in Pall Mall, now occupied by Messrs. Ransom, Morland, and Co. bankers.[3]

No. 65 is Arthur's Club-house, another subscription house, on the same elegant and select plan as White's, Boodle's, and Brookes's. Some years ago, these houses had other titles. One was called the Jockey Club; another the *Savoir vivre*, and the third the *Sans Souci*. The jockies dropt [204] their appellation after the appearance of a humorous satirical poem which assumed it: the title of Sans Souci was sneered out of fashion by a wit who altered it to *sans six sous;* and the *savoir vivre* was probably dropt because the members were conscious that their *vivre* was not quite adequate to their *savoir*.[4]

[1] **Jordan's Hotel** – listed by Tallis as Symon's Hotel in 1838 – was demolished before 1865, when Alfred Waterhouse's New University Club was built on the site.
[2] **Brooks's** (not Brookes's) Club, at no. 60 St James's, west side, was built in 1776-78 and continues in operation today.
[3] The **Cocoa Tree** was originally a chocolate house in Pall Mall, known from at least 1698; it was later converted to a subscription club and in 1799 moved to no. 64 St James's. It ceased to exist in 1932, and the building itself was replaced shortly thereafter (*SL* 30, pp. 461-63).
[4] **Arthur's Club** was founded in 1811 at no. 69 (not 65); the clubhouse – rebuilt as nos. 69-70 in 1826-27 – was taken over by the Carlton Club in 1940 (*SL* 30, pp. 464 and 474; *BoE Westminster*, p. 640). The **Jockey Club**, founded around 1750, initially met at the Star and Garter, Pall Mall (*SL* 29, p. 352), but soon moved to Newmarket, where it continues today. The **Savoir Vivre Club** (sometimes spelt 'Scavoir Vivre') was established at the Star and Garter in 1772, and soon after moved to

Tomlins's Jelly House.

At the corner of Ryder Street and Bury Street, St. James's, is Tomlins's (late Oswald's) Royal Jelly-house, wholesale and retail. This is the only house in London that confines its business to jellies strictly. Mr. Tomlins supplies the article in the highest flavour, the most pellucid purity, and the firmest consistence as well as in all its varieties, to the distinguished houses above-mentioned. This jelly manufactory has existed here for more than a century, so that the last generation knew a little of what the stomach was good for, as well as the present.[1]

Clarke and Sons.

On the east side of St. James's Street, No. 14, is Messrs. Clarke and Sons, Coffee-house and Tavern. The proprietors are re- [205] spectable wine and brandy merchants, and if the quality of their wines and liquors be equal to that of the viands, displayed in their larder down the passage, they must be great men indeed.[2]

Dawson's Fruit Shop.

At No. 7, is Dawson's, (late Fitzwater's) Fruit and Confectionery-shop. Mr. Dawson has warrants for supplying their Majesties with the articles in which he deals.

premises on the west side of St James's; a grand new club house was built on the east side in 1775-76, but by 1782 the Savoir Vivre had dissolved and the building was taken over by Boodle's Club. I have found no other reference to a London club known as the **Sans Souci**. The 'satirical poem' referred to here was more likely a prose work, *The Jockey Club, or a Sketch of the Manners of the Age*, published anonymously in 1792 and often reprinted, in which Charles Pigott savagely attacked members of the aristocracy and men of fashion.

[1] In the C18 jelly houses were frequently mentioned as the resort of prostitutes (and men seeking them), but there is no suggestion here that **Tomlins** was anything other than a respectable purveyor of sweet and savoury jellies.

[2] The site of **Clarke's** (no. 14 St James's Street, east side) was rebuilt in 1910-12; the 'passage' referred to here can be seen on the Horwood map just north of Little King Street.

Thatched House.

No. 80, is the Thatched House Tavern, kept by Mr. Willis. In one of the large rooms of this first-rate house are the celebrated Kit Kat Pictures – Portraits of the members of a club, once so called, which was held here. These Portraits ought to be, and surely are, engraved upon the hearts of the unfortunate; numbers of whom confined for small debts are liberated every month from a fund raised for the purpose, by the noblemen and gentlemen of this society.[1]

Below the Thatched House on the same side of St. James's Street are four other houses of great celebrity; the Albion Hotel; the Smyrna; Parloe's; and the St. James's coffee- [206] house, which last is a splendid new building, that handsomely terminates St. James's Street and Cleveland Row.[2]

Union Club House.

In St. James's Square, in the very mansion built for the Duke of Leeds, the elegance of which mansion is set forth in a posie written by one of his

[1] The **Thatched House Tavern** was at no. 74 (not 80) St James's Street, west side. Established around 1705, the tavern existed on this site until 1842, when it moved to no. 85; both buildings have since been demolished (*SL* 30, p. 466). The large public rooms of the Thatched House were heavily used for school and university dinners, Masonic meetings, and meetings of clubs and societies, but the *Almanack* errs in mentioning the Kit Kat Club and its portraits: it was the Society of the Dilettanti who from 1811 until 1861 hung their collection of pictures in one of the tavern's rooms.

[2] The list of the remaining establishments in St James's Street suggests confusion or haste. The **Albion Club** (not Hotel) was at no. 85, which had earlier been home to Saunders's chocolate house and later to a subscription house run by Joseph Parsloe; the Albion took over in 1811 and was succeeded from 1842 to 1861 by the relocated Thatched House Tavern (see *SL* 30, pp. 466-68, for all these establishments). **Parsloe's** was particularly known as a chess club – in 1795, shortly before his death, Philidor played three blindfold matches there – and the Albion seems to have continued the tradition. The **Smyrna**, at no. 86, was originally in Pall Mall, but relocated in 1769; it closed in 1817 and the building was demolished in 1862 (*SL* 30, p. 469). There were two concerns calling themselves the **St James's Coffee House**. That at no. 87 St James's Street was established in 1705 and rebuilt about 1765; it was later sometimes known as Graham's Club. The *Almanack*, however, was describing the establishment at no. 88, at the corner of Cleveland Row. Earlier known as Gaunt's Coffee House, the building was taken over by Samuel Miller (of Miller's Hotel in Jermyn Street) in 1801, but was completely destroyed by fire in 1813 – hence the 'splendid new building', which may be seen in Tallis's view of 1838. Both no. 87 and no. 88 were demolished shortly after 1900 (*SL* 30, pp. 470-71).

Grace's domestics, and favourably spoken of by that learned critic Doctor Johnson, the Union Club hold their meetings. This Club dates its establishment from the Union of Great Britain with Ireland, and thence takes its name. It originally met at the Palace, called Cumberland House, in Pall Mall; but Government, having made choice of that edifice for the office of Ordnance, the members of the Union purchased this elegant mansion.[1]

Royal Hotel.

At No. 95, in Pall Mall, is the Royal Hotel, an extensive establishment, for the reception and accommodation of gentlemen and families of distinction; and this is the only Hotel left in Pall Mall. A few years ago, near this spot, was the Star and Garter Tavern, celebrated for vending the best claret in [207] England. The house somehow or other got out of fashion, and dwindled into an office for the Light and Heat Company, but the light also dwindling and the heat of the company becoming lukewarm it again changed hands and was degraded into a manufactory of shoe-blacking.[2]

THE BOROUGH OF SOUTHWARK.

The order of our tour was adopted in conformity to the usual courtesy which required us to pay our respects first to the City of London, next to the City and Liberties of Westminster, and lastly to the auncient Borough of Southwerke. If we had obeyed the impulse of our own feelings of veneration for the literary renown of the metropolis, we should not have hesitated to commence our tour through London at the very "INN WHERE SIR GEOFFRY CHAUCER KNIGHT AND NINE AND TWENTY PILGRIMS LODGED ON THEIR JOURNEY TO CANTERBURY IN 1383." What more auspicious commencement

---

[1] The **Union Club**, catering to merchants, lawyers, members of Parliament, and 'gentlemen at large' (Timbs, *Clubs*, p. 216) occupied no. 21 St James's Square from 1807 to 1815; the building had been demolished by July 1934 (*SL* 29, pp. 179-80), but the Club itself, founded in 1800, survived until 1964. The lines on the marriage of the Duke of Leeds, which mention his house in St James's Square, are printed in Boswell's *Life of Johnson* (iv:14).

[2] The **Royal Hotel**, at nos. 92-93 Pall Mall, south side, was established in 1777-78, but James Weston, the proprietor, became bankrupt in 1809 and died in 1816. Lilly-white found no later references to the hotel, and the building itself was demolished *c.* 1846. The **Star and Garter** at nos. 94-95 was known as early as 1743 and closed around 1800; see *SL* 29, pp. 351-52, for both establishments.

could we have made, than by invoking the shade of that accomplished gourmand, the father of English poetry; and conjuring him to tell us which of the pilgrims won the *supper* by telling the best tale.

When we reflect on the many claims which [208] this ancient borough has on our preference, we hold ourselves almost inexcusable in having slighted them. It was in Southwark that Mr. William Shakspeare made his debut on the boards, or rather the rushes of the Globe. – It was at the Windmill, in St. George's Fields,¹ that he and Marlow and Big Ben, with Alleyn, Drayton, Peele*, [209] Burbage, Heminge, and Condell, smoked their pipes and quaffed their canary. According to the testimony of some of the fraternity there was so much wit spoken at these meetings, that after the guests had retired, the drawers, who came to put the chamber to rights, became witty merely by respiring the fumes of the tobacco and the ambrosial effluvia with which the poets had impregnated the air. The sacred walls of St. Mary Overy enclose the shrines of old Gower, of Massinger, and we believe of Beaumont and Fletcher, all clever poets and sound epicures in their day. At a short and convenient distance from that sanctuary, the weary and distressed disciples of Apollo may repose themselves in a retreat assigned to them by Royal authority.

* In our city tour we took some pains, but without success, to ascertain the site of the tavern mentioned in the following interesting letter from George Peele, a fellow of Christ Church College, Oxford, and a dramatic poet, who belonged to the club at the *Globe*, to one Marle, an intimate of his. We insert the letter on account of the first sentence, which proves that the poets of those days were not indifferent to the pleasures of the table, and that by them a culinary treatise was perhaps preferred to a *Gradus ad Parnassum*.

Friend Marle,

I must desyr that my syster hyr watch and the *cookerie booke*, you promised, may be sent by the man. I never longed for thy company more than last night. We were all very merrye at the Globe, when Ned Alleyn did not scruple to affirm pleasauntely to thy friend Will, that he had STOLEN his speech about the qualityes of an actor's excellencye in Hamlet, hys tragedye, from conversations manyfold whych passed between them, and opynions given by Alleyn touching the subject. Shaks- [209] peare did not take this talk in good sorte, but Johnson

---

¹ The **Windmill** in St George's Fields is recalled by Justice Shallow in Act III of Shakespeare's 2 *Henry IV*, and is usually taken by editors to refer to an inn, or brothel, in Paris Garden Lane, somewhat west of today's Tate Modern. The letter from 'George Peele' printed as a footnote is a fabrication that first appeared in the *Theatrical Review* in 1763; the hoaxer was almost certainly the Shakespeare editor George Steevens.

put an end to the stryfe by wittylye remarking: "This affaire needeth no contentione; you stole it from Ned no doubte: do not marvel: have you not *seen him act* tymes out of number?"

Beleeve me, most syncerilie, your's,
G. Peele

These contemplations, however, are leading us far astray from our subject; therefore, with the permission of the Marshal of the King's Bench, we will postpone our *reconnoissance* of his establishment until we obtain [210] an official letter of introduction to him, an honour of which we are by no means ambitious;[1] and in honour of the aforesaid Sir Geoffry Chaucer we will give his Hotel the preference, as our point of departure on our progress through Southwerke.

The Taberd is now called the Talbot, and is kept by Mr. Willoughby, who is truly proud of the honour. He has not the humour of Harry Baillie; but, his lodgings are of the best; his fare good and his charges reasonable. You may have a dinner or a hot lunch here on the shortest notice.[2]

Having satisfied our consciences by beginning with Chaucer's Inn, we will now proceed to London Bridge, and from thence reconnoitre the other houses of entertainment in the Borough, without respect of persons and in the mere order of locality.

A few doors on the left of the Bridge at the bottom of White Hart Court, is the Southwark Auction Mart, to which is attached a respectable coffee-house.[3]

Wright's.

No. 310, on the right hand, is Wright's à-la-mode Beef-shop and Eatinghouse. Its accommodations are neat, and the charges very reasonable.

[1] A debtor or other offender consigned to the **King's Bench Prison** in Southwark might be said to have received an 'official letter of introduction' to its Marshal.

[2] The yard of the old **Tabard Inn**, renamed the **Talbot** at the end of the C16, is shown on the east side of Borough High Street on the Rocque and Horwood maps. Rendle and Norman (*Inns of Old Southwark* (1888), pp. 169-201) dated the original inn to *c.* 1306; it was rebuilt about 1630 and again after being levelled in the devastating fire that swept through Southwark in May 1676. The Talbot of George Shepherd's 1810 watercolour, reproduced by Rendle and Norman, was demolished in 1875 and replaced by 'a gin palace of the most approved modern type' (Bowers 1905, p. 391), now also vanished. In Chaucer's *Canterbury Tales* the host is named as Herry Bailly in the prologue to the Cook's tale.

[3] The coffee house was probably among the buildings demolished in 1830 when new approaches to London Bridge were laid out.

[211]

Baxter's.

No. 19 is Baxter's Chop-house. The department of cooking in this house is deemed, by the proprietors, of inferior consideration to that of administering to the thirst of the customers, so that the carving knife yields precedence to the corkscrew. The house is interesting on account of its antiquity; it is part of a palace where Henry the Eighth, the King of English Gourmands, once held his court. It is decorated externally with the remains of the royal insignia. Some of the rooms, now occupied by a hop-merchant, have ceilings richly embossed with the arms of royal Harry. It is said that from this palace the portly monarch took a trip to Bermondsey-fair,* along with Cardinal Wolsey, and there [212] fell in love with Anna Bullen, who appeared there in her gayest attire, by appointment of the holy Cardinal and prime-minister himself. The hop-merchant and his customers little think that in all probability the beautiful Miss Anna Bullen was handed into these very apartments through a whole court of ladies and barons bold, who occupied the very places now filled with a goodly row of pockets of hops.[1]

*The Marquis of Salisbury has in his collection at Hatfield House, a fine and curious picture representing the royal gallant at Bermondsey-fair. He is seen leaning on that pillar of the church and state, Cardinal Wolsey, leering at the ladye, with that amorous old courtier Lord Sands, and a number of other noble attendants in waiting. In the back ground the yeomen of the guard are carrying an entertainment of the finest viands out of the kitchen into the royal tent. Certainly, no better [212] subject could be chosen for a frontispiece to this our almanack. Around, and in the distance, are represented the Cotswold games and sports, with other delectable pastimes, characteristic of the fair of Bermondsey.

The antiquarian society, some years ago, with the permission of the noble Marquis, employed that celebrated artist, Mr. Grimon, to make a reduced copy of this curious picture in water colours.

[1] **Baxter's**, at no. 19 on the east side of Borough High Street, may not have had quite as ancient a history as the *Almanack* would have us believe, but it does appear that at least some of the interior decorations were Elizabethan (see Rendle and Norman, pp. 101-08, with a sketch). Baxter's too was demolished during the 1830 upheaval. The picture discussed in the note is Joris Hoefnagel's 'Fête at Horsley-down [or Bermondsey]', *c.* 1569; the Society of Antiquaries' copy was by Grignon, not Grimon. Although the painting was described in *The Beauties of England and Wales* (vol. 7, 1808) and elsewhere as representing Henry VIII and Anne Boleyn at a country fair, it in fact depicts an Elizabethan wedding feast.

Those noted inns the White Hart and George are of very ancient and established renown for substantial cheer and comfortable accommodations.[1] The same praise may be justly bestowed on the Queen's Head Inn, kept by J. Shore, from the Roebuck, at Maidstone, and also on the Catherine Wheel Inn, which stand on the right hand side from St. Margaret's Hill.[2]

[213]

Three Tuns.

No. 87, in the Borough High Street, is the Three Tuns Tavern and Chophouse kept by Mr. Taylor. It gives dinners to parties of any number, as well as to individuals. Its Burton, Windsor, and other ales are celebrated; and many persons dine here for the purpose of tasting them.[3]

---

[1] The **White Hart** is shown by Rocque and Horwood on the east side of Borough High Street; for its history, see Rendle and Norman, pp. 128-48, with a sketch groundplan and illustrations. The original building, which served as the headquarters of Jack Cade during his rebellion of 1450, was destroyed in the 1676 Southwark fire. Rebuilt, the White Hart continued as a coaching inn through the 1830s, and was well described by Charles Dickens in chapter ten of *The Pickwick Papers*. The south side was replaced by a modern tavern in 1865-66, and the building was demolished in 1889. Just south of the White Hart was the **George**, known from the early C16 and rebuilt after the 1676 fire following the original plan of a courtyard enclosed on three sides by galleried structures (see *SL* 22, pp. 16-21, and Hunter 1989). In 1889 the northern and eastern galleries were demolished, but the southern portion of the building survives, since 1937 owned by the National Trust and still maintained as a public house at no. 77 Borough High Street.

[2] Immediately to the south of the George was the Talbot, followed by the **Queen's Head**. Earlier called the Crossed or Crowned Keys, the inn had changed its name by 1588, and some fifty years later it formed part of the inheritance of the young John Harvard; it escaped the 1676 fire and continued as an inn until 1886. The galleried portion was demolished around 1897, but part of the structure (renewed *c.* 1855) remains at no. 103 Borough High Street, where it served for many years as the headquarters of the National Secular Society (see Rendle and Norman, pp. 204-11, and Collins 1966). The **Catherine Wheel** is shown by Rocque and Horwood on the west side of the street, with the entrance just north of no. 190. It was mentioned in a will as early as 1534, and was described by Strype in 1720 as 'very large and well resorted unto' (11.4.30). The inn was in operation until about 1870, when the buildings were pulled down (see *SL* 25, p. 7, and Rendle and Norman, pp. 278-83).

[3] The tavern and chop house were presumably part of the **Three Tuns** inn on the east side of Borough High Street, shown on the Horwood and Bacon maps; it was

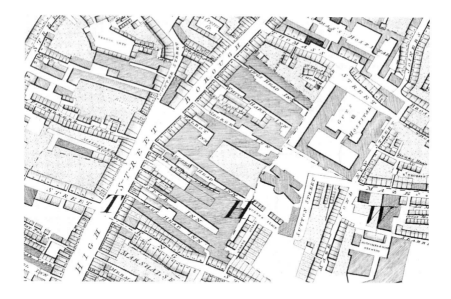

Spur and Nag's Head.

The Spur Inn with a coffee-room attached is kept by Mr. James Foot from the White Hart, River-head, in Kent. This, and the Nag's Head and Tavern, kept by Mr. H. Wissenden may be regarded as equally comfortable and well conducted houses.[1]

earlier called the Black Bull or the Bull and had ceased to function as an inn by 1870 (Rendle and Norman, pp. 212-17).

[1] The **Spur** is shown on the east side of Borough High Street on the Rocque, Horwood, and Bacon maps; as the 'Spore' it appears on a plan of the street made in about 1541 (National Archives MPC 1/64), which also names the Tabard, the White Hart, and the George. The Spur ceased operating as an inn in 1848, but the building was still standing forty years later (Rendle and Norman, pp. 219-21). The **Nag's Head**, on the east side of Borough High Street, is the 'Horse Hede' of the 1541 plan, and is shown under its modern name by Rocque, Horwood, and Bacon; see *SL* 22, p. 26, and Rendle and Norman, pp. 221-25. Rebuilt at some time after Strype referred to it as 'old and sorry', the inn continued into the C20 as a public house. In 1905 Bowers (p. 391) claimed that it was among the establishments now 'bereft of their picturesque features', but in 1950 *SL* noted that the original roof and dormers remained, and that the building was still in use as 'the Nag's Head Inn and booking offices'.

Half Moon.

No. 131, the Half Moon Inn kept by Mr. Nettleship is a large establishment, having an excellent larder well stored with every thing in season. Its convenient accommodations for entertaining and lodging its guests extend on either side the inn yard, and are connected by a well contrived covered bridge from gallery to gallery.[1]
[214]

Horse Shoe.

At the Stones' end opposite the King's Bench, is the Horse Shoe Inn and Chop-house.[2] It has a larder of steaks and other prompt dishes constantly at command, and gives an ordinary at four o'clock every Monday, Wednesday, and Friday, throughout the year, for the accommodation of persons attending the corn and haymarkets from various parts of Surrey and Kent, who usually put up their horses and vehicles at the stables of this inn.

Those of our readers whom business or amusement may lead down King Street and Kent Street, will be sure to meet with several refectories of the humbler sort; and, if their eyes and stomachs be too delicate to encounter and tolerate the smell and sight of the larders, they may walk on to the end of the latter street, and there find, at the Bricklayer's Arms, a most comfortable repast either in the style of a hasty dinner or a flying lunch.[3] The passengers

[1] The **Half Moon** at no. 131 Borough High Street, east side, is shown on the Rocque and Horwood maps; see Rendle and Norman, pp. 245-47. The inn was rebuilt after a fire of 1689, and still flourished in 1888, 'being nowadays much frequented by foreigners' (p. 246), though by 1905 Bowers listed it with the Nag's Head as an inn that had lost its 'picturesque features'. Later known as the White Horse and Half Moon, it closed in 1922 (*The Times*, 13 March, with picture).
[2] The **Horse Shoe** was at the Stones' End – the end of the paved road from London Bridge – at the point where Blackman Street (now part of Borough High Street) gave way to Newington Causeway. The inn is shown by Rocque on the east side of the road, just above Horsemonger Lane (now Harper Road); the King's Bench Prison, demolished in 1880, was northwest of the junction of Blackman Street and Borough Road. By 1738 the Horse Shoe was a major coach stop, and when Rendle and Norman wrote in 1888, giving the address as no. 7 Newington Causeway, they noted that it still had 'extensive stabling', and that despite some rebuilding 'part of the interior is of considerable age' (p. 349). The Horse Shoe was still in business as late as 1944.
[3] Shown on the Horwood and Bacon maps, the **Bricklayer's Arms** was on the east side of the Kent Road, at the corner of Bermondsey New Road; a major coach stop, the tavern was rebuilt *c.* 1880-81 (no. 37 Old Kent Road). The site was exten-

by the numerous Kent and Surrey stages, are regaled here in the readiest manner.

Returning by the Grange Road to Newington Butts, a similarly varied routine of refreshments presents itself to the appetite of the stranger [215] at the Elephant and Castle, where also most of the Surrey and Sussex stages stop.[1]

Cottage of Content.

We ought not to have left the Bricklayer's Arms without bestowing a tribute of applause on the spirited and tasteful exertions of Mr. Holmes, at the Cottage of Content Tavern and Tea Gardens, to render that retreat worthy of the public patronage.[2] Its *local* is a veritable *rus in urbe*, and the refreshments served up there are worthy of the place. The following paragraph copied literatim from one of the most popular journals of the day, and evidently the result of experience and the evidence of facts will testify that our encomiums are not overcharged.

"Cottage of Content, 16th May, 1814.

"A party of twenty-eight having dined a few days back at Mr. Holmes's Cottage Tavern, was highly gratified to find a dinner put on table in a style equal to the first-rate houses in town, with every delicacy of the season, and the wines extremely good. The very moderate charge induced the worthy chairman, who has a knowledge of the style that a dinner ought to be served up in, to take the opportunity to remark, for the good of the [216] community, it should be made public; as, at this season of the year there are very many benefit societies and companies that wish a rural spot to spend a convivial day

sively redeveloped in the late 1960s, and although Bricklayer's Arms still survives on modern maps, it is only as the name for the resulting flyover and roundabout.

[1] There had been an inn at the busy **Elephant and Castle** junction in Newington from the mid-C18, when it replaced the White Horse smithy (see *SL* 25, pp. 46-48). Rebuilt in 1818 and again in 1897-98, the inn survived the extensive bombing of the area in the Second World War, but was cleared away in 1959 during redevelopment. A modern Elephant and Castle public house carries on the name not far away.

[2] I have been unable to find the original of this letter, and it may be Rylance's invention. The rustic **Cottage of Content** tavern and tea gardens was located in the area of Lock's Fields, south of the New Kent Road and east of Walworth Road. An 1834 directory gives the address as no. 1 Park Place (today's Elsted Street), so that the Cottage can be identified as the isolated building so numbered on the original Horwood map (it is less clear in the 1813 version). A public house of the name survived into the late 1970s, latterly at no. 123 Rodney Road, Walworth.

without going a distance from town. The situation is truly rustic; and it not being more than one mile from the three bridges makes it a pleasant retiring distance, after partaking freely of the nectareous libation.

"One of the party."   N.

Surrey Theatre.

Passing on to the Obelisk, we find several houses of entertainment adjoining the Surrey Theatre, or in its immediate vicinity. Contiguous to it are, the Surrey Theatre Coffee-house and Tavern, kept by Mr. Branscomb; and Johnson's Coffee-house and Tavern. Each keeps a larder and soups during the season of the house; and both serve dinners and suppers in a very neat style to the numerous frequenters of this splendid place of amusement, as well as to many of the performers. Opposite the theatre is an establishment called the Theatre Refectory, which is nothing more or less than a cook's-shop.[1]

Will Nickle's.

Distant a few yards from the theatre in [217] what is called by some people the paragon that surrounds the obelisk, are *Will Nickle's supper rooms*. A curious medley of refreshments is here displayed, and announced as always ready: tea, coffee, wines, pastry, a-la-mode beef, ham, fowls, tongues, and fruit. It is at Will Nickle's that some of the fair frail unfortunate females who sojourn in the plains of St. George, now unhappily covered with new streets and brick kilns, sometimes regale. But this is only when they happen to meet with a kind Samaritan, who has sympathy enough to conceive that these goddesses do possess so much of mortality as to require solid food with their nectar, or in the vernacular idiom, Deady's Full Proof and Old Tom.

A purveyor of similar varieties will be found, on turning round the corner into the Westminster-road.

---

[1] The Obelisk, constructed of Portland stone, was erected at the intersection now known as St George's Circus in 1771; it was moved in 1905 to the grounds of the Imperial War Museum, but in 1998 was restored to its original site. The **Theatre Coffee House** and **Johnson's** both adjoined the Surrey Theatre, rebuilt in 1806 after a fire and shown on Horwood's map as the Royal Circus. The theatre burned down again in 1865; its successor closed in 1924 and was demolished ten years later. The 'fair frail unfortunate females' seen at **Will Nickle's** supper rooms would have been inmates of the Magdalen Hospital for Penitent Prostitutes in Great Surrey Street (now Blackfrairs Road), established in 1769 and pulled down around 1870.

Cross Keys.

If you choose now to pass on to the Obelisk over Blackfriars Bridge, you may as well rest yourself in a very respectable Coffee-house and Tavern, at the corner of Albion Street, known by the sign or cognomen of the Cross Keys and Museum Tavern. The premises having been recently under repair, will [218] doubtless restore to this house the fame of being an excellent place of entertainment. It is on a large scale, and has a stable-yard attached to it.[1]

At the corner of Christ Church Yard there is an established eating-house and cook's-shop, where various joints as well as subordinate dishes are kept hot from noon until midnight.

Shell Fish, Ham Shop, and Pastry Cook.

In Great Surrey Street, between Christ Church and the New Road, opposite Rowland Hill's Chapel, we find at No. 6, Baker's Shell-fish and Oyster Rooms. Hard by lives an excellent pastry-cook, and near his manufactory there is a shop famous for its dressed hams, tongues, and occasionally fowls.[2]

Ordnance Tavern.

Such of our readers as go to the Obelisk, by the way of Westminster Bridge, will on the east side of Bridge Street find the Ordnance Coffee-house and Tavern. Here a larder and soups are always at command. The last proprietor was a wine-merchant, and he piqued himself on supplying his guests with genuine and choice juice of the grape of every variety of vintage; we understand that his [219] cellar stock has been transferred to his successor.[3]

---

[1] The **Cross Keys** at no. 1 Albion Street (now part of Blackfriars Road) is shown on Horwood's map at the southwest corner of Upper Ground Street. It survived into the C20 as the Cross Keys and Railway Hotel.

[2] Great Surrey Street is now incorporated in Blackfriars Road. All of the establishments mentioned would have been on the west side near Christ Church, facing the Surrey Chapel that the *Almanack* refers to by its popular name commemorating the preacher Rowland Hill.

[3] Roads led from St George's Circus north to Blackfriars Bridge, northeast to London Bridge, and northwest to Westminster Bridge. The **Ordnance Coffee House and Tavern** was on the 'east' (i.e. north) side of Westminster Bridge Street (now Road), not far from Astley's Royal Amphitheatre; it is presumably identical with the Ordinance [*sic*] named in the 1799 *Boyle's View of London* and the Ordnance Arms listed

New Inn.

On the same side, a few doors from Pedlar's Acre, is the New Inn, a most excellent house, which has invariably maintained the high reputation of its dinners ever since the completion of that magnificent structure, Westminster Bridge. It has also a hotel department, in which persons coming from the country on parliamentary or law business, find the best and most convenient accommodations.[1]

Stangate.

A few yards down Amphitheatre Row, leading to Standgate, we find a very decent à-la-mode beef-shop, which does much business, particularly in the evenings after the close of the tremendous spectacles at Mr. Astley's theatre.

On the road to the Obelisk, and nearly fronting the Lying-in-Hospital, is an Eating-house and Cook's-shop, where the usual fare is to be had from an early hour in the forenoon until late at night.[2]

Red Lion and Dover Castle.

On the east side of the road commences [220] the New Lambeth Marsh Road, or New Cut, as it is called. It commences very respectably with a licensed public-house at each corner; the one called the Red Lion; the other the Dover Castle. Both are houses of a superior class, alike famed for ales. Here chops, kidneys, Welsh-rabbits, and other tit-bits, in the way

in the 1819 *New Picture of London*. The coffee house and tavern may also have ties to the Ordnance Arms public house once at no. 71 York Road; see Peter Walker 1989, but note that York Road itself was not built until 1824, when the area was developed following the construction of the Strand or Waterloo Bridge (opened 1817).

[1] The **New Inn** was also on the north side of Westminster Bridge Street, near Pedlar's Acre (now Belvedere Road); the 1813 Horwood map clearly indicates the 'New Inn Stables'. The Inn was rebuilt in 1895 (no. 254 Westminster Bridge Road) and demolished in 1959; see Walker 1989 for this and other Lambeth establishments.

[2] Amphitheatre Row (now under St Thomas's Hospital) was just west of Astley's, leading south into Stangate, which marked the end of the Roman road leading up to a ford by which one could cross to Westminster. The lying-in hospital mentioned here is shown on the 1813 Horwood map, just past the New Inn Stables.

of a relish to the potent beverage, are served up to a numerous and most respectable range of customers, who are accommodated with several of the morning, evening, and provincial papers. At the Red Lion a whimsical society of humorists, who call themselves the Codgers, hold their lodge.[1]

Here for the present terminates our Trans-Thamesian tour. The several houses of entertainment in the neighbouring villages in the sweet county of Surrey, such as Newington, Kennington, Brixton, Stockwell, Clapham, Camberwell, and Peckham, will be noticed in our circumambulation of the metropolis.

COUNTRY TOUR.

Having finished our alimentary ramble in town, we now proceed with keen stomachs to circumambulate it for the information of those whom business, pleasure, or mere idleness, may prompt to a rural excursion. Let [221] us here premise that we shall for the present attempt nothing more than a rapid survey of the immediate environs; if our labours be well received by the public, we shall be encouraged in future to extend our researches, and enrich the results of them with a variety of interesting particulars, which we cannot at present obtain.

---

[1] The next two taverns were at the junction of Westminster Bridge Road and Lambeth Marsh Road (now Lower Marsh), which with its continuation (the New Cut) connected Westminster Bridge Street with Great Surrey Street. The **Red Lion** is named in a 1794 announcement of the upcoming anniversary meeting of the 'Surrey Hall of Cogers' (*Morning Advertiser*, 21 March; cf. the Barley Mow, p. 73 above), but I have been unable to trace it further. A public house called the **Dover Castle** was in business by 1715 (Gibberd 1992, p. 15), and by the middle of the C19 two establishments of that name were operating on opposite corners: one was by then known as the Old Dover Castle, and both were for some time owned by John Henry Watchorn (see *The Times* of 5 August 1850, advertising the sale of the lease of Watchorn's New Dover Castle together with that of its neighbour). The Old Dover Castle was rebuilt as a hotel in the 1890s; according to Peter Walker it was converted to offices in 1958 (Walker 1989, p. 22). The New Dover Castle, described in 1850 as having been completely rebuilt within the previous eight years, was frequently referred to simply as Watchorn's, but about 1890 became the Red Lion, possibly recalling the earlier establishment of that name, and is now the Walrus Social (no. 172 Westminster Bridge Road).

KNIGHTSBRIDGE.

Departing from Hyde Park corner, we proceed along the great western road, and find ourselves, after a few minutes walk, in the midst of the village of Knightsbridge. Passing the end of Sloane Street, we find, on the left-hand, a very respectable Eating-house, with good accommodations up stairs. Those who choose to regale themselves in better style must go down Sloane Street, as far as Exeter Street, where they will find the Feathers Tavern, a very respectable house.[1] All the rooms are fitted up in good style. There is a large saloon for parties, in which the commissioners for the Hyde Park toll trust* hold their monthly court of direction.

* The commissioners of high-ways are in general adepts in good living, but they never forget their duty to the public in their most convivial hours. [222] A knot of them in one of the midland counties debated during two courses of a grand dinner the knotty and hard question, "to what minimum of size should the stones for mending the roads be broken?" One of the commissioners, a young barrister, at length proposed a standard quite to their taste; and it was unanimously resolved, that no stone, or fragment of rock, used for mending the road, should be left there unbroken if of too large a size to go into the mouth of the greatest gourmand in the commission.

[222]

Resuming the high-road, we find, nearly facing the Horse-barracks, an Eating-house of subaltern class, frequented mostly by the sons of Mars.[2] You may dine here quite à la militaire; and now that the wars are over, you can hardly fail of being entertained, over dinner, by a history of the late campaigns of many a battered veteran —

"Shouldering his crutch to shew how fields were won."

[1] Exeter Street in Knightsbridge is now part of Hans Crescent, but in 1815 it ran between North (now Basil) Street and Sloane Street. A later public house at no. 6 Exeter Street, the Prince of Wales, may be a descendant of the *Almanack*'s **Feathers**, and it is even possible that the Wales feathers on a signboard for the tavern prompted a naming error in 1815.
[2] The horse barracks on the edge of Hyde Park were relatively new in 1815, but have been replaced twice since then; the retired soldier 'shouldering his crutch' appears in Oliver Goldsmith's *The Deserted Village*.

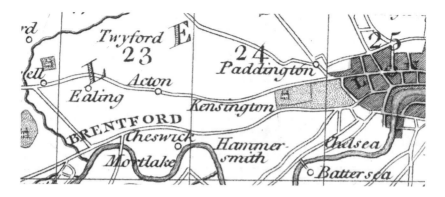

KENSINGTON.

We enter the town of Kensington, and immediately halt at the King's Arms Tavern adjoining the Palace Gate.[1] This establishment serves excellent dinners, to order, at reasonable charges. It has an ordinary on Sunday's, at a very convenient hour, for the numerous parties who go to inhale the gales in the groves [223] and gardens of Kensington. If you prefer dining apart, you may do so to your heart and stomach's content, and not indeed to the great disparagement of your pocket, considering the variety of good things set forth on the bills of fare.

In Young Street, leading to the square, there is an humble Eating-house; and opposite the church another to match it. In the midst of the town is Shepherd's Pastry-shop, long famed for its excellent three cornered cakes. A collation of these cakes, with a bottle of spruce, or soda, is an excellent thing for the throat of any pedestrian who has to encounter the dusty clouds which over-hang his route toward Brentford.

HAMMERSMITH.

As soon as you are through the town you descry, on the left-hand, the Hand and Flower, which gives an ordinary on Sundays, at two o'clock, and will supply you with a hasty dinner at any time.[2] On the right-hand, at the

---

[1] From Knightsbridge our guide travelled west along Kensington Road, stopping at the **King's Arms** near the gate into the grounds of Kensington Palace (no. 1 Kensington High Street).

[2] The **Hand and Flower** at no. 1 Hammersmith Road is shown on Bacon's 1888 map; although considerably rebuilt, it is still in business as a 'Victorian-style pub hotel', just opposite the Olympia exhibition and conference centre. The Hand and Flower

corner of the lane leading to Holland House, is the White Horse, a neat public-house, famous for good ale; to relish which a chop, or steak, is always to be had.[1]

On the same side of the way, close to Hammersmith Turnpike, is the Bell and Anchor, [224] a considerable establishment, where a larder is kept, and any part of its contents sent up dressed in very neat and comfortable style.[2]

Almost facing the church, which is called the Broadway, is the Hammersmith Coffee-house. A little farther, on the same side, are two houses – the Plough and Harrow and the Windsor Castle, both well accustomed by the passengers per stage, or chaise, along the western road. For their service a cold larder, and chops and steaks are kept at either house. Those who do not choose to alight may refresh themselves with cakes, which the waiters always offer at the carriage windows.[3]

CHISWICK.

Having passed through Hammersmith you soon come to the road leading to Chiswick, in which pleasant village you will find good entertainment at the George.[4] Chiswick has the distinction of having given birth to that excellent

was known for many years as Harvey Floorbanger's Hammersmith Charivari, but in 2000 the old name was restored.

[1] The **White Horse**, at the junction of Kensington Road (now Kensington High Street) and Melbury Road, was earlier known as the Horse and Groom; it was rebuilt as the Holland Arms in 1824 and is shown as such on Bacon's map (*SL* 37, p. 106).

[2] The **Bell and Anchor** on the north side of Hammersmith Road is also shown on Bacon's map, at the corner of Blythe Lane (now Road). Writing in 1878, Walford (*ONL*, vi:530) noted that it was 'much patronized by people of fashion in the early part of the reign of George III., though now frequented only by the working population about North End'. A public house of the name was still in business at nos. 38-40 Hammersmith Road into the 1960s; the site is now covered by the Olympia parking lots.

[3] The **Hammersmith Coffee House** is mentioned in newspaper advertisements of 1803 through 1833. The **Plough and Harrow** is shown on Bacon's map on the north side of Hammersmith Road (now King Street), just east of Cambridge Grove. It was rebuilt as a hotel in 1900 and again in 2002, and there is still a Plough and Harrow on the site, at nos. 120-124 King Street. Bacon also shows the mid-C18 **Windsor Castle** a few doors past the Plough on the same side of King Street; the site is now occupied by shops.

[4] Today the **George** at Chiswick is the George and Devonshire, at no. 8 Burlington Lane, next to Fuller's brewery (the 'Devonshire' was added to the name around

comedian Charles Holland, uncle to the present Charles Holland of Drury Lane Theatre. The church-yard of this village contains the ashes of the inimitable Hogarth. We may state also, in honour of the George, that the celebrated champion of liberty, John Wilkes, used to dine there with his constituents during the period in which he represented the County of Middlesex in Parliament.

[225]

Packhorse.

On Turnham Green, which you find on the left, soon after passing Chiswick Lane, stands the Packhorse, a very considerable inn and tavern, constantly stocked with abundance of good cheer.[1]

Roebuck.

Almost facing it is the Roebuck, a neat house, on a small scale, which has an ordinary on Sunday's, of a very superior description.

Upper Packhorse.

On the same side is another Packhorse, called the Upper Packhorse, to distinguish it from the one just mentioned. Dinners for small or large parties are to be had here, and ordinaries, on Sundays, are constant during the season.[2]

1826 to honour the Duke of Devonshire, who then owned Chiswick House). The public house still occupies the Georgian building described here.

[1] The **Packhorse** on Turnham Green was earlier known as the Lower Packhorse and had become the Old Pack Horse by 1838. The original tavern was known as early as 1698 (*VCH Middlesex*, vii:69; for an illustration see Stuart, p. 69), but today's opulent building dates from 1910 (no. 434 Chiswick High Road). The **Roebuck**, on the north side of the road at no. 122, was a coaching inn, licensed from 1732; the original building was demolished in 1890. In the late C20 the establishment was also known as the Chiswick Eyot, the Rat and Parrot, and the Bird Cage; now a gastropub, the Roebuck reverted to its original name in 2006.

[2] The **Upper Packhorse** was the ancestor of the C20 Packhorse and Talbot at no. 145 Chiswick High Road, south side; again, the original inn is known from 1698.

Star and Garter Tavern.

Proceed for Kew Bridge, and just before you come to it, you will find the Star and Garter Tavern, a celebrated house, where all the Kew Bridge stages take up and set down. Here is kept a good larder, and every requisite for good entertainment.[1]

[226]

Royal Village of Kew.

Having passed the bridge you come to the Royal Village of Kew, which, at the time when the Royal Family resided there, was a place of great gaiety. At that period the beautiful gardens attached to the palace, and so tastefully laid out and decorated by Sir William Chambers, with temples, alcoves, and other fanciful things, in the oriental style, were thrown open to the public one day in the week; as were Richmond Gardens every Sunday during the season. This gracious indulgence attracted hosts of cockneys.

The New Palace of Kew.

The New Palace of Kew is a very conspicuous object from the town of Brentford, over the Thames. It has, by some curious unenquiring travellers, been set down as the town jail thereof. It wants one essential quality of the gothic – size.[2]

Dreary Lane.

In going up Dreary Lane that leads to Richmond you pass along the east boundary-wall of Kew Gardens, extending more than a mile in length. This dead wall used to have [227] a most teazing and tedious effect on the eye of a pedestrian; but a poor mendicant crippled seaman, some years ago, enlivened it by drawing on it, in chalk, every man of war in the British navy. He returns annually to the spot to refit his ships, and raises considerable supplies for his

[1] The C18 **Star and Garter** coaching inn at Old Brentford, just north of Kew Bridge, is shown on G. F. Cruchley's 1824 map of the *Environs of London*, and there is an 1881 photograph in Hobhouse 1971, p. 220. By then principally known as a hotel, the Star and Garter was rebuilt in brick and stucco around 1900; it was severely damaged by fire in 1977 and later converted to offices.

[2] The gothic castellated palace, designed by James Wyatt with input from George III himself, was begun in 1800 and never completed nor used; it was demolished in 1827-28.

own victualling board from the gratuities of the charitable, who pass to and from Richmond.

RICHMOND.

At the top of Kew Lane you enter the town of Richmond amidst a colony of butchers, poulterers, fishmongers, and green-grocers, whose well-stocked shops furnish strong indications of the epicurean propensities of the inhabitants. The hopes which these indications generate may be amply satisfied at any of the numerous houses of good cheer in the town. If you be very sharp set on your arrival, turn to the right and you will find the Bowling Green (one of the largest and best-preserved in England); on the left is the Duke's Arms, noted for good cooking, good accommodation, and good punch.[1] If it be the summer season, you will also be sure to find good company. If you be in the merry mood, indeed you can hardly fail – for at that season the Richmond Theatre is open, and [228] this inn is the head-quarters of the company of comedians. The theatre stands on the angle of the Green, leading to the Thames. Near it is a place called the Old Court, being part of the ancient palace of Sheen. This palace, in which Queen Elizabeth died, stood in the gardens, and was razed to the ground by order of his present Majesty.

Castle Inn and Tavern.

Passing again into the main street you soon come to the Castle Inn and Tavern, a most magnificent establishment, with gardens, and a flight of steps to the river. This accessory ensures to the proprietor a considerable share of business, as it is a very convenient landing place for the numerous water-parties which enliven the Thames during the summer season. Among other great personages who disembark here, are frequently to be seen whole crews of opulent citizens, who regularly make several summer voyages hither in

[1] Having walked down 'Dreary Lane' (Kew Road), our guide entered Richmond near the bowling green, now called the Little Green to distinguish it from Richmond Green proper. In 1818 John Hassell called Richmond 'the most fashionable village in England' (*Picturesque Rides and Walks*, ii:68); the Theatre Royal, in operation from 1765 to the early 1880s, attracted such well-known London actors as David Garrick and Edmund Kean. In naming one inn as the **Duke's Arms**, the *Almanack* appears to have erred: no Duke's Arms is known, but it is possible that the establishment meant was the Prince's Head on the Green, which before about 1795 was known as the Duke's Head (Cloake 1999, p. 10).

the city barges. We rather wonder that none of those ingenious and public spirited gentlemen ever conceived the idea of personifying the city of London as a tall, portly dame, seated on the poop of a peterboat, and towed along the Thames like a *Venus anadyomene*, by a pair of lively turtles. Perhaps a certain yachto-nautical baronet will improve upon this hint.[1]

[229] It is needless to add, in speaking of the Castle Tavern, that the fare is in every respect *sumptuous*. The luxurious dainties you *lay-in* here are princely; you cannot grudge, therefore, to *lay-out* (as Sir John Falstaff said to Bardolph) as becomes a prince.

Talbot Inn and Tavern.

A little farther on is the Talbot Inn and Tavern, commanding a beautiful view over the elegant bridge. This large house has an extensive bowling-green, and a well supplied larder for the support of the bowlers during the season. We say during the season, because, after the summer season, Richmond and the houses in it are "as dull as the great thaw." The wines are good; so are the lodging-rooms; so are the stables and every office and appurtenance to the establishment.[2]

[1] In the early C19 the **Castle Inn** was the most important hotel in central Richmond, described by John Evans in 1824 as having 'a handsome front, and extensive accommodations, with a delightful lawn behind it, reaching down to the river' (*Richmond and its Vicinity*, p. 147). The inn had moved from a site in George Street to a mansion in Hill Street about 1760; largely rebuilt in the mid-C19, the Castle closed in 1876 and was converted to offices.

[2] The **Talbot**, on the corner of Hill Street and Ormond Road, was originally the Dog Inn, known from 1702 and renamed in 1735 (a talbot was a large hound used for tracking and hunting). It survived as the Talbot Hotel until 1907, but today a cinema covers the site (Cloake, p. 10).

The Roebuck.

Ascending the hill you find on the left-hand, facing the terrace, the Roebuck, a sort of tavern of ease to that stupendous hotel the Star and Garter, on Richmond Hill. This house commands one of the most extensive and beautiful prospects in the environs of London: it is also remarkable as being a very [230] costly house; so costly that, on the demise or secession of its proprietor, no one could be found of sufficient capital to embark in the concern; the company who frequent it, and on whom it must depend for support, being rather select than numerous – instead of being equally numerous and select.[1]

RICHMOND HILL.

The reader will regard Richmond Hill with veneration as well as delight when he remembers it to have been the sacred and favourite haunt of Thomson's muse. The epicure, also, will not fail to do homage to the manes of Thomson, a true and philosophic lover of good cheer; and so indolent withal, that he was once found in an orchard, on a fine autumn day, under an apple-tree, with his hands in his coat pockets, eating the blooming fruit from the branches on which they grew.

Besides its hill Richmond has many attractions; such as its terrace, its park, its theatre, and its elegant villas, among which those of the Duke of Buccleugh, and of the late Duke of Queensberry, take the first rank in point of elegance. If the stranger cannot acquire an appetite by taking a forenoon's ramble among these places, he may pursue the recreation of rowing on the Thames, which exercise [231] will tend to open his chest, and infallibly strengthen and quicken his digestive organs. These benefits are too important

---

[1] Continuing east along Richmond Hill our guide came to the **Roebuck**, established by 1724 and still in operation at no. 130; rebuilt and recently refurbished, it remains famous for its view of the river. The **Star and Garter Hotel** on Petersham Common is shown on Cruchley's 1824 map, and on Bacon's of 1888. It began as a small inn about 1738, was rebuilt and expanded around 1780, and closed in 1808 following the bankruptcy and death of the owner (see Valentine Ellis 1983). The next owner, Christopher Crean, died in 1815, and the hotel was later taken over and enlarged by Joseph Ellis. The old buildings were totally destroyed by fires of 1870 and 1888, and the remainder of the hotel was demolished in 1919, being replaced in 1924 by the Royal Star and Garter Home for disabled servicemen; it is possible, however, that when the Home moves to Surbiton in 2013 the site may once again host a hotel.

to be foregone from the mere dread of being disabled from carving by a few blisters on the palms and fingers.

RICHMOND BRIDGE.

You may pass the bridge, or, if you dislike the expence of a halfpenny for the toll, you may cross the Thames in a ferry-boat for almost as mere a trifle, and you will then be refreshed by a walk over some delightful meadows to Twickenham. Directly off which place there is a small island in the Thames, occupied by an old fisherman, who takes charge of the oziers that grow, and the swans that swim about there. This fisherman is as much monarch of his little island, as Buonapartè is of Elba; but he has one advantage which the Corsican islander has not – he has his empress to share the toils of dominion with him, and to lighten his cares. This emperor bobs for eels, and his old woman manufactures them into excellent pyes. Few parties of pleasure pass the island without touching at it to refresh. We understand that this monarch derives a great portion of his revenue from the eel-fisheries alone.[1]

[232]

TWICKENHAM.

At Twickenham you may find a variety of good houses of entertainment. The George Inn in particular may be relied on for every thing that an inn ought to afford – good accommodations, good cheer, and kind welcome.[2]

HAMPTON COURT.

From Twickenham you have a most delightful walk, or ride, of about three miles and a half, by that charming, secluded, modern, antique villa, (built

---

[1]   There was a bowling alley, quoits court, and public house – originally the Ship and later the White Cross – on Twickenham Ait by 1740. The popularity of the pies served there eventually led to the renaming of the island itself, and even in 1824, six years before the famous Eel Pie Hotel was built, John Evans referred to it as **Eel Pie Island** (p. 167). Charles Dickens visited the 'eel pie house' and mentioned the island in *Nicholas Nickleby* (1839); in the 1950s and 1960s the hotel became an important venue for jazz, rhythm and blues, and latterly rock, featuring performances by the Rolling Stones, the Who, and other groups until it closed in 1967 (see Van der Vat and Whitby 2009) .

[2]   The **George** at Twickenham (no. 32 King Street) is known as a coaching inn from 1737; the building itself has late C17 origins, but the interior has been modernized.

by the author of the Castle of Otranto and hight Strawberry Hill)[1] and by Teddington (Tide's End Town, because the tide of the Thames flows no further), through the middle of Bushy Park, beneath a row of fine, tall, shady, chestnut-trees, to Hampton Court. Arriving there you cannot do better than go to the King's Arms directly, facing Bushy Park Gate, where Mrs. Hippison, a most obliging hostess, assisted by her son, will entertain you in very respectable style.[2] Having dined there upon some of her barn-door fowls, and her Thames-eels, you may take a view of the palace; you will there see seven of the twelve celebrated cartoons of Raphael, besides a fine collection of paintings by the first masters; among which, one [233] piece, a Madonna and Child, by Parmegiano, is alone well worth going to see, if you went as the pilgrims go to our Lady of Loretto. There are also the Hampton Court beauties of Charles II.; out of whom, if you do not fix upon Miss Pitt as the most beautiful, you must certainly be set down as no connoisseur. You may then amuse yourself in the gardens of the palace, laid out exactly in the old regular style, which, after all, suits the place so well, that Brown himself could find no capability for clumping, belting, lawning, and ponding, or rather sheeting. There is a labyrinth in one corner which is most amusingly perplexing, and affords infinite fun if the party consist of about twelve ladies and gentlemen.

There is another inn, called the Toy, just by the foot of the bridge. It is on a larger scale than the King's Arms, and the charges are rather higher, we believe, but the fare is such as to leave you no shadow of cause to repine at the expence.[3]

---

[1] In the second half of the C18 Horace Walpole (1717-97) transformed his home at **Strawberry Hill** into a miniature Gothic castle, adding towers, battlements, and pinnacles, and creating extensive gardens.

[2] At Hampton Court the **King's Arms** (C18 or possibly older) is still in business, although extended and considerably refurbished since 1815; it backs onto the perimeter wall of Hampton Court Palace, just at the Lion Gate facing Bushy Park.

[3] The **Toy** was on the other side of the Palace grounds, by Hampton Court Bridge, and the name may derive from its location near the tow path. Possibly built in the time of Henry VIII, the Toy was known as a victualling house from the C17 – John Taylor remarked in his *Honorable and Memorable Foundations* (1637) that 'The *Toy* Taverne at *Hampton-Court* needs no signe' – and it can be seen in a drawing by Canaletto made soon after the first bridge opened in 1753. In 1827 Hassell described the Toy as 'much frequented by the Nobility and Gentry' (i:244); it was pulled down in 1857 (Ripley 1885, p. 9).

We will proceed to the town of Hampton and no further. There is a ferry there across the river to Moulsey Hurst, a noted field of battle among the heroes and champions of the fist.

The Bell, at Hampton.

At the Bell, at Hampton, those who are [234] fond of angling in a punt may find good fare and much diversion. In some of the parlours there are portraits drawn on the wall of various remarkable fine fish, with inscriptions underneath, certifying when, and by whom, they were caught – who manufactured the hooks, lines, and baits – how much weighed the fish, and who were the epicures that feasted on them.[1]

Having now exceeded our prescribed excursion of ten miles, we must direct you back to town, and you may either follow the meanderings of the Thames, or go at once to that pleasant village Isleworth, and then saunter through the Duke of Northumberland's beautiful park, at Sion, to Brentford, where several houses of good entertainment offer themselves, such as the Three Pigeons and the Red Lion.[2]

KINGSTON.

If you prefer returning from Hampton by way of Kingston, in Surrey, you will save at least a mile of ground, avoid the pavements in Brentford, Hammersmith, and Kensington, and be delighted with a fine diversity of scenery. If you stand in need of restoration at Kingston, which is one of the assize towns for the sweet county of Surrey, you will find ample [235] means at two or three capital inns – the Sun for one.

---

[1] There is still a **Bell Inn** at Hampton (no. 8 Thames Street), the successor to an ancient establishment with records going back to the mid-C16; the present building replaced one that burned down in 1892 (Sheaf and Howe 1995, p. 102). In the C19 the Bell was popular with visiting anglers, and the portrait gallery of prize catches is mentioned in several accounts.

[2] The Three Pigeons and the Red Lion at Brentford were well-established coaching inns. The **Three Pigeons** is mentioned in Ben Jonson's *The Alchemist* (1610), Thomas Dekker's *Roaring Girl* (1611), and Oliver Goldsmith's *She Stoops to Conquer* (1773), and there is a tradition that Shakespeare stayed – or at least tippled – there while working on *The Merry Wives of Windsor*. Located in the marketplace, the Three Pigeons closed in early 1916 (*The Times*, 8 January). An inn called the Lion, possibly identical with the **Red Lion**, is known as early as 1446 (*VCH Middlesex*, vii:120); today's Red Lion (no. 318 High Street) was built in the mid-1960s.

WIMBLEDON.

Proceeding along that charming vale called Kingston Bottom, you will in good time come to Putney Heath, where you may refresh again at the picture of the Green Man; or turning to the right, you will soon come to the elegant village of Wimbledon, where the Spencer's Arms will receive and entertain you.[1] There is a singularly curious church adjoining, with a mausoleum equally curious and singular. Many beautiful villas give distinction to Wimbledon – such as Lord Spencer's, in the midst of a beautiful park; Lord Melville had a house there; Horne Tooke also here enjoyed the *otium cum dignitate*, and had for his neighbour Sir Francis Burdett. It is said that he wrote here that curious etymological tract called the Diversions of Purley. He died before he had completed it by a Treatise on the Verb, so that grammarians are almost as much at a loss to define that important part of speech as ever they were.

White Lion.

Continuing on your way to town you come to the village of Putney, at the bottom of which, [236] close to Fulham Bridge, is the White Lion.[2] You may have a good dinner drest here to order, in which order you ought not to forget to include stewed eels, or fried flounders. The people here have a live stock of them in the wells of the peter-boats moored off the village.

Seven Stars.

A few yards up the road, by the water, leading to Barnes Common, is the Seven Stars, which house is also famous for dressing fish.[3] Here are two or

---

[1] The **Green Man** on Putney Heath, dating from around 1700, has recently been renovated and extended, but would probably still be recognizable to our guide and to a later habitué, the poet Algernon Charles Swinburne. I have been unable to trace the **Spencer's Arms** at Wimbledon, which from the description given here stood near the C13 parish church of St Mary's, containing the early C17 mortuary chapel of Sir Edward Cecil, Viscount Wimbledon.

[2] The **White Lion** near Fulham Bridge (now Putney Bridge) dated from the early C17 and was rebuilt in 1887; it is still operating, as the 'Australian' Walkabout Inn, at nos. 14-16 Putney High Street.

[3] I have been unable to trace a **Seven Stars** in Putney, and suspect that the house meant was the **Star and Garter**, known from the late C18 and rebuilt a century later. It too is still open, at no. 4 Lower Richmond Road.

three pleasant rooms for small parties; they overhang the towing path by the river side, where there are convenient landing places for guests coming by water.

The Swan, Walham Green.

On the middle of Fulham Bridge, stands the four miles' stone from Hyde Park corner; after dining here the walk may be performed without a single halt; but should the pedestrian stand in need of a half-way house, he may stop at the Swan on Walham Green, which is famous for home-brewed ale, and has always a stock of hasty tit-bits to give a relish to this native Burgundy.[1] If business or inclination prompt you to go to town from Putney through Wandsworth, you will there find, [237] besides many other good houses, the Spread Eagle and the Ram, both of them near Garrat-lane.[2] Should you wish to halt nearer home, you may depend on good accommodations at the Royal Oak, Vauxhall Turnpike, or at the Pilgrim Tavern in Kennington-lane. A few minutes walk from thence will bring you within the limits of our town directory.[3]

---

[1] The **Swan** brewery at Walham Green was established in the 1740s, and by the early C19 offered the patrons of its taproom a recreation ground and gardens (*VCH Middlesex*, ii:176-77). In 1880 the brewery relocated and a new Swan – today an Irish theme pub called Brogans – opened at what is now no. 1 Fulham Broadway.

[2] The present **Spread Eagle**, at no. 71 Wandsworth High Street, is mostly Victorian. The old coaching inn was bought by Young's brewery in 1836 and rebuilt in 1898; it was further altered in the 1980s. The Ram Brewery in Wandsworth High Street, owned by Young's from 1831 until its closure in 2006, traced its history to the C17, when it provided beer not only to the **Ram Inn** but to neighbouring establishments. Both the inn and the brewery were rebuilt in 1883 after a fire, and a Ram Inn, remodelled in the 1930s, continued on the site until 1974 (Brandwood and Jephcote 2008, p. 193).

[3] The **Royal Oak**, Vauxhall Turnpike, is shown on Horwood's map just behind Cumberland Gardens. Described by Heckethorn (1899, p. 151) as 'an old inn with a galleried yard', it is mentioned in an advertisement as early as 1730 (*Daily Post*, 26 June), and in the 1740s was the meeting place of a free-thinking 'Wits' Club' that included Henry Fielding (Coke and Borg 2011, pp. 36-37). The Royal Oak was demolished very soon after the *Almanack* was published, during the construction of approaches to the first Vauxhall Bridge, completed in 1816. The **Pilgrim**, at no. 247 Kennington Lane (corner of Montford Place), was rebuilt in 1952; Peter Walker (*North Lambeth*, p. 79) has found a 1784 reference to the original tavern.

Cumberland Gardens.

We just now omitted to mention Cumberland Gardens, near Vauxhall, which have rooms adapted for large or small parties, and tea-gardens fitted up with boxes for families, and tête à têtes. Here is a convenient landing-place for water-parties, and a suit of colours as well as a battery of cannon to announce them.[1]

Some of our readers may choose to take short excursions into Surrey from the several bridges. They will find on Kennington common, that well-known House, called the Horns, which has an assembly-room, and a suite of spacious apartments attached to it. This house has much of the parochial business of Lambeth, and entertains numerous parties from the Metropolis on public occasions. It has always an extensive larder at command, and the wines and liqueurs are said [238] to be of the best. There is a bowling-green, with other pleasure grounds opposite; indeed the common itself is occasionally converted into one, and marquees are pitched upon it for the accommodation of parties who take the exercise of cricket or trap-ball.[2]

Clapham Common.

If you wish for a rural shady walk to Clapham common, you may pass thither by a foot-path lane, commencing at the Wheat-sheaf in South Lambeth, a very decent house, to the lower Clapham road. At the end of this

[1] **Cumberland Gardens** are shown on Horwood's map, on the south bank of the Thames just south of Vauxhall Bridge; from 1775 to 1783 they had been known as Smith's Tea Gardens. The Gardens were the finishing point for an annual boat race from Blackfriars to Vauxhall, first held in 1786, and Wroth (*London Pleasure Gardens*, pp. 283-85) notes that they were 'much frequented' by south Londoners in the early C19. On 25 May 1825 the tavern and adjoining ballroom were completely destroyed by fire, and the site was later occupied by a waterworks and a gas company. Curiously, the *Almanack* overlooks the much more famous **Vauxhall Gardens** nearby, opened (as Spring Garden) by the early 1660s and enormously popular until 1859; see Coke and Borg 2011.
[2] The **Horns** is shown on Bacon's 1888 map at the junction of Kennington Road and Kennington Park Road, not far from the Oval cricket ground; Peter Walker (pp. 69-70) suggests that it was established by 1725. John Hassell described the Horns in 1827 as being opposite the common where cricket was played, adding that the tavern 'accommodates parties with every necessary for the amusement, even to a marquee; it also sends their refreshments on the ground' (*Picturesque Views*, i:127). The Horns was rebuilt in 1887, but suffered bomb damage in the Second World War and closed in 1962.

retired path, which is called Lark-Hall-lane, you will find Lark-Hall, originally an humble cot-ale-house, which acquired its title and renown from the
extraordinary vocal powers of a caged lark. It has now become a tavern of
some consequence. Mr. Lovett, the late landlord, who improved it, laid out
part of the fortune he had acquired at the Red Lion at Westminster bridge,
in building some houses to serve as a neighbourhood for the support of
Lark-Hall.[1]

The Swan.

On the road leading from the Horns to Clapham common, at the corner
of that lead- [239] ing into Stockwell, you find the Swan, a house built a few
years ago on the site of a very ancient establishment for public accommodation. It is on a very large scale, and entertains small as well as large parties in
a style of great comfort.[2]

Plough Inn.

Going on to the beautiful common of Clapham, which is pleasantly
bounded by a variety of elegant villas, we find, first the Plough, the house
from which most stages start, and further on, that pleasant house, called the
Windmill. At both these Inns dinners are dressed to order, and excellent
ordinaries are provided on Sundays.[3]

[1] There is still a (Victorian) **Wheatsheaf** at no. 126 South Lambeth Road; it has
recently been refurbished and converted to a gastropub. **Lark Hall** appears on
Cary's 1786 *Survey*, and Bacon's map of a century later locates it on the west side
of Lark Hall Lane, at the junction with Priory Grove. Much of the immediate area
has now been transformed into Larkhall Park; a later Larkhall Tavern, at no. 96
Larkhall Lane, closed in 1999.

[2] The Bacon map shows the **Swan** on the east side of Clapham Road at the junction
of Stockwell Road (no. 215). Known from at least 1790, and rebuilt more than once
since then, the tavern is now a prominent venue for live music.

[3] The **Plough** is shown by Bacon at the south end of Clapham High Street facing
Clapham Common: a Plough Inn is known on this site since at least 1729, but the
building described here was completely destroyed by fire in the early hours of
29 May 1816. It was rebuilt in 1820 and a mock-Tudor facade added some hundred
years later; known as Bar SW4 in the early C21, it is today a branch of the 'Irish'
chain O'Neill's (nos. 196-198 Clapham High Street). There was apparently an
alehouse on the site of the **Windmill** on Clapham Common in the late C17, but the
present building dates from about 1797. In 1848 it was purchased by the founder

Balaam Hill.

Passing over the common, we come to Balaam Hill, where we find the George, a superior public-house.[1] Here baiting-refreshments may be had. A mile and a half farther on, at the corner of the lane leading to Wandsworth-common, is a celebrated house provided in the summer seasons with a larder; and at all times a rasher with eggs, or a chop may be procured. Here is good stabling. We now proceed to the two Tootings, the [240] upper and the lower; here are three or four houses where a chance dinner or at least a lunch may be obtained; if you can wait the proper length of time you may even have a tolerably plenteous dinner cooked.

TOOTING AND STREATHAM.

The walk or ride from Tooting to Streatham, is one of the pleasantest in the environs of London. Many of the adjacent villas are elegant, and their pleasure grounds are finely cultivated and laid out. Nor has this part of country been as yet stripped of its venerable and majestic oaks and other forest trees, to make room for those coss-lettuce poplars, which as they afford neither shade, nor shelter nor ornament, form mere apologies for groves.

Nothing can be more foreign to the idea of rural retirement, than the contrivances executed in this country a little nearer town; rows of compact boxes, with here and there a couple of porter's lodges like tea canisters; a counterpane's breadth of grass-plot, with a broad border of yellow gravel trimmed

---

of Young's brewery and extended backwards; further extensions followed in the 1980s (see Osborn 1991, pp. 33-34).
[1] There is still a (rebuilt) **George** public house at nos. 14-16 Balham Hill.

with box and studded with Michaelmas daisy, full-length windows and shade-less verandas, for the admission of road-dust and sun-shine; a wooden ruin with mock gothic casements, and [241] in short such a heterogeneous com-pound of common-place and extravaganza; of wilderness and town, of trade and tillage, of shop and farm, as one would never expect to find any where but in the very limbo of vanity.

White Horse.

Streatham has two or three very good houses of entertainment. Coming down Brixton-Hill, you find the White Horse, many years kept by Mrs. Woods, and now by Mr. Tidlark, who always gives a hearty welcome to his guests, and takes great care as well as great pleasure in making them comfortable. Here the epicure will be agreeably surprised to find a glass of super-excellent port.[1]

Horns Tavern.

Taking the road which terminates opposite the White Horse, we proceed to Norwood, where we find the Horns Tavern, better known by the name of the Gypsey-House. During the summer, here is ample provision made for the refreshment of the many parties who come hither to have their fortunes told.[2]

[242]

NORWOOD.

Norwood is now partly enclosed, but the surrounding scenery is delightful, comprehending views over Sydenham, Beckenham, Sutton, and the adjacent arcadia of Surrey and Kent, on which though our prescribed limits forbid us

---

[1] The **White Horse**, a coaching inn on the road to Streatham Hill, was known from the early C18; the present building at no. 94 Brixton Hill dates from the later C19.

[2] The **Horns**, on the west side of Knight's Hill Common, Norwood, is shown on Rocque's ten-mile map of 1746 and Cary's of 1786. J. B. Wilson (1990, p. 56) states that the original timber-built Horns was demolished for the building of the railway in 1856; its replacement was pulled down in 1937, but today's modern Horns at no. 40 Knights Hill is not far from the site of the original. There were Gypsies at Norwood as early as the C17 – Samuel Pepys's wife visited them to have her fortune told in 1668 (*Diary*, 11 August) – and by the early C19 Norwood was 'perhaps the principal rendezvous of the London Gypsies' (Mayall 1988, p. 35).

to enter, we gaze with a portion of that rapture which Moses felt when he beheld the land of Canaan from the top of Mount Pisgah.

DULWICH.

We come now to the ancient village of Dulwich, the college of which was founded by Edward Alleyn, a contemporary and friend of Shakspeare, and one of the best actors of his day. The rustic tavern, called the Half-moon, though but an humble hedge ale-house, is much frequented on account of its sequestered situation. In Lordship's lane, is the Plough, a house of similar character, and often visited during the summer by what are termed gypsey-ing parties.[1] Here cockney sportsmen during the shooting season repose and regale after enjoying the noble diversions of the field; and in spring, summer, and autumn, another class of sportsmen, whose game [243] are butterflies and moths, meet here to arrange their entomological collections, and exchange those insects of which they have duplicate specimens for others of a different species. It is no uncommon thing on these occasions to see an austere philosopher barter an emperor in his purple robes, for a painted lady; or a sedate stoic exchange a richly clad alderman, for a shabby insignificant looking individual with only a monstrous pair of horns to recommend him. Whilst these fly-fanciers are depositing their tiny spoils in their cork-bottomed boxes, we may roam in search of nobler prey.

Denmark-Hall.

A short walk from this place will bring us to the top of Denmark-hill, where once stood Denmark-Hall, a celebrated house for entertaining rusticatory parties. It was some time ago converted into a private dwelling-house.

---

[1] The **Half Moon** in Herne Hill (no. 10 Half Moon Lane, south side) is shown on Cruchley's 1824 map and on Bacon's of 1888; according to Edwin T. Hall (1917, p. 37) it was established in 1760. The present building dates from 1896, and for the past half century has also been home to a boxing gym. The **Plough** at no. 381 Lordship Lane, east side, was long a terminus for coaches (and later busses); the old Plough was rebuilt in 1865 and after a brief spell as a 'Goose and Granite' has recently reassumed its original name. Like Norwood, the area around Lordship Lane was a popular site for Gypsy encampments.

Champion-Hill.

Adjacent stands Champion-hill, embellished with villas, fermes ornées, and dress-cottages, which have been erected here for the sake of the pleasing and extensive views which the site commands, over some thousand acres of [244] highly cultivated land. About midway down the hill, is a cool retreat by the road side, called the Fox-under-the-Hill; and rightly so, for as you pass down the foot-path on the right bank, you may touch the top of the house. Reynard it seems has excavated a large part of the bank, for the stowage, not of turkies and poults, but of excellent ale, and he is seldom destitute of solid provender to feast you withal.[1]

CAMBERWELL.

Passing several noble or at least elegant mansions, we come to Camberwell; before we enter it however, we will turn a little to the left, up Cole-Arbour-lane, where we shall find the Rising Sun.[2] The artist who painted this sign had obviously a design of supplanting Phœbus, and of giving the reins to the jolly god, for such a bold, full, brazen front never could have fitted the shoulders of Argyrotox. Topers say that the ale suits the sign; it is some of the brown October drawn as Thomson says,

> "Mature and perfect from his dark retreat
> "Of thirty years."

Green Man.

At another turn in the same lane, we find [245] the sign of the Green Man with a gun in his hand. The house to which this sign belongs, was some years

---

[1] The **Fox under the Hill** is shown on Cary's 1786 *Survey* and on Bacon's map, located in Denmark Hill just north of the junction with Champion Hill. According to Walford, the tavern was earlier called Little Denmark Hall, 'there being at that time another house of entertainment known as "Great Denmark Hall," which was subsequently converted into one or more private houses' (*ONL*, vi:284).The old tavern had been demolished by the time Walford wrote; its successor at no. 149 Denmark Hill is now called the Fox *on* the Hill.

[2] Coldharbour Lane runs southwest from Denmark Hill to the centre of Brixton, and the **Rising Sun** would have been located not far west of Denmark Hill. The lines from Thomson's *The Seasons* refer to the strong ale typically brewed in October; the 'jolly god' is Bacchus, and Argurotoxus or Argyrotoxus ('silver-bowed') is one of the many names given to Phœbus Apollo.

ago conducted by Mrs. Webb, and was then renowned even to a proverb for its neatness. Many cits of opulence and genuine taste for the rustique used at that time occasionally to sequester themselves here from the bustle of a town life, and to their supreme satisfaction were regaled by Mrs. Webb, with as good dinners, and as good wines, as they could find at the London coffee-houses.[1]

The Golden Lion.

On our entrance into Camberwell, almost facing the end of this lane, we find on his post a most tremendous golden Lion, who invites us to his den, with a promise of as good fare as might be found in the hole of the Fox-under-the-Hill. The den indeed is capacious, the prey noble, and the ale mighty.[2]

Grove-House Tavern.

We pass Camberwell-Green, and take the road to Peckham, not the turnpike road, but a pleasanter one, up what is termed Grove-hill. We must not pass without notice the Grove-House Tavern, which has an elegant large room for assemblies and large dinner- [246] parties, and several minor apartments for dining smaller parties, with an excellent larder always ready for casual guests.[3] The wines and liquors of this house are good; the lawn and pleasure grounds neatly laid out, and kept in the best order, and the stabling unexceptionable.

---

[1] This **Green Man** may be the ancestor of the late C19 pub of that name at Loughborough Junction (225 Coldharbour Lane, corner of Hinton Road): now closed, gutted, and redeveloped as the 'Green Man Skills Zone', a neighbourhood employment support centre.

[2] The **Golden Lion** at no. 23 Denmark Hill had been rebuilt by 1925, when Wagner mentioned it in a list of 'modern successors of time-honoured taverns' (p. 193); it was demolished about 1985 for the building of a shopping centre (Boast 2000, p. 17).

[3] The original **Grove House Tavern** was popular in the C18 for its tea gardens, bowling green, and large assembly rooms; it was rebuilt in 1927 and continues in business at no. 26 Camberwell Grove. At nearby **Grove Hill** the physician and philanthropist John Coakley Lettsom (1744-1815) had built a separate wing to house his library and extensive collections – but anyone calling in to view them at the *Almanack*'s suggestion would have been disappointed, for Lettsom had left Grove Hill in 1810.

Grove-Hill.

Among the elegant houses at the top of Grove-hill, is one worth particular notice, being laid out in the virtuoso style, by the philanthropic Dr. Lettsom, who never refuses permission for any respectable stranger to view it on proper application. It commands in front a view of London and Westminster with the adjacent hills in Middlesex, and behind, a prospect bounded only by the horizon of the rich region of Surrey and Kent, the thickly navigated Thames, and the various striking objects which adorn and embellish its banks. The doctor's cabinet of curiosities, and his pleasure grounds laid out in a very original style, are liberally left open to the inspection and entertainment of the visitants.

White-Horse.

We now descend the hill by a pleasant foot- [247] path lane, which brings us to the White Horse at Peckham-Rye. This for a country tavern, is a very good one, and is as such often selected by parties from town as the scene of their banquets *champêtres*. In Peckham town there are several houses of entertainment, one of the best frequented of which, we believe is the Greyhound.[1] Those who make choice of the White Horse, above noticed, may, if so inclined after dinner, take a walk or ride up the common to Forest-hill, where of late years a small town has been built by a subscription of gentlemen. The trouble of walking will be amply requited by the view which has recently been further embellished by the completion of the Croydon canal.

Montpellier Gardens.

Those who pass either to Camberwell or Peckham through Walworth, may lunch to advantage at the sign of the famous Sir William Walworth, or proceeding a little farther may be sure of an excellent dinner at the Montpellier Gardens.[2] Here in the summer season some manly sport or other is

[1] The **White Horse** stood near the northernmost edge of the commonland known as Peckham Rye, and is clearly shown on several C19 maps; today's mock-Tudor White Horse was built in the 1930s on the site of the one described here (no. 20 Peckham Rye, west side). The **Greyhound** is known as early as 1636 (John Taylor, *Honorable and Memorable Foundations*, fol. D3r) and again the name lives on, now adorning a late-Victorian pub at no. 109 Peckham High Street, corner of Peckham Hill Street.

[2] The **Sir William Walworth** at no. 297 Walworth Road, east side, survived in some form into the 1970s. **Montpelier Gardens** (not Montpellier) can be seen

almost daily going forward. Not long ago a match of cricket was played here by females who displayed vigour and agility worthy of amazons. [248] On another occasion a purse was made for a match, all Greenwich versus Chelsea, the players being selected from among the Pensioners at the two Royal Hospitals; on each side was an equal number of one-armed and one-legged veterans.

Nun's Head.

  From Peckham Rye, an excursion is frequently made to the Nun's Head, where a rural dinner, with vegetables fresh from the garden may be had in summer. Nun's Head hill commands a very extensive land and water view; by the aid of the telescope, you may even see the Nore.[1] If you wish to lengthen your excursion, you may go from the Nun's Head to the genteel village of

on the 1827 Greenwood map; the name endures in Walworth's Pelier Street and Pelier Park, which itself probably represents the remains of the pleasure gardens. These, complete with a 'maze or labyrinth', had opened by 21 June 1782, when 'genteel company' were invited to partake of tea, coffee, and wines, and to purchase trees, plants, and flowers (*Parker's General Advertiser*). Records survive of cricket matches in the Gardens as early as 1796, when *The Times* (10 August) reported the contest 'between 11 of the Greenwich [sailor] pensioners, wanting an arm each, against the same number of their fellow-sufferers with each a wooden leg'; the 'one-leg men' won by 103 runs (*Oracle and Public Advertiser*, 12 August). If played at all, the women's contest described here was presumably a similar kind of exhibition, but at least one three-day first-class match is recorded in 1802, and in 1845 the Montpelier Cricket Club were responsible for creating the Oval grounds. William Hazlitt mentioned the site as 'deserted' in 1822, saying: 'When I was quite a boy my father used to take me to the Montpelier Tea-Gardens at Walworth. Do I go there now? No; the place is deserted, and its borders and its beds o'erturned' ('Why Distant Objects Please', *Table Talk*); in 1924 Leopold Wagner described the Montpelier Picture and Variety Palace at the foot of Empress Street as 'of old [...] the dance hall of the famous Montpelier Tea-Gardens' (pp. 158-59).

[1] The **Old Nun's Head Tavern** at the edge of Nunhead Green can be traced back to 1690 and may be older, but there is no real evidence to support local claims that it dates to the reign of Henry VIII, is built on the site of a nunnery suppressed at the Reformation, or is haunted (Woollacott, p. 18). The tavern described here is shown on Bacon's 1888 map; it was replaced in 1934 by the present mock-Tudor building, which has recently been refurbished.

Lewisham, where you will find several good houses of entertainment.[1] This village is watered by a pleasant streamlet, which rises on Sydenham common, and falls into the Thames at Deptford. The latter place, though distinguished as the site of his Majesty's victualling office, has few attractions for the bon vivant, and we therefore hasten on to the Royal village of Greenwich, celebrated for its magnificent and munificent hospital, its park and its observatory. The principal house within the village, is the George Inn and [249] Tavern. The two favourite places of resort on the river, are the Ship and the Crown and Sceptre. They are famous for giving good dinners, particularly those parts of a good dinner which the river produces. These they cook most deliciously. Their wines are reputed very good. Mr. Mollard, the landlord of the Crown and Sceptre, is himself, as we have elsewhere stated, a first-rate cook, and deserves every praise for the manner in which he conducts this concern. There are many houses in Greenwich on a smaller scale for the accommodation of those persons and parties whose circumscribed means will not allow them to dine out so expensively as at the Crown and Sceptre.[2]

Greenwich is at all times a favourite spot among all classes, but at the fairs of Easter and Whitsuntide, the afflux of lads and lasses is so great, that one half of the inhabitants are obliged to turn public cooks, to accommodate them.

---

[1] Among the 'several good houses' at Lewisham was the George, built sometime after 1799 at the corner of Rushey Green and George Lane; heavily altered in the C20, it was demolished in 2011 and replaced by a Tesco supermarket.

[2] The **George Tavern** on the river at Greenwich was replaced in 1837 by the Trafalgar, which closed in 1915 but reopened fifty years later following an extensive restoration. The Trafalgar, the Ship, and the Crown and Sceptre are all shown on the Bacon map, and all three are mentioned as locations for dinners attended by Charles Dickens (see Younger 1943). The **Ship**, just behind Greenwich Pier in King William Street, was originally built with a weather-board front, but the old tavern was replaced with a new structure in the mid-C19 (see Matz 1923, p. 211). Just east of the Ship, in Crane Street, was the **Crown and Sceptre**, which according to Timbs (*Clubs*, p. 494) also had a weather-board front and bow windows before it was rebuilt in the mid-C19. The Crown and Sceptre was demolished in the early 1930s, and the Ship destroyed by enemy action on 1 November 1940. For Mollard, see above, p. 147; his successor in 1826 (*The Times*, 27 March) was Samuel Lovegrove of the Horn Tavern in Godliman Street, noticed on p. 11 above. In 1829 Lovegrove opened another popular riverside establishment, the West India Dock Tavern at Coldharbour (*The Times*, 23 May), and in 1834 the Brunswick Tavern at Blackwall; like the Greenwich taverns they were famous through mid-century for their whitebait dinners (for which see above, p. xlix).

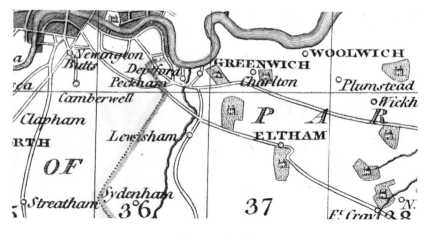

Flamstead-Hill.

The view from Flamstead-hill in the Park, may truly be esteemed unique; and that which presents itself on the side towards Black Heath, though not so splendid and so variously magnificent is truly fine; the heath [250] which is very romantic, is surrounded by elegant villas and mansions, among which is Montague House, lately the favourite residence of Her Royal Highness the Princess of Wales.

Green Man.

The epicure who has regained or improved his appetite by a walk in this direction, will be sure of gratifying it by a good dinner at the Green Man, on Black Heath.[1] About two miles onward, the road being straight before you, stands Shooter's-hill, – having on its summit a most conspicuous landmark,

[1] There had been a bowling green on Blackheath as early as 1629, and an inn known as the Bowling Green House or **Green Man** was in business by the early C18, if not before. Lavishly rebuilt in 1869, it is prominent on Bacon's 1888 map, but was demolished in 1970 (Rhind 1987, p. 70). Lillywhite suggested that the Green Man was the successor of another Blackheath establishment, the Chocolate House, but this was in fact a separate concern, built around 1702 and closed in 1788 or 1789; the building was later used for the Chocolate House Academy, a boys' school (see Kirby 1936).

built in the style of an Asiatic fort, in a general's pleasure ground. The Bull Inn and Tavern on Shooter's-hill, is a very large and well provided establishment.[1]

WOOLWICH.

From this eminence you have before you a pleasant walk, by the Royal Military Academy and the Royal Artillery barracks to Woolwich, a place that abounds in attractions to John Bull and his Family; besides those just mentioned there is the Dock-yard and the Warren; and as a contrast to those objects of national exultation, there is a field open for commiseration and charity in that correctory of human depravity, the convict Hulks.

[251] The number of naval and military officers resident at Woolwich, and that of occasional visitors, require and support many houses of entertainment. All these are inadequate, however, on some occasions, such as the launch of a man of war; or a review of troops; or an engineering experiment in the Warren. At such times hundreds are compelled to forego the gratification of sitting down to a comfortable dinner, until they have retraced their steps to Greenwich, or have ferried over to Blackwall or the Isle of Dogs.

At Blackwall the epicure may, if he chooses, improve his dinner by the addition of a dish of White Bait, a luxury of which naturalists are not agreed as to the origin. Some suppose them to be the spawn of the smelt. Of this opinion is the water-bailiff, who seizes the nets for catching them wherever he finds them, and the Lord Mayor, at his Court of Conservancy, never fails to condemn them. The landlords of the Artichoke and the Folly, the two principal houses, not having the fear of Our Lord, the Mayor, and his Court of Conservancy before their eyes, do not scruple to serve them up, whenever they can be had, on receiving an order from their guests to do so.[2]

[1] Shooters Hill is the highest point in south London, and the 'most conspicuous landmark' mentioned here is still standing: Severndroog Castle, a folly commissioned in 1784 by the widow of Sir William James to commemorate his capture of the pirate fortress of Severndroog on the Malabar coast of India. A large C18 coaching inn, the Bull described here was replaced in 1882 by a new **Bull Inn**, which is still in business at no. 151 Shooters Hill.

[2] The **Artichoke**, built around 1731, was a wooden tavern near Blackwall Stairs on the east side of the Isle of Dogs; both it and the Folly, a half mile or so to the south, are shown on Bacon's map. The Artichoke was famous for whitebait, and in 1765 an early proprietor, Peter Lord, boasted that he was 'the first that brought that fish into repute' (*Gazetteer and New Daily Advertiser*, 10 July). The tavern was demolished for the building of the Blackwall Tunnel, having been purchased by the Metropolitan Board of Works in 1888 and promptly closed down. The **Folly**

Persons whom business or curiosity may lead to the West India Docks, will find some good houses of refreshment in Poplar. Indi- [252] viduals in the employ of the Dock Company, the Customs and the Excise, and seamen as well as labourers engaged in loading or unloading the West India produce, are the principal consumers at the houses in the immediate vicinity. One of the dock restrictions is, that no cooking be done on board whilst the ships are in charge of the company. – We here finish our Surrey and Kent Tour, with an apology for deviating at the end into another county. We now enter upon that of Middlesex.

Copenhagen-House.

There are three distinct roads from the metropolis to the pleasant village of Highgate, whither we now propose to direct our readers in order to their being duly sworn according to the ancient charter of the place, – the road through Islington; the road through Kentish Town; and the middle road at the end of Gray's Inn Lane.¹ About a third of the way up the latter road will be found that well-known place of resort Copenhagen House, to which any large

House Tavern, licensed as early as 1758, sat in a large pleasure garden that included a cockpit; the tavern closed in 1875, but the place name Folly Wall remains to mark its location (see *SL* 44, pp. 551, 536).

¹ What the *Almanack* describes as the 'middle road at the end of Gray's Inn Lane' was known as Maiden Lane (later York Road and now York Way). **Copenhagen House**, shown on Rocque's 1746 map, is known by name from 1695, and had become a tavern and tea gardens by the mid-c18. Standing to the east of Maiden Lane, 'alone on an eminence' and with an 'extensive and uninterrupted […] view of the metropolis' (William Hone, *The Every-Day Book* (1826), i:860), its isolated position is clear from the 1827 Greenwood map. Within the gardens were a fives court, a cricket field, and provision for bowling games such as skittles and Dutch pins. One year after the *Almanack* was published the landlord, one Mr Tooth, lost his license because of the disturbance caused by his less savoury clientele. Hone relates that on Sundays during Tooth's tenancy 'the fives-ground was filled by bull-dogs and ruffians, who lounged and drank to intoxication; so many as fifty or sixty bull-dogs have been seen tied up to the benches at once, while their masters boozed and made match after match, and went out and fought their dogs before the house […]. There was also a common field, east of the house, wherein bulls were baited'. The next landlord restored order and tea-drinking, and Copenhagen House continued until 1853, when the grounds were purchased by the Corporation of London and the buildings pulled down for the creation of the new Metropolitan Cattle Market (see below, p. 246n); this too is now gone, leaving nothing behind but the clock tower in Caledonian Park.

party sending previous order may resort in the full confidence of enjoying a satisfactory dinner. Here is a tennis-court for the benefit of those guests who may wish to whet their appetites by exercise. The ales here are famous, and serve [253] as an excellent invigorating stimulus to those who halt here for a short rest, preparatory to the ascent of Highgate Hill.

From the city, the nearest road to Highgate is through Islington and Hollo-way. When you arrive, by either of the three outlets from London – the City Road, Goswell Road, or St. John's Road, at their point of junction, you are welcomed by the Angel at Islington with an assurance that Mr. Derrell, at the house where the Angel is stationed, has a larder of chops and steaks constantly at your service, and on Sundays an ordinary at two, and another at four o'clock. This house is much frequented by graziers, drovers, and farmers, whose business lies in Smithfield. At this inn and the Peacock most of the northern stages stop a few minutes.[1]

About five minutes walk along the road, leading west from this place will bring you to the Belvidere Tavern, Pentonville, kept by Mr. Blunt, who has always a well stocked larder for the accommodation of his friends, and provides an ordinary in very good style on Sundays, at half past two.[2]

If, when you have arrived at the Green, you take what is called the Lower Road, you will see at a very short distance from its commencement a foot-path leading across a field, to the pleasant tavern called Canonbury [254] House. Here is a noble large room for numerous parties, and various minor apartments; a bowling-green, trap-ball ground, garden, and other pleasure

---

[1] From the C16 a series of inns occupied what is now the northwest corner of Penton-ville Road and Islington High Street, providing lodging for livestock traders on their way to Smithfield and accommodating long-distance coaches. The galleried **Angel Inn** described here was pulled down in 1819 and completely rebuilt, but the Angel survived as a hotel into the C20; today the building houses a bank (see *SL* 47, pp. 441-47, for a thorough account). The **Peacock**, mentioned in *Nicholas Nickleby*, dates from about 1700; it was rebuilt in 1857 and again in 1931, but closed in 1962. A portion of the original building still survives at no. 13 Islington High Street, and a plaque on the adjoining no. 11 commemorates the inn, which at one time occupied those two buildings and no. 9 to the south.

[2] The **Belvidere Tavern**, on the northwest corner of Penton Street and Pentonville Road, was originally Penny's Folly, developed by John Pennie in 1768 and renamed *c.* 1774 (*SL* 47, pp. 351-52). Like Copenhagen House it had large tea gardens with a bowling green, as well as a rackets court and a 'bun house'. The tavern was rebuilt as a public house in 1876 and remained in business at no. 96 Pentonville Road until the 1990s, when it became a tapas bar; relaunched as the Clockwork bar and music venue in 2004, it is now the Lexington.

grounds neatly laid out, and a larder amply stocked in the summer season. Several anniversary dinners are had here, the wines being such as suit the palates and heads of the most considerate persons.[1]

Without returning hence into the Lower Road, you may easily get into the Upper by a path which terminates very near the entrance to Highbury Place. About half a mile distant from the terrace is an establishment similar to Canonbury House, called Highbury Barn. It is much frequented on account of its pleasure grounds or gymnasia, and the good fare served up to the guests who take exercise in them.[2]

From Highbury there is a most pleasant walk across the fields, occasionally along the pleasant banks of the New River, to Hornsey-wood House, a favourite rendezvous for rusticators.[3] The provisions and liquors here served are of the best, and the walks around the spot are as pleasant as any that can be found within the same distance from London in any direction. – About half way between Highbury Barn and this place, stands the Sluice-house, so named from a sluice or water- [255] gate on the New River. This house is

[1] In 1815 **Canonbury House** denoted both the Tudor house itself and the tavern built about 1730 on the eastern side of the mansion. By the early C19 the grounds included a shrubbery and bowling green, with facilities for Dutch pins, trap-ball, fishing, and cricket. The tavern was demolished in 1846 and rebuilt, but today's Canonbury Tavern at no. 21 Canonbury Place still boasts one of London's largest beer gardens.

[2] **Highbury Barn**, shown on Rocque's 1746 map, began life in the early C18 as a cake and ale house (Oliver Goldsmith and his friends were customers), and gradually grew into a tavern with gardens; it was sometimes known as Willoughby's Tea Gardens, after the proprietor who added a bowling green and trap-ball ground in the late C18. Willoughby also expanded the dining rooms, and by the mid-C19 Highbury Barn was a popular venue for large trade and society dinners. In 1869 it was described as 'still a great place of public entertainment, combining an hotel, public gardens, and a regularly licensed theatre, as well as a dancing saloon' (Howitt, p. 475). Complaints by neighbours led to the loss of the dancing license in 1870, and the Barn was closed the following year. Today the late-Victorian Highbury Barn Tavern perpetuates the name only a few hundred yards from the site of the vanished tea gardens (no. 26 Highbury Park).

[3] The **Hornsey Wood House** visited here was a new tavern built around 1800 on the site of an older establishment, known at least from the mid-C18; in 1826 William Hone described it as a 'good, "plain, brown brick," respectable, modern, London looking building' (*The Every-Day Book*, i:759, with illustration). A small artificial lake constructed for angling and boating survives today in Finsbury Park, which opened on the site of the old gardens in 1869.

noted for its good ale and excellent buns. You may also be well supplied here with a hasty dinner in the summer season.[1]

Recurring to our former position, the Angel at Islington, and proceeding thence toward the Green, we find, about half way, the Star and Garter, a superior public house, kept by Mr. Hall, who has an ordinary every day at four o'clock, for the convenience of several respectable persons, who choose to take a walk thither for the improvement of their appetite.[2]

Almost facing it is the Gun, kept by Mr. J. Marler, who dresses dinners to order, and has an ordinary on Sundays, at two o'clock.[3] There are several other houses in Islington which have similar announcements.

Passing on toward the church, we find on the left, the Pied Bull Inn, chiefly frequented by graziers and farmers, for whose convenience, or rather for that of their beasts, there are behind the house a number of pens, to serve as resting places on the way to Smithfield.[4]

[1] The **Sluice House** tavern and tea gardens, located on the New River near an actual sluice house, or water gate, was also known as the **Eel Pie House**: see the *Morning Chronicle* of 14 August 1809, advertising the sale of the 'Eel Pie-house or Sluice-house', an 'old established Tea-house and gardens' near Hornsey Wood. Among the features listed were 'two large tea rooms, 33 feet long, recently built at a considerable expence', a 'capital eel well', two tea gardens, and a ground for Dutch pins. According to *VCH Middlesex*, vi:158, by 1847 the establishment was known as the Highbury Sluice-House Tavern, surviving into the 1870s. Its late Victorian successor was the Sluice House Tavern at no. 175 Blackstock Road, now the Arsenal Tavern.

[2] The **Star and Garter** is known from 1748 (see *VCH Middlesex*, viii:46), and a later public house at no. 44 Upper Street continued under that name until the mid-1970s. Next known as the Champion – it was kept for a time by the former light heavyweight Len Harvey – it had become the Passage by 1985 and today, recently enlarged and refurbished, is the Steam Passage.

[3] The late C18 **Gun** became the Duke of Sussex in 1834; today it is Frederick's restaurant, no. 106 Islington High Street (Manley 1990, p. 77).

[4] The **Pied Bull** has also lived through several name changes, having become the Sir Walter Raleigh in 1988, next the Finnock and Firkin, and finally simply the Bull (still in business at no. 100 Upper Street, corner of Theberton Street). The C17 inn described here, pulled down in 1826-27 and replaced by the present building, has often been identified as either the home, temporary residence, or property of Sir Walter Ralegh, but this tradition seems to go back only to the mid-C18, and is usually dismissed by modern historians. Among those who did believe the story were William Hone and George Cruikshank, who paid a last visit to the 'dreary' and 'neglected' Pied Bull on 21 May 1825, toasting Sir Walter and smoking a pipe

Facing the church is the King's Head Tavern, kept by Mr. Smith. Here is an excellent larder in front, with an announcement that dinners are drest for large and small [256] parties on the shortest notice. This house is in every point of view a respectable one.[1]

Adjoining is an excellent pastry shop kept by Mr. Bracebridge, who prepares soups of various kinds, savoury patties and confectionery in all its branches.

Having left Islington, we pass by Highbury, and soon enter Holloway, where several public houses capable of regaling us with a glass of ale and a biscuit, present themselves. They who wish for a higher relish may try at the Half Moon, the Crown, or Mother Black Cap's.[2] At Lower Holloway, you may turn to the right into Duval's Lane, vulgarly called Devil's Lane, which leads to Hornsey, and you will, a short way up it, find a house capable of supplying

'in the same room that the man who first introduced tobacco smoked in himself' (F. W. Hackwood, *William Hone: His Life and Times* (1912), pp. 249-51).

[1] There was a **King's Head** in Islington as early as 1594 (*VCH Middlesex*, viii:45), possibly rebuilt in the C17, as Thomas Cromwell described it in 1835 as 'probably as old as the reign of James I. or Charles I.' (p. 254). The house that Samuel Pepys recalled visiting for cakes and ale in his youth (*Diary*, 27 March and 25 April 1664) was taken down and replaced by a modern tavern about 1864. Remodelled in the 1890s, the King's Head is still in business at no. 115 Upper Street, and since 1970 has also been home to a small theatre.

[2] From Upper Street our guide turned northwest into Holloway Road. The **Half Moon**, opposite the entrance to Tollington Way, was noted for its cheesecakes in the early C18; struck by lightning in 1846 and rebuilt in the same location, it is today known as The Quays (no. 471 Holloway Road). Close to the Half Moon was the **Crown**, built in the early C17 and traditionally once the residence of Oliver Cromwell. Writing in 1869, William Howitt remarked that the Crown had 'long disappeared' (*The Northern Heights of London*, p. 466); a more recent Crown continues in business at no. 622 Holloway Road. The *Almanack*'s Mother Black Cap's is almost certainly **Mother Red Cap's**, a bit farther north along Holloway Road and shown on Cruchley's 1824 map. The inn was mentioned in *Barnabae Itinerarium* (1638) by Richard Brathwait, who described encountering a 'troupe of Trulls', or prostitutes, there, and Samuel Pepys referred to it in his diary entry for 24 September 1661: 'drinking at Halloway at the sign of a woman with Cakes in one hand and a pot of ale in the other'. According to Thomas Cromwell the Mother Red Cap was rebuilt about 1820 (p. 329); the Victorian public house at no. 665 Holloway Road, just south of Archway underground station, retains the old name.

your alimentary wants.[1] At Upper Holloway commences the road leading to the celebrated Highgate archway.

Half way up the hill, from Holloway to Highgate, at the corner of the road leading to Crouch End, will be found a superior public house, which commands an extensive view over London, into Surrey and Kent, as well as over part of Middlesex and Essex. We believe it is called the Prospect House. The prospect within, over the bar and larder is too good to be neglected.[2]

When you have gained the summit of High- [257] gate a complete galaxy of inns and taverns invites the eye. We distinguish among them as stars of superior order, first the Gate House, facing the chapel, attached to which house are the Highgate Assembly Rooms.[3] Here, when any military are quartered or on their march through Highgate, the head-quarters of the officers are established; a pretty sure proof of the goodness of the cheer. – To the right, a little farther on, is the Castle Inn, where many anniversary parties of pleasure dine and entertain themselves.[4] It is worth while to take a summer-afternoon's walk to this house, for the sake of enjoying the diversion of its neat, well ordered bowling-green. This moreover is the evening club-house for the Highgate politicians. Those persons who ride or drive hither will find good stabling for their horses.

[1] The house in 'Duval's Lane' was known under the name Lower Place in the mid-C16 and as the **Devil's House** by 1586 (see *VCH Middlesex*, viii:63). It is shown on Cary's 1786 *Survey* at the southeast corner of Devil's Lane (later Tollington Lane and today Hornsey Road) and Hearne Lane (now Seven Sisters Road), and seems to have become a place of entertainment by the early C18. A wooden structure with a moat – partly filled in around 1811 – the house was still in existence in the 1840s, although described by Cromwell in 1835 as 'of late years […] somewhat modernized' (pp. 341-42); it was gone when mentioned by Thornbury in 1874 (*ONL*, ii:275). Both the house and the lane were variously known as Devil's and Duval's, the latter probably a corruption referring to the highwayman Claude Duval (1643-70), who operated in the area of Holloway and Highgate.

[2] The 'superior public house' believed by the *Almanack* to be called **Prospect House** was almost certainly the **Archway Tavern**, located at the junction of Archway Road (built in 1813 and leading to Crouch End) and Holloway Road, which here becomes Highgate Hill. The present Archway Tavern, built in the late 1880s, is the third on the site.

[3] There has been an inn on the site of the **Gate House** since the late C17; the present mock-Tudor building (no. 1 North Road) dates from 1905, but the old inn can be seen in a photograph of 1885 (Richardson 1989, p. 152).

[4] The **Castle**, at the southwest corner of Castle Yard and North Road, was licensed by 1719 and fifty years later added a bowling green; it closed around 1872 and was demolished in 1928 (Richardson 1989, p. 75).

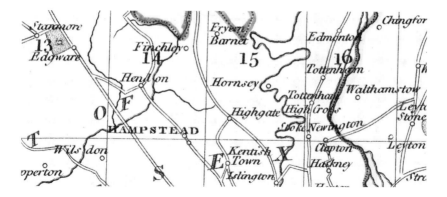

The next house for business is the Red Lion, at which most of the mails and long stages used to stop. On the same side, a little farther on is the Wrestlers public house, where passengers, by the return chaises, generally take refreshment.[1] At the above, and at almost all other public houses in Highgate, is kept a huge pair of horns attached to a long staff, being the ensign or symbol on which the famous oath is administered to those who choose to be sworn at Highgate. [258] Persons of the most tender consciences may, without offence, take this oath, because the wisdom of its framers hath provided so many saving clauses that a case of perjury is hardly to be made out from it. You swear never to eat boiled meat if you can get roast, unless you like boiled meat better; never to eat brown bread when you can get white, unless you like brown bread better; never to drink small beer when you can get strong, unless you like small beer better; and never to kiss the maid when you can kiss the mistress, unless you like the maid better. After swearing all this and much more, you kiss the horns – pay the fees, generally half a crown or more, and call for a gallon of ale.

Descending the northern side of Highgate Hill, and proceeding about a mile and a half you come to Finchley Common, on the verge of which, by the road side, is the Bald-faced Stag, a good house with a decent larder and

[1]   The **Red Lion**, a major coach stop from the mid-C17, is indicated on Bacon's 1888 map (no. 90 North Road) but closed twelve years later. When the **Wrestlers** (no. 98 North Road) was rebuilt in 1922, it was described as more than 300 years old, but no record of it survives prior to 1721 (Richardson 1989, p. 153). The tradition of swearing a whimsical oath before a pair of horns can be traced back to the late C17, and is occasionally still revived in Highgate pubs, including the Wrestlers.

pretty good cooking.¹ The left hand road, from the Bald-faced Stag, leads to Finchley, that right onward to Whetstone and Barnet; and those to the right to Southgate, Colney Hatch, and Friar's Barnet, all beyond our present limits.

Returning to the Gate House at Highgate, we direct you to that delightful place, Southwood Lane, just behind the chapel, com- [259] manding one of the finest views in Middlesex. Passing down it, you come to Muswell Hill and Hornsey, one of the pleasantest villages in the vicinity of London, not only on account of its rural site and charming prospects, but of its numerous neat houses of refreshment, where the best meat in season and some of the delicacies of the season may be had at a reasonable expense.

The road turning to the west from the Gate House, leads to Hampstead, passing by the highly cultivated estate of Fitzroy Farm, the property and residence of the Earl of Southampton; and the villa and extensive pleasure grounds called Caen Wood, the residence of the Earl of Mansfield. A little farther stands the noted tavern called the Spaniards, commanding a noble view without, and affording excellent entertainment within.²

We shall now pass over the ridge of the hill toward Hampstead, and on Hampstead Heath shall halt at the Castle Inn and Tavern,³ much frequented

¹ Continuing northwest from Highgate on the route now designated North Road and North Hill, the traveller would have reached the Great North Road, which led on to Whetstone and Barnet; to the northwest, along what is now East End Road, was Finchley, and slightly to the east were other roads leading north to Colney Hatch, Friern Barnet, and Southgate. The **Bald Faced Stag** dates from the mid-C18 and was called the Jolly Blacksmiths until about 1780; it was rebuilt around 1886 and is still in business at the junction of East End Road and the High Road to Barnet (no. 69 High Road, East Finchley).

² Both the Spaniards and the Castle on Hampstead Heath were popular from the mid-C18. The **Spaniards Inn** is frequently described as dating from 1585 and often said to have once been the residence of Count Gondomar, Spanish Ambassador to James I. The latter story is generally discounted by serious writers, and *BoE North*, p. 235, describes the building succinctly as 'a whitewashed C18 pub'. Alan Farmer (1984, p. 158), noting that licensing records show a Francis Porero as landlord in 1721, has suggested that Porero was in fact the 'eponymous Spaniard'.

³ Even before 1815 the Castle was sometimes called **Jack Straw's Castle**, although there is no historical evidence for a connection between the inn and the leader of the Peasants' Revolt. Famed for its panoramic views, in the later C19 the Castle counted among its guests Charles Dickens, Karl Marx, and Friedrich Engels. The inn known to them was extensively damaged by bombing during the Second World War, and in 1963-64 was rebuilt in what *BoE* terms 'Georgian Gothick [...] but on a scale that is unmistakably C20' (*North*, p. 234). In 2003 the building was converted to flats.

during the summer season on account of its excellent larder and cellar, as well as of its views, which in every direction are delightful. A telescope is kept at the house for the use of the guests; by its aid you may, in clear serene weather, with a right light, see Gravesend, and the vessels in the river down even to the Nore. If you descend [260] the hill by the Castle you will infallibly come to North End; there at the Hare and Hounds you may rely on having a good dinner if you order one. Continue along the same road, and you will come to Hendon and Mill Hill. Half way to Hendon, at Golden Green, is a very pleasant road-side-house called the Cock and Hoop.[1]

Returning to Hampstead Heath, and proceeding from the Castle Inn you soon come to the town, where, as at Highgate, you have great choice of houses of entertain you. The Long Room is said to take the lead, being qualified, as its name imports, to accommodate large as well as small parties. The Flask, down Flask Lane, possesses similar qualifications. The Yorkshire Grey is frequented on Sundays by a very joyous company.[2] Such is the intercourse between this village and London, that stages go every half hour.

If from Hampstead you take either the road that leads from the church, or a pleasant foot-path in the same direction, you will come to Child's Hill and West End; the latter place is celebrated for its annual fair. Here is a house at which you may dine very comfortably;[3] after that you may hold

[1] The **Hare and Hounds**, in North End Avenue just off Sandy Heath, is mentioned as early as 1730 (Wade 2000, p. 83). The public house was twice bombed in 1940 and operated for a time from caravans; rebuilt in 1968, it was closed in 2002 and demolished. I have been unable to identify the 'road-side-house' at Golders Green described here, and suspect that Rylance's memory of the name as the **Cock and Hoop** results from confusion with the establishment at West End described below.

[2] The *Almanack*'s reference to the **Long Room** at Hampstead is curious, for this had been converted to private residences by about 1803; an earlier assembly room of the same name had become a chapel by 1725, and neither building survives today (*VCH Middlesex*, ix:19). By the early c18 water from the Hampstead wells was being taken to the **Flask** (then called the Thatched House), where it was bottled and sold on the spot or carted into London (Osborn 1991, p. 57). The Flask, at no. 14 Flask Walk, was rebuilt in 1873-74, and, refurbished in 2007, continues in business. The **Yorkshire Grey** was just west of Hampstead High Street, to the north of Church Row: today Yorkshire Grey Place commemorates the old coaching inn, licensed as early as 1723 and demolished in the 1880s (Wade 2000, p. 67).

[3] At West End (now West Hampstead) the 'comfortable' house described was without doubt the **Cock and Hoop**, the only tavern in the tiny village. Established by 1720, it closed in 1896 and was demolished four years later; the site, near the intersection of Mill Lane and West End Lane, is now covered by a mansion block (see Redley 1981, with photograph).

your course for Kilburn Wells, and take a pot of hot coffee or tea; a bottle of ale; or any other evening beverage that you may happen to [261] prefer at the moment.[1] Or if you feel disposed you may dine again, and depend upon being well served. Many cockneys undertake an expedition to this place on summer Sundays, for no other purpose, except the walk hither and home again. Adjoining the gardens is a play ground for cricket and trap-ball; the amateurs of those sports who visit Kilburn Wells for an afternoon's diversion, commonly return by Maida Hill, to Oxford Street, where we shall leave them, and returning to Hampstead, find our way home by Kentish Town and Camden Town.

Coming down the hill from Hampstead, we find on the left, at the corner of Pond Street, the George public-house, to which is attached a pleasant garden furnished with rural seats and shady arbours, in which are served tea, coffee, ales, and cakes.[2] We then proceed to Haverstock Hill, where we notice a small white cottage, said to have once belonged to Sir Richard Steele, in which retreat Addison is said to have written some of the rural spectators. At the sign of the Load of Hay,[3] here, you may take a draught of Addison's favourite beverage (when with Sir Roger) bottled ale, to help you down the hill, at the bottom of which, on the right, is a lane that leads to Chalk Farm, well

[1] The pleasure gardens at **Kilburn Wells** were located on the site of an abandoned Benedictine priory, and were advertised to Londoners in 1773 as 'at an easy Distance, being but a Morning's Walk from the Centre of the Metropolis, two miles from Oxford-street; the footway from Mary-bone across the Fields still nearer' (*Public Advertiser*, 3 July). The wells themselves were in the rear of the **Bell Inn**, located on the east side of the old Roman road, just south of Belsize Road; the inn was pulled down around 1863 and the present Old Bell public house erected on the same spot (no. 38 Kilburn High Road).
[2] The **George** at Hampstead was licensed as early as 1715 (Richardson 1985, p. 154); it was extensively repaired in 1889 and described by Wagner in 1925 as 'still preserv[ing] much of its antiquated character', though 'wholly lacking the tea gardens formerly associated with it' (p. 176). The public house, called 'recently rebuilt' by J. H. Preston in 1948 (p. 66), is still in business at no. 250 Haverstock Hill.
[3] The **Load of Hay** was licensed as early as 1721 (Richardson 1985, p. 154); several writers describe it as having been a quaint timbered inn until it was rebuilt in an Italianate style in 1863, by which time it had lost most of its surrounding gardens. From 1965 to 1974 the pub was called the Noble Art, a reference to the boxing gymnasium behind the building. Closed in 2000, the premises re-opened in 2002 as a gastropub known simply as The Hill (no. 94 Haverstock Hill).

frequented by reason of its proximity to Primrose Hill.[1] [262] Chalk Farm is capacious enough to entertain parties however numerous; it has a large room for public tea drinking, an oven for baking hot rolls, and a stock of milch cows for the supply of milk for syllabubs. During one period of the late war, Chalk Farm was the field for sham-fights of riflemen, sharpshooters, and volunteers. It has also been the theatre of real fights between duellists.

You have a pleasant walk over the fields, or along the road from Chalk Farm to Camden Town, where you may bait either at Mother Red Cap's or at the Britannia.[2]

We now resume our point of departure at Highgate, and descend to Kentish Town, not by the high road, but by a beautiful shaded foot-path along the side of Holly Terrace. From this path the view of London is truly panoramic.[3] – Arriving in Kentish Town, we find on the right, the Bull and Gate, which we mention by way of eminence, as being the rendezvous of politicians, who hold

[1] Chalk Farm, on the way to Primrose Hill, takes its name from the manor of Chalcot, and the **Chalk Farm Tavern** is often identified with the White House at Lower Chalcot to which Sir Edmund Godfrey's body was carried after his murder in 1678. By the 1790s the tavern was operating under its modern name, and Anthony Cooper notes an advertisement of 1793-94 that mentions 'real' wines, 'liquors of a superior kind', and 'tea and hot rolls as usual' (Cooper 1978, p. 2). Chalk Farm was indeed a popular site for duels, and a portion of the gardens served as a military practice ground during the Napoleonic Wars. The old tavern was extended several times before being demolished and rebuilt in 1853-54; it survived as a public house – briefly known as Pub Lotus in the early 1970s – until the 1990s, when it was replaced by a Greek restaurant (no. 89 Regent's Park Road).

[2] **Mother Red Cap's** – now in central Camden Town but once only a stopping point on the north-south road – is shown on Rocque's 1746 ten-mile map and Cary's 1786 *Survey;* the Bacon map of 1888 shows both the Mother Red Cap, on the east side of what is now Camden High Street, and the **Britannia Tavern** opposite it (southwest corner of Camden High Street and Parkway). The Mother Red Cap, which once had extensive tea gardens, was rebuilt in 1875, and is now called the World's End, at no. 174 High Street (*BoE North*, p. 384). Its former neighbour, known from at least 1777, was succeeded by the Britannia Hotel, which closed in 1962; the name survives in Britannia Junction, the complicated intersection of Camden High Street, Parkway, Camden Road, and Kentish Town Road (Denford and Woodford 2003, p. 19).

[3] Returning to Highgate, this time our guide goes south to Kentish Town, taking a footpath leading past Holly Lodge, a country villa built in 1798. The **Bull and Gate** in Kentish Town – the name is perhaps a corruption of 'Boulogne Gate' – is known from the C18; rebuilt in 1871 (*BoE North*, pp. 394-95), it is today a popular music venue at no. 389 Kentish Town Road.

their councils under the presidency of Mr. Finch, the worthy and opulent proprietor of the ham and beef shop in St. Martin's Court, of whose place we have elsewhere spoken. The rumours of the day are usually communicated by a German furrier who arrives at his country house from his shop in town, every day to dinner; and these rumours are confirmed or [263] contradicted by a stock-broker, who arrives an hour or two later, with a Courier in his pocket, from the Royal Exchange.

Lower down, on the other side of the way, is the Assembly House, which, as may be supposed, is capable of accommodating a great number of guests and of regaling them with whatever good things the town affords. Lower down is the Castle, a good old house with a tea-room and gardens.[1] This tea-room, as well as the Assembly Room, is converted occasionally into a theatre for an itinerant company of comedians who annually visit this place for a few weeks.

A walk of five minutes from the Castle will bring us to Camden Town, where, at either the Bedford or the Southampton Arms, there are good accommodations and pleasant tea-gardens.[2] At the boundary of the Regent's Park, there has lately been erected a new Jews Harp Tavern, which is rapidly improving, and is much frequented by promenaders in this quarter.[3] In terminating our tour at Tottenham Court Road, we may just take a parting

[1] Just to the south of the Bull and Gate was the **Assembly House**, a large early C18 inn with gardens and provision for trap-ball, skittles, etc. (Wroth 1896, pp. 129-30); this was pulled down in 1853, but in 1898 a new Assembly House tavern opened on part of the site (now nos. 292-94 Kentish Town Road, east side). The old **Castle Tavern**, taken down in 1849 (Timbs, *Clubs*, p. 468), was a large inn with tea gardens standing back from the Kentish Town Road on the west side; it has left its name on nearby Castle Road and Castle Place.

[2] The **Bedford Arms** can be seen on the 1827 Greenwood map at the point where Grove Street becomes Arlington Road; when the latter street absorbed the former the address of the public house, once no. 1 Grove Street, became no. 80 Arlington Road. The extensive tea gardens were a popular site for balloon ascents, and in 1861 the Bedford's 'Long Room' was transformed into the Bedford Music Hall (knocked down in 1898, reopened in 1899, demolished in 1969; see Kamlish 1995). A Bedford Arms public house survived in Arlington Road until about 1970. The **Southampton Arms**, somewhat to the southeast, is shown on the 1746 ten-mile Rocque map as the Crown (see Denford and Woodford 2003, p. 16). It was renamed in the 1780s, rebuilt in the mid-C19, and is now called the Crescent (no. 1 Camden High Street, at the corner of Mornington Crescent).

[3] The new **Jew's Harp Tavern** was successor to an earlier establishment of the same name, shown on Rocque's 1745 map and the first edition of the Horwood map in a position north of the top of what is today Portland Place. In about 1812 the formation of Regent's Park forced a move to a new location just south of the Regent's

glass of wine and biscuit, at either the Adam and Eve or the King's Head, both which houses have been immortalized by Hogarth, who introduced portraits of them into his inimitable picture of the march of the Guards to Finchley.[1]

[264] Had we returned by way of Pancras, we should have given the same preference to Mr. George Skillicorn, of the Adam and Eve, adjoining the church of St. Pancras, who brews excellent ale, and is one of the best caterers for the larder in or near town.[2]

Park Barracks, at no. 1 Edward (now Redhill) Street, as shown on the 1827 Greenwood map. The Jews's Harp continued at this address into the C20.

[1] Both the Adam and Eve and the King's Head are pictured in William Hogarth's 'March of the Guards to Finchley' (1750), although the artist has transformed the latter into a brothel, with the well-known bawd 'Mother Douglas' and her prostitutes filling the windows (George 1967, p. 41). The **Adam and Eve**, on the western corner of what is now Hampstead Road and Euston Road, is known as early as 1718, and was probably older (Wroth 1896, pp. 77-80). In the early C19 at least some of the gardens, which had contained grounds for skittles and Dutch pins, were dug up, and in 1831 William Hone described it as 'now denominated a coffee-house' (*Year Book of Daily Recreation*, col. 47). A modern Adam and Eve public house was built on the site in 1869 (no. 1 Hampstead Road) and demolished when the area was redeveloped in the 1960s (Swinley 1975, p. 4). The **King's Head** – later the Old King's Head – was opposite the Adam and Eve to the east (no. 282 Euston Road), but the sites of both public houses are now covered by late C20 buildings.

[2] The *Almanack*'s second **Adam and Eve**, adjoining St Pancras Old Church, is shown on the 1827 Greenwood map. According to Wroth the tea gardens were in existence as early as 1730, and Clinch (p. 157) prints the text of a 1786 advertisement extolling the grounds and the larder. In 1805 the original Adam and Eve was demolished during the construction of the St Giles in the Fields burial ground adjoining Old St Pancras churchyard; its replacement, somewhat to the south, gradually declined into an ordinary public house, and had been taken down by the time Clinch wrote in 1890, shortly before the opening of the St Pancras Gardens that now cover the site.

REVIEW OF ARTISTS WHO ADMINISTER
TO THE WANTS AND CONVENIENCES
OF THE TABLE.

The proverb most frequently repeated by John Bull is, that "God sends meat; but the Devil sends cooks." Whether John means any slur upon the French or the German *cuisine*, in thus likening them by implication to the *bureau des affaires étrangères* of his infernal majesty, is best known to John's self; but the sarcasm seems to point that way. There is something uncharitable and indeed unjust in the reflection, for the whole system of English cookery is much inferior in economy, and variety of resources to either the French or the German. As it is now the rage with the continental nations to new-model their constitutions à l'Anglaise, it would be [265] only polite in us to return the compliment by copying whatever is exemplary in their culinary institutions; if John Bull has any regard to his constitution, he must, physically speaking, repeal some of the statutes of Elizabeth Raffald,[1] and commence a fundamental reform in the lower house, commonly called the kitchen.

It is a matter of serious surprise to all foreigners who visit this country, that blest as we are with the primest beef, the finest flavoured mutton, the richest variety of fish, the most luxuriant crop of pulse, sallads, and table vegetables in the world, we should be comparatively novices in cookery. Let us take an instance from among the lower classes of society, to demonstrate the deplorable want of economy that exists in families where economy ought most strictly to be practised. An artisan sends his wife to Newport market to lay in a dinner for the family. She purchases a leg of mutton; sends it to the baker's for the sake of saving time, trouble, and fire: the baker puts it in his oven to be baked, or in other words, to have its most nutritious juices evaporated and dried up; out of mere politeness and regard for the health of his customers, he will perhaps pour off part of the fat before he sends the joint home. It serves to dine a family of hungry labourers [266] and children; and stands a very poor chance of appearing next day, the raw-boned spectre of its former self. A Frenchman with the same *materiel*, and the proper allowance of vegetables,

---

[1] Elizabeth **Raffald** (1733-81), confectioner and inn-keeper of Manchester, was the author of *The Experienced English Housekeeper, for the Use and Ease of Ladies, Housekeepers, Cooks, &c.*, first published in 1769 and still popular in the early C19.

would produce a dinner sufficient for double the number of persons; he would extract from the bones, the cartilage, and the superabundant fat, a stock of nutriment wherewith to conjure up a multitudinous variety of delicious repasts.

We need not ascend higher in the scale of society for the purpose of finding examples to strengthen our argument. The quantity of kitchen-stuff obtained by the chandlers, from great families, in the course of a season, speaks volumes. Our present business is to prove that we have the means of effecting a culinary revolution in our own power; and if we neglect to avail ourselves of them, we deserve to suffer the penalty of that neglect more than we do.[1]

To begin fundamentally with the great business of culinary reform, the kitchen fireplace must be re-organized. Here a host of patents, for improved cooking apparatus, presses upon us, each patent having some plea for priority of recommendation. We have examined some specimens, and shall endeavour to do impartial justice to their merits.

[267]

Coombs's Patent Kitchen Range.

At No. 22 Holborn, there is an improved cooking apparatus in actual use. The patentee, Mr. Coombe, announces on his card that it has the united advantages of economy, cleanliness, and simplicity; and a minute examination of it will satisfy any person that these pretensions are well founded. This kitchen range is so constructed as by means of one small fire to roast, boil, bake, stew, and fry at the same time. We saw, (what may be seen here every day from eleven until four o'clock), an ample dinner undergoing the above processes. There was a fine piece of beef roasting, a pudding in the oven, a kettle of fish boiling, and the usual accompaniments of vegetables and melted butter. There was a copper containing several gallons of boiling-water with a cock in front of the range for drawing it off when wanted, and two chambers for warming plates. The grate is so contrived that the fire may be increased or diminished, raised, or lowered at pleasure; and meat may be roasted by it either on a horizontal or a vertical spit. By sliding back the plate of iron over the grate you have a fine hot space for boiling or frying, without the possibility of annoyance from [268] smoke or ashes, since the stream of air from the fire passes under the oven and boiler, and the ashes subside of themselves

---

[1] Further details of some of the shopkeepers and suppliers not discussed in individual notes may be found in the index entries.

to a box so contrived as to separate and preserve the cinders without permitting a particle to escape. The surface of the range appears a perfect floor of iron, and the range of clean pans and other vessels upon it appears the neater, by being matched with an entire coating of white porcelain, with which the sides and back of the chimney are lined. Another advantage, pointed out by the patentee, is the evident saving in the saucepans, stewpans, and other vessels, which, never coming in contact with the fire, are exempt from the wear and tear of burning and scouring. This saving, and that in the important article of fuel, would, in a twelvemonth, compensate the expense of substituting this range for any common fireplace.[1]

Deakin's Philosophical Kitchen Range.

We also went to Mr. Deakin's, 47, Ludgate Hill, for the purpose of inspecting his Philosophical Kitchen Range, which also combines economy with simplicity.[2] It contains an improved oven for bread or pies; a capacious boiler, a space for the several stewpans and saucepans, with the addition of a moveable [269] steaming apparatus, by which meat, fish, poultry, vegetables, and other viands, are cooked and kept warm at any distance from the fire. This range, as well as the last-mentioned, constitutes a certain cure for any smoky chimney to which it may be affixed. The boiler may be applied to a chemical apparatus for distilling simple waters for domestic use. Mr. Deakin furnishes his visitants with cards of prices, which, considering the effects produced, and the savings effected by his ranges, appear very reasonable.

The limits of this work do not allow us to enumerate all the inventions and improvements in culinary apparatus which are constantly advertised as well worth the attention of epicures and economists; but we cannot omit mentioning one which bids fair to become the *ne plus ultrà* of cheap and expeditious cooking. At the corner of Catherine Street, in the Strand, is manufactured

[1] Benjamin Merriman **Coombs**, ironmonger, patented his 'improved apparatus for the cooking or dressing of victuals, and possessing other advantages in lessening the consumption of fuel' in March 1813. By early 1817, when he advertised his patented 'winding front cooking apparatus' in the *Morning Post* (15 March), he had moved to no. 66 Holborn.

[2] Thomas **Deakin** patented his kitchen range – 'philosophical' in the sense of scientific or experimental – in 1811; an advertisement in *The Times* of 13 September 1815 recommends it to 'the Nobility, Gentry, and Public'. Two years later, now operating as Deakin and Duncan, he announced prices ranging from eleven to twenty guineas (*The Times*, 27 January 1817).

and sold a travelling kitchen for dressing beef-steaks, mutton-chops, and veal-cutlets, without any other fuel than a sheet of brown paper cut into shreds and tied up as a faggot. The patentee recommends it as very convenient in warm weather for gentlemen in chambers; for sportsmen and for parties on the water. We believe it is called the conjuror, having inherited, not usurped, that title from the tea-kettle con- [270] structed on a similar principle, and ushered into notice a few years ago.[1]

Armstrong and Folkard.

Messrs. Armstrong and Folkard of No. 76, Great Queen Street, Lincoln's Inn Fields, are manufacturers of the Rumford stoves, ovens, roasters, boilers, and steam kitchens;[2] and likewise of an improved kitchen apparatus, which will roast, boil, bake, and steam simultaneously by one small fire. These kitchens are on the most economical plan. They also manufacture and furnish complete sets of culinary apparatus at very reasonable rates. The metal is either tin, Britannia, wrought-iron, or copper. They are all constructed on the most improved economical principle.

The empyreal air stoves for warming large rooms, invented by these gentlemen, ought to excite the gratitude of every person who duly appreciates the blessings of a good and genial digestion, and dreads the evils of obstructed perspiration. These empyreal stoves ensure the one and obviate the other. Their sanative warm baths, steam-baths, and shower baths, are beyond all praise. We hesitate not to aver, that a philosopher might select, in a few minutes, from the ample stores of this [271] repository, materials for the construction of a complete temple of health.[3]

---

[1] For the **travelling kitchen** or **conjuror** exhibited at the corner of Catherine Street and the Strand, see Thomas Webster, *An Encyclopædia of Domestic Economy* (1844), p. 838, where this portable apparatus, also called a camp kettle, is described and illustrated.

[2] The American-born Sir Benjamin Thompson, Count Rumford (1753-1814) is known principally for his **Rumford stove**, an improved chimney that minimized the escape of heat upward; he also experimented with cooking ranges, most of which proved impractical for common domestic use.

[3] The **empyreal air stove** was patented in 1786 for the purpose of 'purifying the air of churches, theatres, gaols, sick and other rooms, and enclosed buildings' (*Dictionary of Traded Goods*); Armstrong and Folkard's 'sarcophagus warm and cold sanative baths' were advertised as suitable for hospitals, hotels, dressing rooms, 'or any other situation' (*Morning Post*, 7 August 1811).

There has been recently invented an improved broiler for steaks and chops, somewhat resembling a frying-pan. The bottom is embossed, or convexed, so as to permit the fat as it melts to flow off in all directions into a groove, which forms the circumference of the vessel. Thus the fat and gravy are saved; the steak or chop is kept free from grease or flare over any kind of fire, and comes clean and sweet to table.

We cannot dismiss this part of the subject without strongly recommending the strictest attention to be paid to the state of the vessels in which viands are cooked. These, particularly if made of brass or copper, should be constantly kept well tinned. The fatal accident at Salt Hill some years ago is still fresh in the memory of the public. Five or more persons were poisoned there by eating a made dish which had been cooked in a copper stew-pan.[1] This melancholy catastrophe gave a stimulus to the ingenuity of many artists; among whom Mr. Bent, of St. Martin's Lane, distinguished himself by inventing a method of lining copper stew-pans with an enamel similar to that on the dial plates of watches. This was found too expensive. Subsequently [272] a method has prevailed of lining these vessels with zinc, which is more durable than tin.

Let us now pass from the subject of culinary apparatus to that of condiments, and examine the vast variety of good things which generally form the stock of what is called an Italian warehouse.[2] The usual catalogue of them must naturally excite the appetite of all epicures, and render them anxious to know where they are to be had. We will endeavour to satisfy them.[3]

As soups generally take the lead at table, we take the liberty of recommending vermicelli; that from Genoa is esteemed the best. The Anderina and Cagliari pastes are excellent ingredients for thickening soups, and for converting veal-broth into delicious white soup.[4] The flavour will be much

[1] In 1773 several men fell ill and died after attending a public dinner at a tavern at Salt Hill, near Staines; the deaths were universally attributed to their having eaten a stew kept overnight in an inadequately lined copper vessel. The incident was frequently mentioned in early C19 cookery books, which often included warnings on the dangers of unlined copper utensils (see, for example, the appendix on 'culinary poisons' in John Farley's *London Art of Cookery*). The Mr Bent mentioned here was **William Bent**, ironmonger.
[2] An **Italian warehouse** typically sold not only foodstuffs and other goods imported from Italy, but also oil, tea and coffee, spices and prepared sauces, pulses, cheese, dried fruits and vegetables, etc.; see Allen 1992 and Riello 2006.
[3] For items not discussed in notes here, see the Glossary.
[4] Cagliari (Sardinia) is one of the places where pasta was supposedly invented. For Anderina, read Andria (in Apulia).

improved by the addition of lean ham fried. For the convenience of those whom travel or business compels to dine hastily, there are tablets of portable soup to be had of various flavours, which dissolve quickly in hot water, and form an extemporaneous dish of the most nutritious kind.

For fish, the next article in succession, a great variety of materials for sauce present themselves: some, in the state of extracts, as essence of lobster, of anchovies, zoobditty mutch, and sauce royale; Japan soy, lemon- [273] pickle, walnut and mushroom ketchups, oyster ketchup, and various articles prepared, so as to require only the admixture of melted butter.

For ragouts, hashes, and made dishes in general, as well as for fowls, a great choice of sauces presents itself. We may instance cavice sauce, Hanoverian sauce for game, Quin's sauce, camp sauce, Harvey's sauce, coratch, &c. Several curious flavoured vinegars may be said to belong to this department; such as red and white French vinegar, Tarragona, and garlic vinegar, cayenne and Chili vinegar. There are also kept essences of parsley, celery, mint, thyme, marjoram, sage, onion, &c., for flavouring soup. These essences are much preferable to the herbs themselves used after the common way in their dried state.

Of materials for puddings we notice millet, semolina, patna rice. Of cheeses we have the Parmesan, the gruyère, the chapsigre, and our famous English Stilton. That delicious and nutritive article, macaroni, forms, with grated cheese, a fine after-dish. Morells, foreign and English, truffles, dry, green, and preserved; mushrooms and champignons dried or in powder; dried artichoke-bottoms, curry-powder, beans and lentils for making haricots; and that highly prized luxury, the *sauer kraut* [274] must complete our summary of those infinite catalogues which issues from the warehouse of

Messrs. Bartovalle, and Co. No. 21, Haymarket.[1]

Mr. Price, successor to Badioli, No. 3, do.[2]

Messrs. Burgess and Son, near Exeter Change, Strand.[3]

Messrs. Pressy and Co., Oxford Street.

Messrs. Thomas and Son, No. 40. Conduit Street, Bond Street.

[1] **Bartho Valle**'s warehouse was established around 1750, and the family business survived into the C20 (Riello, pp. 206-11).

[2] **John Badioli**'s Italian warehouse was operating as early as 1775 (*Morning Post*, 19 June); **Edward Price** had taken over the business by the end of 1800 (*The Times*, 22 December)

[3] **John Burgess** was one of the first non-Italians to set up in the business; his shop at no. 107 Strand was established in 1760 and remained there until 1908 (Riello, pp. 215-17; for a photograph see Davies 2009, p. 154).

Messrs. Mackay and Co. 176, Piccadilly.

Mr. John Plaistowe, 133, Pall Mall.

Mr. R. Hodgson, 287, Strand.

Mr. Hickson, 170, near Surrey St. Strand.

Mr. Haggers, 88, Oxford Street.

Messrs. Frisby and Howis, 220, Piccadilly.

Mr. J. Kohler's, corner of Mary-le-Bone and Sherrard
    Streets, Golden Square.

Mr. Collier, St. James's Market.

Mr. S. Wix, Leadenhall Street.

Mr. Hornby's Italian Warehouse, 184, Strand.

Mr. Golding, late Holland's, 56, Strand.

Italian Warehouse, 451, Strand.

Messrs. Fortnum and Co. 183, Piccadilly.[1]

There is a warehouse for very superior and tasteful dishes and covers, plated, and with silver edges, at Mr. Wilson's, Swallow Street, corner of Vigo Lane. Such of our readers whose revenues enable them to have these articles in silver may find them manufactured, [275] in the most elegant style, at Messrs. Rundell and Bridges, Ludgate Hill; Garrard, Panton Street; Hamlet, Sidney's Alley, Leicester Square; Drury, 32, Strand; Gilbert, Cockspur Street; Barnard, corner of the Adelphi; Fearn, 73, Strand; Brown and Wilkinson, 38, Piccadilly; Sydenham, New Bond St.; and Wirgman, St. James's Street.

No table service can be complete without a good carver and keen cutting knives. Several eminent cutlers vend these essential weapons of the best steel, warranted town-made, and so tempered as long to retain a keen edge.

Messrs. Thornhill and Morley, Bond Street, near Giblet's;

Mr. Salter, 35, Strand;

Mr. Rees, 9, Red Lion Passage, Red Lion Square;

Mr. Rotton, corner of Sackville Street and Vigo Lane;

Mr. Priest, Cockspur Street;

Messrs. Smith and Simpson, 17, Strand;

Are among the most eminent in this class of tradesmen. We must also enumerate among them Mr. Clarke, of Exeter 'Change, who sells table and dessert knives, with improved carvers, elegantly finished and mounted in

[1] Of the eighteen warehouses listed only **Fortnum** survives today, having occupied premises more or less on the same site since 1756 (the present building dates from the 1920s). Founded in nearby Duke Street in 1707, the firm has been known as Fortnum and Mason since 1808.

ivory, silver, &c., warranted; and if not approved of exchanged. His prices are most reasonable.

[276] When a dinner has been well dressed, the cook's next step is to send it up in proper style and condition to table; for which purpose he ought to be provided with water-dishes in the winter season, and in all seasons with neat covers.

So great have been the improvements in our porcelain manufactories of late, that they now produce dishes with cavities for hot water under them, and with wells and channels for the gravy. These, though generally denominated venison dishes, are fit for the reception of any joint whatever; and an assortment of them for common use may be purchased at any of the respectable earthenware-shops Those for splendid entertainments are to be had in the greatest perfection at the Worcester and Colebrook Dale china warehouses. The perfection to which the manufacture of porcelain has been brought in our own manufactories, has almost entirely terminated the importation of that article from China. At Worcester, and at Colebrook Dale, the most elegant services are made in every possible variety of fashion and device. The painting and colouring are executed in a style purely classical: this branch of the manufacture gives employment to some thousands of ingenious and eminent artists. One of the great incentives to the encouragement of this flourishing [277] branch of our domestic trade is, that families may have their services characteristically enriched with their proper arms, crests, or ciphers, in the most correct manner. Repositories of these elegant requisites for the table are established in almost every quarter of the town. Some of the most considerable are those of

Messrs. Flight and Barr, corner of Coventry Street, Leicester Fields.

Messrs. Wedgwood and Co. St James's Sq.

Messrs. Chamberlain, Piccadilly.

Mr. Sharpus, Cockspur Street, Charing Cross.

Mr. Shirley, 53, Great Mary-le-Bone Street.

Mr. Assen, 406, Strand.*

Mr. Hargrave, St. Alban's Street, Chinaman to the Price Regent.

Messrs. Pellatt and Green, St. Paul's Church Yard.

Mr. Mist, Fleet Street, corner of Salisbury Court.

Most of these repositories have promenades for the exhibition of their splendid and elegant productions.

* Mr. Assen furnishes crates assorted for families at all prices, from two guineas to fifty.

With respect to covers for dishes, those articles which contribute so essentially to the [278] comforts of the table; they are to be found at all the superior tin manufactories in complete sets, made either of block-tin or Britannia metal. Among the eminent furnishers of them we may mention Mr. Dare, of Cockspur Street, Charing Cross; Messrs. Hill, Holborn Hill; and Messrs. Barron and Son, 476, Strand.

It will be quite proper in this place to advert to the article dining-tables, and mention the recent improvements made in them.

Mr. George Oakley, of Bond Street, exhibits many fashionable varieties of this essential article of furniture.[1]

Mr. Pocock, of Southampton Street, Strand, has a patent for a sympathetic dining-table, which one person can with ease enlarge or contract at pleasure. It is thus calculated alike for the cottage or *ferme ornée*; for the hospitable mansion; and for the spacious saloon, appropriated to the entertainments of a host of nobles. This table can be constructed so as to unite with a fashionable sideboard, or made so portable as to pack with the baggage of a regiment for the officers' mess.[2]

Messrs. Morgan and Sanders, No. 16 and 17, Catherine Street, Strand, have a patent for manufacturing imperial dining-tables, so constructed as to dine from four to one hundred guests, and capable of being folded up [279] into the compass of a large Pembroke table. They have another patent for a Trafalgar sideboard and dining-table, combined to form one elegant piece of furniture: and they also make portable chairs for routes [*sic*] and other entertainments. A dozen of these chairs may be packed in the compass of two ordinary chairs.[3]

Lamps and tapers are now as indispensable to a grand dinner, as tables and chairs. Most of the superior silversmiths whom we have mentioned

[1] **Oakley** (no. 8 New Bond Street) has been described as 'one of the most famous cabinet-makers and upholsterers in Regency London' (Gilbert 1996, pp. 42-43).

[2] William **Pocock** (no. 26 Southampton Street) patented his 'sympathetic' extending dining table in 1805; it operated by means of a pulley mechanism that lifted a leaf from the centre of the table (Gilbert, pp. 44-45).

[3] **Morgan and Sanders** formed their partnership in 1800 (Gilbert, p. 41), and specialized in portable military furniture as well as items for domestic use. They advertised their Trafalgar sideboards as being 'as well calculated for small rooms as for the first nobleman's mansion, as they can be made from the smallest dimensions to the very largest size'. Thus, as Margarette Lincoln remarks, '[p]urchasers were led to believe that it was not only patriotic to purchase the sideboard but that by doing so they were also emulating the aristocracy' (Lincoln 2002, pp. 103-04).

above, manufacture a variety of elegant candelabra and candlesticks. Some of the latter are on the plan of sliding telescopes, and are raised or lowered at pleasure. There are almost innumerable venders of wax and sperm-candles, but proportionably few of them really manufacture those articles. Some of the most eminent are Mr. Barret, of the Haymarket; Mr. Glassop, of Compton Street, Soho; and Mr. Field, of Lambeth Marsh. Their bleaching grounds and manufactories are very extensive, and at convenient distances from town.*

* Many chandlers now manufacture mould candles of tallow with waxed wicks. In Little Britain there is a manufactory of candles with hollow wicks, a contrivance which effectually prevents the candle from guttering.

Chandeliers and lustres are very essential [280] appendages to all dining-rooms which have any pretensions to elegance. These are made either of *or-moulu*, bronze, petit-or, or elegantly cut-glass, some adapted for candles, and others for lamps.[1]

One of the most extensive and brilliant assortments of these articles is exhibited at the spacious establishment of Messrs. Hancock and Shepherd, Cockspur Street. These premises, when lighted up, form a coup d'œil the most superb. Every article of glass in the all possible degrees of finish and elegance, from five guineas to five hundred, is to be had here.

Messrs. Pellatt and Green, on the south side of St. Paul's Church Yard, No. 16, and Messrs. Neale and Bailey, No. 8, same place, have a very extensive stock of these elegant articles. In Ludgate Hill Mr. Blades, at No. 5, and Messrs. Jackson and Co. No. 38. In Fleet Street Messrs. Parker and Perry, near Salisbury Square. In the Strand Mr. Collings, at No. 227, Mr. Blakeway, No. 37, and Mr. Furniss, No. 125; all exhibit a very elegant assortment. In most parts of the west end of the town there are displays of glasswork equally brilliant.

Among the numerous manufacturers of fashionable lamps our limits only permit us to notice a few. The lamp originally called [281] the Argand lamp was the basis of all subsequent improvements; but, we believe, the artist whose name it bears was defrauded of the profit of his invention. The patent of the Liverpool lamp belongs to Mr. Turmeau, 125, Drury Lane. The variation consists in an enlargement of the cylinder and the addition of a reflector.[2]

[1] Ormolu refers either to gilt brass or bronze, or to a gold-coloured alloy of copper, zinc and tin; petit-or is another name for pinchbeck, a goldish alloy of copper and zinc.
[2] Both of these lamps were oil-burning. The **Argand lamp**, with an improved tubular wick that facilitated combustion and greatly increased the amount of light produced, was invented by François-Pierre-Ami Argand in the early 1780s and

MARKETS.

That sagacious observer who pronounced the English to be the most thinking people in the world, would have added much to his own reputation as a philosopher, by discovering and revealing what they are oftenest and most intensely thinking upon. Doctor Johnson, either sarcastically or seriously, declared, that the subject on which a man thought most earnestly, and most frequently, was *his dinner;* and certainly, if we consider the present habits and manners of the people of London, we must conclude that the doctor's position is defensible, at least within the compass of our bills of mortality. No body of men meet on any public occasion, or on any occasion that is alike interesting to every individual composing that body, without eating and drinking together. A dinner seems to be the test by [282] which a man's social qualities are tried; and he who should refuse this test might as well excommunicate himself at once, and say, with old Shylock the Jew, "I will buy with you; sell with you; talk with you; walk with you; and so following: but I will not eat with you, drink with you, or pray with you." To dine, and to give a dinner, may now be deemed an essential part of a liberal education; and proper lectures for the acquisition of this accomplishment ought to be included in the prospectus of every professor who undertakes to "prepare youth for the pulpit, bar, or senate."

The Athenians, the most thinking people among the ancients, had their *academus:* the English, who have acquired the like distinction among the moderns, have also their public walks laid out with care, and furnished with every thing that art and nature can produce; to rouse, stimulate, and exercise their thinking faculties. In these walks are stationed proper officers, who, like the flappers of Laputa, use, not indeed bladders, but short emphatical words and signs to fix the attention of the passing philosopher to what is before him. The words *"what d'ye buy,"* have an import almost as solemn as the warning which a monarch of ancient times used to hear every hour of the

patented by him in England in 1784; in France his lamp was copied by Antoine Arnoult Quinquet, and it was there generally known as a *quinquet.* John Turmeau of Liverpool and Charles Seward of Lancaster patented the **Liverpool lamp** in 1811; Turmeau (1776-1846) is principally known as a miniaturist and portrait painter, but his role in the development of the lamp is mentioned in an obituary (*Liverpool Mercury*, 18 September 1846).

day: "Remember that you are mortal! remember that you must dye!" We wish we [283] had a better and more classical name* for these sacred haunts, than "market," or "shambles," as we could then report the survey we have made of them in a style that might better suit the dignity of the subject.

   *The homeliness of the English language is observable even in the nomenclature of state-offices and princely residences. Some of the most important jurisprudential questions are settled in a *cock-pit:* the great law officers of the crown transact business in an *inn*, and one of the princes of the blood royal lives in a *stable-yard*. Nay, the lord chancellor himself, and the judges, when attending in the house of peers, are accommodated with no better seats than *wool-sacks*. Some of our first courtiers are designated by the humble name of *ushers* and *grooms;* and the most noble order of knighthood acknowledged in Britain, is said to have originated in that precious bagatelle a *lady's garter*.

   Leadenhall Market, independently of the sales of hides and leather effected there, is by far the most considerable market in London.[1] The articles sold here are town and country killed meats of every sort, and of the primest quality. In addition to the usual variety of fine beef, veal, and mutton, some of the first rate butchers here expose, during the winter season, specimens of very delicate house-lamb, which is usually sold by the quarter, at Christmas tide from fifteen to twenty-five shillings each. Here also are exhibited capital [284] joints of country-fed pork, as cut up from what are called porkers; and delicate fillets, spare-ribs, loins, and griskins, transmitted from the country manufacturers of bacon. There are parts of the market appointed for the

---

[1] There was a market in the courtyard of the **Leadenhall** – a lead-roofed mansion belonging to the Neville family – by 1321. By the close of the century the market had come under the control of the City of London, who took over the Leadenhall itself in 1411 and by mid-century had erected new buildings on the site, including a granary or garner, a chapel, a school, and new market houses (see Samuel and Milne 1992). These largely survived the 1666 fire, which destroyed most of the other City markets, with the result that the Leadenhall Market, previously a 'white' market in which poultry and all flesh except beef was sold, was considerably expanded, with cattle butchers, fishmongers, and fruit and vegetable sellers joining the Leadenhall traders. In 1720 John Strype hailed the market as 'one of the greatest, the best, and the most general for all Provisions in the City of London, nay of the Kingdom; and if I should say of all Europe, I should not give too great a Praise' (II.5.89), and the market that he described in detail had changed little by 1815. In the 1870s there were proposals to abolish the market and move traders to the new Central Meat Market at Smithfield, but it was decided instead to demolish the old buildings and start anew; today's glass-roofed Leadenhall Market, designed by Horace Jones, opened in December 1881.

wholesale vending of carcases: here come lots of country-fed veal and pork packed in clean cloths, and thus consigned to the salesmen; and from these supplies most of the porkmen in and about town stock their shops. Another part of the market is allotted to the sale of live and dead poultry of every variety; the weekly supplies of which are to an amount scarcely conceivable. The poulterers throughout London resort hither for stock. Not only turkies, bustards, geese, peacocks and peahens, guinea fowls, pullets, capons, pigeons, ducks, wild and tame, widgeons, teal, plovers, quails, woodcocks, snipes, larks, and all other lawful game are sold here; but hares, pheasants, partridges, and other game prohibited by the game acts, form the basis of a secret but very considerable traffic. These are enquired after by the several names of longs and shorts, lions and owls; and under shelter of these metonymies the penalty is evaded.[1] Perhaps the city-epicures wink at the subterfuge for the sake of the luxuries it adds to their tables. Around the wholesale poultry-market are the shops of several retail poulterers of [285] great fame, such as Messrs. Mott's. Here are roasting-pigs, eggs, and fresh-butter, in great abundance: nor is there wanting a proportionate supply of the finest fish in season. Here also are two or three excellent tripe-shops. This is the most considerable market in London for tame and wild-rabbits, wild in particular, which arrive every day during the season from the several warrens in Essex, Herts, and Suffolk.

As a general market that of Newgate stands next in estimation, being well supplied with carcases of town and country-fed meat, and occupied by many excellent cutting-butchers. The division allotted for poultry is much smaller than that at Leadenhall. In the interior there is a district set apart for the sale of vegetables. This is one of the principal emporiums of fresh butter in London. Here are a few fishmongers and poulterers, and an excellent shop for tripe, calves' feet, and sheep-trotters. This is an open market every week-day; but the country supplies arrive for the most part on Saturdays, when Newgate-street, early in the morning, is thronged with carts waiting to take in and distribute the various articles of the market all over town.[2]

[1] See p. l in the introduction for a discussion of laws relating to the sale of game; and for the terms used here, the Glossary.
[2] **Newgate Market** was descended from an ancient market in Newgate Street, shown on the 'Agas' map of the 1560s, but moved after the 1666 fire to a purpose-built site at the heart of the area bounded by Newgate Street, Ivy Lane, Paternoster Row, and Warwick Lane. Already a centre for retail or cutting butchers in the early C19, Newgate took over most of the trade in dead meat when the sale of live animals was moved from Smithfield to Islington in 1855 (see below). This trade was

If we had observed the order of locality, and not that of precedence, we should have placed Whitechapel Market next to that of [286] Leadenhall. This market extends for nearly half-a-mile along that wide street called White-chapel, and is crowded with butchers of both the carcase and the cutting class; but its shambles frequently display very indifferent meats. Indeed Whitechapel is almost proverbial for bull and cow-beef, and ewe mutton. It can, however, boast of a good supply of country killed veal from the Essex dairies. This is a daily market; but the supply of meat from the country is chiefly on Saturdays.[1]

Fleet Market, extending from Fleet-street to Holborn Bridge, is a very considerable retail market for meats; but few of the butchers (in number about 100) can rank with the first rate.[2] To this rank Mrs. Heath, No. 50, (on the left-hand, soon after you have passed the covered part of the market) has an undoubted claim. Her expository is surrounded by what some people call mere keg-meg shops;[3] so that she shines like the moon *inter minora sidera*. The prime joints which she constantly exhibits and sells, would not disgrace the magazine of a Giblet, or a Pope. The Holborn end of Fleet Market is a sort of miscellaneous emporium for fish, vegetables, and roots. Here are two or three poulterers, and about the same number of fishmongers. Near the Fleet Prison

transferred back to Smithfield in 1868 when the new London Central Meat Market opened, and the Newgate market buildings were demolished the following year. Known as Paternoster Square by 1872, the site of the market was destroyed in the Blitz.

[1] The **Whitechapel** (or **Aldgate**) meat market consisted of a number of shops at the eastern end of Aldgate High Street, south side, housing both carcase butchers who did the actual slaughtering, and cutting butchers who dismembered the carcases and sold the meat. In the C19 Whitechapel was also a major market for hay and straw, but today's Whitechapel Market, operating six days a week somewhat to the east, has moved away from its agricultural origins and accommodates stalls selling everything from electrical goods to sari silks, alongside Asian spices and exotic vegetables.

[2] **Fleet Market** was formed in the mid-1730s when that portion of the Fleet River from Holborn to Fleet Street was completely covered over by arches: the former riverside wharves became roadways, and the central strip was converted to a market consisting of two rows of shops selling meat, fish, and vegetables. In the 1820s – by which time the lower portion of the river had also been covered over, creating New Bridge Street leading to Blackfriars Bridge – the entire thoroughfare from Holborn to the Thames was widened, necessitating the removal of the market to a site west of Farringdon Street. The new Farringdon Market opened in 1826 and continued until 1892, when the remaining stalls were transferred to Smithfield.

[3] A variant of *cagmag*, referring to unwholesome or decaying meat.

there is a very considerable fruit-market; the supplies for which from Kent, [287] Essex, Surrey, and Middlesex, are mostly landed at Blackfriars Bridge. In the market are two good tripe-shops, and two repositories of medicinal herbs.

Spital Market, in Spital Fields, is a general market for meats, poultry, and fish. It is well supplied with fruits and vegetables, and particularly well with that inestimable root the potatoe. In this article there are several wholesale as well as retail dealers.[1]

The Borough Market is situated near the church of St. Mary Overy, and partially extends into the high street. Here are to be purchased meats of every sort; but the chief traffic consists in fruit and vegetables.[2]

---

[1] The fruit and vegetable market at **Spitalfields** was established by royal license in 1682, and by the early C18 meat and poultry were also being sold at this large market located in the area bounded by Lamb Street, Red Lion Street (lost in the construction of Commercial Street), Paternoster Row (now part of Brushfield Street), and Crispin Street. When the original cruciform market building was destroyed by fire in the early C18 it was not replaced, and wooden market stalls remained the norm until the late C19 (see *SL* 27, pp. 127-36). In 1875 the leasehold interest in the market was purchased by Robert Horner, who was responsible for new glass-roofed market buildings erected between 1885 and 1893, and in 1920 Spitalfields came under the control of the City of London. Horner's buildings continue to house a thriving market specializing in fashion, art, and antiques (Old Spitalfields), but the main market for fruit, vegetables, and flowers was moved to Leyton in 1991 (New Spitalfields). Potatoes, incidentally, long remained a feature of the market: writing in 1935, W. J. Passingham noted that of the produce sold daily, 'potatoes constitute at least one-half' (p. 95).

[2] There was a market in **Borough High Street**, Southwark, as early as the C13. Originally held near the present-day junction of the High Street with Southwark Street, the market was moved north towards London Bridge in the late C17, and then west in 1756 to a triangular site bounded by Stoney Street, Church (now Cathedral) Street, and Rochester Street (now Walk). It was expanded in the C19 and again in the C20, covering what is shown on the Horwood map as Three Crown Court and spreading east to the High Street and north to Winchester Street (now Walk). A major redevelopment of the site, begun in 1995, has seen the restoration of some buildings and the demolition and replacement of others, culminating in 2004 with the opening of a new building that incorporates the Victorian portico from Covent Garden's abandoned Floral Hall (see the essays by Ptolemy Dean and Jo French in *The Borough Market Book*, 2005).

Honey Lane Market lies off Cheapside, between Milk-street and Laurence-lane. It boasts some very excellent butchers, poulterers, fishmongers, butter-men, and green-grocers.[1]

Billingsgate is the grand mart from whence this vast metropolis is sup-plied with fish,[2] either by the established fishmongers who exhibit their stores on trays of marble or of lead; or by the silver-voiced and "trumpet-tongued" nymphs and matrons who gracefully transport their *cophini* of mackarel, flounders, and soles, on their heads from street to street, and from house to house. Every tide brings up to Billingsgate whole fleets of vessels freighted with spoils from Neptune's wide dominion: Ber- [288] wick smacks laden with salmon packed in ice; Dutch schuyts with their wells filled with luxurious turbots, or delicious eels; boats and barges almost sinking with their plentiful cargoes of cod, haddock, skate, soles, herrings, or mackarel, according to the season; oysters, crabs, lobsters, crawfish, &c. &c. Hither the Brighton mackarel and soles, at the commencement of the season, are forwarded by land-carriage, and occasionally those welcome guests at the tables of the great and opulent, the john dory and the mullet, both grey and scarlet. Bounties are given to encourage the supply of fish to this market; and the traffic is under proper regulations. Oysters, mussels, cockles, sprats, and other fish that are sold by measure, are subject to the inspection of the

[1] **Honey Lane Market** was created after the 1666 fire to replace the street markets of Cheapside; just east of Milk Street, it took in land formerly belonging to All Hallows, Honey Lane, and St Mary Magdalen, Milk Street (see Masters 1974, pp. 37-39). The original market building, described by Strype in 1720 as containing 135 covered stalls for butchers, was replaced in 1787-88 by a new structure designed by George Dance. In 1835 Honey Lane Market was closed for the building of the City of London School, which opened two years later. Following the removal of the school to Blackfriars in 1883 the old name was restored, and until the Second World War a number of retail food shops clustered around the old market site. The last remnants of Honey Lane Market were absorbed by new developments in the 1950s.

[2] Everything from coal to wine was once traded at Billingsgate Wharf, but by the C16 **Billingsgate** had become the principal market for fish, a status formally acknow-ledged by an Act of Parliament passed in 1698. Until 1850, when the first permanent building was erected, fish and seafood were sold from stalls and sheds in the various lanes and alleyways south of Lower Thames Street, roughly at the bottom of St Mary at Hill. The first market building was demolished in 1873 to make way for the one that still stands in Lower Thames Street (designed by Horace Jones, recently renovated by Richard Rogers); Billingsgate fish market itself, owned and operated by the City of London, moved to Docklands in 1982.

city-meters. Around Billingsgate and in its vicinity are numerous dealers in salt and dried fish; such as salmon, cod, ling, and herrings. In the spring and summer seasons the supply from Newcastle of that great delicacy, pickled salmon, is very considerable. The money expended annually in the purchase of fish landed at this place is of enormous amount: it has been said that the Dutch used to take yearly from our current coin fifty thousand guineas for turbot only! The principal market day at Billingsgate is Monday.

Smithfield Market supplies the whole town [289] and its environs with cattle.[1] The weekly returns are about 3000 beeves, and 30,000 sheep and lambs, besides calves and pigs. The weekly supply of country killed meat to London is computed to fall little short of this in weight. What a carnivorous nation we are! The improvements and additions at present making in Smithfield Market will remedy many inconveniences, and remove many annoyances which have for centuries been endured in that capital part of the metropolis. Slaughter-houses are erecting for the purpose of slaying the beasts on the spot, instead of driving them through the streets to the shops and shambles of the purchasers.

In taking leave of the city markets, we must not omit the mention of one which is held in Duke's Place, Houndsditch, principally for the supply of the Jews.[2] Here may be purchased beef, mutton, veal, and lamb, slaughtered and

[1] Cattle and horses were being sold at **Smithfield** – a 'smooth field' just outside the city walls – as early as the C10, and since 1327 the City of London has controlled the market there. Just north of St Bartholomew's Hospital, the large open area known as West Smithfield was also used for tournaments and sporting events, and was long a place of execution. By the late C17 the once rural site was surrounded by houses and shops, but the tradition of driving cattle through the streets to the market, where they were held in pens before being slaughtered, continued into the mid-C19. Following vigorous protests it was decided in 1852 to move the live cattle market, and three years later new facilities were opened in Copenhagen Fields, Islington (see above, p. 217n). A new London Central Meat Market opened at West Smithfield in 1868; expanded and in part rebuilt, it continues today as the principal London market for meat and poultry.

[2] As shown on the Horwood map, **Duke's Place** was a large square yard at the rear of the Great Synagogue, north of Aldgate High Street and just west of Houndsditch; it was renamed St James's Place in the mid-C19 and today is Creechurch Place. By Victorian times the market, still controlled by Jewish merchants, dealt principally in fruit – especially oranges – and nuts, and was sometimes referred to as the Orange Market, a name often encountered in descriptions of the 1888 'Jack the Ripper' murder committed in nearby Mitre Square. Writing in *Household Words* in April 1854, John Capper compared the 'open-air shops, piled up with ripe, luscious radiant fruit' with Indian bazaars, and Henry Mayhew devoted three columns to

duly sealed according to the law of Moses; but by no means so *well dressed* (to use the butchers' phrase), or exhibited in shops so neat and clean as our own. In and about the market are several Jewish fish-merchants, who vend very prime fish, as well live and fresh, as in the salted, dried, or smoked state. They also sell anchovies, either in barrels or glass squares, and Dutch herrings in tubs. Many of these Jewish fishmongers [290] daily ply about the Bank, the Exchange, and the adjacent alleys. In this market are to be purchased lentils and Turkey fruits; eggs raw or cooked; and various articles of confectionery from itinerant confectioners, who, during the time of the passover, sell also unleavened cakes and biscuits. Here and in the parts adjacent inhabited by the Jews are to be bought fish of various kinds, deliciously cooked, in a cold state. It is said that the method of cooking them is boiling them in oil, which makes them appear delicately brown. They certainly look very tempting and savoury.

Of the markets out of the city the first we shall notice is Brook's Market, up Brook Street, Holborn. It is small, and only calculated to supply the immediate neighbourhood with flesh. The butchers who inhabit it sell in general very good meat.[1]

Clare Market is situated between Drury Lane and Portugal Street, Lincoln's Inn.[2] Here are several excellent butchers, poulterers, fishmongers, greengrocers, potatoe-men, and two or three good tripe-men. From this market many shops in the west end of the town are supplied with butter. The principal salesmen of that essential article are Messrs. Cullums'.

the market in his *London Labour and the London Poor*, describing it in less glowing terms (Mayhew, i:86-87).

[1] Brook or Brooke Street runs north from Holborn between Gray's Inn Road and Leather Lane. The name **Brookes Market** still appears on modern maps; the market itself, which survived into the C20, is now gone, but the old market square has been preserved as a public open space.

[2] **Clare Market** also remains on today's maps, indicating a short passage abutting the London School of Economics, whose buildings now cover the old market site. Located at the southwest corner of Lincoln's Inn Fields, the market was established about 1657 on land belonging to the Earl of Clare; it was mentioned with approval by Strype, but even in the C18 its proximity to Drury Lane meant that here, as at Covent Garden, gin shops, brothels, and gaming houses sprang up to accommodate theatre-going rakes. At the end of the C19 the market, which by then catered almost exclusively to the poorest shoppers, was described by H. B. Wheatley as 'a cluster of narrow dirty streets [...] a crowded, noisy, and unsavoury place on market days and Saturday nights' (*London Past and Present*, i:407), and in the first years of the C20 Clare Market was swept away during the building of Aldwych.

Newport Market, situated at the head of St. Martin's Lane, and in the vicinity of Lei- [291] cester Square, is principally occupied by butchers, some of whom are very respectable.[1] The sale of fish has of late been wholly transferred from it to Lumber Court, in its vicinity, which has risen to such consequence as a fish-market, that it now ranks second to Billingsgate.[2] It was in Newport Market that the father of the celebrated John Horne Tooke kept a poulterer's shop, from which he supplied fowls to the table of his present Majesty's father, when resident in Leicester Square. John Horne himself was some part of his life a fishmonger.

Carnaby Market, situated between Golden Square and Great Marlborough Street, is a general market, though the greatest proportion of its occupants are butchers.[3] In Tyler's Court and Major Foubert's Passage, which are accessories to it, there are two or three first-rate poulterers, porkmen, and fishmongers. Mr. J. Phillips, the celebrated fishmonger of Bond Street, formerly kept his shop in this market.

[1] **Newport Market**, created by royal letters patent in 1686 as a market for all merchandise except live cattle, lay in the area bounded by Litchfield Street, Porter Street (now vanished), Newport Court, and Grafton Street (also gone), somewhat south of today's Cambridge Circus. By the early 1840s, when shares in the market were being offered for sale (*The Times*, 22 November 1841 and 27 June 1842), there were two market buildings, a cattle pound, and a slaughter house, as well as numerous shops and other buildings, but it is not clear to what extent the meat market was still operating (see SL 34, pp. 365-70). As at Clare Market, the surrounding area had filled with thieves and prostitutes, and in the 1860s the larger market building became a refuge for the destitute. Newport Market was cleared away in the 1880s, during the formation of Shaftesbury Avenue and Charing Cross Road.

[2] **Lumber Court** (shown on the Horwood map as Lomber Court, and now called Tower Court) runs northeast from Tower Street toward Seven Dials. The fish market was still operating in 1851 (Weale, p. 612), but by 1877, when John Thomson and Adolphe Smith published their photographic essay on *Street Life in London*, the principal trade in Lumber Court seems to have been in second-hand clothes and furniture (p. 43).

[3] **Carnaby Market** was opened in 1725 as Lowndes Market and changed its name about ten years later. It was located south of Great Marlborough Street, between Carnaby Street and Marshall Street, and could be approached from the west though Lowndes Court and Marlborough Court, still surviving today as pedestrian passages (Major Foubert's Passage was lost in the building of Regent Street, and Tyler's Court is now part of Foubert's Place). The market was demolished in 1820 and almost the whole area was rebuilt soon after (SL 31, pp. 190-91).

Oxford Market, in Oxford Street, nearly opposite the Pantheon, is another general market, of good repute, for flesh, fish, fowls, and vegetables of all sorts. Here are two tripe-shops, a few considerable cheesemongeries, and one medicinal herb-shop.[1]

Shepherd's Market, between Piccadilly and [292] May Fair, is in most respects similar to Oxford Market.[2]

Grosvenor Market, between South Moulton Street and Davies Street, considered relatively to its site, is a very inferior market. It has dwindled into obscurity; scarcely half a dozen butchers' shops remain, and these are so seldom provided with prime meats, that the epicure would scarcely regret their secession.[3]

St. George's Market, in Oxford Street, at a very short distance from the last-mentioned, and with the exception of a few shops in front, is deserving of a like censure.

St. James's Market, situated between St. James's Square and the Haymarket, is in high repute for good meats, and can boast within its precincts several first

---

[1] **Oxford Market** was just north of Oxford Street in an area bounded on the east by Market (now Great Titchfield) Street and on the other three sides by what is today called Market Place. Developed by Edward Harley, second Earl of Oxford, the market opened in 1731; the original hexagonal market building, designed by James Gibbs, was replaced around 1815 (see *ONL* iv:463, with an illustration of Gibbs's market house). The market was closed and demolished in 1880 (Mackenzie 1972, p. 40).

[2] **Shepherd Market**, tucked away between Piccadilly and Curzon Street, takes its name from the architect and builder Edward Shepherd, who began developing the area – formerly the site of the rowdy annual May Fair – in the 1730s. According to *BoE Westminster*, p. 570, the upper floor of the original market building was also used as a theatre. The main buildings seen today date from 1860, and the market traders have given way to boutiques and restaurants.

[3] **Grosvenor Market**, which the *Almanack* describes as having 'dwindled into obscurity' by 1815, had opened only thirty years earlier on a triangular plot at the junction of Davies Street and South Molton Street, and was, according to the *Survey of London*, 'a failure from the beginning'. This was in part because of competition from the nearby **St George's Market**, a meat market set up about the same time in a yard between Davies Street and James (now Gilbert) Street, with entrances from Oxford Street and Chandler (now Weighhouse) Street (*SL* 40, pp. 68-69). By the 1840s only a few tenants remained in Grosvenor Market, but butchers and cheesemongers continued to cluster in the St George's Market area for several decades more.

rate fishmongers, poulterers, fruiterers, and green-grocers. From hence the households of most of the branches of the Royal Family are supplied.[1]

Hungerford Market, in the Strand, once so eminent, has fallen away, and at present scarcely supports half a dozen butchers. Here still remains a very good shop for fine tripe, calves' feet, and trotters.[2]

Bloomsbury Market, between Holborn and Bloomsbury Square, is very small but well supplied.[3]

[293] St. George's Market, in Surrey, was established for the convenience of families migrating to that new and thriving part of the metropolis.[4] Though

[1] **St James's Market** opened in 1664 just south of Jermyn Street, extending west to Market (now St Alban's) Street and east to the now-vanished Market Lane, which closely paralleled Haymarket; by 1666 a market house had been erected, described as 'commodious' in 1720 by John Strype, who also praised the 'good Provisions' of the market (11.6.83). St James's Market was demolished in 1816-18, during the construction of Waterloo Place and Lower Regent Street, and was replaced by a smaller market slightly to the north. This was razed after the First World War, leaving only a street name to mark the spot (*SL* 29, pp. 215-20).

[2] **Hungerford Market** was established under a 1678 private Act of Parliament on the site of a mansion owned by the Hungerford family, but despite its prime location between the Thames and the Strand, just above Craven Street, it seems never to have been very prosperous (see *SL* 18, pp. 40-45). By 1815 the market had indeed 'fallen away', and although it was completely rebuilt in 1831-33 the new market too was a failure. In 1854 some of the buildings were destroyed by fire, and in the early 1860s Hungerford Market was completely demolished to make way for the Charing Cross railway station and hotel.

[3] **Bloomsbury Market** was set up in 1662 as a meat and fish market, and the outline of the market square survives today as the area bounded by Bloomsbury Way (earlier Hart Street), Bury Place, and – recalling the former use – Barter Street. The Rocque map of 1738 shows two market buildings, one devoted to fish, but neither appears on Horwood's 1799 map, suggesting that by then Bloomsbury Market had declined into a street market; fifty years later the market site had been built over (see Gage 1986).

[4] New roads were built in Lambeth and Southwark in the later C18, and the great open space then known as St George's Fields was rapidly developed (see *SL* 25, pp. 49-64: a comparison of the Rocque and Horwood maps gives an idea of the magnitude of the changes). In late 1789 James Hedger, owner of a local refreshment house called the Dog and Duck, took out newspaper advertisements announcing the opening of **St George's Market**, which he had established on land east of London Road and south of Borough Road, 'for the conveniency of the adjacent neighbourhood' (*Morning Post*, 12 December, naming the opening day as the 19th). There was immediate opposition from the body that controlled the nearby Borough Market, but a settlement of some sort was reached, and the market,

erected on the most improved plan, and furnished with every accommodation, it has not apparently met with much encouragement. Here are several
butchers; but the vegetable department is scantily supplied.

Tothill Street, since the demolition of the Westminster Market to make
room for the New Sessions House, has become almost a market, since nearly
one half of the houses in it may be said to victual the numerous inhabitants
of the lower Liberties of Westminster.[1]

Chelsea Market, near Sloane Square, was established to supply the genteel
and improving neighbourhood of Sloane Street and Hans Town, but it has
hitherto been poorly encouraged.[2]

Last of all

> Centric in London noise and London follies;
> Proud Covent Garden blooms in smoky glory
> For coachmen, coffee-rooms, piazzas, dollies,
> Cabbages, and comedians, fam'd in story.

Perhaps in the whole world there is not a market for vegetables so well
supplied as this. The principal days are Tuesday, Thursday, [294] and Saturday. Almost all the principal market gardeners within ten or twelve miles
of the metropolis, rent a stand in Covent Garden, where every esculent
vegetable in or out of season, indigenous or exotic, natural or forced, may
be purchased. Among the superior fruiterers we notice Mr. Cook at the
lemon-tree, Mr. Moulder, Mr. Bunting, Mr. Grange, Mr. Mabbot, Messrs.
Best and Strudwiche. In their windows are often displayed precocious fruits
and vegetables, produced into full bloom and maturity by the skill and care of
scientific botanists: delicious pine-apples, for instance, and grapes, vieing in
growth and flavour with those of warmer climates; strawberries and cherries

---

clearly visible on the Horwood map, continued to operate. By 1832 it was in 'so
dilapidated and dangerous a state, that it has been for a long time considered a
public nuisance' (*Morning Chronicle*, 26 November), but plans by Hedger's son
to build an abbatoir and new market buildings came to nothing. The market can
still be seen on Bacon's map of 1888; today the site is covered by the South Bank
University buildings fronting on London Road.

[1] North of Westminster Abbey, **Westminster Market** or **King Street Market**,
described by Strype in 1720 as 'well served and resorted unto', was displaced in
1804 for the building of a Sessions House, the predecessor of the early C20 Middlesex Guildhall that now occupies the site and is home to the Supreme Court of the
United Kingdom. Tothill Street is directly to the west.

[2] **Chelsea Market** is shown on the Horwood map south of Sloane Square. Established by the 1790s (Annabel Walker 1987, p. 153), the market was removed in the
late 1880s, and today the site is covered by the lawns and houses of Sloane Gardens.

ripened in defiance of the snow and nipping blasts of spring; cucumbers and asparagus forced under frames in mid-winter; early French beans grown in pots, and early peas in warm banks, which epicures may at times procure at as low a rate as two or three guineas a pint; early peaches and nectarines ripened in forcing-houses, and a thousand other delicacies which our limits will not allow us to enumerate. Here are also several orange-merchants who sell not only the finest China, Seville, and St. Michael, but lemons also, and exotic grapes, chestnuts, filberts, and hazelnuts. Here are shops of medicinal herbs, roots, simples, and seeds, as well as the ge- [295] nuine stramonium,[1] now so much recommended by some of the faculty. Flowers of various genera and species, and aromatic plants for drawing-rooms, verandas, and balconies, may be had here. In the centre of the market is a spot for the sale of Staffordshire earthenware, of various patterns and devices. In short this spot is well worth the attention of the epicure and the bon-vivant; nor is it without its charms to the philosopher, who loves to ruminate on the wants, passions, and habitudes of his species, and who delights in the associations which classic spots like this inspire. Hither the SPECTATOR resorted to witness the humours of a market-morning; and the facetious Tom Brown pourtrayed and dramatized the colloquial sallies of the market folks: this scene was depicted by Hogarth in his Rake's Progress: it is this scene which Farquhar and Vanburgh frequently chose in their comedies as the rendezvous of intriguants. In all probability it will continue to be what it has been – the academus of epicures, dramatists, and comic philosophers.[2]

[1] Stramonium was a narcotic prepared from the plant *Datura stramonium* or thorn apple, a member of the nightshade family; in the early C19 it was principally used in cases of asthma, epilepsy, and mania, and Rylance's mention of the drug suggests that it may have been prescribed for him.

[2] For the early development of **Covent Garden** see above, pp. xxxii. The market building of 1828-30, designed by Charles Fowler, still survives, and is described by *BoE* as 'the best-preserved Late Georgian market-house in England' (*Westminster*, p. 342). The glass roof over the outer pavilions of the market was added in the later C19, a floral hall opened in 1860, and two flower markets – one, Jubilee Market, specifically for 'foreign flowers' – were built between 1871 and 1904. Covent Garden continued as London's principal market for fruit and vegetables until 1974, when operations were moved to Nine Elms, Battersea. Today Fowler's market building houses boutiques and restaurants, the old flower market is home to the London Transport Museum, and traders in Jubilee Market specialize in antiques and arts and crafts. The 1860 Floral Hall, never a commercial success, was converted to use as a ballroom venue in the 1870s, and later became a fruit market; badly damaged

ALIMENTARY CALENDAR.

JANUARY.

The commencement of the year, in England, has from time immemorial been a season of festivity; and accordingly the month of January is one of the most distinguished in the calendar for good cheer.[1] At no time is the metropolis more abundantly stocked with provisions of every kind, or the stomachs of its inhabitants in better plight for consuming them. The bracing air of winter promotes exercise and quickens appetite; the gloom of the season, its long nights and short days, create a relish for social and domestic enjoyments; of which dinner, being the most substantial, is most generally interesting; nor can any thing more splendidly and durably attractive than this repast be found in the whole circle of our summer pleasures. Following the close of that joyous festival Christmas, which, as Sir Roger De Coverly goodnaturedly observes, could not have been contrived to take place at a better time[2] – this month commences with a series of convivial meetings, which rarely terminates before the feast of the Epiphany, when twelfth night, the jubilee of the pastry-cooks, affords another oc- [297] casion of mirth and revelry. At this period of the year a brisk interchange of presents is kept up between the citizens and their friends in the country, from whom profuse supplies of turkies, pheasants, hares, geese, and partridges, are received in return for barrels of oysters and baskets of Billingsgate fish. So plenteous and diversified are the arrivals of poultry and game, that an epicure who might covet a repast of that kind, could scarcely imagine a more satisfactory bill of fare, than the way-bill

---

by fire in 1956, the remains of the structure – minus the portico now at Borough Market (see above, p. 244n) – were incorporated into the Royal Opera House in the 1990s. The lines quoted here are from George Colman the Younger's 'Please to Ring the Bell'.

[1] As mentioned in the introduction, much of the information in this section is based on that in the marketing guides appended to contemporary cookery books. Considerable sections of Rylance's own text were adapted – with no acknowledgement – by William Hone in his 1832 *Year Book of Daily Recreation and Information*.

[2] The fictional English squire Sir Roger de Coverly frequently appeared in the *Spectator* essays written by Joseph Addison and Richard Steele; his remarks on the timing of Christmas are in the *Spectator* for 8 January 1712 (no. 269).

of one of the Norwich coaches. The supply of fish is equally various and abundant: it consists of sea salmon, haddock, cod, skate, whitings, soles, lobsters, and oysters. The meats in season are beef, veal, mutton, pork, and house-lamb; to which may be added, Westphalia and north-country hams, Canterbury and Oxfordshire brawn, salted chines and tongues. Of the feathered tribe, besides fowls and turkies, there are capons, guinea-fowls, pea-hens, wild-ducks, widgeons, teal, plovers, and a great variety of wild waterfowl, as well as woodcocks, snipes, and larks. Notwithstanding the rigour of the season, a profusion of vegetables is found to accompany this treasure of viands; the skill and industry of our horticulturists having enlivened the sterility of winter with the verdure of spring. Not only potatoes, savoy cabbages, sprouts, [298] broccoli, kale, turnips, onions, and carrots, but even forced small sallads are in season; and some epicures boast of having so far anticipated the course of vegetable nature, as to regale their friends at Christmas with asparagus and green-peas. To complete this catalogue of luxuries, there is an infinite variety of puddings and pastry, among which the plum-pudding holds, by national preference, the first rank, being the inseparable companion, or rather follower of roast beef: puddings also of semolina, millet, and rice; tarts of preserved fruit, apple-pyes, and last, though not least in estimation, that delicious medley the mince-pye. When the appetite has been satiated by these solid viands, it may be further amused by a succession of custards and jellies; and lastly, by a dessert of Portugal grapes, oranges, apples, pears, walnuts, and other fruits indigenous or exotic, crude or candied.

From this rapid glance at the supplies of the table for January, it must be evident, that they comprehend a great proportion of the alimentary productions of the year, and, indeed, many of the main articles of solid fare are in season either perennially, or for several months in succession. Of the former are beef, mutton, veal, and house-lamb; sea-salmon; turbot, flounders, soles, whitings, Dutch [299] herrings, lobsters, crabs, shrimps, eels, and anchovies; fowls, chickens, pullets, tame pigeons, and tame rabbits. Grass-lamb is in season in April, May, June, July, August, September, and October, pork in the first three months and four last months of the year, buck-venison in June, July, August, and September; and doe-venison in October, November, December, and January. There is scarcely one article of diet, animal or vegetable, the appearance of which, at table, is limited to a single month, and of course in forming a calendar of meats, it becomes necessary so to class and distribute them, that each shall be mentioned under the month, when it is in greatest request, with an indication of the entire period, during which it continues in season.

Beef.

The derivation of this term from the French word bœuf, may account for the preference which is generally given to the flesh of the ox, though according to some tastes that of the heifer is better if well fed. Good beef should have a smooth open grain, delicately marbled with streaks of fat; the flesh should look red and feel tender, and the colour of the fat should be rather white than yellow; the latter [300] hue being a strong indication that the beast has been fed on oil-cake, in which case the meat will have by no means so fine a flavour, and the fat will almost wholly melt away in the cooking. Cow-beef has a closer grain and whiter fat than ox-beef, from which it may also be distinguished by the udder, when viewed in the whole or in quarters. The sweetest and best flavoured beef, is that of the little Scotch bullock, when fed to a proper condition in English pasture. Northamptonshire is noted for good beef of a larger size, and Leicestershire for very large oxen, but their flesh is by no means in high repute for fine flavour, the quality being almost in an inverse ratio to the quantity.

Veal.

The flesh of a bull-calf is firmer than that of a cow-calf, but not so white; the fillet of the latter is generally preferred on account of the udder. The whitest veal is not the most juicy, having been made so by frequent bleeding. In the choice of this meat, one of the best indications is, that the kidney be covered with white dense fat. In the loin the kidney first becomes putrescent, and the fat in that case loses its firm consistence. If the vein in the shoulder appear blue or of a bright red, [301] it is to be presumed that the beast has been recently killed; if the meat is clammy and spotted, it is stale and bad. It is to be remarked, that on account of the great demand for milk in the metropolis, the calves produced in the immediate vicinity, are sent to a distance to be suckled; Essex is the general nursery for them, and from thence they are brought to market at a proper age in high condition for the table.

Mutton.

The flesh of the wether should always be preferred to that of the ewe, which is paler, and of closer grain. It is in greatest perfection at six years old; the lean should be of a good colour, and the fat firm and white. The flavour of ram-mutton is disagreeably strong, the flesh of a deep red, and the fat spongy. Mutton fed on mountains and downs, where the herbage is short and fine, is better than that fed on rich pasture. Hence the preference given to the south down, to the small Welsh mutton, and that of the Highlands of Scotland. Leicestershire and the marshes of Kent produce the largest and fattest sheep.

[302]

Lamb.

In the choice of lamb one of the first objects of attention is the eye, which should be bright and full; if it be sunk and wrinkled the meat will be stale. The vein in the neck should be of a fine blue, and not green or yellow. If there be a faint disagreeable smell near the kidney, and the knuckle be very flexible, it is no longer fit for the table.

Pork.

A thin rind is a good indication in all pork; a thick tough one not easily impressed with the finger is a sign of age. If the flesh be clammy it is tainted. The lean of young pork will break on being pinched. Measly pork, which is very unwholesome, is easily distinguishable from sound pork, by the fat being full of kernels. London is supplied with the best pork from the dairy farms in Essex.

Hams are chosen by the shortness of the shank. To judge of their quality a sharp thin knife is stuck under the bone; if it come out clean and smell sweet the ham is unobjectionable; if it be daubed and have a fetid smell the meat will prove bad.

[303] Bacon should have a thin rind; the fat should be firm and of a red tinge, the lean tender and well coloured, adhering to the bone. If there be yellow streaks, it is either already rusty or very soon will be.

Poultry.

Barn-door fed fowls are preferable to those fatted in coops. Much experience and personal observation are requisite in forming a judgment of their freshness and goodness. It may be observed generally that any appearance of greenness about the rump is a sure sign of putrescency. Young poultry may be distinguished by the pellucid appearance and peculiar feel of the flesh, and by the flexibility of the breast bone: many poulterers, aware of the latter criterion, take care to break the breast-bone of every fowl they expose for sale. Young cocks have short spurs, but those of old ones may be scraped so as to deceive any but a very accurate observer. The bill and feet of a goose when young are yellow; they turn red as the bird grows old. To ascertain that a goose has been fresh killed, the legs and feet must be examined; they ought to be limber: if stiff, the bird is not fresh. The same observations apply to ducks. Of the [304] many varieties of wild ducks, those with red legs are held in highest estimation.

Game.

The animals which come under the description of game, seldom arrive in a bad state, since a little keeping improves their flavour. Partridges, when young, have yellowish legs and dark-coloured bills; blue legs and a white bill are signs of age. Hares, when old, have blunt and rugged claws; their bones are hard, and they are very difficult to case. The ears also are dry and tough, and the cleft between the lips wide and large, the contrary indications denote a hare to be young. A leveret is chiefly distinguished from a hare by a small bony protuberance on the fore-leg near the foot.

Fish.

Turbot, eels, flounders, carp, tench, pike, and sometimes soles, as also lobsters, oysters, crabs and other shell-fish are usually brought and delivered to the cook alive. Some of the latter species, however, may be kept so long alive, after being caught, that their flesh shall be almost wasted away. Cod, skate, maids, [305] and thornback, should be in a state fit to crimp, and are so when the flesh rises again on being pressed with the finger.[1] Salmon, haddock, whiting, and all other fish, whether of the sea, pond, or river, may be judged, as to freshness, by the red lively colour of the gills, the brightness of the eyes, the closeness and regular undisturbed position of the scales, and a plumpness of body almost amounting to stiffness. A dead eye, livid gills, and flabby condition of flesh are sure signs that the meat is stale. Soles, John Dories, mullets,

---

[1] Maids are young skates or thornback rays; fish were crimped by slashing their flesh – sometimes before they were dead – to make it contract.

gurnets, and other delicate fish that come to market gutted and packed by land carriage must be judged by the smell. The freshness of mackarel may be ascertained by the stiffness of the body and the prismatic brilliancy of its colours; that of herrings and sprats by the brightness of the scales.

The fish in season this month are sea-salmon, turbot, thornback, skate, soles, flounders, plaice, haddock, cod, whitings, eels, sprats, lobsters, crabs, crayfish, oysters, muscles [sic], cockles, Dutch herrings, and anchovies. There is also a small supply of mackarel in this and the preceding month.

The poultry and game are turkies, capons, fowls, pullets, geese, ducklings, wild ducks, widgeons, teal, plovers, woodcocks, snipes, larks, tame pigeons, hares, herns,[1] partridges, [306] pheasants, wild and tame rabbits, and grouse. Of fowls the game breed is most esteemed for flavour. The Poland breed is the largest. Dorking in Surrey, and Epping in Essex, are alike famed in the metropolis for good poultry. In the neighbourhood of Bethnal Green and Mile End, are several large establishments for fattening all kinds of domestic fowls, for the supply of Leadenhall market and the shipping in the port of London; these repositories have every convenience, such as large barns, enclosed paddocks, ponds, &c.; but, however well contrived and managed they may be, every person of taste will prefer a real barn-door fed fowl to those fed in them. The county of Norfolk has the reputation of breeding the finest turkies; they are in season from November to March, at which period they are succeeded by turkey-poults. The various birds of passage, such as wild-ducks, widgeons, teal, plovers, &c., which arrive here in the cold season, are to be found in most parts of England; but London is chiefly supplied from the fens of Lincolnshire and Cambridgeshire. There are said to be more than a hundred varieties of the duck tribe alone; those with red legs are accounted the best. The plover's eggs, seen in such abundance in the poultry shops, are generally picked up by shepherds and cottagers on the moors and [307] commons, where they have been dropped by the birds during their temporary sojourn to this country. They are considered a very great delicacy.

FEBRUARY.

The viands for this month differ little from those cited under the last; but with respect to the article game, it must be observed, that by act of parliament, none of any kind is permitted to appear on table after the 13th. The long

[1] An archaic form of *heron*.

fast of Lent, which usually commences in February, occasions an increased demand for fish of all kinds, and so abundantly various is the supply that this season set apart for self-denial and penitence is signalized rather by a change of Epicurean enjoyment. The standing dish for all fast days is salt-fish (commonly barrelled cod) with parsnips and egg sauce; but they who choose to mortify themselves more devoutly, do penance on a dinner of princely turbot plain boiled, or stewed with wine, gravy and capers, or perhaps chastise their appetites with a dish of soles, haddock, or skate. Poultry are by no means totally excluded from table, a capon, a duckling, or even a pidgeon-pye being regarded as merely innocent transitions from the legitimate diet, and some persons will at times be [308] tempted, after a struggle between the conscience and the stomach, to indulge the latter with a repast of roast beef, in direct offence against the ordinances of the church, an offence which is perhaps visited on the culprit in the shape of an indigestion. Codlings and herrings are now in season and continue until the end of May; peacocks, pea-hens, and guinea-fowls until July. The vegetables of February, besides that never-failing root, the potatoe, are coleworts, cabbages, savoys, cresses, lettuces, chards, beets, celery, endive, chervil, and also forced radishes, cucumbers, kidney-beans, and asparagus. Green geese and ducklings are fit for table this month, and continue to be admissible, the former until the end of May, the latter until that of April.

MARCH.

The continuance of Lent, generally through the whole of this month, confines us principally to a course of fish diet, interrupted, however, by two national festivals which are observed in the metropolis with the most cordial demonstrations of joy and merriment. The one is the first of March, St. David's Day, when all the Cambro-Britons in London assemble in large parties for the purpose [309] of dining together. The 17th of this month is equally dear to the sons of Erin, who celebrate the anniversary of their patron saint on a dinner somewhat better than lenten fare. We know not that any particular national dish is brought forward on these occasions, though Irish pork and Welsh mutton are mentioned with the same kind of distinction as English beef. The turbot, though in season all the year, is now in great request, and large quantities are brought by Dutch fishermen from the sandbanks on the coast of Holland, which are most congenial to the breed of this fine fish. The boats which bring them are provided with wells in which the fish are kept alive. The vast sums paid annually for turbot by the citizens of London afford a striking proof of their good taste and spirit in whatever concerns the glory of the table. Turbots are also brought occasionally from Scotland packed in ice. That delicate fish the whiting, is now in great perfection, and smelts during this and the two following months are in particular request. The best smelts are taken in the Thames: when perfectly fresh they are stiff and smell like a fresh cut cucumber. They are sold by tale, and vary in price from six to fifteen shillings a hundred. The usual mode of dressing is to [310] fry them and serve them up with melted butter, and a Seville orange or lemon.

The John Dory makes his first appearance this month, and notwithstanding the uncouthness of his physiognomy and the ugliness of his person, is a welcome guest at the most elegant tables until the end of June. This gracious reception he owes to his intrinsic merits, which more than atone for the disadvantages of his exterior, and are of so high an order that Quin the celebrated epicure bestowed on him the title of King of Fish.[1] The gurnet is in season for the same period, as also is the jack.

Leverets are fit for table from this month until about midsummer. Dovecote and wood-pigeons, together with a variety of wild fowl are in high request as well as wild and tame rabbits.

The approach of spring now begins to be marked by an increasing supply of vegetables for sallads. Early radishes form an agreeable accompaniment to the new cheeses now introduced, the most noted of which are the Bath and York, with those cream cheeses manufactured in the vicinity of the metropolis. Custard and tansy puddings, stewed eggs with spinach, and mock green peas formed of the tops of forced asparagus are among the lighter [311] dishes which characterize this season; and the strong winter soups give place to spring soups which are flavoured with a variety of esculent and aromatic herbs.

APRIL.

The festival of Easter which generally takes place toward the commencement of this month is the epoch at which grass-lamb and turbot are in particular demand. Green-geese and turkey-poults also come into notice. Pork in this month disappears from all polite tables, but roasting pigs are in request.

---

[1] See above, p. 161.

Holibut, in this and the two following months is in perfect condition; it comes in, as an acceptable variety at the close of Lent, along with carp, tench, and perch, which continue in season until the end of June.

The novelty which most distinguishes this month, however, is that royal fish the sturgeon, whose value has recently been enhanced by the discovery of a mode of dressing him which places him almost on a par with turtle in richness of flavour. His flesh partakes much of the nature of veal, and admits of being roasted as such. The weight of sturgeon varies from 50lb. to 400; the price of young ones from 3s. 6d. to 5s. per lb.

Mackarel is in season during this and the [312] two following months. The first supply is caught off Brighton, and brought to London in light vehicles hung on springs, and drawn by four horses at the same rate as the stage coaches. The fish are packed in wicker baskets called pots. The mackarel brought in boats are generally taken off Margate, and in such quantities, that shortly after the commencement of the season, the market is glutted with them, and they fall rapidly in price. Immense numbers are caught at Torbay, in Devonshire, where they are often sold two or three for a penny, and sometimes the glut is so great that they are thrown on the land as manure.

Mullets are in season only during this and the following month. Brighton soles are at this time in request, and are brought up by the same rapid conveyance which is used for early mackarel. In warm weather the precaution is taken of gutting them. Herrings at this season appear in abundance, and in full roe, on which account they are not so much esteemed by epicures, as at their second appearance, late in the autumn, when they have cast their spawn.

Although ham be as much in season at any other time, yet we may notice it here, as being the almost inseparable escort of most kinds of white meat, the prevailing ingredient [313] of sandwiches, and the most convenient article of occasional refection. The hams of Bayonne and Westphalia, are held in highest estimation; but those of Yorkshire, if well cured, scarcely yield to them in goodness and flavour. In boiling them it is desirable to throw in coarse fresh meat and vegetables, the juices of which, insinuating themselves between the fibres, dislodge the salt and render the meat rich and tender.

This is the last of the spring months in which the various classes of wild fowl, except wild pigeons, are admissible at table.

MAY.

Grass-lamb continues through this month a prevailing dish, being now in high condition, and deriving an additional relish from the profusion of sallad herbs that enliven the table by their refreshing verdure, and form a salubrious article of diet in the spring and summer months.

Asparagus, if favoured by a genial alternation of warm weather and light showers, may now be expected in abundance. The districts on which the metropolis chiefly depends for its supply are Battersea and Gravesend. From the latter place it arrives by the tilt-boats, every tide during the season, at Billings- [314] gate, where in Dark-House Lane there is a kind of market for it.

Dovecote-pigeons are in great request, during the continuance of asparagus, which is usually served up with them. Those destined for table are always taken before they can fly, and must be cooked soon after they are killed.

The season for river-salmon holds from this month to September. It is held in higher estimation than sea-salmon, from which it is distinguished by the paler and more delicate hue of the flesh. The best which comes to the metropolis is caught in the Thames and the Severn.

The 13th of May is the period at which the oyster season terminates.

Toward the latter end of this month, if the weather have been genial, green peas begin to make their appearance, and are welcomed with more general satisfaction than any vegetable which comes to table. Early potatoes constitute at this epoch another favourite novelty, but they are far less nutritive now, than at a more advanced period of the season when they begin to be farinaceous.

In the course of this month that portly vegetable the cauliflower attains its full maturity.

Poultry of almost every kind are now in [315] high and plump condition. The turkey however yields his place at table to the turkey-poult, who may be said to retain it until the end of August, when, being no longer a minor, he succeeds to the title of turkey. The green goose about this time casts his first feathers, and becomes a goose; the duckling after the same change of uniform ranks as a duck.

The table is supplied during this month with a great variety of sea and fresh-water fish. Of the latter description the most considerable in point of magnitude is the jack, a very formidable free-booter in ponds and rivers, who is generally admissible at table from March to July. He makes a striking figure there, but his flesh is coarse, and if it have any merit, it is that of calling forth the talents of the cook in the preparation of a seasoning that may relish with it. Carp, tench, and perch, are in season until the end of June.

As butter is an indispensable ingredient in almost all culinary preparations, we may remark that at this time it is peculiarly fragrant and balsamic, being perceptibly impregnated with the juices of fresh herbage and flowery pasture.

JUNE.

That far-famed West Indian luxury, turtle, [316] generally arrives about the latter end of May, or the beginning of June, though from the uncertainties of a sea-voyage no exact period for its first appearance can be fixed. In the year 1814 it was so unusually late, that at the magnificent banquet given in Guild-hall to the Emperor of Russia and the King of Prussia, on the 18th of June, there was no turtle to be had.[1] A supply was announced at Portsmouth on the very day, but as this civic dignitary, like other great personages, requires much time to dress, he could not possibly be present on the occasion. Great, indeed, must have been the disappointment of the corporation: not an alder-man among them who might not have apostrophized with as much fervor as Macbeth did on the absence of Banquo at supper, and with much more sincerity,

> Here had we now our table's honour roof'd
> Were the grac'd person of our turtle present.[2]

The disappointment however would be in some measure allayed by the satis-factory assurance that this long-expected guest, having braved the perils of the sea, would speedily afford a pretext for another feast, for the express purpose of welcoming him, and of presenting him in all his glory to the illus-trious strangers.

The great emporium for live turtle, as we [317] have elsewhere observed, is at Mr. Bleaden's, the King's Head, in the Poultry, from whence supplies are sent all over London.[3] The weight of a turtle varies from 30 to 500, or 600lb.; and the price from 2s. 6d. to 5s. per lb. The cooking is generally performed by a professed artist, whose fee is from one to two guineas. Some epicures of note have been known to prefer it cut into steaks and broiled, to be eaten with melted butter, Cayenne pepper, and the juice of a Seville orange, and say that the flesh thus simply dressed retains more of its true flavour than when made into callipash and callipee.

[1] The banquet took place on 18 June 1814, during the visit by the Allied Sovereigns to celebrate the abdication of Napoleon.
[2] An adaptation of Macbeth's speech in Act 3, Scene 4: 'Here had we now our coun-try's honour roof'd,/Were the grac'd person of our Banquo present'.
[3] See above, p. 16.

Calf's head, which is susceptible of as many culinary variations as the head of an ingenious cook can devise, forms the basis of a soup called mock turtle, and, in cases of emergency, may serve as an augmentative ingredient to real turtle soup.

Buck venison is now introduced at polite tables, and continues in season until the end of September. The price of a prime haunch is from three to five guineas. The next best joint is the neck, which is proportionably lower in value. The shoulders, breasts, and scrags, generally fetch from ten to fourteen pence a pound. Forest venison is the smallest and finest flavoured. In the choice of this rich meat the principal criterion [318] is the fat, which in a young buck will be thick, bright, and clear, the cleft smooth and close: a very wide tough cleft denotes age.

Salmon, sturgeon, lobsters, turbot, haddock, eels, and whitings, as well as crabs, prawns, and shrimps, continue generally through the summer season. After the close of this month the john dory and the gurnet are no longer admissible. In addition to eels, carp, tench, and perch, that prince of freshwater fish the trout is now produced, and forms a very favourite repast during the remainder of the summer.

JULY.

The heats of the season now impose the necessity of occasionally substituting a light vegetable diet for the more solid gratification of animal food, and nature has provided ample and various means of effecting this change without imposing any grievous penance on the organs of taste. Cauliflowers, artichokes, green-peas, French-beans, Windsor[1] and other garden beans, frequently form a conspicuous part of the family dinner; to which butcher's meat, in moderate quantities, may be said to serve merely as an auxiliary stimulant. Ham, bacon, and tongues, as well as ducks and geese, are the most seasonable viands for this [319] purpose, as their high flavour counteracts agreeably the insipidity of vegetables, and provokes the appetite to a greater consumption of them. On festive occasions venison and turtle retain their pre-eminent station at the tables of the opulent, where also the fawn, received now and then as a present forms an elegant dish, when roasted whole and served up with rich gravy. Veal, having now been fed on milk, in its richest state, is peculiarly fine and well flavoured; but care should be taken that it be delivered fresh to the cook, as it is more liable to suffer from the heat of the

[1] Broad beans.

weather and from flies than any other kind of meat. Ragouts of sweetbreads, oxpalates, lambs' bits, fat livers, and cocks'-combs, are among the light dishes introduced at superior tables; where also various preparations of curry afford a delectable repast to those who have acquired a taste for this Indian diet.

Quails, during this and the following months, are brought in considerable numbers from France in low wicker cages, and on account of their rarity in this country fetch a high price. The ortolan, a delicate little bird of the quail tribe, is imported from Germany either alive, or in a potted state, and being a great rarity is still dearer than the quail.

To those epicures whose taste is not exclusively formed for the more solid enjoyments [320] of the table, a plenteous and varied dessert presents itself at this season; consisting of pines, melons, peaches, cherries, grapes, currants, gooseberries and raspberries, as well as early apples and pears. Fruit is certainly most salubrious in hot weather; but, if the opinion be well founded that it does most good when taken before dinner, the dessert ought to take place of that spurious meal called the lunch, which, being usually made of animal food, too often banishes the appetite irrecoverably for the day.

AUGUST.

This month is remarkable for numerous migrations from the metropolis in all directions. The great and opulent either visit their estates, or make excursions to the fashionable watering places, or perform a tour on the continent. The lawyers are either on the circuit, or enjoying the long vacation; and the citizens, among whom may be classed the commercial and trading part of the community, relax their minds and renovate their health by a trip to Margate, Ramsgate, or the more distant bathing places on the Welsh and Yorkshire coasts. London, in short, after the Regent's birthday, on the 12th, becomes so *thin* that it [321] looks like the ghost of its former self, and remains in this state of exhaustion until the close of autumn; when its recovery begins to be manifested in the ruddy complexions of its sons, and the renovated bloom of its daughters, returning from a course of sea-bathing, fish diet, and rural air. Among the many maladies, some real and some imaginary, which furnish a pretext for these marine excursions, the only one that concerns us is loss of appetite; for which the sea air is a prompt and efficient remedy. Many, who on their setting out from London after a luxurious season would turn away in languid apathy from turtle and venison, have been known, after a morning's ramble on the coast, not only to relish a fried sole, or a broiled whiting, but to call loudly for beef-steaks or rashers of bacon. Happy change in the tone of the digestive organs; amply compensating all the expense, bustle, and inconvenience of travelling to attain it! Small need have we to lament the paucity of alimentary novelties in the month of August, when we recognize it to be the season for procuring a sauce of higher value than all that have been in fashion from the days of Apicius to those of Peter Harvey; a sauce alike suited to fish, flesh, and fowl, and without which the most costly and scientific preparations in cooking fail of their effect. [322] Of this sauce, proverbially the best, and vulgarly called hunger, a stock may be obtained at most parts of the coast, to serve with proper management and œconomy the whole year. The mountains of Wales, the lakes of Westmorland, and the highlands of Scotland, are also noted for producing it.

This may be considered the first of the sporting months. According to the terms fixed by the game laws, the shooting of red-game, or grouse, commences on the 12th, and of black-game, or heathfowl, on the 20th, and both continue until the 20th of December. As these birds chiefly frequent the moorlands in Scotland and the north of England, they are seldom received as presents in London until the cold weather admits of their being sent so great a distance; for though some time must elapse between the killing and the cooking of them, yet there is a point of mortification, which, if they are suffered in the least to exceed, they are no longer fit for the table.

The oyster season commences on the 5th of August, when a large supply from Feversham, Whitstable, and other nurseries in Kent arrives, and is eagerly bought up by the expectant public. This first supply being quite fresh is palatable, but for some weeks afterwards the fish are in poor condition: those who would eat oysters in perfection must wait [323] the approach of cold weather. It is a remarkable fact, that these and all shellfish are best at the full of the moon.

River-salmon forms a leading dish during this month: the salmon-trout is also considered as a seasonable delicacy. Eels, roach, dace, and trout, are the fresh-water fish principally in request. London is mostly supplied with the latter, from the Wandle and other mill-streams and rivulets, in Surrey and Sussex. Turbot, whiting, skate, soles, and flounders, as well as lobsters, crabs, and crayfish, are still supplied in great plenty.

Leverets are now introduced at table, and roasting pigs obtain a distinguished place there occasionally. As French-beans attain to full maturity during this and the following month, there is no very apparent diminution in the consumption of bacon and hams. Fruits for the dessert are now produced in great abundance and variety.

SEPTEMBER.

The first of this month is the period fixed by law for the commencement of partridge shooting; but if there be a late harvest, it is commendable in sportsmen not to take the field so early, since they will have ample time [324] before the first of February to signalize themselves in this noble diversion.

Although the season for carp and tench expires in June, yet the dragging of the ponds, which usually takes place in this month, affords a short supply of those fish.

Wild rabbits are now brought in great numbers from the warrens in Essex, and appear at table under various modes of cookery, but most commonly boiled and smothered in onions.

Doe venison is in season from this month until January.

Michaelmas is the high season for geese. The low fenny lands in the counties of Lincoln and Cambridge produce them in greatest quantities, but as the geese brought from thence have sometimes a fishy taste, a preference is always given to those bred on inland greens and commons, with the run of a farmyard and the indispensable convenience of water. The flavour of roasted goose is much improved by pouring into the body, immediately before it is sent up, a savoury sauce composed of a table-spoonful of made mustard, half a tea-spoonful of Cayenne pepper, and three spoonfuls of port wine, made hot.

The fruits in season are apples, pears, peaches, nectarines, plums, native grapes, filberts, and hazel nuts, to which are sometimes added ripe figs of English growth.

[325] The dulness of this month in town is somewhat enlivened by the opening of the summer theatres, and by a series of civic dinners, which are given on the occasion of swearing in the sheriffs and electing a Lord Mayor. Bartholomew Fair, which commences on the 3d, and continues three days, is a kind of carnival for the populace, distinguished by every gradation of broad humour and boisterous merriment. Smithfield, where it is held, exhibits a motley assemblage of raree-shows, travelling menageries, moveable theatres, conjurors, tumblers, merry andrews, toymen, pye-men, and gingerbread merchants; every avenue to this centre of attraction is crowded to excess, and the currents of people moving in opposite directions within it frequently form a vortex of uproar, confusion, and noise. In addition to the piles of fruit, sweetmeats, and pastry, which abound on such occasions, this fair has to boast the singular luxury of a hot supper in the open air, which is almost exclusively served up to one class of the community – the chimney-sweepers.

It consists of fried, or rather frizzled sausages, which these knights of the brush eat hot from the trays on which they are cooked, without cloth, plate, knife, or fork. A long alley of these trays with charcoal fires under them, is observed in one part of the fair, and at night, [326] when it is most frequented, presents a coup d'œil, to which no parallel can be found on the *face* (at least) of the globe.[1]

OCTOBER.

The temperate weather that prevails this month (there are always fourteen fine days in it) is peculiarly favourable to the brewing of malt liquor, being neither too hot nor too cold. For ales, however, which require long keeping, the month of March is by some deemed the preferable season.

At this time the range of alimentary productions begins to extend itself; chickens, pullets, capons, and turkies, are in high order for the spit. Beef and mutton improve in quality, while hares, pheasants, wild ducks, widgeons, teal, plovers, woodcocks, snipes, and larks, are added to the former list of viands, and continue in season for the remainder of the year. In the department of fish it is observable that cod, which has been absent from table since April, now re-appears for the winter season: herrings also, having cast their spawn, are held by some connoisseurs in higher estimation than in the spring of the year: and oysters, particularly the native Milton and Colchester, are full fed and in high flavour. [327] Of esculent vegetables there is no sensible diminution; peas and beans indeed have disappeared, but potatoes having now attained their proper growth are become mealy; and carrots, with which London is chiefly supplied from Sandwich, in Kent, now arrive in large quantities. The dessert of this period chiefly consists of peaches, grapes, apples, pears, and plums.

NOVEMBER.

Though this be proverbially the gloomiest month in the year, it is not to the lovers of good eating the most cheerless, being conspicuously rich in beef, mutton, veal, pork, and house-lamb, as well as in fish, poultry, game,

---

[1] Originally a cloth fair or market, held since the c12 near the priory of St Batholomew, Smithfield, by the mid-c17 Bartholomew Fair was more famous for the entertainment provided by conjurors, clowns, fire-eaters, and rope-dancers, and notorious as well because of the hordes of rowdy visitors and the opportunities for crime. The last fair was held in 1855.

and wild fowl. Thus, by an admirable provision in the economy of nature, at the season when the human appetite is increasing in strength, the means of gratifying it are multiplied. Among the infinite variety of dishes formed, or compounded of these elements, it is difficult to distinguish any one which peculiarly belongs to this division of the year; the difference of taste or choice being most observable at the period when its objects are most diversified. We may remark that pork during the winter months is in universal re- [328] quest, not only as being of itself an excellent plain dish either roast or boiled, but as affording the chief ingredient in the composition of sausages, &c. When boiled its usual escort is peas-pudding. In the important department of soups, hare-soup may be noticed as the most luxurious, since, in the opinion of a learned epicure, "no gravy can be extracted from the flesh of any animal equal in richness to what the hare affords."[1]

There is now a great consumption of oysters, as well in their simple state as scolloped, stewed, roasted, or served up in sauce for fowls, beef-steaks, &c.

The season for sprats commences on Lord Mayor's day, the 9th of November, which is more eminently distinguished by the magnificent and sumptuous dinner given in Guildhall, in honour of the chief magistrate of the city of London, who now enters upon his office for the year. At this dinner the choicest dishes in season, and every delicacy which wealth can procure, or culinary skill devise, are produced in a style worthy the great occasion. The different city companies are feasted at their respective halls; and those companies which have no halls dine severally at the first rate taverns, in a style equally sumptuous. Some idea of the grandeur of this festival may be formed, when it is understood [329] that the aggregate expenses of all the dinners amount to upwards of twelve thousand pounds.

On the 30th, St. Andrew's day, the Caledonians, resident in London, assemble in various parties to hold a national anniversary, or in other words, to dine together. Among the good things served up on this occasion, it is not to be supposed that haggis and sheep's-head broth will be forgotten, as these native dishes, in addition to their intrinsic merits, have the effect of reviving early associations, and of cherishing the *amor patriæ.*

[1] The quotation is from Alexander Hunter, *Culina famulatrix medicinæ* (1804), p. 90.

DECEMBER.

The fish in season this month are turbot, skate, soles, mackarel, (a small supply) haddock, cod, whiting, holibut, lampreys, (chiefly for potting) lobsters, oysters, and other shellfish.

Of game, wild fowl, and poultry, may be mentioned hares, partridges, pheasants, wild and tame rabbits, grouse, wild-ducks, widgeons, teal, plovers, woodcocks, snipes, larks, turkies, capons, pullets, chickens, geese, and ducks.

The various kinds of butchers' meat are to be had in great perfection. Toward the 20th of the month there is an annual prize shew of [330] cattle in Barbican, than which no sight can surely be more interesting to the epicure, except that of a good dinner, and such a one is generally given as a suitable sequel to the exhibition.

As Christmas advances the arrivals from the country of poultry and game become more frequent and abundant. At this season also the metropolis is supplied with large quantities of brawn, chiefly from Canterbury and Oxfordshire. Brawn is manufactured from the flesh of large boars, which are suffered to live in a half wild state, and when put up to fatten, are strapped and belted tight round the principal parts of the carcase, in order that their flesh may become dense and brawny. This article comes to market in rolls about two feet long, and ten inches in diameter, packed in wicker baskets. It is commonly vended by the fishmongers, who at this season generally expose, along with it, a boar's head, with a lemon stuck between the tusks.

The close of the year, being Christmas week, is a season of festivity among all ranks of people. The middling classes, who are for the most part immersed in the cares of business throughout the year, welcome and celebrate it as a period of holiday enjoyment; while the rich, who "fare sumptuously every day," comply with the general custom, by [331] adding the established national dishes to their bills of fare; and distribute to their dependants, their tenantry, and the poor around them, a portion wherewithal to eat, drink, and be merry. At their tables the refinements of foreign invention are for once superseded by the simpler products of old English cookery: roast beef and plum-pudding, turkies and chines, ham and fowls, capons and sausages, saddles and haunches of mutton, with a profusion of custards and pyes, among them that characteristic luxury the mince-pye, present a range of viands, which, though all of the solid kind, are rendered easy of digestion by proportionate draughts of ripe port and mellow October,[1] and perhaps more so by the mirth and laughter

---

[1] A strong ale typically brewed in October.

which the gambols of the season excite, and which in no unimportant degree aid the stomach and intestines in the discharge of their functions.

As Christmas completes this alimentary circle of the year, we here take leave of our readers with the usual compliments of that season, wishing them also most earnestly those inestimable blessings, a good appetite and a plentiful choice of good fare. The latter part of our wish, we trust, the Directory, which precedes this Calendar, will help to realize.

FINIS.

GLOSSARY

Drinks

Burton ale: not necessarily brewed in Burton, this was a 'strong ale, dark in colour, made with a proportion of highly dried or roasted malts' (*OED*).

Capillaire: an infusion of maidenhair fern sweetened with sugar or honey, and often flavoured with orange-flower water; a kind of mock capillaire was made with the orange-flower water alone.

Chocolate ('Spanish chocolate'): in 1815 almost exclusively a drink, made from mixing chocolate sold as wafers or tablets with hot water or sometimes milk. Chocolate reached England in the 1650s, and by the end of the eighteenth century the manufacturing process was semi-industrialized, but true 'Spanish' chocolate was hand-ground by specialists (see Coe and Coe 1996).

Deady's Full Proof: a gin, probably sweet, produced by Deady's distillery. Signs advertising both Deady's Cordial and Old Tom (see below) appear in George Cruikshank's 1829 caricature 'The Gin Shop', illustrated in Brandwood 2004, p. 33.

Marasquin: maraschino, a strong sweet liqueur based on Marasca cherries.

Meux's entire: a porter from the Meux brewery, entire being an early name for porter. In an account of a 'dreadful accident' of 1814, in which one of the giant vats in Meux's brewery near Tottenham Court Road burst, causing eight deaths, entire was defined as 'beer that was 10 months brewed' (*Examiner*, 23 October).

Noyau: an almond-flavoured liqueur made from peach or apricot kernels.

October: a strong ale typically brewed in October.

Old Tom: a kind of sweetened gin (cf. Deady's Full Proof).

Orgeat: a drink made by mixing water or barley water with syrup of orgeat, prepared from almonds, sugar, and rose water or orange-flower water.

Porter: 'a dark-brown or black bitter beer, brewed from malt partly charred or browned by drying at a high temperature' (*OED*).

Saloop: originally a drink consisting of an infusion of powdered salep, 'made from the dried tubers of various orchidaceous plants, chiefly those of the genus *Orchis*' (*OED*), mixed with sugar and water or milk. By 1815 saloop was more commonly made from sassafras.

Spruce beer: 'a fermented beverage made with an extract from the leaves and branches of the spruce fir' (*OED*), mixed with treacle or sugar. According to the *Dictionary of Traded Goods* it was a 'medicinal drink believed to have antiscorbutic properties and to have an effect on the kidneys'.

Stout: a dark beer, with the term usually referring to the strongest – either in terms of flavour or alcohol content – of the porters.

Syllabub: a drink or dish containing liquor (usually wine or brandy) and milk or cream, flavoured with sugar and spices.

Windsor ale: a highly-esteemed ale from the Windsor brewery of Rams-bottom and Baverstock (later Nevile Reid).

Foodstuffs and Prepared Dishes

Alamode beef: see above, p. xlviii.

Bouilli: boiled or stewed meat, especially beef.

Cachou à la rose (*à l'orange, à la violette*): a lozenge-shaped sweetmeat.

Callipash, callipee (calipash, calipee): parts of a turtle, the calipash being the meat adjacent to the upper shell, and the calipee the meat adjacent to the plastron, the bony plate that forms the underside of a turtle's shell.

Camp sauce: a prepared sauce, claimed by one Mr Skill, an Italian ware-houseman at no. 15 Strand, as his invention. An advertisement in the *Morning Chronicle* (14 September 1791) refers to the sauce as 'Skill's Newly Invented Camp Sauce, or Essence of Beef, for enriching Game, Poultry, and all kinds of Stews, Hashes, and Ragouts – gives a peculiar flavour to Beef-steaks, Chops, and Cutlets; is an article very convenient for the Side-board and Kitchen; and is of indispensible utility to Officers of the Navy and Army, Captains of Ships, and Families in general'.

Cavice sauce: a prepared sauce, possibly related to caveach, a West Indian form of spiced and pickled mackerel (see *OED*). Recipes calling for cavice sauce sometimes give substitutions of anchovy sauce or Harvey's sauce.

Chapsigre (also known as Schabzieger or sapsago): a hard, green cheese from Switzerland, flavoured with blue fenugreek.

Cheesecakes: tarts filled with sweetened custard or soft cheese, which was often flavoured with almonds or citrus.

Chine: a joint (such as a saddle of mutton) that consists of all or part of an animal's backbone, together with the adjoining flesh.

Collared beef: a thin piece of steak wrapped in cheesecloth and boiled for several hours in a spiced broth.

Coratch: another highly flavoured prepared sauce. Skill's advertisement of 1791 (see camp sauce, above) recommends it for use on steaks, chops, and cutlets.

Curry powder: the earliest English recipe to 'make a Currey the India way' appeared in Hannah Glasse's 1747 *Art of Cookery*, and by 1776 ready-made curry powder was being advertised in London newspapers (*Gazetteer and New Daily Advertiser*, 18 December).

Esculent vegetables: those suitable for eating.

Green geese: young geese, usually killed when less than four months old.

Hanoverian sauce: an 1866 recipe for this sauce, which especially recommends it as an accompaniment to wild duck, includes sugar, lemon, port, and the zest of a lemon or Seville orange (*Dainty Dishes: Receipts Collected by Lady Harriett St Clair*, p. 22).

Harvey's sauce: a bottled sauce introduced in the late eighteenth century, which remained popular throughout the nineteenth and was still available in the early years of the twenty-first. The sauce was the invention of Peter Harvey, landlord of the Black Dog at East Bedfont, near Staines, who is said to have given the recipe as a present to his sister Elizabeth in 1776, on her marriage to the London grocer John Lazenby. This much-imitated condiment, by 1900 also known as Lazenby's sauce (advertisement, *Morning Post*, 16 October), included among its ingredients anchovies, mushroom or walnut ketchup, soy, and vinegar.

Jack: a young pike.

Ketchup: various forms of ketchup were available in British shops by the 1740s, and the three types named in the *Almanack* – walnut, mushroom, and oyster – were among the most popular. For an exhaustive account of the condiment and typical recipes, see Smith 1996.

Mock turtle soup: the principal ingredient of the soup was a calf's head, which when stewed had something of the texture and flavour of turtle meat. Recipes for artificial or imitation mock turtle soup replaced the head with calf's feet and cow heels.

Olla, olio: a stew of meat and vegetables (from the Spanish *olla*, or pot).

Papillotes avec devises: small candies wrapped in papers containing jokes, sentiments, or rebuses.

Pâte de guimauve: marshmallow confections.

Pine: pineapple.

Portable soup (also known as pocket soup, soup squares, and veal glue): the ancestor of today's bouillon cube, portable soup was made by thoroughly degreasing a meat broth and reducing it to a gluey consistency; the jelly-like result was then cut into squares and further dried, and could be reconstituted by the addition of boiling water. Mid-eighteenth-century cook books frequently included recipes for homemade squares, and a commercial 'portable gravy soup' was advertised as early as 1747 (*London Evening Post*, 19 September).

Pudding: often used here in the sense of a stuffed entrail, or sausage, rather than a sweet.

Quin's sauce: a sauce for fish, probably named after the actor and epicure James Quin (see above, p. 161). A recipe of 1817 includes anchovies, walnut liquor, garlic, shallots, and spices (William Kitchiner, *Apicius Redivivus; or, The Cook's Oracle*, sauce no. 424).

Sauce royal[e]: in 1788 the Italian warehouseman John Burgess advertised his 'new-invented sauce royal', claiming that it was suitable for all kinds of fish and would 'keep years in any climate' (the *World*, 19 April)

Whitebait: see above, p. xlix.

Zoobditty mutch (much, match): another prepared sauce for fish. The earliest advertisement that I have found for it describes zoobditty mutch as 'a Curious East India Fish Sauce [i.e. a sauce for fish], which for its peculiar rich Flavour exceeds every thing of the kind hitherto made use of' (*Public Advertiser*, 10 May 1776). The ingredients remain a mystery.

Other terms

Abbess: a bawd or procuress.

Baiting refreshments: 'to bait' was to stop for food or rest during a trip.

Body snatcher: a contemptuous slang term for a bailiff employed in making arrests.

Britannia metal: a pewter-like alloy of tin, antimony, and copper, resembling silver in appearance.

Court of conservancy: until 1857 a court of conservancy was held eight times a year before the Lord Mayor to investigate infringements of the laws governing the preservation of the Thames and its fish.

Cyprian: a prostitute.

Gentlemen of the long robe: lawyers.

Hummums: see above, p. xli.

Knights of the sock and buskin: actors.

Lion: a name used for a hare, to evade the game laws (see above, p. l).

Long: the 1811 *Lexicon Balatronicum* defines 'long one' as another term for a hare, used by poachers.

Nun: a prostitute.

Ordinary: a fixed-price meal, commonly offered only at a specified time.

Owl: a poacher's term for a partridge (cf. lion).

Pil. hydrag.: a shortened form of *pilulæ hydrargyri chloridi compositæ*, a preparation of mercury often used in the treatment of venereal diseases, and sometimes called Plummer's pills.

Red-tail knight: another slang term for a bailiff.

Shambles: used here to mean a stall or counter where meat is sold, rather than a slaughterhouse.

Short: another poacher's term, of uncertain meaning.

Trap-ball: a game in which a ball, placed on one end of a wooden box, or trap, is propelled into the air by a batsman striking the other end of the trap, and then batted toward a goal.

SURVIVORS

The following taverns, public houses, and eating houses listed in the *Epicure's Almanack* remain in business today in essentially the same premises described in 1815; see above, p. ix.

Central London
>The Seven Stars, no. 53 Carey Street: p. 150
>The Bell (now the Old Bell), no. 96 Fleet Street: p. 74
>The Cheshire Cheese (Ye Olde Cheshire Cheese), Wine Office Court, no. 145 Fleet Street: p. 72
>The George and Vulture, George Yard: p. 28
>Simpson's, Ball Court: p. 28
>The Cock and Woolpack, no. 6 Finch Lane: p. 23

Outer London
>The George, no. 77 Borough High Street, Southwark: p. 184
>The George, no. 32 King Street, Twickenham: p. 200
>The Green Man, Putney Heath: p. 203
>The King's Arms, Hampton Court: p. 201
>The Town of Ramsgate, no. 62 Wapping High Street: p. 57
>The Spaniards, Hampstead Heath: p. 224
>The Windmill, Clapham Common: p. 206
>The Hand and Flower, no. 1 Hammersmith Road: p. 193
>The George (now the George and Devonshire), no. 8 Burlington Lane, Chiswick: p. 194

WORKS CITED

In citing works in the notes, short titles have generally been used. Works mentioned frequently have been identified by the following abbreviations:

BoE	*Buildings of England*
DNB	*Dictionary of National Biography*
ODNB	*Oxford Dictionary of National Biography Online*
OEC	Westminster City Archives, *One on Every Corner*
OED	*Oxford English Dictionary Online*
ONL	Thornbury and Walford, *Old and New London*
SL	*Survey of London*
VCH	*Victoria County History of England*

1. Maps

1541   Plan of Southwark, *c*.1541, showing streets and many named buildings (National Archives, MPC 1/64). Reproduced in *SL* 22, plate 8.

1560s   The 'Agas' map, a woodcut map of central London, produced probably between 1561 and 1570 and widely misattributed to the Elizabethan surveyor Ralph Agas (1545-1621). Reproduced as *The A to Z of Elizabethan London*, compiled by Adrian Prockter and Robert Taylor, with introductory notes by John Fisher (Lympne Castle, 1979); also available online at mapco.net/agas/agas.htm

1676   John Ogilby and William Morgan, *A Large and Accurate Map of the City of London*. Reproduced as *The A to Z of Restoration London*, with introductory notes by Ralph Hyde and an index compiled by John Fisher and Roger Cline (Lympne Castle, 1992).

1746   John Rocque, *An Exact Survey of the Citys of London, Westminster, ye Borough of Southwark and the Country near Ten Miles Round*.

1746   John Rocque, *A Plan of the Cities of London and Westminster and Borough of Southwark*. Reproduced as *The A to Z of Georgian London*, with introductory notes by Ralph Hyde (Lympne Castle, 1981); available online at www.motco.com/map/81002/

1786   John Cary, *Cary's Actual Survey of the Country Fifteen Miles round London*. Two versions are available online: www.motco.com/map/81001/ and www.oldlondonmaps.com/cary/carymain.html

1799   Richard Horwood, *Plan of the Cities of London and Westminster, the Borough of Southwark, and Parts Adjoining*. First edition, published in thirty-two sheets over the years 1792-99. Reproduced, with introduction by James Howgego, by the London Topographical Society in 1967 (Publication no. 106); available online at www.motco.com/map/81005/ and www.oldlondonmaps.com/horwoodpages/horwoodmain.html

1813   Richard Horwood, *Plan of the Cities of London and Westminster, the Borough of Southwark, and Parts Adjoining*. Third edition, completed by William Faden; like the second edition of 1807 this contains eight additional sheets, extending the area covered eastward to the new docks. Reproduced as *The A to Z of Regency London*, with introduction by Paul Laxton and index compiled by Joseph Wisdom (Lympne Castle, 1985).

1818   William Faden, *A Plan of London and Westminster, with the Borough of Southwark*. First published in 1818 as an index to the earlier Horwood *Plan* and known in many later editions, 1819-46. Copies of the 1823, 1831, and 1836 maps from the British Library's Crace Collection of Maps of London may be viewed at www.bl.uk/onlinegallery/onlineex/crace/

1824   George Frederick Cruchley, *Cruchley's Environs of London Extending Thirty Miles from the Metropolis*.

1827   John Greenwood and Christopher Greenwood, *Map of London … from an Actual Survey Made in the Years 1824, 1825, and 1826*. There are two versions available online: users.bathspa.ac.uk/greenwood/index.html and www.oldlondonmaps.com/greenwoodpages/greenwoodmain.html

1888   George W. Bacon, *New Large-Scale Ordnance Atlas of London & Suburbs*. Reproduced as *The A to Z of Victorian London*, with introductory notes by Ralph Hyde (Lympne Castle, 1987)

1945   *The London County Council Bomb Damage Maps, 1939-1945*, ed. Ann Saunders (2005). London Topographical Society Publications, 164.

II. Manuscripts

De Castro, John Paul. Manuscript dictionary of London taverns since the Restoration, compiled *c*.1930. 4 vols. London Metropolitan Archives, Guildhall MS 3110.

Foster, D. 'Inns, Taverns, Alehouses, Coffee Houses, etc. in and around London', an 82-volume scrapbook compiled *c*.1900. City of Westminster Archives Centre.

Longman (publishers). Records of the Longman Group. University of Reading Special Collections, MS 1393.

Marylebone rate books. City of Westminster Archives Centre.

Rylance, Ralph. Letters to John Dovaston, Shropshire Archives (Shrewsbury), MS 1662, and Princeton University Library, MS C0764; letters to William Roscoe, Liverpool Record Office, MS 920 ROS.

III. Printed Works

Allen, Brigid. 1992. 'Foreign Flavours: The Italian Warehouse and its Near Relations in England, 1720-1880', in Harlan Walker, ed., *Spicing up the Palate: Studies of Flavourings, Ancient and Modern*, pp. 23-27 (Proceedings of the Oxford Symposium on Food and Cookery, 1992).

Altick, Richard D. 1978. *The Shows of London: A Panoramic History of Exhibitions, 1600-1862*. Cambridge, Mass.

Anon. 1851. *London at Table; or How, When, and Where to Dine*. A new edition, retitled *London at Dinner; or Where to Dine*, appeared in 1858 (facsimile reprint, 1969).

Anon. 1968. *Historic and New Inns of Interest: City of London, Wining and Dining*. Halifax, Yorks.

Berry, Herbert. 2006. 'The Bell Savage Inn and Playhouse in London'. *Medieval and Renaissance Drama in England*, 19:121-43.

Boast, Mary. 2000. *The Story of Camberwell* . Rev. ed.

Boswell, James. 1934-50. *Boswell's Life of Johnson*, ed. George Birkbeck Hill and revised by L. F. Powell. 6 vols. Oxford.

Bowers, Robert Woodger. 1905. *Sketches of Southwark Old and New*.

Boyle, Patrick. 1799. *Boyle's View of London and its Environs*.

Brandwood, Geoffrey K., Andrew Davison, and Michael Slaughter. 2004. *Licensed to Sell: The History and Heritage of the Public House*. Swindon.

Brandwood, Geoff, and Jane Jephcote. 2008. *London Heritage Pubs: An Inside Story*. St Albans.

The Buildings of England:
    Bridget Cherry and Nikolaus Pevsner. *London: South.* 1983.
    Bridget Cherry and Nikolaus Pevsner. *London: North-West.* 1991.
    Simon Bradley and Nikolaus Pevsner. *The City of London.* 1997.
    Bridget Cherry and Nikolaus Pevsner. *London: North.* 1998.
    Simon Bradley and Nikolaus Pevsner. *Westminster.* 2003.
    Bridget Cherry, Charles O'Brien, and Nikolaus Pevsner. *London: East.* 2005.
Burke, Thomas. 1937. *Dinner Is Served! Or, Eating Round the World in London.*
Burn, Jacob Henry. 1853. *A Descriptive Catalogue of London Traders, Tavern, and Coffee-House Tokens ... in the Corporation Library, Guildhall.*
Burnett, John. 1966. *Plenty and Want: A Social History of Diet in England from 1815 to the Present Day.*
Burnett, John. 1969. *A History of the Cost of Living.*
Burnett, John. 1999. *Liquid Pleasures: A Social History of Drinks in Modern Britain.*
Burton, J. G. 1819. *The Critics' Budget; or, A Peep into the Amateur Green Room.*
Callow, Edward. 1899. *Old London Taverns: Historical, Descriptive and Reminiscent; with Some Account of the Coffee Houses, Clubs, etc.*
Chambers, E. K. 1923. *The Elizabethan Stage.* 4 vols. Oxford.
Chancellor, E. Beresford. 1912. *The Annals of Fleet Street: Its Traditions and Associations.*
Charlton, Ferrier H. 1987. *The Swan with Two Necks: Linklaters & Paines.*
Clinch, George. 1890. *Marylebone and St. Pancras.*
Cloake, John. 1999. 'Public Houses in Richmond, 1790-1880'. *Richmond History,* 20:9-18.
Coe, Sophie D., and Michael D. Coe. 1996. *The True History of Chocolate.*
Coke, David, and Alan Borg. 2011. *Vauxhall Gardens: A History.*
Collins, Elizabeth. 1966. *103 Borough High Street: History of a House.*
Collingham, Lizzie. 2005. *Curry: A Biography.*
Colsoni, Francesco Casparo. 1951. *Le guide de Londres (1693),* ed. Walter H. Godfrey.
Cooper, Anthony. 1978. 'Old Chalk Farm Tavern'. *Camden History Review,* 6:2-5.
Cromwell, Thomas Kitson. 1835. *Walks through Islington, Comprising an Historical and Descriptive Account of that Extensive and Important District.*
Cruickshank, Dan. 2009. *The Secret History of Georgian England.*
Cunningham, George H. 1927. *London: Being a Comprehensive Survey of the History, Tradition & Historical Associations of Buildings and Monuments Arranged under Streets in Alphabetical Order.*
Cunningham, Peter. 1849. *Hand-book of London, Past and Present.* 2 vols.

Curl, James Stevens. 2010. *Spas, Wells, & Pleasure-Gardens of London.*

David, Elizabeth. 1994. *Harvest of the Cold Months: The Social History of Ice and Ices.*

Davies, Philip. 2009. *Lost London: 1870-1945.* Croxley Green, Herts.

Dean, Ptolemy, et al. 2005. *The Borough Market Book: From Roots to Renaissance.*

Denford, Steven, and F. Peter Woodford. 2003. *Streets of Camden Town.*

Dickens, Charles. 1965-2002. *The Letters* [1820-70], ed. Madeline House, Graham Storey, and Kathleen Tillotson. 12 vols.

Dictionary of National Biography. 1885-1901. 66 vols.

Ehrman, Edwina, et al. 1999. *London Eats Out: 500 Years of Capital Dining.*

Ellis, Markman. 2004a. 'Pasqua Rosee's Coffee-House, 1652-1666'. *London Journal*, 29:1-24.

Ellis, Markman. 2004b. *The Coffee House: A Cultural History.*

Ellis, Markman. 2009. 'Coffee-House Libraries in Mid-Eighteenth-Century London'. *The Library*, 7th ser., 10:3-40.

Ellis, Valentine. 1983. 'John Ellis and the Star & Garter'. *Richmond History*, 4:2-13.

Endelman, Todd M. 1979. *The Jews of Georgian England, 1714-1830: Tradition and Change in a Liberal Society.* Ann Arbor.

Evans, John. 1824. *Richmond and its Vicinity, with a Glance at Twickenham, Strawberry Hill, and Hampton Court.* Richmond upon Thames.

Evelyn, John. 1959. *The Diary* [1620-1706], ed. E. S. de Beer. Oxford.

Farmer, Alan. 1984. *Hampstead Heath.*

Fisher, Michael H. 1996. *The First Indian Author in English: Dean Mahomed (1759-1851) in India, Ireland, and England.*

Freeman, Janet Ing. 2010. '"Poor Ralph": The Precarious Career of a Regency Hack'. *The Library*, 7th ser., 11:197-226.

Gage, John. 1986. 'Bloomsbury Market: A Unit in the Earl of Southampton's Pioneer Town Planning'. *Camden History Review*, 14:20-23.

George, M. Dorothy. 1967. *Hogarth to Cruikshank: Social Change in Graphic Satire.*

Gibberd, Graham. 1992. *On Lambeth Marsh: The South Bank and Waterloo.*

Gigante, Denise, ed. 2005. *Gusto: Essential Writings in Nineteenth-Century Gastronomy.*

Gilbert, Christopher. 1996. *Pictorial Dictionary of Marked London Furniture, 1700-1840.*

Grimod de la Reynière, Alexandre Balthazar Laurent. 1802-12. *Almanach des gourmands.* 8 vols. Paris.

Gronow, Rees. 1862. *Reminiscences of Captain Gronow … being Anecdotes of the Camp, the Court, and the Clubs, at the Close of the Last War with France.*

[Grose, Francis]. 1811. *Lexicon Balatronicum: A Dictionary of Buckish Slang, University Wit, and Pickpocket Eloquence.* An adaptation of Grose's *Classical Dictionary of the Vulgar Tongue* (1785).

Hall, Edwin T. 1917. *Dulwich: History and Romance, A.D. 967-1916.*

Harben, Henry A. 1918. *A Dictionary of London: Being Notes Topographical and Historical Relating to the Streets and Principal Buildings in the City of London.*

Harding, Vanessa, and Priscilla Metcalf. 1986. *Lloyd's at Home.* Colchester.

Hassell, John. 1817-18. *Picturesque Rides and Walks, with Excursions by Water, Thirty Miles Round the British Metropolis.* 2 vols.

Heckethorn, C. W. 1899. *London Souvenirs.*

Hobhouse, Hermione. 1971. *Lost London: A Century of Demolition and Decay.*

Howitt, William. 1869. *The Northern Heights of London; or, Historical Associations of Hampstead, Highgate, Hornsey, and Islington.*

Hunter, Judith. 1989. *The George Inn, London.*

Kamlish, Marian. 1995. '"The Alhambra of Camden Town": The Rise and Fall of Sickert's Dear Old Bedford'. *Camden History Review,* 19:30-33.

King, Alexander Hyatt. 1986. 'The Quest for Sterland – 1. The London Tavern: A Forgotten Concert Hall.' *Musical Times,* 127:382-85.

Kirby, John William. 1936-53. 'The Green Man on Blackheath and the Chocolate House in the Grove.' *Transactions of the Greenwich & Lewisham Antiquarian Society,* 4:169-72.

Kynaston, David. 1994. *The City of London, I: A World of Its Own, 1815-1890.*

Lamb, Charles. 1975-78. *The Letters of Charles and Mary Anne Lamb,* ed. Edwin W. Marrs, Jr. 3 vols. Ithaca, New York.

Lane, John. 1889. *A Handy Book to the Study of the Engraved, Printed, and Manuscript Lists of Lodges of Ancient, Free, and Accepted Masons of England, from 1723 to 1814.*

Larwood, Jacob, and John Camden Hotten. 1866. *The History of Signboards.*

Lehmann, Gilly. 2002. 'Meals and Mealtimes, 1600-1800', in Harlan Walker, ed., *The Meal,* pp. 139-54 (Proceedings of the Oxford Symposium on Food and Cookery, 2001).

Lillywhite, Bryant. 1963. *London Coffee Houses: A Reference Book of Coffee Houses of the Seventeenth, Eighteenth and Nineteenth Centuries.*

Lincoln, Margarette. 2002. *Representing the Royal Navy: British Sea Power, 1750-1815.*

MacDonogh, Giles. 1987. *A Palate in Revolution: Grimod de La Reynière and the Almanach des gourmands.*

Macfie, A. L. 1973. *The Crown and Anchor Tavern: The Birthplace of Birkbeck College.*

Mackenzie, Gordon. 1972. *Marylebone: Great City North of Oxford Street.*

Macmichael, J. Holden. 1906. *The Story of Charing Cross and its Immediate Neighbourhood.*

McMurray, William. 1910. 'London Taverns in the Seventeenth Century'. *Notes and Queries,* 11th ser., 1:190-191 (5 March 1910).

Manley, Bill. 1990. *Islington Entertained: or, A Pictorical History of Pleasure Gardens, Music Halls, Spas, Theatres and Places of Entertainment.*

Martin, Benjamin Ellis. 1890. *In the Footprints of Charles Lamb.* New York.

Masters, Betty R. 1974. *The Public Markets of the City of London, Surveyed by William Leybourn in 1677.* London Topographical Society Publications, 117.

Matz, B. W. 1922. *The Inns and Taverns of 'Pickwick'.* 2d ed.

Matz, B. W. 1923. *Dickensian Inns and Taverns.* 2d ed.

Mayall, David. 1988. *Gypsy-travellers in Nineteenth-century Society.* Cambridge.

Mayhew, Henry. 1861-62. *London Labour and the London Poor.* 4 vols.

Metcalf, Priscilla. 1977. *The Halls of the Fishmongers' Company: An Architectural History of a Riverside Site.*

Morton, H. V. 1951. *In Search of London.*

Munsche, P. B. 1981. *Gentlemen and Poachers: The English Game Laws 1671-1831.* Cambridge.

Newnham-Davis, Nathaniel. 1899. *Dinners and Diners: Where and How to Dine in London.*

Nichols, John. 1812-16. *Literary Anecdotes of the Eighteenth Century.* 9 vols.

Norman, Philip. 1898. 'Old Bell Inn, Holborn.' *Middlesex and Hertfordshire Notes and Queries,* 4:101-10.

Norman, Philip. 1905. *London: Vanished and Vanishing.*

Nowell-Smith, Simon. 1958. *The House of Cassell, 1858-1958.*

Osborn, Helen. 1991. *Inn and around London: A History of Young's Pubs.*

Passingham, William John. 1935. *London's Markets, their Origin and History.*

Pepys, Samuel. 1970-83. *The Diary* [1660-69], ed. Robert Latham and William Matthews. 11 vols.

Popham, H. E. 1937. *The Taverns in the Town.*

Postgate, Raymond, ed. 1968. *The Good Food Guide to London.*

Preston, J. H. 1948. *The Story of Hampstead.*

Procter, Bryan Waller. 1820. 'The Cider Cellar'. *London Magazine,* 2:384-88. The essay is sometimes misattributed to Charles Lamb.

Pugh, David ('David Hughson'). 1817. *Walks through London, including Westminster and the Borough of Southwark, with the Surrounding Suburbs; ... Forming a Complete Guide to the British Metropolis.*

Redley, Mike. 1981. 'The End of the Cock and Hoop'. *Camden History Review,* 9:9-12.

Rendle, William, and Philip Norman. 1888. *The Inns of Old Southwark and their Associations.*

Rhind, Neill. 1987. *The Heath: A Companion Volume to Blackheath Village and Environs.*

Richards, Timothy M., and James Stevens Curl. 1973. *City of London Pubs.*

Richardson, John. 1985. *Hampstead One Thousand: A Book to Celebrate the Hampstead Millennium A.D. 986-1986*. New Barnet.

Richardson, John. 1989. *Highgate Past: A Visual History of Highgate.*

Riello, Giorgio. 2006. 'A Taste of Italy: Italian Businesses and the Culinary Delicacies of Georgian London.' *London Journal*, 31:201-22.

Ripley, Henry. 1885. *The History and Topography of Hampton-on-Thames.*

Roach, James, *publisher*. 1793. *Roach's London Pocket Pilot, or Stranger's Guide through the Metropolis.*

Roden, Claudia. 1997. *The Book of Jewish Food: An Odyssey from Samarkand and Vilna to the Present Day.*

Rogers, Kenneth. 1928. *The Mermaid and Mitre Taverns in Old London.*

Rogers, Kenneth. 1931. *Old Cheapside and Poultry: Ancient Houses and Signs.*

Sala, George Augustus. 1894. *Things I Have Seen and People I Have Known*. 2 vols.

Samuel, Mark, and Gustav Milne. 1992. 'The "Ledene Hall" and Medieval Market', in Gustav Milne, ed., *From Roman Basilica to Medieval Market: Archaeology in Action in the City of London*, pp. 39-50.

Saunders, Hilary St George. 1951. *Westminster Hall.*

Sheaf, John, and Ken Howe. 1995. *Hampton and Teddington Past.*

Shelley, Henry C. 1909. *Inns & Taverns of Old London.*

Simpson, J. P. 1906. 'Old City Taverns and Freemasonry'. *Ars Quatuor Coronatorum*, 19:8-30.

Smith, Andrew F. 1996. *Pure Ketchup: A History of America's National Condiment.* Columbia, South Carolina.

Spang, Rebecca. 2000. *The Invention of the Restaurant: Paris and Modern Gastronomic Culture*. Cambridge, Mass.

Stanley, Louis T. 1957. *The Old Inns of London.*

Stow, John. 1598. *A Survey of London.*

Strype, John. 1720. *A Survey of the Cities of London and Westminster*. 2 vols. An expanded and updated edition of John Stow's *Survey.*

Stuart, Donald. 2004. *London's Historic Inns and Taverns*. Derby.

Survey of London. 1900 - . A continuing work, with forty-seven volumes published to date. All but the most recently published volumes are available online at www.british-history.ac.uk

Swinley, Jim. 1975. 'Hogarth and the "March to Finchley"'. *Camden History Review*, 3:4-6.

Sygrave, Jon. 2004. 'From Medieval Malt House to 20th Century Pub: Excavations at 9-11 Poplar High Street, London, E14'. *London Archaeologist*, 10:215-21.

Tallis, John. 2002. *John Tallis's London Street Views, 1838-1840*, ed. Peter Jackson. London Topographical Society Publications, 160.

Taylor, John. 1636a. *Taylors Travels and Circular Perambulation, through, and by More then Thirty Times Twelve Signes of the Zodiack, of the Famous Cities of London and Westminster.* Reprinted by the Spenser Society in 1876.

Taylor, John. 1636b. *The Honorable, and Memorable Foundations, Erections, Raisings, and Ruines, of Divers Cities, Townes, Castles, and other Pieces of Antiquitie, within Ten Shires and Counties of this Kingdome.* Reprinted by the Spenser Society in 1877.

Taylor, John. 1637. *The Carriers Cosmographie.* Reprinted by the Spenser Society in 1873.

Taylor, Rosemary. 1991. *Blackwall, the Brunswick, and Whitebait Dinners: A Short Historical Account of a Forgotten Corner of East London.*

Thompson, John, and Adolphe Smith. 1877. *Street Life in London.* Reprinted 1994 as *Victorian London Street Life in Historic Photographs.*

Thornbury, George Walter, and Edward Walford. 1873-78. *Old and New London: A Narrative of its History, its People, and its Places.* 6 vols. Published in parts, with each volume completed as follows: vol. 1, 1873; vol. 2, 1874; vol. 3, 1875; vol. 4, 1876; vol. 5, 1877; vol. 6, 1878.

Timbs, John. 1865. *Walks and Talks about London.*

Timbs, John. 1868. *Curiosities of London: Exhibiting the Most Rare and Remarkable Objects of Interest in the Metropolis.*

Timbs, John. 1872. *Clubs and Club Life in London, with Anecdotes of its Famous Coffee-houses, Hostelries, and Taverns, from the Seventeenth Century to the Present Time.*

Trusler, John. 1786. *The London Adviser and Guide.*

Van der Vat, Dan, and Michele Whitby. 2009. *Eel Pie Island.*

Victoria County History of England. 1900 - . A large number of the *VCH* volumes have been digitized and are available online at www.british-history.ac.uk

Wade, Christopher. 2000. *The Streets of Hampstead.* 3d ed.

Wagner, Leopold. 1924. *London Inns and Taverns.*

Wagner, Leopold. 1925. *More London Inns and Taverns.*

Walker, Annabel. 1987. *Kensington and Chelsea: A Social and Architectural History.*

Walker, Peter. 1989. *The Pubs of North Lambeth.* Croydon.

Waller, J. G. 1855. 'Remains of Mediaeval London'. *Gentleman's Magazine*, new ser., vol. 43 (April 1855), 359-65.

Weale, John. 1851. *London Exhibited in 1851.*

Webb, David. 1990. 'Guide Books to London before 1800: A Survey'. *London Topographical Record*, 26:138-52.

Weinreb, Ben, and Christopher Hibbert, eds. 1983. *The London Encyclopaedia.*

West, William. 1825. *Tavern Anecdotes, and Reminiscences of Signs, Clubs, Coffee-Houses, Streets.*

Westminster City Archives. 2002. *One on Every Corner: The History of Some West-minster Pubs.*

Wheatley, Henry B. 1891. *London Past and Present: Its History, Associations, and Traditions.* 3 vols.

Wilson, C. Anne. 1994. 'Luncheon, Nuncheon and Related Meals', in C. Anne Wilson, ed., *Luncheon, Nuncheon and Other Meals: Eating with the Victorians,* pp. 33-50. Stroud.

Wilson, J. B. 1990. *The Story of Norwood.* New ed.

Woollacott, Ron. 2002. *Nunhead & Peckham Pubs Past and Present: A Pub Crawl through Time.*

Wroth, Warwick William, and Arthur Edgar Wroth. 1896. *The London Pleasure Gardens of the Eighteenth Century.*

Younger, G. W. 1943. 'Greenwich Taverns'. *The Dickensian,* 39:193-96.

IV. Electronic resources

Cox, Nancy, and Karin Dannehl. 2007. *Dictionary of Traded Goods and Commodities, 1550-1820* (www.british-history.ac.uk/source.aspx?pubid=739)

Old Bailey Proceedings Online (www.oldbaileyonline.org)

Oxford Dictionary of National Biography Online (www.oxforddnb.com)

Oxford English Dictionary Online (www.oed.com)

INDEX

As stated above on pp. x-xi, the index is in four parts. The first, which lists establishments, proprietors, and purveyors of drinks, foodstuffs, and other goods, often includes information supplementary to that in the main text and notes, and occasionally corrects the *Almanack*'s spelling of personal names. This index also includes (to the extent of my knowledge) the names of both earlier and later establishments on the site of the one described in the 1815 *Almanack*. The second index covers places: churches and markets are grouped under those headings, and counties are indexed only when the reference is to an establishment or other feature within the county (thus, mentions of a 'Surrey stage' or a 'splendid view over Surrey' have not been indexed under Surrey). The third index, covering food and drink, excludes the following unless discussed at length or qualified by variety: ale, beef, breadstuffs, cakes, chicken, confectionery, fish, fruit, ham, lamb and mutton, pastries and pies, pork, pudding, soup, tarts, vegetables, and wine. In the final index of persons, places, topics, and terms that did not otherwise find a place, I have been fairly selective, generally not including the names of the many writers quoted by Rylance, nor passing mentions of artists, noblemen, historical events, etc.

1. Establishments, Proprietors, and Purveyors

11. Towns, Counties, Districts, Major London Streets & Buildings

III. Food and Drink

Eggs, xliii, 39, 70, 106, 154, 157n, 207, 242, 247, 258, 260; egg sauce, 259; omelettes, 135

Endive, 7, 259

Figs, 267

Fish, choosing, 257-58; crimping, 257; dried, 57, 246, 247; salted, 135, 246, 247, 259; smoked, 247. *See also* specific varieties

Flounder, 203, 245, 254, 257, 258, 266

Flying dishes (*assiettes volantes*), 4, 13

Fowl, *see* Poultry and wildfowl

French confectionery, 120

French food and cookery, xlviii-xlix, 109, 110, 117, 132, 133, 134, 136n, 230-31

Fruit, candied, 254; exotic, 159, 251, 254; foreign, 39, 247; preserved, 108, 254. *See also* specific varieties

Game, choosing, 257; illegal traffic in, l, 135, 242; laws, l, 135, 242, 258, 266, 267. *See also* specific game

German food, xlviii, 132, 230

Gin, 58, 72, 146; Deady's Full Proof, 188, 272; Old Tom, 167n, 188, 272

Ginger, 91

Ginger beer, 71, 107

Gingerbread, 267

Goose, 80, 153, 242, 253, 257, 258, 259, 260, 262, 264, 267, 270, 274

Gooseberries, 265

Grapes, 251, 252, 254, 265, 267, 268

Grouse, 258, 266, 270

Gudgeon, 160

Guimauve, pâte de, 108, 274

Guinea fowl, 242, 254, 259

Gurnet [gurnard], 161, 257, 260, 264

Haddock, 245, 253, 257, 258, 259, 264, 270; rizzod (i.e. rizzared or dried) haddock, 28

Haggis, 269

Halibut, 135, 261, 270

Ham, Bayonne, 261; bear, 43; choosing, 256; north country, 254; reindeer, 61; Westmorland, 136; Westphalian, 61, 254, 261; Yorkshire, 136, 261

Hanoverian sauce, 235, 274

Hares and leverets, 135, 242, 257, 258, 260, 266, 268, 269, 270

Harvey's sauce, 235, 266, 274

Hearts, 97; sheep's, 112

Heathfowl, 266

Herbs, essences of, 235; medicinal, 244, 249, 252; oriental (for smoking in a hookah), 111

Herons, 258

Herring, 245, 246, 247, 254, 257, 258, 259, 261, 268; preserved, 51, 246

Horsemeat, 7

Ice and ices, 30, 77, 82, 92, 108, 112, 114, 160, 166, 170, 174

Indian food, xlix, 110-11, 265

Italian food, xlviii, 132, 134

Jack (fish), 160, 260, 262, 274

Jam, 108

Jelly, 11, 77, 108, 160, 170, 178, 254

Jewish food, 38-39, 246-47

John Dory, 161, 245, 257-58, 260, 264

Kale, 254

Ketchup, 274

Kidneys, 32, 69, 97, 122, 154, 191

Lamb, choosing, 256. *See also* Mutton

Larks, 242, 254, 258, 268, 270

Lemons, 17, 252, 260; lemon pickle, 235

Lemonade, 17

Lenten food, 259-60

Lentils, 39, 235, 247

Lettuce, 259

Ling, 246

Liqueurs, 133, 160, 170, 205

Liquors, *see* Spirits

Liver, 135, 265

Lobster, 161, 245, 254, 257, 258, 264, 266, 270; essence of, 235

Macaroni, 135, 235

Macaroons, 108

Mackarel, 161, 245, 257, 258, 261, 270

Made dishes, 60, 235

Madeira, 122, 149

Maids (fish), 257

Marasquin, 133, 272

Marmalade, 170

Matzoh ('Passover biscuit'), 39, 247

Melons, 265

Millet, 235

Mince pies, 254, 270

Mineral water, artificial, li, 19, 167, 169; spa, li, 167, 169, 225n

Stage-coaches, 10, 13, 31, 44n, 64, 76, 78n, 86n, 89, 90n, 115, 124, 126, 127, 128, 159, 184n, 186-87, 194, 196, 206, 218, 223, 225
Steam (for keeping food warm), xxxix, 111, 232
Steam baths, 233
Steele, Richard, 226, 253n
Steevens, George, 181n
Stockbrokers, 20, 21
Stow, John, *Survey of London* (1598), 37n
Stramonium, 252
Straw, Jack, 224n
Strype, John, *Survey of London* (1720), 43n, 52n, 67n, 76n, 78n, 184n, 185n, 241n, 245n, 247n, 250n, 251n
Subscription houses, 23-24, 30, 61-62, 173, 176, 177, 179
Suburbia, observations on, xxxv-xxxvi, 207-08
Supper, xliv, 61, 109, 121, 128, 142, 143, 151, 156, 163, 181, 188, 267
Swearing on the horns, 217, 223
Swinburne, Algernon Charles, 203n
Syphilis, cure for, 59-60, 276
Tables, dining, 108, 238
Tatler, 105n
Taverns in general, xxxix-xl
Taylor, John: *Carriers Cosmographie* (1637), xiv, 36n, 61n; *Honorable and Memorable Foundations* (1636), xiv, 201n, 212n; *Taylors Travels* (1636), xiii-xiv, 19n, 76n
Tea gardens and pleasure grounds, xxxv, xlii, 187-88, 205, 211, 212-13, 217-20
Telford, Thomas, 88n
Tennis, 218

Tennyson, Alfred, 70n
Thackeray, William Makepeace, 23n
Theatrical performances and entertainment, xliv, 31n, 36n, 78n, 99n, 109, 143, 145, 152, 155, 175, 197, 221n, 228, 249n, 267
Thomson, James, 199, 210
Tilt boats, 57
Tipping, xlv, 9, 28, 71, 74
Tooke, John Horne, 203, 248
Trap-ball, 205, 218, 219n, 226, 228n, 276
Trusler, John, *London Adviser and Guide* (1786), xv, xlv
Turner, Sir Gregory Page, 96
Turpin, Dick, ix
Vaccari, Francesco, 144
Valets, xl, 172
Vanburgh, John, 252
Victoria, Queen, 163n
Waiters, 9, 15, 28, 55, 68, 71, 72, 74, 77, 118, 120, 129, 138, 162, 167, 194
Waitresses, barmaids, and 'maid-cooks', 87, 117, 151, 167
Walpole, Horace, xxxv, 201
Wellington, Arthur Wellesley, 1st Duke, 171
Westmorland, Sarah Fane, Countess of, 165
Wilkes, John, 195
William IV, xlix
Wolsey, Thomas, 183
Women, xliv-xlv, 16, 39, 60, 82, 92, 139, 143, 144n, 160, 161, 188, 213, 245. *See also* Prostitutes; Waitresses
Wool traders, 61
York and Albany, Frederick, Duke of, 108, 163